2001

LLEWELLYN'S

Moon Sign Book & Gardening Almanac

With Lunar Forecasts by Gloria Star

Copyright © 2000 Llewellyn Publications.
All rights reserved. Printed in the U.S.A.
Editor/Designer: Sharon Leah
Cover Design: William Merlin Cannon
Cover Art: Kristi Schaeppi / RKB Studios
Special thanks to Leslie Nielsen
for astrological proofreading.

LLEWELLYN PUBLICATIONS
P.O. Box 64383 Dept. 953-9
St. Paul, MN 55164-0383 U.S.A.

Table of Contents

How to Use This Book

A re you ready to harness the power of the Moon? With the *Moon Sign Book* you can do just that. The *Moon Sign Book* provides you with four essential tools to reap the benefits of the Moon. You can use these tools alone or in any combination to help you achieve success in 2001. The first tool is our unique, easy-to-use Astro Almanac: a list of the best dates in 2001 to begin important activities. The second tool is a complete how-to on using the Moon to fine-tune your timing. This takes the Astro Almanac one step further and teaches you how to choose the best dates for your activities. The third tool consists of insightful lunar astrological forecasts by astrologer Gloria Star. The fourth tool is a mass of informative articles on using the Moon in the home, business, garden, and everywhere you go. Read on to find out more about how to use each of these features.

The Astro Almanac

The simplest method for using the *Moon Sign Book* in lunar timing is to turn straight to the Astro Almanac, beginning on page 12. The Astro Almanac lists the best days to perform sixty different activities, based on the sign and phase of the Moon and on lunar aspects. All you need to do is find the particular activity that you are interested in, and the best dates for each month will be listed across the page. When working with the Moon's energies we consider two things—the inception, or beginning of an activity, and the desired outcome. We begin a project under a certain Moon sign and phase in order to achieve certain results. The results are influenced by the attributes of the sign and phase under which we started the project. Therefore, the Astro Almanac lists the best times to begin many activities.

The Moon Tables

The Astro Almanac is a general guide to the best days for the listed activities, but the Astro Almanac can't take everyone's special needs into account. For a more in-depth exploration of lunar timing, the *Moon Sign Book* provides the Moon Tables. Although we can provide generally favorable dates for everyone, not everyone will have the same goal for each activity that they start. Therefore, not everyone will want to start every activity at the same time. For example, let's say you decide to plant a flower garden. Which attributes would you like most in your flowers? Beauty? Then you may want to plant in Libra, because Libra is ruled by Venus, which in turn governs appearance. How about planting for quantity or abundance? Then you might try Cancer or Pisces, the two most fertile signs. What if you were going to be transporting the flowers somewhere, either in pots or as cut blooms? Then you might want to try Scorpio for sturdiness, or Taurus for hardiness. The Astro Almanac also does not take into account retrogrades, Moon void-of-course, or favorable and unfavorable days.

The procedure for using the Moon Tables is more complex than simply consulting the Astro Almanac, but we encourage you to try it so that you can tailor the *Moon Sign Book* information to your needs and fully harness the potential of the Moon. The directions for using the tables to choose your own dates are in the section called "Using the Moon Tables," which begins on page 22. Be sure to read all of the directions, paying special attention to the information on the signs, Moon void-of-course, retrogrades, and favorable and unfavorable days. The sections titled "The Moon's Quarters & Signs" (page 52), "Retrogrades" (page 54), and the Moon Void-of-Course Tables (page 56) are provided as supplementary material and should be read as well. These sections will give you a deeper understanding of how the process of lunar planning works, and give you background helpful in making use of the articles in this book.

Personal Lunar Forecasts

The third tool for working with the Moon is the Personal Lunar Forecasts section, written by Gloria Star. This section begins on page 375. Here Gloria tells you, based on your Moon sign, what's in store for you for 2001. This approach is different than that of other astrology books, including Llewellyn's *Sun Sign Book,* which make forecasts based on Sun sign. While the Sun in an astrological chart represents the basic essence or personality, the Moon represents the internal or private you—your feelings, emotions, and subconscious. Knowing what's in store for your Moon in 2001 can give you great insight for personal growth. If you already know your Moon sign, go ahead and turn to the corresponding section in the back of the book (forecasts begin on page 379). If you don't know your Moon sign, you can figure it out using the procedure outlined beginning on page 62.

Articles, Articles, Articles

Scattered throughout the *Moon Sign Book* are articles on using the Moon for activities from fishing to business. These articles are written by people who successfully use the Moon to enhance their daily lives, and are chosen to entertain you and enhance your knowledge of what the Moon can do for you. The articles can be found in the Home, Health, & Beauty section; the Leisure & Recreation section; the Business section; and the Gardening section. Check the table of contents for specific topics.

Some Final Notes

We get a number of letters and phone calls every year from readers asking the same types of questions. Most of these have to do with how to find certain information in the *Moon Sign Book* and how to use this information.

The best advice we can give is to read the *entire* introduction (pages 5–74), in particular the section on how to use the tables. We provide examples using the current Moon and aspect tables so that you can follow along and get familiar with the process. At first, using the Moon tables may seem confusing because there are several factors to take into account, but if you read the directions carefully and practice a little bit, you'll be a Moon sign pro in no time.

Remember, for quick reference for the best dates to begin an activity, turn to the Astro Almanac. To choose special dates for an activity that are tailor-made just for you, turn to "Using the Moon Tables." For insight into your personal Moon sign, check out Gloria Star's lunar forecasts. Finally, to learn about the many ways you can harness the power of the Moon, turn to the articles in the Home, Health & Beauty; Leisure & Recreation; Business & Legal; and Farm, Garden, & Weather sections.

Important!

All times given in the *Moon Sign Book* are set in Eastern Standard Time (EST). You must adjust for your time zone. There is a time zone conversions chart on page 8 to assist you. You must also adjust for Daylight Saving Time where applicable.

Time Zone Conversions

World Time Zones

(Compared to Eastern Standard Time)

(R) EST—Used

(S) CST—Subtract 1 hour

(T) MST—Subtract 2 hours

(U) PST—Subtract 3 hours

(V) Subtract 4 hours

(V*) Subtract 4½ hours

(W) Subtract 5 hours

(X) Subtract 6 hours

(Y) Subtract 7 hours

(Q) Add 1 hour

(P) Add 2 hours

(P*) Add 2½ hours

(O) Add 3 hours

(N) Add 4 hours

(Z) Add 5 hours

(A) Add 6 hours

(B) Add 7 hours

(C) Add 8 hours

(C*) Add 8½ hours

(D) Add 9 hours

(D*) Add 9½ hours

(E) Add 10 hours

(E*) Add 10½ hours

(F) Add 11 hours

(F*) Add 11½ hours

(G) Add 12 hours

(H) Add 13 hours

(I) Add 14 hours

(I*) Add 14½ hours

(K) Add 15 hours

(K*) Add 15½ hours

(L) Add 16 hours

(L*) Add 16½ hours

(M) Add 17 hours

(M*) Add 17½ hours

Important!

All times given in the *Moon Sign Book* are set in Eastern Standard Time (EST). You must adjust for your time zone. You must also adjust for Daylight Saving Time where applicable.

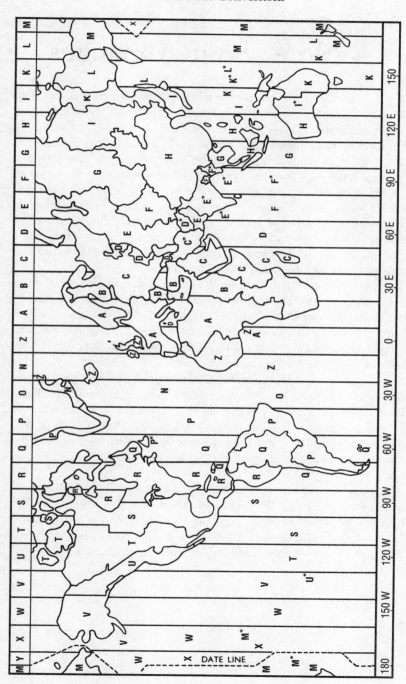

A Note about Almanacs

It is important for those people who wish to plan by the Moon to understand the difference between the Moon Sign Book and most common almanacs. Most almanacs list the placement of the Moon by the constellation. For example, when the Moon is passing through the constellation of Capricorn, they list the Moon as being in Capricorn.

The *Moon Sign Book*, however, lists the placement of the Moon in the zodiac by *sign*, not constellation. The zodiac is a belt of space extending out from the earth's equator. It is divided into twelve equal segments: the twelve signs of the zodiac. Each of the twelve segments happens to be named after a constellation, but the constellations are not in the same place in the sky as the segment of space (sign) named after them. The constellations and the signs do not "match up."

For astronomical calculations, the Moon's place in almanacs is given as being in the constellation. For astrological purposes, like planning by the Moon, the Moon's place should be figured in the zodiacal sign, which is its true place in the zodiac, and nearly one sign (30 degrees) different from the astronomical constellation. The *Moon Sign Book* figures the Moon's placement for astrological purposes.

To illustrate: If the common almanac gives the Moon's place in Taurus (constellation), its true place in the zodiac is in Gemini (zodiacal sign). Thus it is readily seen that those who use the common almanac may be planting seeds when they think that the Moon is in a fruitful sign, while in reality it would be in one of the most barren signs of the zodiac. To obtain desired results, planning must be done according to *sign*.

Some common almanacs confuse the issue further by inserting at the head of their columns "Moon's Sign" when they really mean "Moon's Constellation." In the *Moon Sign Book*, however, "Moon's sign" means "Moon's sign!" Use the *Moon Sign Book* to plan all of your important events and to grow a more beautiful, bountiful garden.

Using the Astro Almanac

L lewellyn's unique Astro Almanac (pages 12–21) is provided for quick reference. Use it to find the best dates for anything from asking for a raise to buying a car!

By reader request, we have included several new categories in the Astro Almanac relating to business, from hiring and firing staff to the best time to advertise on the internet. We hope you will find them useful. If you have suggestions for other activities to be added to the Astro Almanac, please write us at the address listed on the title page of this book.

The dates provided are determined from the sign and phase of the Moon and the aspects to the Moon. These are approximate dates only. We have removed dates that have long Moon void-of-course periods from the list (we did not do this before 1998). Although some of these dates may meet the criteria listed for your particular activity, the Moon void would nullify the positive influences of that day. We have not removed dates with short Moon voids, however, and we have not taken planetary retrogrades into account. To learn more about Moon void-of-course and planetary retrogrades, see pages 54–61.

This year we have also removed eclipse dates and days with lots of squares to the Moon. Like Moon voids, squares could nullify the "good" influences of a given day. Eclipses lend an unpredictable energy to a day, so we have removed eclipse dates so that you may begin your activities on the strongest footing possible.

Another thing to bear in mind when using the Astro Almanac is that sometimes the dates given may not be favorable for your Sun sign or for your particular interests. The Astro Almanac does not take personal factors into account, such as your Sun and Moon sign, your schedule, etc. That's why it is important for you to learn how to use the entire process to come up with the most beneficial dates for you. To do this, read the instructions under "Using the Moon Tables" (page 22). That way, you can get the most out of the power of the Moon!

Astro Almanac

Activity	Jan.	Feb.	Mar.	Apr.	May	Jun.	Jul.	Aug.	Sep.	Oct.	Nov.	Dec.
Advertise Sale	6, 10, 14, 15, 20, 24, 29, 31	7, 12, 17, 20, 21, 25, 26	2, 3, 6, 10, 12, 17, 20, 22, 25, 29	3, 11, 16, 21, 23, 26, 28, 30	3, 5, 14, 19, 20, 24, 28	1, 2, 11, 12, 16, 21, 25, 29	9, 14, 19, 23, 24, 30	6, 11, 15, 19, 24, 30	2, 7, 10, 12, 15, 16, 19, 20, 29, 30	5, 12, 14, 16, 18, 20, 25, 27	1, 4, 6, 9, 10, 14, 19, 24, 25, 28	3, 5, 7, 10, 11, 15, 20, 21, 26, 30
Advertise New Venture	6, 10, 14, 15, 20, 24, 29, 31	7, 12, 17, 20, 21, 25, 26	2, 3, 10, 12, 17, 20, 22, 25, 29	3, 16, 21, 23, 26, 28, 30	3, 5, 14, 19, 20, 24, 28	1, 2, 11, 12, 16, 21, 25, 29	9, 14, 19, 23, 24, 27	6, 11, 15, 19, 24, 30	2, 7, 10, 12, 15, 16, 19, 20, 29, 30	5, 12, 14, 16, 18, 20, 25, 27	1, 4, 6, 9, 10, 14, 19, 24, 25, 28	3, 5, 7, 10, 11, 15, 20, 21, 26, 30
Advertise in the Newspaper	5, 6, 10, 14, 15, 20, 24, 26, 29, 31	2, 5, 7, 11, 12, 17, 20, 21, 25, 26	3, 6, 10, 12, 17, 22, 28, 29	2, 3, 7, 11, 16, 17, 21, 23, 26, 28, 30	3, 5, 14, 19, 20, 24, 28, 29	1, 2, 11, 12, 16, 21, 25, 29	9, 14, 19, 23, 24, 27, 29	6, 10, 11, 15, 19, 24, 30	2, 7, 10, 12, 15, 16, 19, 20, 29, 30	5, 12, 14, 16, 20, 25, 27	1, 4, 6, 9, 10, 14, 19, 24, 25, 28	3, 5, 7, 10, 11, 15, 20, 21, 26, 30
Advertise on TV, Radio, Internet					24	21						
Apply for Job	6, 14, 24, 29	2, 11, 20, 25	2, 6, 10, 12, 20, 26, 30	3, 16, 21, 26, 30	5, 14, 19, 20, 24, 28	1, 11, 12, 16, 21, 22, 25, 29	7, 9, 12, 14, 19, 22, 26, 29	6, 11, 15, 19, 24, 25	2, 10, 12, 15, 16, 20, 24, 30	5, 10, 14, 18, 19, 25, 27	1, 4, 6, 9, 10, 14, 19, 24, 28	4, 7, 9, 14, 19, 21, 25, 26, 30
Apply for Copyrights/patents	5, 6, 10, 14, 20, 24, 29, 31	2, 5, 7, 12, 20, 21, 25, 26	2, 3, 6, 10, 17, 22, 28, 29	2, 3, 7, 11, 16, 17, 23, 26, 28, 30	3, 5, 14, 19, 20, 24, 28, 29	1, 2, 11, 16, 25, 29	9, 14, 19, 23, 24, 29	6, 10, 11, 15, 19, 24, 30	2, 7, 10, 12, 15, 16, 19, 20, 29, 30	5, 12, 14, 16, 18, 20, 25, 27	1, 4, 6, 9, 10, 14, 19, 24, 25, 28	3, 5, 7, 10, 11, 15, 20, 21, 26, 30

Astro Almanac

Activity	Jan.	Feb.	Mar.	Apr.	May	Jun.	Jul.	Aug.	Sep.	Oct.	Nov.	Dec.
Ask for Raise	6, 14, 22, 23	1, 2, 7, 10, 20	10, 29	3, 7, 21, 26, 30	5, 14, 19, 24, 28	1, 11, 16, 21, 25, 27, 29	9, 14, 19, 23, 24, 27	6, 11, 15, 19, 24	7, 12, 16, 20, 30	5, 10, 14, 18, 27	1, 6, 10, 14, 24, 29	3, 7, 11, 21, 26, 30
Bid on Contracts	5, 26	21	28	11	14, 29		9	24	15, 29	12, 25	9	5, 26
Brewing	9, 10, 17, 18	14, 15, 23	23, 24	19, 20	16-18	12-14	10, 11, 19, 20	6-8, 16, 17	2-4, 12, 13	9, 10	5-7	3, 4, 31
Buy Stocks	6, 23	2, 19, 20	19, 29	15	13			11	7	5	1, 28	26
Buy Animals	2, 29-31	11, 12, 17, 20, 21, 28	3, 10, 20, 25, 29	16, 21, 23, 28	5, 14, 19, 20, 24	1, 2, 7, 10, 11, 16, 22, 24, 27-29	7, 9, 12, 14, 19, 21, 22, 24-26	5, 9, 13, 16, 19, 22, 24, 31	1, 6, 19, 24	15, 19, 21, 23, 25, 26	1, 4, 6, 9, 12, 15-17, 19, 24, 27	3, 4, 9, 11, 14, 19, 21, 26
Buy Antiques	9, 10, 17, 18, 22, 23	5, 6, 13-15, 18-20	5, 6, 13, 14, 18, 19	1, 2, 9, 10, 14, 15, 28, 29	7, 8, 11-13, 25-27	3, 4, 8, 9, 22, 23, 30	1, 5, 6, 19, 20, 27-29	1-3, 16, 17, 24, 25, 28-30	12, 13, 20, 21, 25, 26	9, 12, 14, 17, 19, 20, 24	6, 7, 14, 15, 19, 20	3, 4, 11, 12, 16, 17

Astro Almanac

Activity	Jan.	Feb.	Mar.	Apr.	May	Jun.	Jul.	Aug.	Sep.	Oct.	Nov.	Dec.
Buy Appliances	7, 15, 25	12, 22	3, 12, 21, 31	17, 27	5, 10, 14, 15, 20, 24	1, 2, 6, 11, 12, 16, 21, 25, 29	4, 9, 13, 14, 18, 19, 24, 26, 31	5, 6, 10, 11, 14, 15, 19, 24, 27, 30	1, 2, 6, 9, 11, 12, 15, 16, 19, 20, 23, 24, 28, 30	3, 5, 8, 10, 14, 16, 18, 20, 25, 27, 30	1, 4, 8, 10, 13, 14, 17, 19, 22, 24, 26, 27, 29	1, 3, 5, 7, 10, 11, 14, 15, 20, 21, 24, 26, 29
Buy Cameras	2, 6, 14, 19, 29	3, 11, 15, 25	2, 10, 15, 25, 29	7, 11, 21, 26	4, 9, 19, 23	5, 15, 19, 28	2, 12, 17, 25, 29	8, 13, 21, 26	5, 9, 18, 22	2, 7, 5, 19, 29	3, 11, 16, 25, 30	9, 13, 23, 28
Buy a Car	3, 15, 20, 26, 30	4, 16	3, 16, 30	11, 12, 27	10, 24	6, 20	4, 18, 31	14, 15, 27	11, 23	8, 20	4, 17	1, 14, 15, 29
Buy Electronics	7, 15, 25, 26	4, 12, 21, 22	3, 11, 21, 22, 30	8, 17, 27	5, 14, 15, 24	2, 11, 20, 29	8, 18, 26	14, 15, 22	1, 10, 19, 28, 29	8, 16, 25	4, 12	1, 10, 19, 20, 29
Buy a House	5, 6, 24	2	1, 27-29	1, 2, 24, 25, 28-30	25-29	22-25	21, 22	18, 19, 31	1, 27, 29	25, 26	21, 22, 28, 29	18, 19, 26, 27
Buy Real Estate	4, 5, 9, 10, 21, 22	1, 2, 5, 6, 18, 19	1, 5, 6, 18, 19, 27, 28	1, 2, 14, 15, 24, 25, 28, 29	11, 12, 21, 22	8, 9, 18, 19	5, 6, 15, 16	1, 2, 11, 12, 29, 30	8, 9, 12, 13, 25, 26	5, 6, 9, 10, 22, 23	1, 2, 6, 19, 20	3, 4, 16, 17, 26, 27, 30, 31

Astro Almanac

Activity	Jan.	Feb.	Mar.	Apr.	May	Jun.	Jul.	Aug.	Sep.	Oct.	Nov.	Dec.
Canning	10	23, 24	5, 6, 23, 24	19, 20	16, 17, 21, 22	13, 14, 18, 19	10, 11, 15, 16, 19, 20	6, 7, 16, 17	3, 4, 12, 13	1, 9, 10	1, 2, 5-7	3, 4, 30, 31
Collect Money	2, 3, 9, 10, 15, 16, 22, 23, 30, 31	6, 7, 11, 12, 18, 19, 26, 27	5, 6, 11, 12, 18, 19, 25, 26	1, 2, 7, 8, 14, 15, 22, 23, 28, 29	5, 6, 11, 12, 19, 26, 27	1, 2, 8, 9, 15, 16, 22, 23, 28, 29	5, 6, 12-14, 19, 20, 25, 26	1, 2, 9, 10, 16, 17, 22, 23, 28, 29	5, 6, 12, 13, 18, 19, 25, 26	2, 3, 9, 30	6, 12, 13, 18, 19	3, 4, 9, 10, 16, 17, 23-25, 30, 31
Cut Hair-Decrease Growth	13, 14	9, 10	10	21-23	19, 20	15, 16, 20, 21	12-14, 17, 18	9, 10, 13-15	5, 6, 10, 11, 16, 17	3, 4, 7, 8, 13-15	3, 4, 10, 11	1, 2, 7, 8
Cut Hair Increase Growth	1, 27, 28	24, 25	5, 6	1, 2, 28, 29	25-27	22, 23			30	1, 27, 28	23, 24	21, 22, 30, 31
Cut Hair for Thickness	5, 6, 9	1, 2, 5-8	5-9	2-4, 8	1, 7	6, 18, 19	5, 15, 16, 21, 22	4, 11, 12, 18, 19	2, 8, 9, 14, 15	2, 5, 6, 12, 13	1, 2, 28-30	5, 6, 26, 27, 30
Cut Timber	11-16, 20-26	3, 4, 8-12, 16-22	7-12, 15-21, 25-31	3-8, 12-18, 21-27	1-5, 9-15, 19-24, 28-31	1, 2, 5-11, 15-21, 24-29	3-9, 12-18, 21-26, 30, 31	1-5, 9-15, 18-22, 26-31	1, 2, 5-11, 14-19, 22-29	2-8, 11-16, 20-26, 30, 31	2-4, 8-13, 16-22, 26-30	1, 2, 5-10, 13, 14, 15-19, 23-29

Astro Almanac

Activity	Jan.	Feb.	Mar.	Apr.	May	Jun.	Jul.	Aug.	Sep.	Oct.	Nov.	Dec.
Dock or Dehorn Animals	1-8, 11, 12, 25-31	1-6, 21-28	1-7, 20-31	1-4, 17-30	1, 14-28	10-25	1-22	5-18, 31	4-15, 27-30	3-12, 25-31	3-8, 21-30	1-6, 18-29
End a Relationship	10, 14-17, 19-24	10-13, 15-21, 23-28	10-13,15-20, 22, 23	8, 9, 11-17, 21-23	7-16, 19-21, 23	6-11, 14-17, 19, 21	5-9, 11-15, 17-20	4, 5, 8-11, 13, 15-17, 19	5-15, 17	3, 4, 6-9, 11-13, 15, 16	3-7, 9, 11-13, 15	1-5, 8-11, 14, 31
Entertain	7, 8, 15, 16, 24, 26	3, 4, 7, 11, 12, 21	2-4, 7, 11, 12, 20, 22, 30, 31	3, 7, 8, 16, 17, 26, 27, 30	1, 4-6, 14, 15, 23, 24, 28	1, 2, 10, 11, 20, 21, 24, 25, 28, 29	7-9, 17, 18, 21, 22, 25, 26	4, 5, 13-15, 18, 19, 22, 23, 31	1, 10, 14, 15, 19, 27-29	7, 8, 11, 12, 17, 24-26	3, 4, 8, 9, 12, 13, 21, 22	1, 2, 5, 9, 10, 18, 20, 29
Extract Teeth	7, 8, 27, 28	3, 4, 23, 24	3, 4, 30, 31	5, 6, 26, 27	2, 3, 23, 24, 30, 31	5, 26, 27	3, 4, 23, 24, 30, 31	20, 21, 26, 27	22-24, 30	20, 21, 27, 28	10, 16, 17, 23, 24	14, 15, 21, 22
Get a Perm		2, 7	7	3, 25, 30	28	17, 19	22	11	15	5	9	
Fire Staff	10, 14, 15, 19-24	9-12, 15-21	10-12, 15, 17, 19, 20, 24	8, 11, 12, 15-17, 21-23	9, 10, 12-14, 19, 20	6-8, 10, 11, 15, 16, 19, 20, 21	6-8, 14, 17-21	5, 9, 10, 13-19	6, 9, 11, 13-15, 17	3, 6, 7, 9, 11-13, 15	3-6, 9, 11, 13, 30	1-6, 8, 10, 14, 31

Astro Almanac

Activity	Jan.	Feb.	Mar.	Apr.	May	Jun.	Jul.	Aug.	Sep.	Oct.	Nov.	Dec.
Hire Staff	2, 5, 6, 24, 26, 29, 31	25, 26	2, 3, 6, 28, 29	3, 7, 23, 26, 28, 30	3, 5, 24, 28	1, 2, 21, 25, 29	23, 24, 29	19, 24	19, 20, 30	16, 18, 20, 25, 27	19, 25, 29	15, 20, 21, 26, 30
Legal Matters	2, 6, 10, 14, 24, 29	2, 7, 11, 20, 25	2, 6, 10, 20, 25	3, 7, 8, 16, 21, 26, 30	5, 14, 19, 24, 28	1, 11, 16, 21, 25, 29	9, 14, 19, 23, 27	6, 11, 15, 19, 24	2, 7, 12, 16, 20, 30	5, 14, 18, 27	1, 6, 10, 14, 24, 29	3, 7, 11, 21, 26, 30
Marriage Ceremony	1, 4-6, 8, 24, 28, 29	2, 6, 7, 16, 17, 25, 26, 28	1, 2, 5-7, 24, 25, 29	1-3, 7, 23, 25, 26, 28, 30	2, 5, 22, 26-31	1, 2, 22, 25, 26, 29	20-22, 24, 26	18-20, 23, 26-31	2, 18, 22-30	16, 20, 23-25, 28, 29-31	16-30	14-27, 30, 31
Marry for Happiness	4, 8, 24, 29	2, 7, 16, 26	2, 7, 25	3, 25, 30	5	1, 22, 29	20-22, 26	18-20, 23	7, 30	25, 27	19, 24	14, 19, 21, 25, 26, 30
Marry for Longevity	5, 6	1, 2	1, 28, 29	24, 25	21, 22	18, 19	15, 16	11, 12	8, 9	5, 6	1, 2, 28, 29	26, 27
Mow Lawn for Less Growth	1-8, 24-31	1-7, 23-28	1-8, 25-31	1-7, 23-30	1-6, 23-31	1-5, 21-30	1-4, 20-31	1-3, 19-31	1, 17-30	1, 16-31	15-30	14, 30

Astro Almanac

Activity	Jan.	Feb.	Mar.	Apr.	May	Jun.	Jul.	Aug.	Sep.	Oct.	Nov.	Dec.
Neutering or Spaying Animals	1-8, 11, 12, 25-31	1-6, 21-28	1-7, 20-31	1-4, 17-30	1, 14-28	10-25	1-22	5-18, 31	4-15, 27-30	3-12, 25-31	3-8, 21-30	1-6, 18-29
Open a Business	5, 6, 13, 14, 22, 23	1, 2, 9, 10, 18, 19, 27, 28	1, 9, 10, 18, 19, 27, 28	5, 6, 14, 15, 24, 25	2, 3, 11, 12, 21, 22, 30, 31	26, 27	5, 23, 24	1, 2, 20, 21, 29, 30	17, 25, 26	22, 23	1, 18, 19, 28, 29	16, 17, 26, 27
Paint House	9-24	1-8, 23-28	9-25	8-23	7-23	1-21	1-20	1-19	1-17	1-16	1-15	1-14
Pour Concrete		8			7			4			1	
Remodel a Business	1, 3, 6, 10, 14, 15, 20, 24, 27-30	6, 7, 11, 20, 21, 25, 26	6, 10, 20, 25	3, 6, 7, 16, 17, 21, 22, 30	1, 4, 5, 13, 14, 18, 19, 27, 28	1, 10, 11, 15, 16, 24, 25, 28, 29	8, 9, 12-14, 21, 23, 25, 27	4, 6, 9, 11, 18, 19, 22, 24, 31	2, 5, 7, 14, 16, 18, 20, 27, 28, 30	2, 5, 12, 14, 16, 18, 25, 27, 30	1, 8, 10, 12, 14, 21, 24, 26	7, 9, 21, 23, 24, 26
Remodel a House	1, 3, 6, 10, 11, 14, 15, 20, 24, 27, 28-30	6, 7, 11, 20, 21, 25, 26	6, 10, 20, 25	3, 6, 7, 16, 17, 21, 22, 30	1, 4, 5, 13, 14, 18, 19, 27, 28	1, 10, 11, 15, 16, 24, 25, 28, 29	8, 9, 12-14, 21, 23, 25, 27	4, 6, 9, 11, 18, 19, 22, 24, 31	2, 5, 7, 14, 16, 18, 20, 27, 28, 30	2, 5, 12, 14, 16, 18, 25, 27, 20	1, 8, 10, 12, 14, 21, 24, 26	7, 9, 21, 23, 24, 26

Astro Almanac

Activity	Jan.	Feb.	Mar.	Apr.	May	Jun.	Jul.	Aug.	Sep.	Oct.	Nov.	Dec.
Repair a Car	3, 7, 20, 30	4, 17, 27	12, 16, 26, 31	8, 13, 22	5, 10, 15, 20, 24	2, 6, 11, 16, 21, 29	4, 13, 18, 26	10, 22, 27	1, 6, 19, 28	3, 8, 30	4, 13, 17, 27	1, 10, 14, 19, 24, 29
Repair Electronics	3, 13	10, 20	16, 21, 26	4, 18, 23	1, 10, 29	11	8, 13, 18, 31			5		
Roofing	11, 12, 17, 18	8, 14, 15, 21, 22	13, 14, 20-22	9, 10, 16-18	7, 8, 14, 15, 21, 22	10, 11, 17-19	7-9, 15, 16	4, 5, 11, 12, 18, 19	7-9, 14, 15	5, 6, 11, 12	2, 8, 9, 14, 15	5, 6, 11, 12
Seek Favors or Credit	24	20	15, 20	16, 30	14	12	7	6	2, 15			14
Set Fence Posts	11, 12, 24	21, 22	20, 21	17, 18	14, 15, 21, 22	10, 11, 18, 19	7, 8, 15, 16	4, 5, 11, 12, 18	8, 9, 14, 15	5, 6, 12, 13	1, 2, 8, 9	5, 6
Sign Contracts			28	2		29		30	19			10

Astro Almanac

Activity	Jan.	Feb.	Mar.	Apr.	May	Jun.	Jul.	Aug.	Sep.	Oct.	Nov.	Dec.
Sell Items	2, 6, 9, 10, 13-15, 17, 20, 23, 26, 29, 31	2, 5-7, 10-12, 15, 17, 20, 25, 26	2, 3, 6, 7, 10-12, 15, 17, 20-22, 25, 26, 28	2-4, 7, 8, 11, 13, 16-18, 21, 23, 26, 28, 30	5, 10, 14, 15, 19, 20, 24, 28, 29	1, 2, 6, 11, 12, 16, 21, 24, 25, 28, 29	3, 8, 9, 13, 14, 19, 23, 24, 26, 27, 29, 30	4, 6, 10, 11, 15, 18, 22, 24, 27, 30	1, 2, 6, 7, 10, 12, 15, 16, 19, 20, 29, 30	5, 8, 10, 12, 14, 16, 18, 20, 25, 27, 29	1, 3, 4, 6, 9, 10, 14, 16, 19, 24, 25, 27, 29	2, 3, 5, 7, 10, 11, 15, 20, 21, 26, 30
Sell Real Estate	2, 6, 9, 10, 13-15, 17, 20, 23, 29, 31	2, 5, 6, 7, 10-12, 15, 17, 20, 25, 26	2, 3, 6, 7, 10-12, 15, 17, 20-22, 25-28	2, 3, 7, 8, 13, 16, 17, 21, 23, 26, 28-30	5, 10, 14, 18-20, 24, 28	1, 2, 6, 11, 16, 21, 24, 25, 28, 29	3, 8, 9, 13, 14, 19, 24, 26, 27, 29, 30	4, 10, 11, 15, 18, 22, 24, 27, 30	1, 2, 6, 7, 10, 12, 15, 19, 20, 29	5, 8, 10, 12, 16, 18, 25, 28, 29	1, 3, 4, 6, 9, 14, 16, 19, 24, 25, 27, 29	2, 3, 5, 10, 11, 15, 20, 26, 30
Sports	2, 6, 10, 13, 14, 17, 23, 23, 24, 28, 29	7, 11, 15, 20, 25	2, 6, 10, 15, 20, 25, 26, 29	3, 7, 8, 13, 16, 26, 30	1, 5, 6, 10, 14, 15, 20, 28	1, 2, 11, 16, 21, 25, 28, 29	3, 9, 14, 19, 21, 26	15, 18, 19, 22, 24, 27	1, 20		1, 3, 6, 16, 24, 27	11, 15, 26
Start Diet	11, 16, 20-24	8-13, 15-22	9-13, 15-21	12-18, 22, 23	9-15, 19-23	6-12, 15-21	5-9, 13-18	9-15, 18, 19	1, 5-12, 14-17	2-8, 12-16	1-4, 8-13	1, 5-10, 14
Start House Building	6, 7	21	20	17	14, 15, 23	10, 11, 19	7	4, 18	14	12, 13	8	5
Start Savings Account	6, 24, 28, 29	2, 7, 26	2, 3, 6, 7, 25, 29	3, 25, 26, 30	24, 28	1, 7, 21, 22, 27, 29	22, 23, 26, 27	19, 24, 25	19, 20, 30	18, 19, 27	19, 24, 29	14, 19, 21, 25, 26

Astro Almanac

Activity	Jan.	Feb.	Mar.	Apr.	May	Jun.	Jul.	Aug.	Sep.	Oct.	Nov.	Dec.
Stop a Bad Habit	11-14	8-10	9, 10			20	17, 18	14, 15, 18, 19	10, 11, 14, 17	7, 8, 11-26	3, 4, 8-11	1, 5, 8
Travel	6, 8, 10, 14, 15, 23, 24, 28, 29, 31	5, 7, 11, 16, 20, 21, 25, 26	3, 6, 12, 16, 17, 20, 25	11, 16, 17, 21, 23, 30	5, 9, 14, 19, 20	1, 2, 7, 11, 16, 21, 22, 29	9, 14, 24, 26, 29	15, 16, 19, 24, 30	10, 12, 15, 19, 23, 24, 29	8, 25	1, 4, 6, 9, 19, 24	3-5, 9-11, 15, 19, 26
Visit Dentist	10, 13, 14, 17, 28	6, 10, 15, 20, 25	1, 6, 7, 10, 11, 21, 24	4, 21, 23, 30	1, 6, 10, 27, 29, 31	2, 10, 11, 15, 24, 28	7, 8, 12, 13, 21, 26	4, 9, 18, 22, 31	1, 5, 6, 14, 18, 20, 30	3, 5, 12, 18, 25	3, 8, 12, 16, 21, 26, 27	5, 15, 26, 30
Visit Physician	23	19	19		3, 31		24	20			19	
Work with Consultants	2, 5, 6, 10, 14, 20, 29	2, 4, 5, 6, 7, 11, 12, 17, 20, 21, 25, 26	2, 3, 6, 10, 12, 17, 22, 28, 29	2, 3, 11, 16, 17, 21, 23, 28, 30	3, 5, 14, 19, 20, 24, 28, 29	1, 2, 11, 12, 16, 21, 25, 29	9, 14, 19, 23, 24, 27, 29	6, 10, 11, 15, 19, 24, 29	2, 7, 10, 12, 15, 16, 19, 20, 24, 29, 30	5, 8, 10, 14, 16, 18, 20, 25, 27	1, 4, 6, 9, 10, 14, 19, 24, 29	3, 5, 7, 10, 15, 20, 21, 26, 30
Write Letters	3,.5-7, 15, 19, 20, 24, 29, 31	3, 5, 11, 12, 17, 21, 26, 27	2, 3, 10, 12, 15-17, 21, 22, 25, 26, 28, 29, 31	2, 7, 8, 11, 13, 16, 17, 21-23, . 26-28	3-5, 9, 10, 14, 15, 19, 20, 23, 24, 29	1, 2, 5, 6, 10-12, 15, 16, 19, 21, 25, 28, 29	2, 4, 7, 9, 12-14, 17, 18, 24-26, 29, 31	3, 5, 8, 10, 13-15, 20-22, 24, 26, 27, 30	5, 6, 9, 10, 15, 18, 19, 22-24, 27, 29	3, 7, 8, 12, 15, 16, 19, 20, 24, 25, 29, 30	4, 9, 12, 16, 17, 19, 20, 22, 25, 27, 30	1,5,7,9,10, 13,14,18-20,23,24, 26,28,29,30

Using the Moon Tables

Timing your activities is one of the most important things you can do to ensure success. In many Eastern countries, timing by the planets is so important that practically no event takes place without first setting up a chart for it. Weddings have occurred in the middle of the night because that was when the influences were best. You may not want to take it that far, but you can still make use of the influences of the Moon whenever possible. It's easy and it works!

In the *Moon Sign Book* you will find the information you need to plan just about any activity: weddings, fishing, buying a car or house, cutting your hair, traveling, and more. Not all of the things you do will fall on favorable days, but we provide the guidelines you need to pick the best day out of the several from which you have to choose. The primary method in the *Moon Sign Book* for choosing your own dates is to use the Moon Tables that begin on page 28. Following are instructions for choosing the best dates for your activities using the *Moon Sign Book,* several examples, directions on how to read the Moon Tables themselves, and more advanced information on using the Favorable and Unfavorable Days Tables, Void-of-Course, and Retrograde information to choose the dates that are best for you personally. To enhance your understanding of the directions given below, we highly recommend that you read the sections of this book called "A Note about Almanacs" (page 10), "The Moon's Quarters & Signs" (page 52), "Retrogrades" (page 54), and "Moon Void-of-Course" (page 55). It is not essential that you read these before you try the examples below, but reading them will deepen your understanding of the date-choosing process.

The Four Basic Steps

Step One: Use the Directions for Choosing Dates

Look up the directions for choosing dates for the activity that you wish to begin. The directions are listed at the beginning of the following sections of this book: Home, Health, & Beauty; Leisure & Recreation; Business & Legal; and Farm, Garden, & Weather. Check the Table of Contents to see in what section the directions for your specific activity are listed. The activities contained in each section are listed in italics after the name of the section in the Table of Contents. For example, directions for choosing a good day for canning are listed in the Home,

Health, & Beauty Section, and directions for choosing a good day to throw a party are in the Leisure Section. Read the directions for your activity, then go to step two.

Step Two: Check the Moon Tables

Next, turn to the Moon Tables that begin on page 28. In the Moon Tables section, there are two tables for each month of the year. Use the Moon Tables to determine what dates the Moon is in the phase and sign listed in the directions for your particular activity. The Moon Tables are the tables on the left-hand pages, and include the day, date, the sign the Moon is in, the element of that sign, the nature of the sign, the Moon's phase, and the times that it changes sign or phase.

If there is a time listed after a date, such as Sun. 4:32 pm on January 2, that time is the time when the Moon moves into the zodiac sign listed for that day (which in this case would be Sagittarius). Until then, the Moon is considered to be in the sign for the previous day (Scorpio in this example).

The abbreviation Full signifies Full Moon and New signifies New Moon. The times listed directly after the abbreviation are the times when the Moon changes sign. The times listed after the phase indicate when the Moon changes phase.

If you know the specific month you would like to begin your activity, turn directly to that month. When you begin choosing your own dates, you will be using the Moon's sign and phase information most often. All times are listed in Eastern Standard Time (EST). You need to adjust them according to your own time zone. (There is a time zone conversion map on page 8.)

When you have found some dates that meet the criteria for the correct Moon phase and sign for your activity, you may have completed the process. For certain simple activities, such as getting a haircut, the phase and sign information is all that is needed. For other activities, however, we need to meet further criteria in order to choose the best date. If the directions for your activity include information on certain lunar aspects, you should consult the Lunar Aspectarian. An example of this would be if the directions told you that you should not perform a certain activity when the Moon is square (Q) Jupiter.

Step Three: Turn to the Lunar Aspectarian

On the pages opposite the Moon Tables you will find the Lunar Aspectarian and the Favorable and Unfavorable Days Tables. The Lunar

Aspectarian gives the aspects (or angles) of the Moon to the other planets. In a nutshell, it tells where the Moon is in relation to the other planets in the sky. Some placements of the Moon in relation to other planets are favorable, while others are not. To use the Lunar Aspectarian, which is the left half of this table, find the planet that the directions list as favorable for your activity, and run down the column to the date desired. For example, if you are planning surgery and the Health & Beauty section says that you should avoid aspects to Mars, you would look for Mars across the top and then run down that column looking for days where there are no aspects to Mars (as signified by empty boxes). If you want to find a favorable aspect (sextile [X] or trine [T]) to Mercury, run your finger down the column under Mercury until you find an X or T. Negative or adverse aspects (square or opposition) are signified by a Q or O. A conjunction, C, is sometimes good, sometimes bad, depending on the activity or planets.

Step Four: Use the Favorable and Unfavorable Days Tables

The Favorable and Unfavorable Days Tables are helpful in choosing your personal best dates, because they consider your Sun sign. All Sun signs are listed on the right-hand side of the Lunar Aspectarian table. Once you have determined which days meet the criteria for phase, sign, and aspects for your activity, you can find out if those days are positive for you. To find out if a day is positive for you, find your Sun sign and then look down the column. If it is marked F, it is very favorable. If it is marked f, it is slightly favorable. U means very unfavorable and u means slightly unfavorable. Once you have selected good dates for the activity you are about to begin, you can go straight to the examples section beginning on the next page. However, if you are up to the challenge and would like to learn how to fine-tune your selections even further, read on!

Step Five: Check for Moon Void-of-Course and Retrogrades

This last step is perhaps the most advanced portion of the procedure. It is generally considered a bad idea to make decisions, sign important papers, or start special activities during a Moon void-of-course period or during a planetary retrograde. Once you have chosen the best date for your activity based on steps one through four, you can check the Void-of-Course Table on page 56 to find out if any of the dates you have chosen have void periods. The Moon is said to be void-of-course after it has made its last aspect to a planet within a particular sign, but before it has moved into the next sign. Put simply, during the void-of-course period the Moon is "at rest," so activities initiated at this time generally don't come to fruition. You will notice that there are many void periods during the year, and it is nearly impossible to avoid all of them. Some people choose to ignore these altogether and do not take them into consideration when planning activities.

Next, you can check the Planetary Retrogrades Table on page 54 to see what planets are retrograde during your chosen date(s). A planet is said to be retrograde when it appears to move backward in the sky as viewed from the Earth. Generally, the farther a planet is away from the Sun, the longer it can stay retrograde. Some planets will retrograde for several months at a time. Avoiding retrogrades is not as important in lunar planning as avoiding the Moon void-of-course, with the exception of the planet Mercury. Mercury rules thought and communication, so it is important not to sign papers, initiate important business or legal work, or make crucial decisions during these times. As with the Moon void-of-course, it is difficult to avoid all planetary retrogrades when beginning events, and you may choose to ignore this step of the process. Following are some examples using some or all of the steps outlined above.

Using What You've Learned

Example Number One

Let's say you need to make an appointment to have your hair cut. Your hair is thin and you would like it to look thicker. You look in the Table of Contents to find the section of the book with directions for hair care. You find that it is in the Home, Health, & Beauty section. Turning to that section you see that for thicker hair you should cut hair while the Moon is Full and in the sign of Taurus, Cancer, or Leo. You should avoid the Moon in Aries, Gemini, or Virgo. We'll say that it is the month of January. Look up January in the Moon Tables (page 28). The Full Moon falls on January 9 at 3:24 pm. The Moon moves into the sign of Cancer January 8 at 8:09 am, and remains in Cancer until January 10, so January 9 meets both the phase and sign criteria.

Example Number Two

That was easy. Let's move on to a more difficult example using the sign
and phase of the Moon. You want to buy a house for a permanent home.
After checking the Table of Contents to see where the house purchasing
instructions are, look in the Home, Health, & Beauty section under
House. It says that you should buy a home when the Moon is in Taurus,
Leo, Scorpio, or Aquarius (fixed signs). You need to get a loan, so you
should also look in the Business & Legal section under Loans. Here it
says that the third and fourth Moon quarters favor the borrower (you).
You are going to buy the house in January. Look up January in the Moon
Tables. The Moon is in the third quarter from January 9–16, and in the
fourth quarter from January 16–24. The best days for obtaining a loan
would be January 10–12 while the Moon is in Leo or January 16–18
while it is in Scorpio. Just match up the best signs and phases (quarters)
to come up with the best dates. With all activities, be sure to check the
Favorable and Unfavorable Days for your Sun sign in the table adjoining
the Lunar Aspectarian. If there is a choice between several dates, pick
the one most favorable for you (marked F under your Sun sign). Because
buying a home is an important business decision, you may also wish to
see if there are Moon voids or a Mercury retrograde during these dates.

Example Number Three

Now let's look at an example that uses signs, phases, and aspects. Our
example this time is fixing your car. We will use January as the example
month. Look in the Home, Health, & Beauty section under automobile
repair. It says that the Moon should be in a fixed sign (Taurus, Leo, Scorpio, or Aquarius) in the first or second quarter and well aspected to
Uranus. (Good aspects are sextiles and trines, marked X and T. Conjunctions are also usually considered good if they are not conjunctions to
Mars, Saturn, or Neptune.) It also tells you to avoid negative aspects to
Mars, Saturn, Uranus, Neptune, and Pluto. (Negative aspects are squares
and oppositions, marked Q and O.) Look in the Moon Tables under
October. You will see that the Moon is in the second quarter October
1–2, and in the first and second quarters October 16–31. The Moon is in
Aquarius on October 23 at 8:26 pm through October 26 at 8:56 am.
Now, looking to the Lunar Aspectarian, we see that October 25 has a
positive aspect to Uranus (conjunction), but that none of the other cho-

sen dates do. In addition, there are no negative aspects to Mars, Saturn, Neptune, and Pluto on October 25. There is a Moon void-of-course to avoid after 2:32 pm. Otherwise, if you wanted to fix your car in October, this would be the best date.

Use Common Sense!

Some activities depend on outside factors. Obviously, you can't go out and plant when there is a foot of snow on the ground. You should adjust to the conditions at hand. If the weather was bad during the first quarter when it was best to plant crops, do it during the second quarter while the Moon is in a fruitful sign. If the Moon is not in a fruitful sign during the first or second quarter, choose a day when it is in a semi-fruitful sign. The best advice is to choose either the sign or phase that is most favorable when the two don't coincide.

To summarize, in order to make the most of your activities, check with the *Moon Sign Book*. First, look up the activity under the proper heading, then look for the information given in the tables (the Moon Tables, Lunar Aspectarian, or Favorable and Unfavorable Days). Choose the best date considering the number of positive factors in effect. If most of the dates are favorable, there is no problem choosing the one that will fit your schedule. However, if there aren't any really good dates, pick the ones with the least number of negative influences.

Key of Abbreviations for the Moon Tables

X:	sextile/positive	F:	very favorable
T:	trine/positive	f:	slightly favorable
Q:	square/negative	U:	very unfavorable
O:	opposition/negative	u:	slightly unfavorable
C:	conjunction/positive, negative, or neutral depending on planets involved; conjunctions to Mars, Saturn, or Neptune are sometimes negative.	Full:	Full Moon
		New:	New Moon

January Moon Table

Date	Sign	Element	Nature	Phase
1 Mon. 5:14 pm	Aries	Fire	Barren	1st
2 Tue.	Aries	Fire	Barren	2nd 5:31 pm
3 Wed.	Aries	Fire	Barren	2nd
4 Thu. 1:57 am	Taurus	Earth	Semi-fruit	2nd
5 Fri.	Taurus	Earth	Semi-fruit	2nd
6 Sat. 6:44 am	Gemini	Air	Barren	2nd
7 Sun.	Gemini	Air	Barren	2nd
8 Mon. 8:09 am	Cancer	Water	Fruitful	2nd
9 Tue.	Cancer	Water	Fruitful	3rd 3:24 pm
10 Wed. 7:44 am	Leo	Fire	Barren	3rd
11 Thu.	Leo	Fire	Barren	3rd
12 Fri. 7:26 am	Virgo	Earth	Barren	3rd
13 Sat.	Virgo	Earth	Barren	3rd
14 Sun. 9:05 am	Libra	Air	Semi-fruit	3rd
15 Mon.	Libra	Air	Semi-fruit	3rd
16 Tue. 2:02 pm	Scorpio	Water	Fruitful	4th 7:35 am
17 Wed.	Scorpio	Water	Fruitful	4th
18 Thu. 10:35 pm	Sagittarius	Fire	Barren	4th
19 Fri.	Sagittarius	Fire	Barren	4th
20 Sat.	Sagittarius	Fire	Barren	4th
21 Sun. 9:57 am	Capricorn	Earth	Semi-fruit	4th
22 Mon.	Capricorn	Earth	Semi-fruit	4th
23 Tue. 10:43 pm	Aquarius	Air	Barren	4th
24 Wed.	Aquarius	Air	Barren	1st 8:07 am
25 Thu.	Aquarius	Air	Barren	1st
26 Fri. 11:39 am	Pisces	Water	Fruitful	1st
27 Sat.	Pisces	Water	Fruitful	1st
28 Sun. 11:35 pm	Aries	Fire	Barren	1st
29 Mon.	Aries	Fire	Barren	1st
30 Tue.	Aries	Fire	Barren	1st
31 Wed. 9:21 am	Taurus	Earth	Semi-fruit	1st

January

Lunar Aspectarian   Favorable and Unfavorable Days

	Sun	Mercury	Venus	Mars	Jupiter	Saturn	Uranus	Neptune	Pluto	Aries	Taurus	Gemini	Cancer	Leo	Virgo	Libra	Scorpio	Sagittarius	Capricorn	Aquarius	Pisces
1					X	X					f	u	f		U		f	u	f		F
2	Q							X	T	F		f	u	f		U		f	u	f	
3		Q					X			F		f	u	f		U		f	u	f	
4			X	O				Q		F		f	u	f		U		f	u	f	
5	T	T				C	Q				F		f	u	f		U		f	u	f
6		Q			C			T			F		f	u	f		U		f	u	f
7							T		O	f		F		f	u	f		U		f	u
8			T	T						f		F		f	u	f		U		f	u
9	O						X			u	f		F		f	u	f		U		f
10		O			X			O		u	f		F		f	u	f		U		f
11			Q		Q	O			T	f	u	f		F		f	u	f		U	
12			O	Q						f	u	f		F		f	u	f		U	
13	T			X		T			Q		f	u	f		F		f	u	f		U
14		T			T			T			f	u	f		F		f	u	f		U
15							T		X	U		f	u	f		F		f	u	f	
16	Q									U		f	u	f		F		f	u	f	
17		Q	T	C				Q			U		f	u	f		F		f	u	f
18	X					O	Q				U		f	u	f		F		f	u	f
19					O			X		f		U		f	u	f		F		f	u
20		X	Q				X		C	f		U		f	u	f		F		f	u
21										f		U		f	u	f		F		f	u
22				X						u	f		U		f	u	f		F		f
23			X			T				u	f		U		f	u	f		F		f
24	C				T			C		f	u	f		U		f	u	f		F	
25				Q	Q	C			X	f	u	f		U		f	u	f		F	
26		C			Q					f	u	f		U		f	u	f		F	
27									Q	f	u	f		U		f	u	f		F
28			C	T		X					f	u	f		U		f	u	f		F
29	X				X			X		F		f	u	f		U		f	u	f	
30							X		T	F		f	u	f		U		f	u	f	
31		X							Q	F		f	u	f		U		f	u	f	

February Moon Table

Date	Sign	Element	Nature	Phase
1 Thu.	Taurus	Earth	Semi-fruit	2nd 9:02 am
2 Fri. 3:56 pm	Gemini	Air	Barren	2nd
3 Sat.	Gemini	Air	Barren	2nd
4 Sun. 7:00 pm	Cancer	Water	Fruitful	2nd
5 Mon.	Cancer	Water	Fruitful	2nd
6 Tue. 7:21 pm	Leo	Fire	Barren	2nd
7 Wed.	Leo	Fire	Barren	2nd
8 Thu. 6:35 pm	Virgo	Earth	Barren	3rd 2:12 am
9 Fri.	Virgo	Earth	Barren	3rd
10 Sat. 6:46 pm	Libra	Air	Semi-fruit	3rd
11 Sun.	Libra	Air	Semi-fruit	3rd
12 Mon. 9:51 pm	Scorpio	Water	Fruitful	3rd
13 Tue.	Scorpio	Water	Fruitful	3rd
14 Wed.	Scorpio	Water	Fruitful	4th 10:23 pm
15 Thu. 5:02 am	Sagittarius	Fire	Barren	4th
16 Fri.	Sagittarius	Fire	Barren	4th
17 Sat. 3:59 pm	Capricorn	Earth	Semi-fruit	4th
18 Sun.	Capricorn	Earth	Semi-fruit	4th
19 Mon.	Capricorn	Earth	Semi-fruit	4th
20 Tue. 4:53 am	Aquarius	Air	Barren	4th
21 Wed.	Aquarius	Air	Barren	4th
22 Thu. 5:45 pm	Pisces	Water	Fruitful	4th
23 Fri.	Pisces	Water	Fruitful	1st 3:21 am
24 Sat.	Pisces	Water	Fruitful	1st
25 Sun. 5:20 am	Aries	Fire	Barren	1st
26 Mon.	Aries	Fire	Barren	1st
27 Tue. 3:06 pm	Taurus	Earth	Semi-fruit	1st
28 Wed.	Taurus	Earth	Semi-fruit	1st

February

Lunar Aspectarian — Favorable and Unfavorable Days

	Sun	Mercury	Venus	Mars	Jupiter	Saturn	Uranus	Neptune	Pluto	Aries	Taurus	Gemini	Cancer	Leo	Virgo	Libra	Scorpio	Sagittarius	Capricorn	Aquarius	Pisces
1	Q							Q			F		f	u	f		U		f	u	f
2		Q	X	O	C	C					F		f	u	f		U		f	u	f
3	T							T	O	f		F		f	u	f		U		f	u
4		T	Q			T				f		F		f	u	f		U		f	u
5										u	f		F		f	u	f		U		f
6				T	X	X				u	f		F		f	u	f		U		f
7			T					O	T	f	u	f		F		f	u	f		U	
8	O		O	Q	Q	Q	O				f	u	f		F		f	u	f		U
9									Q		f	u	f		F		f	u	f		U
10				X	T	T					f	u	f		F		f	u	f		U
11			O					T	X	U		f	u	f		F		f	u	f	
12	T	T						T		U		f	u	f		F		f	u	f	
13								Q			U		f	u	f		F		f	u	f
14	Q	Q				O	Q				U		f	u	f		F		f	u	f
15				C	O			X			U		f	u	f		F		f	u	f
16		X	T				X		C	f		U		f	u	f		F		f	u
17	X									f		U		f	u	f		F		f	u
18			Q							u	f		U		f	u	f		F		f
19						T				u	f		U		f	u	f		F		f
20				X	T			C		u	f		U		f	u	f		F		f
21		C	X						X	f	u	f		U		f	u	f		F	
22					Q	Q	C			f	u	f		U		f	u	f		F	
23	C			Q						f	u	f		U		f	u	f		F
24						X		Q		f	u	f		U		f	u	f		F
25				T	X			X		f	u	f		U		f	u	f		F
26		X	C			X			T	F		f	u	f		U		f	u	f	
27										F		f	u	f		U		f	u	f	
28	X	Q						Q			F		f	u	f		U		f	u	f

March Moon Table

Date	Sign	Element	Nature	Phase
1 Thu. 10:36 pm	Gemini	Air	Barren	1st
2 Fri.	Gemini	Air	Barren	2nd 9:03 pm
3 Sat.	Gemini	Air	Barren	2nd
4 Sun. 3:24 am	Cancer	Water	Fruitful	2nd
5 Mon.	Cancer	Water	Fruitful	2nd
6 Tue. 5:30 am	Leo	Fire	Barren	2nd
7 Wed.	Leo	Fire	Barren	2nd
8 Thu. 5:44 am	Virgo	Earth	Barren	2nd
9 Fri.	Virgo	Earth	Barren	3rd 12:23 pm
10 Sat. 5:47 am	Libra	Air	Semi-fruit	3rd
11 Sun.	Libra	Air	Semi-fruit	3rd
12 Mon. 7:43 am	Scorpio	Water	Fruitful	3rd
13 Tue.	Scorpio	Water	Fruitful	3rd
14 Wed. 1:17 pm	Sagittarius	Fire	Barren	3rd
15 Thu.	Sagittarius	Fire	Barren	3rd
16 Fri. 11:02 pm	Capricorn	Earth	Semi-fruit	4th 3:45 pm
17 Sat.	Capricorn	Earth	Semi-fruit	4th
18 Sun.	Capricorn	Earth	Semi-fruit	4th
19 Mon. 11:36 am	Aquarius	Air	Barren	4th
20 Tue.	Aquarius	Air	Barren	4th
21 Wed.	Aquarius	Air	Barren	4th
22 Thu. 12:28 am	Pisces	Water	Fruitful	4th
23 Fri.	Pisces	Water	Fruitful	4th
24 Sat. 11:43 am	Aries	Fire	Barren	1st 8:21 pm
25 Sun.	Aries	Fire	Barren	1st
26 Mon. 8:50 pm	Taurus	Earth	Semi-fruit	1st
27 Tue.	Taurus	Earth	Semi-fruit	1st
28 Wed.	Taurus	Earth	Semi-fruit	1st
29 Thu. 4:01 am	Gemini	Air	Barren	1st
30 Fri.	Gemini	Air	Barren	1st
31 Sat. 9:23 am	Cancer	Water	Fruitful	1st

March

Lunar Aspectarian · **Favorable and Unfavorable Days**

Day	Sun	Mercury	Venus	Mars	Jupiter	Saturn	Uranus	Neptune	Pluto	Aries	Taurus	Gemini	Cancer	Leo	Virgo	Libra	Scorpio	Sagittarius	Capricorn	Aquarius	Pisces
1	Q					C	Q				F		f	u	f		U		f	u	f
2	Q	Q	X	0	C	C		T		f	F	F	f	f	u	f	U	U	f	f	u
3	T	T	X				T	T	0	f		F		f	u	f		U		f		u
4		T	Q					T		f		F		f	u	f		U		f		u
5	T		Q				X			u	f		F		f	u	f		U		f	
6				T	X	X		0		u	f		F		f	u	f		U		f	
7		0	T			Q	0	0	T	f	u	f		F		f	u	f	U			
8	0	0		Q	Q	Q	0			f	u	f		F		f	u	f	U			
9	0					T			Q		f	u	f		F		f	u	f		U
10				X	T	T		T			f	u	f		F		f	u	f		U
11		T	0	X			T	T	X	U		f	u	f		F		f	u	f	
12	T	T					T	Q		U		f	u	f		F		f	u	f	
13							Q	Q			U		f	u	f		F		f	u	f
14	T	Q			0	0	Q				U		f	u	f		F		f	u	f
15			T	C	0			X	C	f	U	U	f	f	u	f	F	F	f	f	u
16	Q	X	T				X		C	f		U		f	u	f		F		f	u
17	X									u	f	U	U	f	f	u	f	F	F	f	f
18			Q							u	f		U		f	u	f		F		f
19	X				T	T				u	f		U		f	u	f		F		f
20			X	X	T			C	X	f	u	f	U	U	f	f	u	f	F	F	f
21		C	X			Q	C			f	u	f		U		f	u	f		F	
22		C			Q	Q	C			f	u	f		U		f	u	f		F	
23	C		Q						Q		f	u	f		U		f	u	f		F
24	C						X		Q		f	u	f		U		f	u	f		F
25			C	T	X			X	T	F	f	f	u	f	U	U	f	f	u	f	F
26	X	C					X		T	F		f	u	f		U		f	u	f	
27								Q		F	F	f	f	u	f	U	U	f	f	u	f
28	X	X				C	Q	Q			F		f	u	f		U		f	u	f
29	X		X		C			T			F		f	u	f		U		f	u	f
30		Q		0			T		0	f		F		f	u	f		U		f	u
31			Q							f		F		f	u	f		U		f	u

April Moon Table

Date	Sign	Element	Nature	Phase
1 Sun.	Can.	Water	Fruitful	2nd 5:49 am
2 Mon. 12:54 pm	Leo	Fire	Barren	2nd
3 Tue.	Leo	Fire	Barren	2nd
4 Wed. 2:46 pm	Virgo	Earth	Barren	2nd
5 Thu.	Virgo	Earth	Barren	2nd
6 Fri. 3:57 pm	Libra	Air	Semi-fruit	2nd
7 Sat.	Libra	Air	Semi-fruit	3rd 10:22 pm
8 Sun. 6:01 pm	Scorpio	Water	Fruitful	3rd
9 Mon.	Scorpio	Water	Fruitful	3rd
10 Tue. 10:47 pm	Sagittarius	Fire	Barren	3rd
11 Wed.	Sagittarius	Fire	Barren	3rd
12 Thu.	Sagittarius	Fire	Barren	3rd
13 Fri. 7:21 am	Capricorn	Earth	Semi-fruit	3rd
14 Sat.	Capricorn	Earth	Semi-fruit	3rd
15 Sun. 7:11 pm	Aquarius	Air	Barren	4th 10:31 am
16 Mon.	Aquarius	Air	Barren	4th
17 Tue.	Aquarius	Air	Barren	4th
18 Wed. 8:00 am	Pisces	Water	Fruitful	4th
19 Thu.	Pisces	Water	Fruitful	4th
20 Fri. 7:18 pm	Aries	Fire	Barren	4th
21 Sat.	Aries	Fire	Barren	4th
22 Sun.	Aries	Fire	Barren	4th
23 Mon. 3:56 am	Taurus	Earth	Semi-fruit	1st 10:26 am
24 Tue.	Taurus	Earth	Semi-fruit	1st
25 Wed. 10:11 am	Gemini	Air	Barren	1st
26 Thu.	Gemini	Air	Barren	1st
27 Fri. 2:49 pm	CAN	Water	Fruitful	1st
28 Sat.	CAN	Water	Fruitful	1st
29 Sun. 6:25 pm	Leo	Fire	Barren	1st
30 Mon.	Leo	Fire	Barren	2nd 12:08 pm

April

Lunar Aspectarian   Favorable and Unfavorable Days

	Sun	Mercury	Venus	Mars	Jupiter	Saturn	Uranus	Neptune	Pluto	Aries	Taurus	Gemini	Cancer	Leo	Virgo	Libra	Scorpio	Sagittarius	Capricorn	Aquarius	Pisces
1	Q							Q		u	f		F	u	f	u	f		U	u	f
2		T	X	0	C	X				u	f		F	u	f	u	f		U	u	f
3	T		T		X			0	T	f	u	f		F	u	f	u	f		U	u
4		T	Q	T		Q	0			f	u	f		F	u	f	u	f		U	u
5					Q				Q	u	f	u	f		F	u	f	u	f		U
6		0	0	Q	X	T				u	f	u	f		F	u	f	u	f		U
7	0		T		T			T	X	U	u	f	u	f		F	u	f	u	f	
8	0	0		X	Q	Q	T			U	u	f	u	f		F	u	f	u	f	
9								Q	Q		U	u	f	u	f		F	u	f	u	f
10				X	T	0	Q				U	u	f	u	f		F	u	f	u	f
11		T	T		0			X	X	f		U	u	f	u	f		F	u	f	u
12	T	T		C			X		C	f		U	u	f	u	f		F	u	f	u
13			Q					Q		f	U	U	f	f	u	f	F	F	f	f	u
14	Q	Q					0	Q		u	f		U	u	f	u	f		F	u	f
15	Q		X	C	0	T		X		u	f		U	u	f	u	f		F	u	f
16		X	T		T		X	C	C	f	u	f		U	u	f	u	f		F	u
17	X	X		X		C			X	f	u	f		U	u	f	u	f		F	u
18	X		Q		Q					f	u	f	U	U	f	f	u	f	F	F	f
19					Q	T			Q	u	f	u	f		U	u	f	u	f		F
20			C	Q	T	X		C		u	f	u	f		U	u	f	u	f		F
21		C	X		X			X	T	F	u	f	u	f		U	u	f	u	f	
22				T	Q	Q	X			F	u	f	u	f		U	u	f	u	f	
23	C	C		Q				Q		F	f	f	u	f	U	U	f	f	u	f	F
24						X			Q		F	u	f	u	f		U	u	f	u	f
25			X	T	X	C	Q	X			F	u	f	u	f		U	u	f	u	f
26		X	C		C		X	T	0	f		F	u	f	u	f		U	u	f	u
27			Q	0			T			f		F	u	f	u	f		U	u	f	u
28	X	X						Q		u	f		F	u	f	u	f		U	u	f
29						X				u	f		F	u	f	u	f		U	u	f
30	Q		T		X			0	T	f	u	f		F	u	f	u	f		U	u

May Moon Table

Date	Sign	Element	Nature	Phase
1 Tue. 9:16 pm	Virgo	Earth	Barren	2nd
2 Wed.	Virgo	Earth	Barren	2nd
3 Thu. 11:50 pm	Libra	Air	Semi-fruit	2nd
4 Fri.	Libra	Air	Semi-fruit	2nd
5 Sat.	Libra	Air	Semi-fruit	2nd
6 Sun. 3:00 am	Scorpio	Water	Fruitful	2nd
7 Mon.	Scorpio	Water	Fruitful	3rd 8:53 am
8 Tue. 8:05 am	Sagittarius	Fire	Barren	3rd
9 Wed.	Sagittarius	Fire	Barren	3rd
10 Thu. 4:10 pm	Capricorn	Earth	Semi-fruit	3rd
11 Fri.	Capricorn	Earth	Semi-fruit	3rd
12 Sat.	Capricorn	Earth	Semi-fruit	3rd
13 Sun. 3:20 am	Aquarius	Air	Barren	3rd
14 Mon.	Aquarius	Air	Barren	3rd
15 Tue. 4:01 pm	Pisces	Water	Fruitful	4th 5:11 am
16 Wed.	Pisces	Water	Fruitful	4th
17 Thu.	Pisces	Water	Fruitful	4th
18 Fri. 3:41 am	Aries	Fire	Barren	4th
19 Sat.	Aries	Fire	Barren	4th
20 Sun. 12:29 pm	Taurus	Earth	Semi-fruit	4th
21 Mon.	Taurus	Earth	Semi-fruit	4th
22 Tue. 6:12 pm	Gemini	Air	Barren	1st 9:46 pm
23 Wed.	Gemini	Air	Barren	1st
24 Thu. 9:42 pm	Cancer	Water	Fruitful	1st
25 Fri.	Cancer	Water	Fruitful	1st
26 Sat.	Cancer	Water	Fruitful	1st
27 Sun. 12:12 am	Leo	Fire	Barren	1st
28 Mon.	Leo	Fire	Barren	1st
29 Tue. 2:38 am	Virgo	Earth	Barren	2nd 5:09 pm
30 Wed.	Virgo	Earth	Barren	2nd
31 Thu. 5:41 am	Libra	Air	Semi-fruit	2nd

May

Lunar Aspectarian **Favorable and Unfavorable Days**

Day	Sun	Mercury	Venus	Mars	Jupiter	Saturn	Uranus	Neptune	Pluto	Aries	Taurus	Gemini	Cancer	Leo	Virgo	Libra	Scorpio	Sagittarius	Capricorn	Aquarius	Pisces
1	Q	Q		T		Q	0			f	u	f	F	F	f	f	u	f	U	U	f
2	T	T	X	0	Q	X			Q	u	f	u	f	u	F	u	f	u	f	u	U
3	T	T	T	Q	X			0	T	f	f	u	f	F	F	f	f	u	f	U	U
4		T	0	T		T	0	T		U	u	f	u	f	u	F	u	f	u	f	u
5					T		T		X	U	f	f	u	f	F	F	f	f	u	f	U
6		0	0	X	X	T		Q		U	f	f	u	f	F	F	f	f	u	f	U
7	0			T		T	Q	T	X	U	U	f	f	u	f	F	F	f	f	u	f
8	0	0	T	X	Q	0		T		U	U	f	f	u	f	F	F	f	f	u	f
9					0			X	C	f	U	U	f	f	u	f	F	F	f	f	u
10				C	T	0	X			f	U	U	f	f	u	f	F	F	f	f	u
11		T	Q		0			X	X	u	f	U	U	f	f	u	f	F	F	f	f
12	T	T		C			X		C	u	f	U	U	f	f	u	f	F	F	f	f
13			Q			T		C		u	f	U	U	f	f	u	f	F	F	f	f
14	Q	T	X		T	0	Q		X	f	u	f	U	U	f	f	u	f	F	F	f
15	Q		X	X	0	Q	C	X		f	u	f	U	U	f	f	u	f	F	F	f
16		X	T		T		X	C	Q	f	f	u	f	U	U	f	f	u	f	F	F
17	X	Q		X	Q			C	X	f	f	u	f	U	U	f	f	u	f	F	F
18	X		Q	Q		X		X		f	f	u	f	U	U	f	f	u	f	F	F
19		X	C			X	T		T	F	f	f	u	f	U	U	f	f	u	f	F
20			C	T	T	X	X	C		F	f	f	u	f	U	U	f	f	u	f	F
21			C	X		X		Q	T	F	F	f	f	u	f	U	U	f	f	u	f
22	C			T	Q	Q	Q			F	F	f	f	u	f	U	U	f	f	u	f
23	C	C		Q		C		T	0	f	f	F	u	f	u	f	f	U	u	f	u
24		C	X	0	C	X	T		Q	f	F	F	f	f	u	f	U	U	f	f	u
25			X	T	X	C	Q	X		u	f	u	F	u	f	u	f	u	U	u	f
26		X	Q		C		X	T	0	u	f	F	F	f	f	u	f	U	U	f	u
27	X		Q	0		X	T	0	T	u	f	F	F	f	f	u	f	U	U	f	f
28	X	X	T	T	X			0	Q	f	u	f	F	F	f	f	u	f	U	U	f
29	Q	X				Q				f	u	f	F	F	f	f	u	f	U	U	f
30	Q		T		Q	Q		0	Q	f	f	u	f	F	F	f	f	u	f	U	U
31		Q				T		T			f	u	f		F			f	u	f		U

June Moon Table

Date	Sign	Element	Nature	Phase
1 Fri.	Libra	Air	Semi-fruit	2nd
2 Sat. 9:56 am	Scorpio	Water	Fruitful	2nd
3 Sun.	Scorpio	Water	Fruitful	2nd
4 Mon. 3:58 pm	Sagittarius	Fire	Barren	2nd
5 Tue.	Sagittarius	Fire	Barren	3rd 8:39 pm
6 Wed.	Sagittarius	Fire	Barren	3rd
7 Thu. 12:23 am	Capricorn	Earth	Semi-fruit	3rd
8 Fri.	Capricorn	Earth	Semi-fruit	3rd
9 Sat. 11:20 am	Aquarius	Air	Barren	3rd
10 Sun.	Aquarius	Air	Barren	3rd
11 Mon. 11:53 pm	Pisces	Water	Fruitful	3rd
12 Tue.	Pisces	Water	Fruitful	3rd
13 Wed.	Pisces	Water	Fruitful	4th 10:28 pm
14 Thu. 12:03 pm	Aries	Fire	Barren	4th
15 Fri.	Aries	Fire	Barren	4th
16 Sat. 9:39 pm	Taurus	Earth	Semi-fruit	4th
17 Sun.	Taurus	Earth	Semi-fruit	4th
18 Mon.	Taurus	Earth	Semi-fruit	4th
19 Tue. 3:42 am	Gemini	Air	Barren	4th
20 Wed.	Gemini	Air	Barren	4th
21 Thu. 6:40 am	Cancer	Water	Fruitful	1st 6:58 am
22 Fri.	Cancer	Water	Fruitful	1st
23 Sat. 7:55 am	Leo	Fire	Barren	1st
24 Sun.	Leo	Fire	Barren	1st
25 Mon. 8:57 am	Virgo	Earth	Barren	1st
26 Tue.	Virgo	Earth	Barren	1st
27 Wed. 11:11 am	Libra	Air	Semi-fruit	2nd 10:19 pm
28 Thu.	Libra	Air	Semi-fruit	2nd
29 Fri. 3:28 pm	Scorpio	Water	Fruitful	2nd
30 Sat.	Scorpio	Water	Fruitful	2nd

June

Lunar Aspectarian   Favorable and Unfavorable Days

	Sun	Mercury	Venus	Mars	Jupiter	Saturn	Uranus	Neptune	Pluto	Aries	Taurus	Gemini	Cancer	Leo	Virgo	Libra	Scorpio	Sagittarius	Capricorn	Aquarius	Pisces
1	T				T				X	U		f	u	f		F		f	u	f	
2		T	0	X				T		U		f	u	f		F		f	u	f	
3								Q			U		f	u	f		F		f	u	f
4								Q			U		f	u	f		F		f	u	f
5	0					0		X	C	f		U		f	u	f		F		f	u
6		0		C	0		X			f		U		f	u	f		F		f	u
7			T							f		U		f	u	f		F		f	u
8										u	f		U		f	u	f		F		f
9			Q							u	f		U		f	u	f		F		f
10						T		C	X	f	u	f		U		f	u	f		F	
11	T	T		X	T		C			f	u	f		U		f	u	f		F	
12			X		Q						f	u	f		U		f	u	f		F
13	Q			Q	Q				Q		f	u	f		U		f	u	f		F
14		Q									f	u	f		U		f	u	f		F
15						X		X	T	F		f	u	f		U		f	u	f	
16	X	X		T	X		X			F		f	u	f		U		f	u	f	
17			C					Q			F		f	u	f		U		f	u	f
18								Q			F		f	u	f		U		f	u	f
19						C		T			F		f	u	f		U		f	u	f
20		C		0	C	T			0	f		F		f	u	f		U		f	u
21	C									f		F		f	u	f		U		f	u
22			X							u	f		F		f	u	f		U		f
23						X		0		u	f		F		f	u	f		U		f
24		X	Q	T					T	f	u	f		F		f	u	f		U	
25	X				X	Q	0			f	u	f		F		f	u	f		U	
26		Q	T	Q					Q		f	u	f		F		f	u	f		U
27	Q				Q						f	u	f		F		f	u	f		U
28				X	T			T	X	U		f	u	f		F		f	u	f	
29		T				T		T		U		f	u	f		F		f	u	f	
30	T							Q			U		f	u	f		F		f	u	f

July Moon Table

Date	Sign	Element	Nature	Phase
1 Sun. 10:13 pm	Sagittarius	Fire	Barren	2nd
2 Mon.	Sagittarius	Fire	Barren	2nd
3 Tue.	Sagittarius	Fire	Barren	2nd
4 Wed. 7:21 am	Capricorn	Earth	Semi-fruit	2nd
5 Thu.	Capricorn	Earth	Semi-fruit	3rd 10:04 am
6 Fri. 6:33 pm	Aquarius	Air	Barren	3rd
7 Sat.	Aquarius	Air	Barren	3rd
8 Sun.	Aquarius	Air	Barren	3rd
9 Mon. 7:05 am	Pisces	Water	Fruitful	3rd
10 Tue.	Pisces	Water	Fruitful	3rd
11 Wed. 7:36 pm	Aries	Fire	Barren	3rd
12 Thu.	Aries	Fire	Barren	3rd
13 Fri.	Aries	Fire	Barren	4th 1:45 pm
14 Sat. 6:13 am	Taurus	Earth	Semi-fruit	4th
15 Sun.	Taurus	Earth	Semi-fruit	4th
16 Mon. 1:26 pm	Gemini	Air	Barren	4th
17 Tue.	Gemini	Air	Barren	4th
18 Wed. 4:56 pm	Cancer	Water	Fruitful	4th
19 Thu.	Cancer	Water	Fruitful	4th
20 Fri. 5:43 pm	Leo	Fire	Barren	1st 2:44 pm
21 Sat.	Leo	Fire	Barren	1st
22 Sun. 5:29 pm	Virgo	Earth	Barren	1st
23 Mon.	Virgo	Earth	Barren	1st
24 Tue. 6:08 pm	Libra	Air	Semi-fruit	1st
25 Wed.	Libra	Air	Semi-fruit	1st
26 Thu. 9:17 pm	Scorpio	Water	Fruitful	1st
27 Fri.	Scorpio	Water	Fruitful	2nd 5:08 am
28 Sat.	Scorpio	Water	Fruitful	2nd
29 Sun. 3:44 am	Sagittarius	Fire	Barren	2nd
30 Mon.	Sagittarius	Fire	Barren	2nd
31 Tue. 1:16 pm	Capricorn	Earth	Semi-fruit	2nd

July

Lunar Aspectarian   **Favorable and Unfavorable Days**

Day	Sun	Mercury	Venus	Mars	Jupiter	Saturn	Uranus	Neptune	Pluto	Aries	Taurus	Gemini	Cancer	Leo	Virgo	Libra	Scorpio	Sagittarius	Capricorn	Aquarius	Pisces
1			0					Q			U		f	u	f		F		f	u	f
2						0		X	C	f		U		f	u	f		F		f	u
3		0		C				X		f		U		f	u	f		F		f	u
4					0					f		U		f	u	f		F		f	u
5	0									u	f		U		f	u	f		F		f
6			T							u	f		U		f	u	f		F		f
7						T		C	X	f	u	f		U		f	u	f		F	
8		T		X				C		f	u	f		U		f	u	f		F	
9			Q		T					f	u	f		U		f	u	f		F	
10	T			Q	Q				Q		f	u	f		U		f	u	f		F
11		Q		Q							f	u	f		U		f	u	f		F
12			X		X			X	T	F		f	u	f		U		f	u	f	
13	Q			T				X		F		f	u	f		U		f	u	f	
14		X			X			Q		F		f	u	f		U		f	u	f	
15											F		f	u	f		U		f	u	f
16	X							Q			F		f	u	f		U		f	u	f
17			C	0	C			T	0	f		F		f	u	f		U		f	u
18					C			T		f		F		f	u	f		U		f	u
19		C								u	f		F		f	u	f		U		f
20	C									u	f		F		f	u	f		U		f
21			X	T	X			0	T	f	u	f		F		f	u	f		U	
22				X				0		f	u	f		F		f	u	f		U	
23		X	Q		Q				Q		f	u	f		F		f	u	f		U
24	X		Q		Q						f	u	f		F		f	u	f		U
25				X		T		T	X	U		f	u	f		F		f	u	f	
26		Q	T					T		U		f	u	f		F		f	u	f	
27	Q				T			Q			U		f	u	f		F		f	u	f
28		T						Q			U		f	u	f		F		f	u	f
29	T							X			U		f	u	f		F		f	u	f
30				C	0				C	f		U		f	u	f		F		f	u
31			0		0			X		f		U		f	u	f		F		f	u

August Moon Table

Date	Sign	Element	Nature	Phase
1 Wed.	Capricorn	Earth	Semi-fruit	2nd
2 Thu.	Capricorn	Earth	Semi-fruit	2nd
3 Fri. 12:53 am	Aquarius	Air	Barren	2nd
4 Sat.	Aquarius	Air	Barren	3rd 12:56 am
5 Sun. 1:30 pm	Pisces	Water	Fruitful	3rd
6 Mon.	Pisces	Water	Fruitful	3rd
7 Tue.	Pisces	Water	Fruitful	3rd
8 Wed. 2:05 am	Aries	Fire	Barren	3rd
9 Thu.	Aries	Fire	Barren	3rd
10 Fri. 1:23 pm	Taurus	Earth	Semi-fruit	3rd
11 Sat.	Taurus	Earth	Semi-fruit	3rd
12 Sun. 9:59 pm	Gemini	Air	Barren	4th 2:53 am
13 Mon.	Gemini	Air	Barren	4th
14 Tue.	Gemini	Air	Barren	4th
15 Wed. 2:55 am	Cancer	Water	Fruitful	4th
16 Thu.	Cancer	Water	Fruitful	4th
17 Fri. 4:25 am	Leo	Fire	Barren	4th
18 Sat.	Leo	Fire	Barren	1st 9:55 pm
19 Sun. 3:53 am	Virgo	Earth	Barren	1st
20 Mon.	Virgo	Earth	Barren	1st
21 Tue. 3:19 am	Libra	Air	Semi-fruit	1st
22 Wed.	Libra	Air	Semi-fruit	1st
23 Thu. 4:50 am	Scorpio	Water	Fruitful	1st
24 Fri.	Scorpio	Water	Fruitful	1st
25 Sat. 9:59 am	Sagittarius	Fire	Barren	2nd 2:55 pm
26 Sun.	Sagittarius	Fire	Barren	2nd
27 Mon. 7:02 pm	Capricorn	Earth	Semi-fruit	2nd
28 Tue.	Capricorn	Earth	Semi-fruit	2nd
29 Wed.	Capricorn	Earth	Semi-fruit	2nd
30 Thu. 6:47 am	Aquarius	Air	Barren	2nd
31 Fri.	Aquarius	Air	Barren	2nd

August

Lunar Aspectarian   **Favorable and Unfavorable Days**

	Sun	Mercury	Venus	Mars	Jupiter	Saturn	Uranus	Neptune	Pluto	Aries	Taurus	Gemini	Cancer	Leo	Virgo	Libra	Scorpio	Sagittarius	Capricorn	Aquarius	Pisces
1										u	f		U		f	u	f		F		f
2										u	f		U		f	u	f		F		f
3		0							C	u	f		U		f	u	f		F		f
4	0			X		T	C		X	f	u	f		U		f	u	f		F	
5						T				f	u	f		U		f	u	f		F	
6			T		Q				Q		f	u	f		U		f	u	f		F
7				Q							f	u	f		U		f	u	f		F
8			Q		Q			X			f	u	f		U		f	u	f		F
9	T	T		T		X	X		T	F		f	u	f		U		f	u	f	
10										F		f	u	f		U		f	u	f	
11			X		X			Q			F		f	u	f		U		f	u	f
12	Q	Q						Q			F		f	u	f		U		f	u	f
13						C		T	0	f		F		f	u	f		U		f	u
14	X			0				T		f		F		f	u	f		U		f	u
15		X			C					f		F		f	u	f		U		f	u
16			C							u	f		F		f	u	f		U		f
17								0		u	f		F		f	u	f		U		f
18	C			T		X	0		T	f	u	f		F		f	u	f		U	
19		C			X				Q	f	u	f		F		f	u	f		U	
20			X	Q		Q					f	u	f		F		f	u	f		U
21					Q			T	X		f	u	f		F		f	u	f		U
22			Q	X		T	T			U		f	u	f		F		f	u	f	
23	X				T			Q		U		f	u	f		F		f	u	f	
24		X					Q				U		f	u	f		F		f	u	f
25	Q		T					X			U		f	u	f		F		f	u	f
26					0				C	f		U		f	u	f		F		f	u
27		Q	C			X				f		U		f	u	f		F		f	u
28	T				0					u	f		U		f	u	f		F		f
29										u	f		U		f	u	f		F		f
30		T	0						C	u	f		U		f	u	f		F		f
31						T			X	f	u	f		U		f	u	f		F	

September Moon Table

Date	Sign	Element	Nature	Phase
1 Sat. 7:32 pm	Pisces	Water	Fruitful	2nd
2 Sun.	Pisces	Water	Fruitful	3rd 4:43 pm
3 Mon.	Pisces	Water	Fruitful	3rd
4 Tue. 7:58 am	Aries	Fire	Barren	3rd
5 Wed.	Aries	Fire	Barren	3rd
6 Thu. 7:18 pm	Taurus	Earth	Semi-fruit	3rd
7 Fri.	Taurus	Earth	Semi-fruit	3rd
8 Sat.	Taurus	Earth	Semi-fruit	3rd
9 Sun. 4:41 am	Gemini	Air	Barren	3rd
10 Mon.	Gemini	Air	Barren	4th 1:59 pm
11 Tue. 11:09 am	Cancer	Water	Fruitful	4th
12 Wed.	Cancer	Water	Fruitful	4th
13 Thu. 2:16 pm	Leo	Fire	Barren	4th
14 Fri.	Leo	Fire	Barren	4th
15 Sat. 2:39 pm	Virgo	Earth	Barren	4th
16 Sun.	Virgo	Earth	Barren	4th
17 Mon. 2:00 pm	Libra	Air	Semi-fruit	1st 5:27 am
18 Tue.	Libra	Air	Semi-fruit	1st
19 Wed. 2:27 pm	Scorpio	Water	Fruitful	1st
20 Thu.	Scorpio	Water	Fruitful	1st
21 Fri. 6:02 pm	Sagittarius	Fire	Barren	1st
22 Sat.	Sagittarius	Fire	Barren	1st
23 Sun.	Sagittarius	Fire	Barren	1st
24 Mon. 1:48 am	Capricorn	Earth	Semi-fruit	2nd 4:31 am
25 Tue.	Capricorn	Earth	Semi-fruit	2nd
26 Wed. 1:05 pm	Aquarius	Air	Barren	2nd
27 Thu.	Aquarius	Air	Barren	2nd
28 Fri.	Aquarius	Air	Barren	2nd
29 Sat. 1:50 am	Pisces	Water	Fruitful	2nd
30 Sun.	Pisces	Water	Fruitful	2nd

September

Day	Lunar Aspectarian									Favorable and Unfavorable Days											
	Sun	Mercury	Venus	Mars	Jupiter	Saturn	Uranus	Neptune	Pluto	Aries	Taurus	Gemini	Cancer	Leo	Virgo	Libra	Scorpio	Sagittarius	Capricorn	Aquarius	Pisces
1				X			C			f	u	f		U		f	u	f		F	
2	0				T				Q		f	u	f		U		f	u	f		F
3						Q					f	u	f		U		f	u	f		F
4		0		Q				X			f	u	f		U		f	u	f		F
5			T		Q	X			T	F		f	u	f		U		f	u	f	
6			T				X			F		f	u	f		U		f	u	f	
7			Q		X			Q			F		f	u	f		U		f	u	f
8	T						Q				F		f	u	f		U		f	u	f
9								T		f		F		f	u	f		U		f	u
10	Q	T	X			C	T		0	f		F		f	u	f		U		f	u
11			0							u	f		F		f	u	f		U		f
12	X	Q			C					u	f		F		f	u	f		U		f
13										u	f		F		f	u	f		U		f
14		X			X			0	T	f	u	f		F		f	u	f		U	
15			C	T			0			f	u	f		F		f	u	f		U	
16					X	Q			Q		f	u	f		F		f	u	f		U
17	C			Q				T			f	u	f		F		f	u	f		U
18					Q	T			X	U		f	u	f		F		f	u	f	
19		C	X				T			U		f	u	f		F		f	u	f	
20				X	T			Q			U		f	u	f		F		f	u	f
21	X		Q			Q					U		f	u	f		F		f	u	f
22				0			X	C		f		U		f	u	f		F		f	u
23		X					X			f		U		f	u	f		F		f	u
24	Q		T	C						f		U		f	u	f		F		f	u
25					0					u	f		U		f	u	f		F		f
26	T	Q								u	f		U		f	u	f		F		f
27					T		C	X		f	u	f		U		f	u	f		F	
28					C					f	u	f		U		f	u	f		F	
29		T								f	u	f		U		f	u	f		F	
30			0	X	T	Q			Q		f	u	f		U		f	u	f		F

October Moon Table

Date	Sign	Element	Nature	Phase
1 Mon. 2:08 pm	Aries	Fire	Barren	2nd
2 Tue.	Aries	Fire	Barren	3rd 8:49 am
3 Wed.	Aries	Fire	Barren	3rd
4 Thu. 1:01 am	Taurus	Earth	Semi-fruit	3rd
5 Fri.	Taurus	Earth	Semi-fruit	3rd
6 Sat. 10:12 am	Gemini	Air	Barren	3rd
7 Sun.	Gemini	Air	Barren	3rd
8 Mon. 5:19 pm	Cancer	Water	Fruitful	3rd
9 Tue.	Cancer	Water	Fruitful	4th 11:20 pm
10 Wed. 9:54 pm	Leo	Fire	Barren	4th
11 Thu.	Leo	Fire	Barren	4th
12 Fri. 11:58 pm	Virgo	Earth	Barren	4th
13 Sat.	Virgo	Earth	Barren	4th
14 Sun.	Virgo	Earth	Barren	4th
15 Mon. 12:26 am	Libra	Air	Semi-fruit	4th
16 Tue.	Libra	Air	Semi-fruit	1st 2:23 pm
17 Wed. 1:03 am	Scorpio	Water	Fruitful	1st
18 Thu.	Scorpio	Water	Fruitful	1st
19 Fri. 3:47 am	Sagittarius	Fire	Barren	1st
20 Sat.	Sagittarius	Fire	Barren	1st
21 Sun. 10:11 am	Capricorn	Earth	Semi-fruit	1st
22 Mon.	Capricorn	Earth	Semi-fruit	1st
23 Tue. 8:26 pm	Aquarius	Air	Barren	2nd 9:58 pm
24 Wed.	Aquarius	Air	Barren	2nd
25 Thu.	Aquarius	Air	Barren	2nd
26 Fri. 8:56 am	Pisces	Water	Fruitful	2nd
27 Sat.	Pisces	Water	Fruitful	2nd
28 Sun. 9:15 pm	Aries	Fire	Barren	2nd
29 Mon.	Aries	Fire	Barren	2nd
30 Tue.	Aries	Fire	Barren	2nd
31 Wed. 7:48 am	Taurus	Earth	Semi-fruit	2nd

October

Lunar Aspectarian   Favorable and Unfavorable Days

	Sun	Mercury	Venus	Mars	Jupiter	Saturn	Uranus	Neptune	Pluto	Aries	Taurus	Gemini	Cancer	Leo	Virgo	Libra	Scorpio	Sagittarius	Capricorn	Aquarius	Pisces
1											f	u	f		U		f	u	f		F
2	0			Q	Q	X		X	T	F		f	u	f		U		f	u	f	
3		0					X			F		f	u	f		U		f	u	f	
4								Q		F		f	u	f		U		f	u	f	
5			T	T	X			Q			F		f	u	f		U		f	u	f
6								T			F		f	u	f		U		f	u	f
7	T					C			0	f		F		f	u	f		U		f	u
8		T	Q					T		f		F		f	u	f		U		f	u
9	Q				C					u	f		F		f	u	f		U		f
10		Q	X	0						u	f		F		f	u	f		U		f
11						X		0	T	f	u	f		F		f	u	f		U	
12	X	X						0		f	u	f		F		f	u	f		U	
13						Q			Q		f	u	f		F		f	u	f		U
14			C	T	X						f	u	f		F		f	u	f		U
15								T	X		f	u	f		F		f	u	f		U
16	C	C		Q	Q	T	T			U		f	u	f		F		f	u	f	
17								Q		U		f	u	f		F		f	u	f	
18				X	T			Q			U		f	u	f		F		f	u	f
19			X					X			U		f	u	f		F		f	u	f
20		X				0	X		C	f		U		f	u	f		F		f	u
21	X									f		U		f	u	f		F		f	u
22		Q	Q		0					u	f		U		f	u	f		F		f
23	Q			C						u	f		U		f	u	f		F		f
24			T					C	X	f	u	f		U		f	u	f		F	
25		T				T	C			f	u	f		U		f	u	f		F	
26	T									f	u	f		U		f	u	f		F	
27					T	Q			Q		f	u	f		U		f	u	f		F
28				X							f	u	f		U		f	u	f		F
29								X		F		f	u	f		U		f	u	f	
30		0	0	Q	X	X			T	F		f	u	f		U		f	u	f	
31				Q				Q		F		f	u	f		U		f	u	f	

November Moon Table

Date	Sign	Element	Nature	Phase
1 Thu.	Taurus	Earth	Semi-fruit	3rd 12:41 am
2 Fri. 4:12 pm	Gemini	Air	Barren	3rd
3 Sat.	Gemini	Air	Barren	3rd
4 Sun. 10:44 pm	Cancer	Water	Fruitful	3rd
5 Mon.	Cancer	Water	Fruitful	3rd
6 Tue.	Cancer	Water	Fruitful	3rd
7 Wed. 3:34 am	Leo	Fire	Barren	3rd
8 Thu.	Leo	Fire	Barren	4th 7:21 am
9 Fri. 6:49 am	Virgo	Earth	Barren	4th
10 Sat.	Virgo	Earth	Barren	4th
11 Sun. 8:53 am	Libra	Air	Semi-fruit	4th
12 Mon.	Libra	Air	Semi-fruit	4th
13 Tue. 10:44 am	Scorpio	Water	Fruitful	4th
14 Wed.	Scorpio	Water	Fruitful	4th
15 Thu. 1:51 pm	Sagittarius	Fire	Barren	1st 1:40 am
16 Fri.	Sagittarius	Fire	Barren	1st
17 Sat. 7:40 pm	Capricorn	Earth	Semi-fruit	1st
18 Sun.	Capricorn	Earth	Semi-fruit	1st
19 Mon.	Capricorn	Earth	Semi-fruit	1st
20 Tue. 4:55 am	Aquarius	Air	Barren	1st
21 Wed.	Aquarius	Air	Barren	1st
22 Thu. 4:52 pm	Pisces	Water	Fruitful	2nd 6:21 pm
23 Fri.	Pisces	Water	Fruitful	2nd
24 Sat.	Pisces	Water	Fruitful	2nd
25 Sun. 5:21 am	Aries	Fire	Barren	2nd
26 Mon.	Aries	Fire	Barren	2nd
27 Tue. 4:06 pm	Taurus	Earth	Semi-fruit	2nd
28 Wed.	Taurus	Earth	Semi-fruit	2nd
29 Thu.	Taurus	Earth	Semi-fruit	2nd
30 Fri. 12:04 am	Gemini	Air	Barren	3rd 3:49 pm

November

Lunar Aspectarian   Favorable and Unfavorable Days

Day	Sun	Mercury	Venus	Mars	Jupiter	Saturn	Uranus	Neptune	Pluto	Aries	Taurus	Gemini	Cancer	Leo	Virgo	Libra	Scorpio	Sagittarius	Capricorn	Aquarius	Pisces
1	0				X		Q				F		f	u	f		U		f	u	f
2											F		f	u	f		U		f	u	f
3				T		C		T	0	f		F		f	u	f		U		f	u
4		T	T					T		f		F		f	u	f		U		f	u
5	T									u	f		F		f	u	f		U		f
6						C				u	f		F		f	u	f		U		f
7		Q	Q	0				0		u	f		F		f	u	f		U		f
8	Q				X		0		T	f	u	f		F		f	u	f		U	
9		X	X							f	u	f		F		f	u	f		U	
10	X				X	Q			Q		f	u	f		F		f	u	f		U
11								T			f	u	f		F		f	u	f		U
12			T		Q	T	T		X	U		f	u	f		F		f	u	f	
13			C					Q		U		f	u	f		F		f	u	f	
14		C		Q	T		Q				U		f	u	f		F		f	u	f
15	C										U		f	u	f		F		f	u	f
16				X	0			X	C	f		U		f	u	f		F		f	u
17								X		f		U		f	u	f		F		f	u
18			X							u	f		U		f	u	f		F		f
19		X			0					u	f		U		f	u	f		F		f
20	X								C	u	f		U		f	u	f		F		f
21			Q	C		T	C		X	f	u	f		U		f	u	f		F	
22	Q	Q								f	u	f		U		f	u	f		F	
23					T	Q			Q		f	u	f		U		f	u	f		F
24			T								f	u	f		U		f	u	f		F
25	T	T						X			f	u	f		U		f	u	f		F
26				X	Q	X	X		T	F		f	u	f		U		f	u	f	
27										F		f	u	f		U		f	u	f	
28					X			Q			F		f	u	f		U		f	u	f
29			0	Q				Q			F		f	u	f		U		f	u	f
30	0	0				C		T			F		f	u	f		U		f	u	f

December Moon Table

Date	Sign	Element	Nature	Phase
1 Sat.	Gemini	Air	Barren	3rd
2 Sun. 5:30 am	Cancer	Water	Fruitful	3rd
3 Mon.	Cancer	Water	Fruitful	3rd
4 Tue. 9:15 am	Leo	Fire	Barren	3rd
5 Wed.	Leo	Fire	Barren	3rd
6 Thu. 12:11 pm	Virgo	Earth	Barren	3rd
7 Fri.	Virgo	Earth	Barren	4th 2:52 pm
8 Sat. 2:57 pm	Libra	Air	Semi-fruit	4th
9 Sun.	Libra	Air	Semi-fruit	4th
10 Mon. 6:09 pm	Scorpio	Water	Fruitful	4th
11 Tue.	Scorpio	Water	Fruitful	4th
12 Wed. 10:30 pm	Sagittarius	Fire	Barren	4th
13 Thu.	Sagittarius	Fire	Barren	4th
14 Fri.	Sagittarius	Fire	Barren	1st 3:47 pm
15 Sat. 4:48 am	Capricorn	Earth	Semi-fruit	1st
16 Sun.	Capricorn	Earth	Semi-fruit	1st
17 Mon. 1:43 pm	Aquarius	Air	Barren	1st
18 Tue.	Aquarius	Air	Barren	1st
19 Wed.	Aquarius	Air	Barren	1st
20 Thu. 1:09 am	Pisces	Water	Fruitful	1st
21 Fri.	Pisces	Water	Fruitful	1st
22 Sat. 1:45 pm	Aries	Fire	Barren	2nd 3:56 pm
23 Sun.	Aries	Fire	Barren	2nd
24 Mon.	Aries	Fire	Barren	2nd
25 Tue. 1:12 am	Taurus	Earth	Semi-fruit	2nd
26 Wed.	Taurus	Earth	Semi-fruit	2nd
27 Thu. 9:39 am	Gemini	Air	Barren	2nd
28 Fri.	Gemini	Air	Barren	2nd
29 Sat. 2:40 pm	Cancer	Water	Fruitful	2nd
30 Sun.	Cancer	Water	Fruitful	3rd 5:40 am
31 Mon. 5:09 pm	Leo	Fire	Barren	3rd

December

Lunar Aspectarian — Favorable and Unfavorable Days

Day	Sun	Mercury	Venus	Mars	Jupiter	Saturn	Uranus	Neptune	Pluto	Aries	Taurus	Gemini	Cancer	Leo	Virgo	Libra	Scorpio	Sagittarius	Capricorn	Aquarius	Pisces
1				T				T	0	f		F		f	u	f		U		f	u
2										f		F		f	u	f		U		f	u
3					C					u	f		F		f	u	f		U		f
4			T					0		u	f		F		f	u	f		U		f
5	T	T				X	0		T	f	u	f		F		f	u	f		U	
6		Q		0						f	u	f		F		f	u	f		U	
7	Q	Q			X	Q			Q		f	u	f		F		f	u	f		U
8											f	u	f		F		f	u	f		U
9	X		X		Q	T		T	X	U		f	u	f		F		f	u	f	
10		X	T			T				U		f	u	f		F		f	u	f	
11					T			Q			U		f	u	f		F		f	u	f
12						Q					U		f	u	f		F		f	u	f
13				Q		0	X			f		U		f	u	f		F		f	u
14	C		C				X		C	f		U		f	u	f		F		f	u
15		C		X						f		U		f	u	f		F		f	u
16					0					u	f		U		f	u	f		F		f
17										u	f		U		f	u	f		F		f
18						T		C	X	f	u	f		U		f	u	f		F	
19	X		X				C			f	u	f		U		f	u	f		F	
20		X		C		Q				f	u	f		U		f	u	f		F	
21				T				Q		f	u	f			U		f	u	f		F
22	Q		Q							f	u	f			U		f	u	f		F
23		Q			Q	X		X	T	F		f	u	f		U		f	u	f	
24			T				X			F		f	u	f		U		f	u	f	
25	T				X			Q		F		f	u	f		U		f	u	f	
26		T		X		Q					F		f	u	f		U		f	u	f
27								T			F		f	u	f		U		f	u	f
28				Q		C			0	f		F		f	u	f		U		f	u
29			0				T			f		F		f	u	f		U		f	u
30	0			T	C					u	f		F		f	u	f		U		f
31		0								u	f		F		f	u	f		U		f

The Moon's Quarters & Signs

Everyone has seen the Moon wax and wane through a period of approximately twenty-nine and a half days. This circuit from New Moon to Full Moon and back again is called the lunation cycle. The cycle is divided into parts, called quarters or phases. There are several methods by which this can be done, and the system used in the Moon Sign Book may not correspond to those used in other almanacs.

First Quarter

The first quarter begins at the New Moon, when the Sun and Moon are in the same place, or conjunct. (This means that the Sun and Moon are in the same degree of the same sign.) The Moon is not visible at first, since it rises at the same time as the Sun. The **New Moon** is the time of new beginnings, beginnings of projects that favor growth, externalization of activities, and the expansion of ideas. The first quarter is the time of germination, emergence, beginnings, and outwardly directed activity.

Second Quarter

The second quarter begins halfway between the New Moon and the Full Moon when the Sun and Moon are at right angles (90 degrees). This half Moon rises around noon and sets around midnight, so it can be seen in the western sky during the first half of the night. The second quarter is the time of growth, development, and articulation of things that already exist.

Third Quarter

The third quarter begins at the Full Moon, when the Sun is opposite the Moon and its full light can shine on the full sphere of the Moon. The round Moon can be seen rising in the east at sunset, and then rising a little later each evening. The **Full Moon** stands for illumination, fulfillment, culmination, completion, drawing inward, unrest, emotional expressions, and hasty actions leading to failure. The third quarter is a time of maturity, fruition, and the assumption of the full form of expression.

Fourth Quarter

The fourth quarter begins about halfway between the Full Moon and New Moon, when the Sun and Moon are again at 90 degrees, or square. This decreasing Moon rises at midnight, and can be seen in the east during the last half of the night, reaching the overhead position just about as the Sun rises. The fourth quarter is a time of disintegration, drawing back for reorganization, and reflection.

The Signs

Moon in Aries is good for starting things but lacks staying power. Things occur rapidly but also quickly pass.

Moon in Taurus accent is on things that arre long lasting and tend to increase in value. Things begun now become habitual and hard to alter.

Moon in Gemini is an inconsistent position for the Moon, characterized by a lot of talk. Things begun now are easily changed by outside influence.

Moon in Cancer stimulates emotional rapport between people. It pinpoints need, and supports growth and nurturance.

Moon in Leo accents showmanship, being seen, drama, recreation, and happy pursuits. It may be concerned with praise and subject to flattery.

Moon in Virgo favors accomplishment of details and commands from higher up while discouraging independent thinking.

Moon in Libra increases self-awareness. It favors self-examination and interaction with others, but discourages spontaneous initiative.

Moon in Scorpio increases awareness of psychic power. It precipitates psychic crises and ends connections thoroughly.

Moon in Sagittarius encourages expansionary flights of imagination and confidence in the flow of life.

Moon in Capricorn increases awareness of the need for structure, discipline, and organization. Institutional activities are favored.

Moon in Aquarius favors activities that are unique and individualistic, concern for humanitarian issues, society as a whole, and improvements that can be made.

Moon in Pisces energy withdraws from the surface of life, hibernates within, secretly reorganizing and realigning for a new day.

Retrogrades

When the planets cross the sky, they occasionally appear to move backward as seen from Earth. When a planet turns "backward" it is said to be retrograde. When it turns forward again, it is said to go direct. The point at which the movement changes from one direction to another is called a station.

When a planet is retrograde, its expression is delayed or out of kilter with the normal progression of events. Generally, it can be said that whatever is planned during this period will be delayed, but usually it will come to fruition when the retrograde is over. Of course, this only applies to activities ruled by the planet that is retrograde. Mercury retrogrades are easy to follow.

Mercury Retrograde

Mercury rules informal communications—reading, writing, speaking, and short errands. Whenever Mercury goes retrograde, personal communications get fouled up or misunderstood. The general rule is *when Mercury is retrograde, avoid informal means of communication.*

Planetary Retrogrades for 2001 (EST)

Planet	Begin		End	
Saturn	9/12/00	6:35 pm	1/24/01	7:24 pm
Mercury	2/03/01	8:55 pm	2/25/01	10:42 pm
Pluto	3/17/01	9:36 pm	8/23/00	11:06 am
Neptune	5/10/01	8:13 pm	10/17/01	8:48 pm
Uranus	5/29/01	10:11 am	10/30/01	5:55 pm
Mercury	6/04/01	12:21 am	6/28/01	12:48 am
Saturn	9/26/01	7:04 pm	2/07/02	8:33 pm
Jupiter	11/02/01	10:35 am	3/01/02	10:16 am

Moon Void-of-Course

Kim Rogers-Gallagher

The Moon makes a loop around the Earth in about twenty-eight days, moving through each of the signs in two-and-a-half days (or so). As she passes through the thirty degrees of each sign, she "visits" with the planets in numerical order by forming angles or aspects with them. Because she moves one degree in just two to two-and-a-half hours, her influence on each planet lasts only a few hours, then she moves along. As she approaches the late degrees of the sign she's passing through, she eventually reaches the planet that's in the highest degree of any sign, and forms what will be her final aspect before leaving the sign. From this point until she actually enters the new sign, she is referred to as void-of-course, or void.

Think of it this way: The Moon is the emotional "tone" of the day, carrying feelings with her particular to the sign she's "wearing" at the moment. After she has contacted each of the planets, she symbolically "rests" before changing her costume, so her instinct is temporarily on hold. It's during this time that many people feel "fuzzy" or "vague"—scattered, even. Plans or decisions we make now will usually not pan out. Without the instinctual "knowing" the Moon provides as she touches each planet, we tend to be unrealistic or exercise poor judgment. The traditional definition of the void Moon is that "nothing will come of this," and it seems to be true. Actions initiated under a void Moon are often wasted, irrelevant, or incorrect—usually because information is hidden or missing, or has been overlooked.

Although it's not a good time to initiate plans, routine tasks seem to go along just fine. However, this period is really ideal for what the Moon does best: reflection. It's at this time that we can assimilate what the world has tossed at us over the past few days.

On the lighter side, remember that there are other good uses for the void Moon. This is the time period when the universe seems to be most open to loopholes. It's a great time to make plans you don't want to fulfill or schedule things you don't want to do. See the table on pages 56–61 for a schedule of the 2001 void-of-course Moons.

Moon Void-of-Course

Last Aspect		Moon Enters New Sign		
Date	Time	Date	Sign	Time
		January		
1	6:36 am	1	Aries	5:14 pm
3	5:09 am	4	Taurus	1:57 am
5	9:09 pm	6	Gemini	6:44 am
7	2:19 pm	8	Cancer	8:09 am
10	7:39 am	10	Leo	7:44 am
11	10:08 pm	12	Virgo	7:26 am
13	11:12 pm	14	Libra	9:05 am
16	7:35 am	16	Scorpio	2:02 pm
18	8:44 pm	18	Sagittarius	10:35 pm
20	1:18 pm	21	Capricorn	9:57 am
23	10:38 am	23	Aquarius	10:43 pm
26	12:28 am	26	Pisces	11:39 am
28	2:48 pm	28	Aries	11:35 pm
31	8:36 am	31	Taurus	9:21 am
		February		
2	5:31 am	2	Gemini	3:56 pm
4	3:12 am	4	Cancer	7:00 pm
6	12:30 pm	6	Leo	7:21 pm
8	4:25 pm	8	Virgo	6:35 pm
10	3:18 pm	10	Libra	6:46 pm
12	12:31 pm	12	Scorpio	9:51 pm
14	10:23 pm	15	Sagittarius	5:02 am
17	2:22 pm	17	Capricorn	3:59 pm
19	6:03 pm	20	Aquarius	4:53 am
22	7:18 am	22	Pisces	5:45 pm
24	7:25 pm	25	Aries	5:20 am
26	11:34 pm	27	Taurus	3:06 pm
		March		
1	1:57 pm	1	Gemini	10:36 pm

Moon Void-of-Course

Last Aspect		Moon Enters New Sign		
Date	Time	Date	Sign	Time
3	1:45 pm	4	Cancer	3:24 am
5	10:10 pm	6	Leo	5:30 am
7	10:50 pm	8	Virgo	5:44 am
9	11:01 pm	10	Libra	5:47 am
11	9:44 pm	12	Scorpio	7:43 am
14	7:17 am	14	Sagittarius	1:17 pm
16	10:48 pm	16	Capricorn	11:02 pm
19	9:40 am	19	Aquarius	11:36 am
21	6:03 pm	22	Pisces	12:28 am
24	5:58 am	24	Aries	11:43 am
26	8:10 am	26	Taurus	8:50 pm
28	11:29 pm	29	Gemini	4:01 am
30	9:54 pm	31	Cancer	9:23 am
April				
2	9:26 am	2	Leo	12:54 pm
4	11:46 am	4	Virgo	2:46 pm
6	1:18 pm	6	Libra	3:57 pm
8	7:31 am	8	Scorpio	6:01 pm
10	8:43 pm	10	Sagittarius	10:47 pm
12	8:56 pm	13	Capricorn	7:21 am
15	6:00 pm	15	Aquarius	7:11 pm
18	7:26 am	18	Pisces	8:00 am
20	12:40 pm	20	Aries	7:18 pm
22	10:34 pm	23	Taurus	3:56 am
25	12:08 am	25	Gemini	10:11 am
27	11:12 am	27	Cancer	2:49 pm
28	4:53 pm	29	Leo	6:25 pm
May				
1	6:43 pm	1	Virgo	9:16 pm
3	9:39 pm	3	Libra	11:50 pm

Moon Void-of-Course

Last Aspect		Moon Enters New Sign		
Date	**Time**	**Date**	**Sign**	**Time**
6	1:03 am	6	Scorpio	3:00 am
7	10:25 pm	8	Sagittarius	8:05 am
10	2:20 pm	10	Capricorn	4:10 pm
12	11:17 am	13	Aquarius	3:20 am
15	1:53 pm	15	Pisces	4:01 pm
18	1:18 am	18	Aries	3:41 am
20	9:48 am	20	Taurus	12:29 pm
22	9:06 am	22	Gemini	6:12 pm
24	6:12 pm	24	Cancer	9:42 pm
26	7:44 am	27	Leo	12:12 am
29	12:13 am	29	Virgo	2:38 am
31	4:40 am	31	Libra	5:41 am
		June		
2	9:41 am	2	Scorpio	9:56 am
4	6:29 am	4	Sagittarius	3:58 pm
6	11:41 pm	7	Capricorn	12:23 am
7	1:57 am	9	Aquarius	11:20 am
11	7:38 pm	11	Pisces	11:53 pm
14	5:26 am	14	Aries	12:03 pm
16	1:32 pm	16	Taurus	9:39 pm
18	6:21 pm	19	Gemini	3:42 am
20	10:24 pm	21	Cancer	6:40 am
22	9:11 am	23	Leo	7:55 am
25	2:22 am	25	Virgo	8:57 am
27	5:12 am	27	Libra	11:11 am
29	10:07 am	29	Scorpio	3:28 pm
		July		
1	2:25 pm	1	Sagittarius	10:13 pm
4	3:36 am	4	Capricorn	7:21 am
5	10:04 am	6	Aquarius	6:33 pm

Moon Void-of-Course

Last Aspect		Moon Enters New Sign		
Date	**Time**	**Date**	**Sign**	**Time**
9	5:28 am	9	Pisces	7:05 am
11	7:09 pm	11	Aries	7:36 pm
13	6:52 pm	14	Taurus	6:13 am
16	2:41 am	16	Gemini	1:26 pm
18	6:46 am	18	Cancer	4:56 pm
20	2:44 pm	20	Leo	5:43 pm
22	7:34 am	22	Virgo	5:29 pm
24	2:48 am	24	Libra	6:08 pm
26	10:10 am	26	Scorpio	9:17 pm
28	10:50 pm	29	Sagittarius	3:44 am
31	11:24 am	31	Capricorn	1:16 pm
31	9:21 pm	3 (August)	Aquarius	12:53 am
August				
4	11:52 pm	5	Pisces	1:30 pm
7	12:39 am	8	Aries	2:05 am
9	11:53 pm	10	Taurus	1:23 pm
12	5:32 pm	12	Gemini	9:59 pm
14	2:42 pm	15	Cancer	2:55 am
16	8:03 am	17	Leo	4:25 am
18	9:55 pm	19	Virgo	3:53 am
20	3:21 pm	21	Libra	3:19 am
22	8:34 pm	23	Scorpio	4:50 am
25	6:16 am	25	Sagittarius	9:59 am
27	7:50 am	27	Capricorn	7:02 pm
30	1:28 am	30	Aquarius	6:47 am
September				
1	12:36 pm	1	Pisces	7:32 pm
4	3:37 am	4	Aries	7:58 am
6	5:31 pm	6	Taurus	7:18 pm
8	1:30 pm	9	Gemini	4:41 am

Moon Void-of-Course

Last Aspect		Moon Enters New Sign		
Date	**Time**	**Date**	**Sign**	**Time**
10	8:42 pm	11	Cancer	11:09 am
12	10:16 pm	13	Leo	2:16 pm
15	3:35 am	15	Virgo	2:39 pm
17	5:27 am	17	Libra	2:00 pm
19	11:38 am	19	Scorpio	2:27 pm
21	4:09 pm	21	Sagittarius	6:02 pm
23	7:32 pm	24	Capricorn	1:48 am
26	9:38 am	26	Aquarius	1:05 pm
29	12:27 am	29	Pisces	1:50 am
30	8:02 am	1 (October)	Aries	2:08 pm
October				
3	11:44 pm	4	Taurus	1:01 am
5	5:33 pm	6	Gemini	10:12 am
8	11:23 am	8	Cancer	5:19 pm
10	12:47 pm	10	Leo	9:54 pm
12	11:34 am	12	Virgo	11:58 pm
14	11:52 pm	15	Libra	12:26 am
16	2:23 pm	17	Scorpio	1:03 am
18	5:30 pm	19	Sagittarius	3:47 am
21	6:42 am	21	Capricorn	10:11 am
23	3:11 pm	23	Aquarius	8:26 pm
25	2:32 pm	26	Pisces	8:56 am
27	4:31 pm	28	Aries	9:15 pm
30	2:17 pm	31	Taurus	7:48 am
November				
1	11:20 pm	2	Gemini	4:12 pm
4	2:45 pm	4	Cancer	10:44 pm
7	2:10 am	7	Leo	3:34 am
8	3:30 pm	9	Virgo	6:49 am
10	1:40 pm	11	Libra	8:53 am

Moon Void-of-Course

Last Aspect		Moon Enters New Sign		
Date	Time	Date	Sign	Time
12	7:42 pm	13	Scorpio	10:44 am
15	1:40 am	15	Sagittarius	1:51 pm
17	3:14 am	17	Capricorn	7:40 pm
20	12:57 am	20	Aquarius	4:55 am
22	2:37 am	22	Pisces	4:52 pm
25	12:29 am	25	Aries	5:21 am
26	11:43 pm	27	Taurus	4:06 pm
29	6:21 pm	30	Gemini	12:04 am
		December		
1	8:48 pm	2	Cancer	5:30 am
3	6:04 am	4	Leo	9:15 am
6	9:20 am	6	Virgo	12:11 pm
7	5:57 pm	8	Libra	2:57 pm
10	3:43 am	10	Scorpio	6:09 pm
12	7:48 am	12	Sagittarius	10:30 pm
15	3:24 am	15	Capricorn	4:48 am
16	4:35 am	17	Aquarius	1:43 pm
19	9:41 pm	20	Pisces	1:09 am
22	3:44 am	22	Aries	1:45 pm
24	10:21 pm	25	Taurus	1:12 am
26	7:22 pm	27	Gemini	9:39 am
29	1:24 am	29	Cancer	2:40 pm
31	8:43 am	31	Leo	5:09 pm

Find Your Moon Sign

Every year we give tables for the position of the Moon during that year, but it is more complicated to provide tables for the Moon's position in any given year because of its continuous movement. However, the problem was solved by Grant Lewi in Astrology for the Millions (available from Llewellyn Publications).

Grant Lewi's System

1. Find your birth year in the Natal Moon Tables (pages 65–74).

2. Run down the left-hand column and see if your date is there.

3. If your date is in the left-hand column, run over this line until you come to the column under your birth year. Here you will find a number. This is your base number. Write it down, and go directly to the direction under the heading "What to Do with Your Base Number" on page 63.

4. If your birth date is not in the left-hand column, get a pencil and paper. Your birth date falls between two numbers in the left-hand column. Look at the date closest after your birth date; run across this line to your birth year. Write down the number you find there, and label it "top number." Having done this, write directly beneath it on your piece of paper the number printed just above it in the table. Label this "bottom number." Subtract the bottom number from the top number. If the top number is smaller, add 360 and subtract. The result is your difference.

5. Go back to the left-hand column and find the date before your birth date. Determine the number of days between this date and your birth date. Write this down and label it "intervening days."

6. Note which group your difference (found at 4, above) falls in. If your difference was 80–87, your daily motion was 12 degrees. If your difference was 88–94, your daily motion was 13 degrees. If your difference was 95–101, your daily motion was 14 degrees. If your difference is 102–106, your daily motion is 15 degrees. Note: If you were born in a leap year and use the difference between February 26 and March 5, then the daily motion is slightly different. If you fall into this category and your difference

is 94–99, your daily motion is 12 degrees. If your difference is 100–108, your daily motion is 13 degrees. If your difference is 109–115, your daily motion is 14 degrees. If your difference is 115–122, your daily motion is 15 degrees.

7. Write down the "daily motion" corresponding to your place in the proper table of difference above. Multiply daily motion by the number labeled "intervening days" (found at step 5).

8. Add the result of step 7 to your bottom number (under step 4). This is your base number. If it is more than 360, subtract 360 from it and call the result your base number.

What to Do with Your Base Number

Turn to the Table of Base Numbers on page 64 and locate your base number in it. At the top of the column you will find the sign your Moon was in. In the far left-hand column you will find the degree the Moon occupied at: 7 am of your birth date if you were born under Eastern Standard Time (EST); 6 am of your birth date if you were born under Central Standard Time (CST); 5 am of your birth date if you were born under Mountain Standard Time (MST); or 4 am of your birth date if you were born under Pacific Standard Time (PST).

If you don't know the hour of your birth, accept this as your Moon's sign and degree. If you do know the hour of your birth, get the exact degree as follows:

If you were born after 7 am Eastern Standard Time (6 am Central Standard Time, etc.), determine the number of hours after the time that you were born. Divide this by two, rounding up if necessary. Add this to your base number, and the result in the table will be the exact degree and sign of the Moon on the year, month, date, and hour of your birth.

If you were born before 7 am Eastern Standard Time (6 am Central Standard Time, etc.), determine the number of hours before the time that you were born. Divide this by two. Subtract this from your base number, and the result in the table will be the exact degree and sign of the Moon on the year, month, date, and hour of your birth.

Table of Base Numbers

	♈ (13)	♉ (14)	♊ (15)	♋ (16)	♌ (17)	♍ (18)	♎ (19)	♏ (20)	♐ (21)	♑ (22)	♒ (23)	♓ (24)
0°	0	30	60	90	120	150	180	210	240	270	300	330
1°	1	31	61	91	121	151	181	211	241	271	301	331
2°	2	32	62	92	122	152	182	212	242	272	302	332
3°	3	33	63	93	123	153	183	213	243	273	303	333
4°	4	34	64	94	124	154	184	214	244	274	304	334
5°	5	35	65	95	125	155	185	215	245	275	305	335
6°	6	36	66	96	126	156	186	216	246	276	306	336
7°	7	37	67	97	127	157	187	217	247	277	307	337
8°	8	38	68	98	128	158	188	218	248	278	308	338
9°	9	39	69	99	129	159	189	219	249	279	309	339
10°	10	40	70	100	130	160	190	220	250	280	310	340
11°	11	41	71	101	131	161	191	221	251	281	311	341
12°	12	42	72	102	132	162	192	222	252	282	312	342
13°	13	43	73	103	133	163	193	223	253	283	313	343
14°	14	44	74	104	134	164	194	224	254	284	314	344
15°	15	45	75	105	135	165	195	225	255	285	315	345
16°	16	46	76	106	136	166	196	226	256	286	316	346
17°	17	47	77	107	137	167	197	227	257	287	317	347
18°	18	48	78	108	138	168	198	228	258	288	318	248
19°	19	49	79	109	139	169	199	229	259	289	319	349
20°	20	50	80	110	140	170	200	230	260	290	320	350
21°	21	51	81	111	141	171	201	231	261	291	321	351
22°	22	52	82	112	142	172	202	232	262	292	322	352
23°	23	53	83	113	143	173	203	233	263	293	323	353
24°	24	54	84	114	144	174	204	234	264	294	324	354
25°	25	55	85	115	145	175	205	235	265	295	325	355
26°	26	56	86	116	146	176	206	236	266	296	326	356
27°	27	57	87	117	147	177	207	237	267	297	327	357
28°	28	58	88	118	148	178	208	238	268	298	328	358
29°	29	59	89	119	149	179	209	239	269	299	329	359

Month	Date	1901	1902	1903	1904	1905	1906	1907	1908	1909	1910
Jan.	1	55	188	308	76	227	358	119	246	39	168
Jan.	8	149	272	37	179	319	82	208	350	129	252
Jan.	15	234	2	141	270	43	174	311	81	213	346
Jan.	22	327	101	234	353	138	273	44	164	309	84
Jan.	29	66	196	317	84	238	6	128	255	50	175
Feb.	5	158	280	46	188	328	90	219	359	138	259
Feb.	12	241	12	149	279	51	184	319	90	221	356
Feb.	19	335	111	242	2	146	283	52	173	317	94
Feb.	26	76	204	326	92	248	13	136	264	60	184
Mar.	5	166	288	57	211	336	98	229	21	147	267
Mar.	12	249	22	157	300	60	194	328	110	230	5
Mar.	19	344	121	250	24	154	293	60	195	325	105
Mar.	26	86	212	334	116	258	22	144	288	69	192
Apr.	2	175	296	68	219	345	106	240	29	155	276
Apr.	9	258	31	167	309	69	202	338	118	240	13
Apr.	16	352	132	258	33	163	304	68	204	334	115
Apr.	23	96	220	342	127	267	31	152	299	77	201
Apr.	30	184	304	78	227	354	114	250	38	164	285
May	7	267	40	177	317	78	210	348	126	249	21
May	14	1	142	266	42	172	313	76	212	344	124
May	21	104	229	350	138	275	40	160	310	85	210
May	28	193	313	87	236	2	123	259	47	172	294
Jun.	4	277	48	187	324	88	219	358	134	258	30
Jun.	11	11	151	275	50	182	322	85	220	355	132
Jun.	18	112	238	359	149	283	48	169	320	93	218
Jun.	25	201	322	96	245	11	133	267	57	180	304
Jul.	2	286	57	197	333	97	228	8	142	267	40
Jul.	9	21	160	283	58	193	330	94	228	6	140
Jul.	16	121	247	7	159	291	57	178	330	102	226
Jul.	23	209	332	105	255	18	143	276	66	188	314
Jul.	30	295	66	206	341	105	239	17	151	275	51
Aug.	6	32	168	292	66	204	338	103	237	17	148
Aug.	13	130	255	17	168	301	65	188	339	111	234
Aug.	20	217	341	113	265	27	152	285	76	197	323
Aug.	27	303	77	215	350	113	250	25	160	283	62
Sep.	3	43	176	301	75	215	346	111	246	27	157
Sep.	10	139	263	27	176	310	73	198	347	121	242
Sep.	17	225	350	123	274	35	161	294	85	205	331
Sep.	24	311	88	223	358	122	261	33	169	292	73
Oct.	1	53	185	309	85	224	355	119	256	35	166
Oct.	8	149	271	36	185	320	81	207	356	130	250
Oct.	15	233	359	133	283	44	169	305	93	214	339
Oct.	22	319	99	231	7	130	271	42	177	301	83
Oct.	29	62	194	317	95	233	5	127	266	44	176
Nov.	5	158	279	45	193	329	89	216	5	139	259
Nov.	12	242	6	144	291	53	177	316	101	223	347
Nov.	19	328	109	239	15	140	280	50	185	311	91
Nov.	26	70	203	325	105	241	14	135	276	52	185
Dec.	3	168	288	54	203	338	98	224	15	148	268
Dec.	10	251	14	155	299	61	185	327	109	231	356
Dec.	17	338	118	248	23	150	289	59	193	322	99
Dec.	24	78	213	333	115	249	23	143	286	61	194
Dec.	31	176	296	61	213	346	107	232	26	155	277

Month	Date	1911	1912	1913	1914	1915	1916	1917	1918	1919	1920
Jan.	1	289	57	211	337	100	228	23	147	270	39
Jan.	8	20	162	299	61	192	332	110	231	5	143
Jan.	15	122	251	23	158	293	61	193	329	103	231
Jan.	22	214	335	120	256	23	145	290	68	193	316
Jan.	29	298	66	221	345	108	237	32	155	278	49
Feb.	5	31	170	308	69	203	340	118	239	16	150
Feb.	12	130	260	32	167	302	70	203	338	113	239
Feb.	19	222	344	128	266	31	154	298	78	201	325
Feb.	26	306	75	231	353	116	248	41	164	286	60
Mar.	5	42	192	317	77	214	2	127	248	26	172
Mar.	12	140	280	41	176	311	89	212	346	123	259
Mar.	19	230	5	136	276	39	176	308	87	209	346
Mar.	26	314	100	239	2	124	273	49	173	294	85
Apr.	2	52	200	326	86	223	10	135	257	35	181
Apr.	9	150	288	51	184	321	97	222	355	133	267
Apr.	16	238	14	146	286	48	184	318	96	218	355
Apr.	23	322	111	247	11	132	284	57	181	303	96
Apr.	30	61	208	334	96	232	19	143	267	43	190
May	7	160	296	60	192	331	105	231	4	142	275
May	14	246	22	156	294	56	192	329	104	227	3
May	21	331	122	255	20	141	294	66	190	312	105
May	28	69	218	342	106	240	29	151	277	51	200
Jun.	4	170	304	69	202	341	114	240	14	151	284
Jun.	11	255	30	167	302	65	200	340	112	235	11
Jun.	18	340	132	264	28	151	304	74	198	322	114
Jun.	25	78	228	350	115	249	39	159	286	60	209
Jul.	2	179	312	78	212	349	122	248	25	159	293
Jul.	9	264	39	178	310	74	209	350	120	244	20
Jul.	16	349	141	273	36	161	312	84	206	332	123
Jul.	23	87	237	358	125	258	48	168	295	70	218
Jul.	30	187	321	86	223	357	131	256	36	167	302
Aug.	6	272	48	188	319	82	219	360	129	252	31
Aug.	13	359	150	282	44	171	320	93	214	342	131
Aug.	20	96	246	6	133	268	57	177	303	81	226
Aug.	27	195	330	94	234	5	140	265	46	175	310
Sep.	3	281	57	198	328	90	229	9	138	260	41
Sep.	10	9	158	292	52	180	329	102	222	351	140
Sep.	17	107	255	15	141	279	65	186	312	91	234
Sep.	24	203	339	103	244	13	149	274	56	184	319
Oct.	1	288	68	206	337	98	240	17	148	268	52
Oct.	8	18	167	301	61	189	338	111	231	360	150
Oct.	15	118	263	24	149	290	73.	195	320	102	242
Oct.	22	212	347	113	254	22	157	284	65	193	326
Oct.	29	296	78	214	346	106	250	25	157	276	61
Nov.	5	26	177	309	70	197	348	119	240	7	161
Nov.	12	129	271	33	158	300	81	203	329	112	250
Nov.	19	221	355	123	262	31	164	295	73	202	334
Nov.	26	305	88	223	355	115	259	34	165	285	70
Dec.	3	34	187	317	79	205	359	127	249	16	171
Dec.	10	138	279	41	168	310	89	211	340	120	259
Dec.	17	230	3	134	270	40	172	305	81	211	343
Dec.	24	313	97	232	3	124	267	44	173	294	78
Dec.	31	42	198	325	87	214	9	135	257	25	181

Month	Date	1921	1922	1923	1924	1925	1926	1927	1928	1929	1930
Jan.	1	194	317	80	211	5	127	250	23	176	297
Jan.	8	280	41	177	313	90	211	349	123	260	22
Jan.	15	4	141	275	41	175	312	86	211	346	123
Jan.	22	101	239	3	127	272	51	172	297	83	222
Jan.	29	203	325	88	222	13	135	258	34	184	306
Feb.	5	289	49	188	321	99	220	359	131	269	31
Feb.	12	14	149	284	49	185	320	95	219	356	131
Feb.	19	110	249	11	135	281	60	181	305	93	230
Feb.	26	211	334	96	233	21	144	266	45	191	314
Mar.	5	297	58	197	343	107	230	8	153	276	41
Mar.	12	23	157	294	69	194	328	105	238	6	140
Mar.	19	119•	258	19	157	292	68	190	327	104	238
Mar.	26	219	343	104	258	29	153	275	70	200	323
Apr.	2	305	68	205	352	115	240	16	163	284	51
Apr.	9	33	166	304	77	204	337	114	247	14	149
Apr.	16	130	266	28	164	303	76	198	335	115	246
Apr.	23	227	351	114	268	38	161	285	79	208	331
Apr.	30	313	78	214	1	123	250	25	172	292	61
May	7	42	176	313	85	212	348	123	256	23	160
May	14	141	274	37	173	314	84	207	344	125	254
May	21	236	359	123	277	47	169	295	88	217	339
May	28	321	88	222	11	131	259	34	181	301	70
Jun.	4	50	186	321	94	220	358	131	264	31	171
Jun.	11	152	282	45	182	324	93	215	354	135	263
Jun.	18	245	7	134	285	56	177	305	96	226	347
Jun.	25	330	97	232	20	139	268	44	190	310	78
Jul.	2	58	197	329	103	229	9	139	273	40	181
Jul.	9	162	291	54	192	333	101	223	4	144	272
Jul.	16	254	15	144	294	65	185	315	104	236	355
Jul.	23	338	106	242	28	148	276	54	198	319	87
Jul.	30	67	208	337	112	238	20	147	282	49	191
Aug.	6	171	300	62	202	341	110	231	15	152	281
Aug.	13	264	24	153	302	74	194	324	114	244	4
Aug.	20	347	114	253	36	157	285	65	206	328	95
Aug.	27	76	218	346	120	248	29	156	290	59	200
Sep.	3	179	309	70	213	350	119	239	25	161	290
Sep.	10	273	32	162	312	83	203	332	124	252	13
Sep.	17	356	122	264	44	166	293	75	214	337	105
Sep.	24	86	227	354	128	258	38	165	298	70	208
Oct.	1	187	318	78	223	358	128	248	35	169	298
Oct.	8	281	41	170	322	91	212	340	134	260	23
Oct.	15	5	132	274	52	175	303	85	222	345	115
Oct.	22	97	235	3	136	269	46	174	306	81	216
Oct.	29	196	327	87	232	7	137	257	44	179	307
Nov.	5	289	50	178	332	99	221	349	144	268	31
Nov.	12	13	142	283	61	183	313	93	231	353	126
Nov.	19	107	243	12	144	279	54	183	315	91	225
Nov.	26	206	335	96	241	17	145	266	52	189	314
Dec.	3	297	59	187	343	107	230	359	154	276	39
Dec.	10	21	152	291	70	191	324	101	240	1	137
Dec.	17	117	252	21	153	289	63	191	324	99	234
Dec.	24	216	343	105	249	28	152	275	60	199	322
Dec.	31	305	67	197	352	115	237	9	162	285	47

Month	Date	1931	1932	1933	1934	1935	1936	1937	1938	1939	1940
Jan.	1	60	196	346	107	231	8	156	277	41	181
Jan.	8	162	294	70	193	333	104	240	4	144	275
Jan.	15	257	20	158	294	68	190	329	104	239	360
Jan.	22	342	108	255	32	152	278	67	202	323	88
Jan.	29	68	207	353	116	239	19	163	286	49	191
Feb.	5	171	302	78	203	342	113	248	14	153	284
Feb.	12	267	28	168	302	78	198	339	113	248	8
Feb.	19	351	116	266	40	161	286	78	210	332	96
Feb.	26	77	217	1	124	248	29	171	294	59	200
Mar.	5	179	324	86	213	350	135	256	25	161	306
Mar.	12	276	48	176	311	86	218	347	123	256	29
Mar.	19	360	137	277	48	170	308	89	218	340	119
Mar.	26	86	241	10	132	258	52	180	302	69	223
Apr.	2	187	334	94	223	358	144	264	34	169	315
Apr.	9	285	57	185	321	95	227	355	133	264	38
Apr.	16	9	146	287	56	178	317	99	226	349	128
Apr.	23	96	250	18	140	268	61	189	310	80	231
Apr.	30	196	343	102	232	7	153	273	43	179	323
May	7	293	66	193	332	103	237	4	144	272	47
May	14	17	155	297	64	187	327	108	235	357	139
May	21	107	258	28	148	278	69	198	318	90	239
May	28	205	351	111	241	17	161	282	51	189	331
Jun.	4	301	75	201	343	111	245	13	154	280	55
Jun.	11	25	165	306	73	195	337	117	244	5	150
Jun.	18	117	267	37	157	288	78	207	327	99	248
Jun.	25	215	360	120	249	28	169	291	60	200	339
Jul.	2	309	84	211	353	119	254	23	164	289	64
Jul.	9	33	176	315	82	203	348	125	253	13	160
Jul.	16	126	276	46	165	297	87	216	336	108	258
Jul.	23	226	8	130	258	38	177	300	69	210	347
Jul.	30	317	92	221	2	128	262	33	173	298	72
Aug.	6	41	187	323	91	211	359	133	261	21	170
Aug.	13	135	285	54	175	305	97	224	346	116	268
Aug.	20	237	16	138	267	49	185	308	78	220	355
Aug.	27	326	100	232	10	136	270	44	181	307	80
Sep.	3	49	197	331	100	220	8	142	270	31	179
Sep.	10	143	295	62	184	314	107	232	355	125	278
Sep.	17	247	24	147	277	58	194	317	89	228	4
Sep.	24	335	108	243	18	145	278	55	189	316	88
Oct.	1	58	206	341	108	229	17	152	278	40	188
Oct.	8	151	306	70	193	322	117	240	4	134	288
Oct.	15	256	32	155	287	66	203	324	100	236	13
Oct.	22	344	116	253	27	154	287	64	198	324	98
Oct.	29	68	214	350	116	239	25	162	286	49	196
Nov.	5	161	316	78	201	332	126	248	12	145	297
Nov.	12	264	41	162	298	74	212	333	111	244	22
Nov.	19	353	125	262	36	162	296	73	207	332	108
Nov.	26	77	222	0	124	248	33	172	294	58	205
Dec.	3	171	325	87	209	343	135	257	19	156	305
Dec.	10	272	50	171	309	82	220	341	120	253	30
Dec.	17	1	135	271	45	170	306	81	217	340	118
Dec.	24	86	231	10	132	256	43	181	302	66	214
Dec.	31	182	333	95	217	354	142	265	27	167	313

Month	Date	1941	1942	1943	1944	1945	1946	1947	1948	1949	1950
Jan.	1	325	88	211	353	135	258	22	165	305	68
Jan.	8	50	176	315	85	219	348	126	256	29	160
Jan.	15	141	276	50	169	312	87	220	340	123	258
Jan.	22	239	12	133	258	52	182	303	69	224	352
Jan.	29	333	96	221	2	143	266	32	174	314	75
Feb.	5	57	186	323	95	227	358	134	265	37	170
Feb.	12	150	285	58	178	320	96	228	349	131	268
Feb.	19	250	20	142	267	62	190	312	78	234	359
Feb.	26	342	104	231	11	152	274	43	182	323	83
Mar.	5	65	196	331	116	236	8	142	286	46	179
Mar.	12	158	295	66	199	328	107	236	10	139	279
Mar.	19	261	28	150	290	72	198	320	102	243	8
Mar.	26	351	112	242	34	161	281	53	204	332	91
Apr.	2	74	205	340	125	244	16	152	294	55	187
Apr.	9	166	306	74	208	337	117	244	19	148	289
Apr.	16	270	36	158	300	81	206	328	112	252	17
Apr.	23	360	120	252	42	170	290	63	212	340	100
Apr.	30	83	214	350	133	254	25	162	302	64	195
May	7	174	316	82	217	346	127	252	27	158	299
May	14	279	45	166	311	90	215	336	123	260	26
May	21	9	128	261	50	179	299	72	221	349	110
May	28	92	222	1	141	263	33	173	310	73	204
Jun.	4	184	326	91	226	356	137	261	36	168	307
Jun.	11	287	54	174	322	98	224	344	134	268	34
Jun.	18	17	137	270	60	187	308	81	231	357	119
Jun.	25	102	231	11	149	272	42	183	318	82	213
Jul.	2	194	335	99	234	7	145	269	44	179	316
Jul.	9	296	63	183	332	106	233	353	144	277	43
Jul.	16	25	147	279	70	195	318	89	241	5	129
Jul.	23	110	240	21	157	280	52	192	327	91	224
Jul.	30	205	343	108	242	18	153	278	52	190	324
Aug.	6	304	71	192	341	115	241	3	153	286	51
Aug.	13	33	156	287	80	203	327	98	251	13	138
Aug.	20	119	250	30	165	289	63	201	336	99	235
Aug.	27	216	351	117	250	28	162	287	61	200	332
Sep.	3	314	80	201	350	125	249	13	161	296	59
Sep.	10	41	165	296	90	211	336	108	260	21	146
Sep.	17	127	261	39	174	297	74	209	345	107	246
Sep.	24	226	359	126	259	38	170	295	70	209	341
Oct.	1	323	88	211	358	135	257	22	170	306	67
Oct.	8	49	174	306	99	220	344	118	269	30	154
Oct.	15	135	272	47	183	305	84	217	353	116	256
Oct.	22	236	8	134	269	47	180	303	80	217	351
Oct.	29	333	95	220	7	144	265	31	179	315	75
Nov.	5	58	181	317	107	229	352	129	277	39	162
Nov.	12	143	283	55	192	314	94	225	1	125	265
Nov.	19	244	18	141	279	55	189	311	90	225	0
Nov.	26	343	104	229	16	153	274	39	189	323	84
Dec.	3	67	189	328	115	237	360	140	284	47	171
Dec.	10	153	292	64	200	324	103	234	9	136	274
Dec.	17	252	28	149	289	63	199	319	100	234	9
Dec.	24	351	112	237	27	161	282	47	199	331	93
Dec.	31	76	198	338	123	246	9	150	293	55	180

Month	Date	1951	1952	1953	1954	1955	1956	1957	1958	1959	1960
Jan.	1	194	336	115	238	6	147	285	47	178	317
Jan.	8	297	67	199	331	107	237	9	143	278	47
Jan.	15	30	150	294	70	200	320	104	242	9	131
Jan.	22	114	240	35	161	284	51	207	331	94	223
Jan.	29	204	344	124	245	17	155	294	55	189	325
Feb.	5	305	76	207	341	116	246	18	152	287	56
Feb.	12	38	159	302	80	208	330	112	252	17	140
Feb.	19	122	249	45	169	292	61	216	340	102	233
Feb.	26	215	352	133	253	27	163	303	63	199	333
Mar.	5	314	96	216	350	125	266	27	161	297	75
Mar.	12	46	180	310	91	216	351	121	262	25	161
Mar.	19	130	274	54	178	300	86	224	349	110	259
Mar.	26	225	14	142	262	37	185	312	72	208	356
Apr.	2	324	104	226	358	135	274	37	169	307	83
Apr.	9	54	189	319	100	224	360	131	271	34	170
Apr.	16	138	285	62	187	308	97	232	357	118	269
Apr.	23	235	23	150	271	46	194	320	82	217	5
Apr.	30	334	112	235	6	146	282	48	177	317	91
May	7	62	197	330	109	232	8	142	279	42	177
May	14	146	296	70	196	316	107	240	6	127	279
May	21	243	32	158	280	54	204	328	91	225	15
May	28	344	120	244	15	155	290	55	187	326	100
Jun.	4	71	205	341	117	241	16	153	288	51	186
Jun.	11	155	306	79	204	325	117	249	14	137	288
Jun.	18	252	42	166	290	63	214	336	101	234	25
Jun.	25	354	128	253	26	164	298	63	198	335	109
Jul.	2	80	214	351	125	250	24	164	296	60	195
Jul.	9	164	315	88	212	335	126	259	22	147	297
Jul.	16	260	52	174	299	72	223	344	110	243	34
Jul.	23	3	137	261	37	173	307	71	209	343	118
Jul.	30	89	222	2	134	258	33	174	304	68	205
Aug.	6	174	324	97	220	345	134	268	30	156	305
Aug.	13	270	62	182	308	82	232	353	118	254	42
Aug.	20	11	146	269	48	181	316	79	220	351	126
Aug.	27	97	232	11	143	267	43	183	314	76	215
Sep.	3	184	332	107	228	355	143	278	38	166	314
Sep.	10	280	71	191	316	92	241	2	127	265	50
Sep.	17	19	155	278	58	189	325	88	230	359	135
Sep.	24	105	242	20	152	274	54	191	323	84	225
Oct.	1	193	341	116	237	4	152	287	47	174	324
Oct.	8	291	79	200	324	103	249	11	135	276	58
Oct.	15	27	163	287	68	198	333	98	239	8	143
Oct.	22	113	252	28	162	282	64	199	332	92	235
Oct.	29	201	350	125	245	12	162	295	56	182	334
Nov.	5	302	87	209	333	114	256	19	144	286	66
Nov.	12	36	171	297	76	207	341	109	247	17	150
Nov.	19	121	262	37	171	291	73	208	341	101	244
Nov.	26	209	0	133	254	20	173	303	65	190	345
Dec.	3	312	95	217	342	124	265	27	154	295	75
Dec.	10	45	179	307	84	216	348	119	255	27	158
Dec.	17	129	271	46	180	299	82	218	350	110	252
Dec.	24	217	11	141	263	28	184	311	73	199	355
Dec.	31	321	103	225	352	132	273	35	164	303	84

Month	Date	1961	1962	1963	1964	1965	1966	1967	1968	1969	1970
Jan.	1	96	217	350	128	266	27	163	298	76	197
Jan.	8	179	315	89	217	350	126	260	27	161	297
Jan.	15	275	54	179	302	86	225	349	112	257	36
Jan.	22	18	141	264	35	189	311	74	207	359	122
Jan.	29	105	225	1	136	275	35	173	306	85	206
Feb.	5	188	323	99	225	360	134	270	35	171	305
Feb.	12	284	64	187	310	95	235	357	121	267	45
Feb.	19	26	150	272	46	197	320	81	218	7	130
Feb.	26	113	234	11	144	283	45	182	315	93	216
Mar.	5	198	331	109	245	9	142	280	54	180	313
Mar.	12	293	73	195	332	105	244	5	142	277	54
Mar.	19	34	159	280	71	205	329	90	243	15	139
Mar.	26	122	243	19	167	291	54	190	338	101	226
Apr.	2	208	340	119	253	18	151	290	63	189	323
Apr.	9	303	82	204	340	116	252	14	150	288	62
Apr.	16	42	167	288	81	213	337	99	253	23	147
Apr.	23	130	253	28	176	299	64	198	347	109	235
Apr.	30	216	349	128	261	27	161	298	71	197	333
May	7	314	90	213	348	127	260	23	158	299	70
May	14	51	176	298	91	222	345	109	262	32	155
May	21	137	263	36	186	307	74	207	357	117	245
May	28	225	359	137	270	35	172	307	80	205	344
Jun.	4	325	98	222	357	137	268	31	168	309	78
Jun.	11	60	184	308	99	231	353	119	270	42	163
Jun.	18	146	272	45	195	315	82	217	6	126	253
Jun.	25	233	10	145	279	43	183	315	89	214	355
Jul.	2	336	106	230	6	147	276	40	178	318	87
Jul.	9	70	191	318	108	241	1	129	279	51	171
Jul.	16	154	281	56	204	324	91	227	14	135	261
Jul.	23	241	21	153	288	52	193	323	98	223	5
Jul.	30	345	115	238	16	156	286	47	188	327	97
Aug.	6	79	200	327	116	250	10	138	288	60	180
Aug.	13	163	289	66	212	333	99	238	22	144	270
Aug.	20	250	32	161	296	61	203	331	106	233	14
Aug.	27	353	124	246	27	164	295	55	199	335	106
Sep.	3	88	208	336	126	259	19	147	297	68	189
Sep.	10	172	297	77	220	342	108	249	30	152	279
Sep.	17	260	41	170	304	72	212	340	114	244	23
Sep.	24	1	134	254	37	172	304	64	208	344	115
Oct.	1	97	217	344	136	267	28	155	308	76	198
Oct.	8	180	306	88	228	351	117	259	38	161	289
Oct.	15	270	50	179	312	82	220	350	122	254	31
Oct.	22	10	143	262	47	182	313	73	217	353	123
Oct.	29	105	226	352	146	275	37	163	318	84	207
Nov.	5	189	315	97	237	359	127	268	47	168	299
Nov.	12	281	58	188	320	93	228	359	130	264	39
Nov.	19	19	151	271	55	191	321	82	225	3	131
Nov.	26	113	235	1	157	282	45	172	328	92	215
Dec.	3	197	326	105	245	7	138	276	55	176	310
Dec.	10	291	66	197	328	102	237	7	139	273	48
Dec.	17	30	159	280	63	202	329	91	234	13	139
Dec.	24	121	243	11	167	291	53	183	337	101	223
Dec.	31	204	336	113	254	14	149	284	64	184	320

Month	Date	1971	1972	1973	1974	1975	1976	1977	1978	1979	1980
Jan.	1	335	109	246	8	147	279	56	179	318	90
Jan.	8	71	197	332	108	243	6	144	278	54	176
Jan.	15	158	283	69	207	328	93	240	18	139	263
Jan.	22	244	20	169	292	54	192	339	102	224	4
Jan.	29	344	117	255	17	156	288	64	188	327	99
Feb.	5	81	204	342	116	253	14	153	287	63	184
Feb.	12	167	291	79	216	337	101	251	26	147	271
Feb.	19	252	31	177	300	62	203	347	110	233	14
Feb.	26	353	126	263	27	164	297	72	199	334	109
Mar.	5	91	224	351	124	262	34	162	296	72	204
Mar.	12	176	312	90	224	346	122	262	34	156	203
Mar.	19	261	55	185	309	72	226	356	118	243	37
Mar.	26	1	149	270	37	172	320	80	208	343	130
Apr.	2	100	233	360	134	270	43	170	307	80	213
Apr.	9	184	320	101	232	355	131	273	42	164	302
Apr.	16	271	64	194	317	82	235	5	126	254	46
Apr.	23	9	158	278	47	181	329	88	217	352	139
Apr.	30	109	242	8	145	278	52	178	318	88	222
May	7	193	329	111	240	3	141	282	50	173	312
May	14	281	73	203	324	92	243	14	134	264	54
May	21	19	167	287	55	191	337	97	226	3	147
May	28	117	251	16	156	286	61	187	328	96	231
Jun.	4	201	339	120	249	11	151	291	59	180	323
Jun.	11	291	81	213	333	102	252	23	143	273	63
Jun.	18	29	176	296	64	201	346	106	234	13	155
Jun.	25	125	260	25	167	295	69	196	338	105	239
Jul.	2	209	349	129	258	19	162	299	68	188	334
Jul.	9	300	90	222	341	111	261	32	152	282	72
Jul.	16	40	184	305	72	212	354	115	243	24	163
Jul.	23	133	268	35	176	303	78	206	347	114	248
Jul.	30	217	0	137	267	27	172	308	77	197	344
Aug.	6	309	99	230	350	120	271	40	161	290	83
Aug.	13	51	192	314	81	223	2	124	252	34	171
Aug.	20	142	276	45	185	312	86	217	356	123	256
Aug.	27	225	10	146	276	36	182	317	86	206	353
Sep.	3	317	109	238	360	128	281	48	170	299	93
Sep.	10	61	200	322	90	232	10	132	262	43	180
Sep.	17	151	284	56	193	321	94	228	4	132	264
Sep.	24	234	20	155	284	45	191	326	94	215	2
Oct.	1	325	120	246	9	136	291	56	179	308	103
Oct.	8	70	208	330	101	241	19	140	273	51	189
Oct.	15	160	292	66	202	330	102	238	12	140	273
Oct.	22	243	28	165	292	54	199	336	102	225	10
Oct.	29	334	130	254	17	146	301	64	187	318	112
Nov.	5	79	217	338	112	249	27	148	284	59	197
Nov.	12	169	300	76	210	339	111	247	21	148	282
Nov.	19	253	36	175	300	63	207	347	110	234	18
Nov.	26	344	139	262	25	156	310	73	195	329	120
Dec.	3	87	226	346	122	257	36	157	294	67	206
Dec.	10	177	310	84	220	347	121	255	31	156	292
Dec.	17	261	45	185	308	72	216	356	118	242	28
Dec.	24	355	148	271	33	167	318	81	203	340	128
Dec.	31	95	235	355	132	265	44	166	303	76	214

Month	Date	1981	1982	1983	1984	1985	1986	1987	1988	1989	1990
Jan.	1	226	350	129	260	36	162	300	71	205	333
Jan.	8	315	89	225	346	126	260	36	156	297	72
Jan.	15	53	188	309	73	225	358	119	243	37	168
Jan.	22	149	272	35	176	319	82	206	348	129	252
Jan.	29	234	0	137	270	43	172	308	81	213	343
Feb.	5	324	98	234	354	135	270	44	164	306	82
Feb.	12	64	196	317	81	236	6	128	252	48	175
Feb.	19	157	280	45	185	328	90	217	356	138	260
Feb.	26	242	10	145	279	51	182	316	90	222	353
Mar.	5	332	108	242	15	143	280	52	185	313	93
Mar.	12	74	204	326	104	246	14	136	275	57	184
Mar.	19	166	288	55	208	337	97	227	19	147	268
Mar.	26	250	20	154	300	60	191	326	111	230	1
Apr.	2	340	119	250	24	151	291	60	194	322	103
Apr.	9	84	212	334	114	255	22	144	286	66	192
Apr.	16	175	296	66	216	346	106	237	27	156	276
Apr.	23	259	28	164	309	69	199	336	119	240	9
Apr.	30	349	130	258	33	160	302	68	203	331	113
May	7	93	221	342	124	264	31	152	297	75	201
May	14	184	304	75	225	355	114	246	36	165	285
May	21	268	36	175	317	78	207	347	127	249	18
May	28	358	140	266	41	170	311	76	211	341	122
Jun.	4	102	230	350	135	272	40	160	307	83	210
Jun.	11	193	313	84	234	3	123	255	45	173	294
Jun.	18	277	45	185	325	87	216	357	135	258	27
Jun.	25	8	149	275	49	180	320	85	219	352	130
Jul.	2	110	239	359	146	281	49	169	317	92	219
Jul.	9	201	322	93	244	11	133	263	55	181	304
Jul.	16	286	54	196	333	96	225	7	143	266	37
Jul.	23	19	158	284	57	191	328	94	227	3	138
Jul.	30	119	248	7	155	290	57	178	327	101	227
Aug.	6	210	331	101	254	19	142	272	66	189	313
Aug.	13	294	64	205	341	104	236	16	152	274	48
Aug.	20	30	166	293	66	202	337	103	236	13	147
Aug.	27	128	256	17	164	299	65	187	335	111	235
Sep.	3	218	340	110	264	27	151	281	75	197	321
Sep.	10	302	75	214	350	112	247	24	160	282	59
Sep.	17	40	174	302	74	212	345	112	245	23	156
Sep.	24	138	264	26	172	309	73	197	343	121	243
Oct.	1	226	349	119	274	36	159	292	84	206	329
Oct.	8	310	86	222	359	120	258	32	169	291	70
Oct.	15	50	183	310	84	220	354	120	255	31	165
Oct.	22	148	272	35	181	319	81	206	352	130	251
Oct.	29	234	357	130	282	44	167	303	92	214	337
Nov.	5	318	96	230	8	129	268	40	178	300	79
Nov.	12	58	193	318	93	229	4	128	265	39	175
Nov.	19	158	280	44	190	329	90	214	2	139	260
Nov.	26	243	5	141	290	53	175	314	100	223	345
Dec.	3	327	106	238	16	139	277	49	185	310	88
Dec.	10	66	203	326	103	237	14	136	274	48	185
Dec.	17	167	288	52	200	337	98	222	12	147	269
Dec.	24	252	13	152	298	62	184	324	108	232	355
Dec.	31	337	114	248	24	149	285	59	193	320	96

Month	Date	1991	1992	1993	1994	1995	1996	1997	1998	1999	2000
Jan.	1	111	242	15	145	281	53	185	317	92	223
Jan.	8	206	326	108	244	16	136	279	56	186	307
Jan.	15	289	54	210	337	99	225	21	147	270	37
Jan.	22	18	158	299	61	190	329	110	231	2	140
Jan.	29	119	252	23	155	290	62	193	326	101	232
Feb.	5	214	335	116	254	24	145	287	66	193	315
Feb.	12	298	63	220	345	108	235	31	155	278	47
Feb.	19	29	166	308	69	201	337	119	239	12	148
Feb.	26	128	260	32	164	299	70	202	335	111	240
Mar.	5	222	356	124	265	32	166	295	76	201	337
Mar.	12	306	87	229	354	116	259	39	164	285	72
Mar.	19	39	189	317	77	211	360	128	248	22	170
Mar.	26	138	280	41	172	310	90	212	343	121	260
Apr.	2	230	5	133	275	40	175	305	86	210	345
Apr.	9	314	98	237	3	123	270	47	173	294	83
Apr.	16	49	198	326	86	220	9	136	257	31	180
Apr.	23	148	288	50	180	320	98	221	351	132	268
Apr.	30	238	13	143	284	48	183	315	95	218	353
May	7	322	109	245	12	132	281	55	182	302	93
May	14	57	207	335	95	228	18	144	267	39	190
May	21	158	296	59	189	330	106	230	1	141	276
May	28	247	21	154	292	57	191	326	103	227	1
Jun.	4	330	119	253	21	141	291	64	190	311	102
Jun.	11	66	217	343	105	236	28	152	276	48	199
Jun.	18	168	304	68	199	340	114	238	11	150	285
Jun.	25	256	29	165	300	66	199	337	111	236	10
Jul.	2	339	129	262	29	150	300	73	198	321	111
Jul.	9	74	227	351	114	245	38	160	285	57	209
Jul.	16	177	313	76	210	348	123	246	22	158	293
Jul.	23	265	38	175	309	75	208	347	120	245	19
Jul.	30	349	137	272	37	160	308	83	206	331	119
Aug.	6	83	237	359	123	255	48	169	293	67	218
Aug.	13	186	322	84	221	356	132	254	33	166	302
Aug.	20	273	47	185	318	83	218	356	129	253	29
Aug.	27	358	146	282	45	169	317	93	214	340	128
Sep.	3	93	246	7	131	265	56	177	301	78	226
Sep.	10	194	331	92	231	4	141	263	43	174	311
Sep.	17	281	56	194	327	91	228	5	138	261	39
Sep.	24	8	154	292	53	178	326	102	223	349	137
Oct.	1	104	254	16	139	276	64	186	310	89	234
Oct.	8	202	339	101	241	13	149	273	53	183	319
Oct.	15	289	66	202	337	99	238	13	148	269	49
Oct.	22	16	164	301	61	187	336	111	231	357	148
Oct.	29	115	262	25	148	287	72	195	318	100	242
Nov.	5	211	347	111	250	22	157	283	61	193	326
Nov.	12	297	76	211	346	107	247	22	157	277	58
Nov.	19	24	174	309	70	194	346	119	240	5	159
Nov.	26	126	270	33	156	297	80	203	328	109	251
Dec.	3	220	355	121	258	31	165	293	69	202	334
Dec.	10	305	85	220	355	115	256	31	165	286	67
Dec.	17	32	185	317	79	203	357	127	249	13	169
Dec.	24	135	278	41	166	306	89	211	338	117	260
Dec.	31	230	3	131	266	41	173	303	78	211	343

LLEWELLYN'S

Home,
Health,
& Beauty

Home, Health, & Beauty
How to Choose the Best Dates

Automobile Purchase

The Moon is helpful when in favorable aspect to Mercury and Uranus and in the signs corresponding to travel (Gemini or Sagittarius) or to reliable purchases (Aquarius, Taurus, Leo, and Scorpio).

Automobile Repair

The Moon should be in favorable aspect to Uranus and in the signs of Taurus, Leo, Aquarius, or Virgo. The first and second quarters are best. Avoid any unfavorable aspects between the Moon and Mars, Saturn, Uranus, Neptune, or Pluto.

Baking

Baking should be done when the Moon is in Cancer. Bakers who have experimented say that dough rises higher and bread is lighter during the increase of the Moon (first or second quarter). If it is not possible to bake under the sign of Cancer, try Aries, Libra, or Capricorn.

Beauty Care

For beauty treatments, skin care, and massage, the Moon should be in Taurus, Cancer, Leo, Libra, or Aquarius, and sextile, trine, or conjunct (X, T, C) Venus or Jupiter. Plastic surgery should be done in the increase of the Moon, when the Moon is not square or opposite (Q or O) Mars. Nor should the Moon be in the sign ruling the area to be operated on. Avoid days when the Moon is square or opposite Saturn or the Sun.

Fingernails should be cut when the Moon is not in any aspect with Mercury or Jupiter. Saturn and Mars must not be marked Q or O; this makes the nails grow slowly or thin and weak. The Moon should be in Aries, Taurus, Cancer, or Leo. For toenails, the Moon should not be in Gemini or Pisces. Corns are best cut in the third or fourth quarter.

Brewing

It is best to brew during the Full Moon and the fourth quarter. Plan to have the Moon in Cancer, Scorpio, or Pisces.

Building

Turning the first sod for the foundation of a building marks the beginning of the building. Excavate and pour cement when the Moon is Full in Taurus, Leo, or Aquarius. Saturn should be aspected, but not Mars.

Canning

Can fruits and vegetables when the Moon is in either the third or fourth quarter when it is in Cancer or Pisces. For preserves and jellies, use the same quarters but see that the Moon is in Cancer, Pisces, or Taurus.

Cement and Concrete

Pour cement and concrete during the Full Moon in the fixed signs of Taurus, Leo, or Aquarius.

Dental Work

Pick a day that is marked favorable for your Sun sign. Mars should be marked X, T, or C and Saturn, Uranus, and Jupiter should not be marked Q or O. Teeth are best removed during the increase of the Moon in the first or second quarter in Gemini, Virgo, Sagittarius, Capricorn, or Pisces. Avoid the Full Moon! The day should be favorable for your lunar cycle, and Mars and Saturn should be marked C, T, or X. Fillings should be done in the third or fourth quarters in the signs of Taurus, Leo, Scorpio, or Aquarius. The same applies for plates.

Dieting

Weight gain occurs more readily when the Moon is in a water sign (Cancer, Scorpio, Pisces). Experience has shown that weight may be lost if a diet is started when the Moon is decreasing in light (third or fourth quarter) and when it is in Aries, Leo, Virgo, Sagittarius, or Aquarius. The lunar cycle should be favorable on the day you wish to begin your diet.

Dressmaking

Design, cut, repair, or make clothes in Taurus, Leo, or Libra on a day marked favorable for your Sun sign. First and second quarters are best.

Venus, Jupiter, and Mercury should be aspected, but avoid Mars or Saturn aspects. William Lilly wrote in 1676, "Make no new clothes, or first put them on when the Moon is in Scorpio or afflicted by Mars, for they will be apt to be torn and quickly worn out."

Eyeglasses

Eyes should be tested and glasses fitted on a day marked favorable for your Sun sign and on a day that falls during your favorable lunar cycle. Mars should not be in aspect with the Moon. The same applies for any treatment of the eyes, which should also be started during the increase of the Moon (first or second quarter).

Fence Posts and Poles

Set the posts or poles when the Moon is in the third or fourth quarters. The fixed signs Taurus, Leo, and Aquarius are best for this.

Habits

To end any habit, start on a day when the Moon is in the third or fourth quarter and in a barren sign. Gemini, Leo, or Virgo are the best times, although Aries and Capricorn may be suitable as well. Make sure your lunar cycle is favorable. Avoid lunar aspects to Mars or Jupiter. Aspects to Neptune or Saturn are helpful. These rules apply to smoking.

Hair Care

Haircuts are best when the Moon is in a mutable (Gemini, Sagittarius, Pisces) or earthy sign (Taurus, Capricorn), well placed and aspected, but not in Virgo, which is barren. For faster growth, hair should be cut when the Moon is in Cancer or Pisces in the first or second quarter. To make hair grow thicker, cut it when the Moon is Full or in opposition to the Sun (marked O in the Lunar Aspectarian) in the signs of Taurus, Cancer, or Leo up to and at, but not after, the Full Moon. However, if you want your hair to grow more slowly, the Moon should be in Aries, Gemini, or Virgo in the third or fourth quarter, with Saturn square or opposite the Moon.

Permanents, straightening, and hair coloring will take well if the Moon is in Taurus or Leo and Venus is marked T or X. You should avoid doing your hair if Mars is marked Q or O, especially if heat is to be used.

For permanents, a trine to Jupiter is helpful. The Moon also should be in the first quarter, and check the lunar cycle for a favorable day in relation to your Sun sign.

Health

Diagnosis is more likely to be successful when the Moon is in a cardinal sign (Aries, Cancer, Libra, Capricorn), and less so when in a mutable sign (Gemini, Sagittarius, Pisces, Virgo). Begin a recuperation program when the Moon is in a cardinal or fixed sign and the day is favorable to your sign. Enter hospitals at these times. For surgery, see Surgical Procedures. Buy medicines when the Moon is in Virgo or Scorpio.

House Furnishings

Days when Saturn is aspected make things wear longer and tend to a more conservative purchase. Saturn days are good for buying, and Jupiter days are good for selling.

House Purchasing

If you desire a permanent home, buy when the Moon is in Taurus, Leo, Scorpio, Aquarius, or Cancer, preferably when the Moon is New. If you're buying for speculation and a quick turnover, be certain that the Moon is not in a fixed sign, but in Aries, Cancer, or Libra.

Lost Articles

Search for lost articles during the first quarter and when your Sun sign is marked favorable. Also check to see that the planet ruling the lost item is trine, sextile, or conjunct the Moon. The Moon governs household utensils, Mercury letters and books, and Venus clothing, jewelry, and money.

Marriage

The best time for marriage to take place is during the increase of the Moon, just past the first quarter, but not under the Full Moon. Good signs for the Moon to be in are Taurus, Cancer, Leo, and Libra. The Moon in Taurus produces the most steadfast marriages, but if the partners later want to separate they may have a difficult time. Avoid Aries, Gemini, Virgo, Scorpio, and Aquarius. Make sure that the Moon is well aspected (X or T), especially to Venus or Jupiter. Avoid aspects to Mars, Uranus, or Pluto.

Moving

Make sure that Mars is not aspected to the Moon. Move on a day favorable to your Sun sign, or when the Moon is conjunct, sextile, or trine the Sun.

Mowing the Lawn

Mow the lawn in the first or second quarter to increase growth. If you wish to retard growth, mow in the third or fourth quarter.

Painting

The best time to paint buildings is during the decrease of the Moon. If the weather is hot, do the painting while the Moon is in Taurus; if the weather is cold, paint while the Moon is in Leo. Another good sign for painting is Aquarius. By painting in the fourth quarter, the wood is drier and the paint will penetrate; when painting around the New Moon the wood is damp and the paint is subject to scalding when hot weather hits it. It is not advisable to paint while the Moon is in a water sign if the temperature is below seventy degrees, as it is apt to creep, check, or run.

Pets

Take home new pets when the day is favorable to your Sun sign or the Moon is well aspected by the Sun, Venus, Jupiter, Uranus, or Neptune. Avoid days when the Moon is badly aspected (Q or O) by the Sun, Mars, Saturn, Uranus, Neptune, or Pluto. Train pets when the Moon is in Taurus. Neuter them in any sign but Virgo, Libra, Scorpio, or Sagittarius. Avoid the week before and after the Full Moon. Declaw cats in the dark of the Moon. Avoid the week before and after the Full Moon and the sign of Pisces. When selecting a pet, have the Moon well aspected by the planet that rules the animal. Cats are ruled by the Sun, dogs by Mercury, birds by Venus, horses by Jupiter, and fish by Neptune.

Predetermining Sex

Count from the last day of menstruation to the day of its next beginning, and divide the interval between the two dates into halves. Pregnancy in the first half produces females, but copulation should take place with the Moon in a feminine sign. Pregnancy in the latter half, up to three days of the beginning of menstruation, produces males, but copulation should take place with the Moon in a masculine sign. The three-day period before the next period again produces females.

Romance

The same principles hold true for starting a relationship as for marriage. However, since there is less control of when a romance starts, it is sometimes necessary to study it after the fact. Romances begun under an increasing Moon are more likely to be permanent or satisfying. Those begun on the waning Moon will tend to transform the participants. The tone of the relationship can be guessed from the sign the Moon is in. Romances begun with the Moon in Aries may be impulsive. Those begun in Capricorn will take greater effort to bring to a desirable conclusion, but they may be rewarding. Good aspects between the Moon and Venus are good influences. Avoid Mars, Uranus, and Pluto aspects. Ending relationships is facilitated by a decreasing Moon, particularly in the fourth quarter. This causes the least pain and attachment.

Sauerkraut

The best tasting sauerkraut is made just after the Full Moon in a fruitful sign (Cancer, Scorpio, or Pisces).

Shingling

Shingling should be done in the decrease of the Moon (third or fourth quarter) in a fixed sign (Taurus, Leo, Scorpio, or Aquarius). Shingles laid during the New Moon have a tendency to curl at the edges.

Surgical Procedures

The flow of blood, like ocean tides, appears to be related to Moon phases. *Time* magazine (June, 6, 1960) reported that in 1,000 tonsillectomy case histories, Dr. Edson J. Andrews found that only eighteen percent of hemorrhaging occurred in the fourth and first quarters. To reduce hemorrhage after a surgery, schedule it within one week before or after a New Moon. Avoid surgery within one week before or after the Full Moon. Operate in the increase of the Moon if possible. Select a date when the Moon is not in the sign governing the part of the body involved in the operation. The further removed the Moon sign from the sign ruling the afflicted part of the body, the better. To find the signs and the body parts they rule, turn to the Zodiac Signs & Their Corresponding Body Parts chart on page 83.

Zodiac Signs & Their Corresponding Body Parts

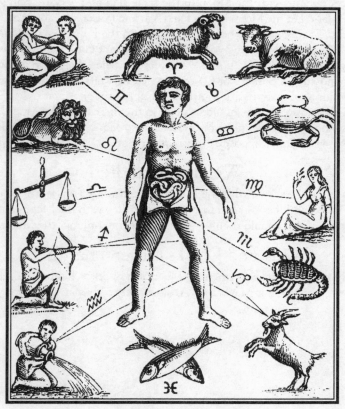

♈	= Aries	♎	= Libra
♉	= Taurus	♏	= Scorpio
♊	= Gemini	♐	= Sagittarius
♋	= Cancer	♑	= Capricorn
♌	= Leo	♒	= Aquarius
♍	= Virgo	♓	= Pisces

For successful operations, avoid lunar aspects to Mars, and look for favorable aspects to Venus and Jupiter. Do not operate when the Moon is applying to any aspect of Mars (this tends to promote inflammation and complications). See the Lunar Aspectarian (pages 28-51) to determine days with negative Mars aspects and positive Venus and Jupiter aspects. Never operate with the Moon in the same sign as a person's Sun sign or ascendant. Let the Moon be in a fixed sign and free of all manner of impediment. There should be no Q or O aspects in the Lunar Aspectarian, and the Moon should not be void-of-course. Do not cut a nerve when Mercury is afflicted (Q or O). Avoid amputations when the Moon is conjunct or opposed the Sun (C or O) or opposed by Mars (O). Good signs for abdominal operations are Sagittarius, Capricorn, or Aquarius.

Cosmetic surgery should be done in the increase of the Moon, when the Moon is not in square or opposition to Mars. Avoid days when the Moon is square or opposite Saturn or the Sun.

Weaning Children

This should be done with the Moon in Sagittarius, Capricorn, Aquarius, or Pisces. Children should nurse for the last time with the Moon in a fruitful sign. Venus should then be trine, sextile, or conjunct the Moon.

Wine and Drinks Other Than Beer

It is best to start brewing when the Moon is in Pisces or Taurus. Good aspects (X or T) to Venus are favorable. Avoid aspects with Mars or Saturn.

The Moon and Aging

Leeda Alleyn-Picotti

Could we, barring the unforeseen events that snipped the threads of the Fates, live as long as we wanted? It is important to realize that we not only believe in immortality, we are smitten with it. We pursue it. Human immortality, though, is not all fanciful fairy tale, legend, or myth. From the cells of our bodies, we sense an unrevealed truth about unending life, beyond the tidy concept of afterlife.

The Fourth House of a horoscope reflects conditions at the end of life. These conditions do not indicate or dictate the death moment, which falls to the rulership of Pluto and the Eighth House. This distinction is important, because the conditions at the end of life may seem contradictory to the actual death moment, such as a solitary period of existence ended through a moment of happiness in the midst of family or friends.

The idea of the end-of-life condition draws from the concept of progressed astrology, which assigns one degree of daily movement by the Sun, Moon, and planets, to equal one year of life. Expanding on this idea, astrologers discovered that the Ascendant also progressed approximately one degree forward each year. About ninety days (equal to ninety years) after birth, the Ascendant reached the Nadir or Fourth House cusp. Because this movement parallelled an "acceptable" lifetime, theorists defined the Fourth House as "conditions at the end of life."

Good thinking prevailed among these investigating astrologers. The square aspect formed by the progressed Ascendant to its original place was not ascribed as a negative, or death. Recognizing the progressed square was complete and losing power, astrological theorists emphasized the next progressed aspect, the trine, which symbolizes fulfillment and rewards. Without death indicated, we assume these thinkers expected the human condition would prevail to encompass a new, but undescribed, vitality, rather than a decline.

Moving through signs, the Moon gives clues about possible developments during different phases of life, and bestows power to alter the scheme of previous existence. Secure in hopeful renewal, we can adopt a new lifestyle, meet changing nutritional demands, and pursue new interests. This can be done without encountering the expectation that life would be dwindling and frail.

The following descriptions of longevity, listed by sign or house, apply to the natal placements of your Moon, Sun, or Ascendant. These descriptions are not promises or predeterminations, and should be considered carefully as you make decisions in preparation for the curtain to rise on a new stage of life. Because few of us are born at the 0 degree of a sign, life progresses through the remaining degrees, before entering subsequent 30 degree periods. Consequently, a person born with an Ascendant at 20 degrees Libra will enter the fourth phase of Capricorn at about age seventy.

Aries or the First House

Ardent Aries starts life with passion and curiosity. Self-involved, he rushes headlong into the Taurus phase where his energy is harnessed into useful, productive ventures. Aries' passion becomes tempered with diplomacy. The Gemini period brings movement and restlessness, causing Aries to relocate to another part of the country, or gravitate to younger people, who are perplexed that aging Aries possesses surprisingly youthful insights.

Under Cancer's influence, in the fourth phase, Aries becomes nostalgic for the past and the old homestead. New sensitivity brings out a surprising dependence, with Aries often seeking comfort and reassurance from a relative.

During the mounting influence of Cancer, Aries can experience health problems relating to the head and sensory organs, as well as the stomach. Imbalanced eating habits are the culprit, especially if high amounts of sugar are consumed, producing an artificial equivalent of adrenaline rush. In particular, the eyes suffer from sugar consumption.

For Aries to fare well under Cancer, focus must be honed into razor-sharp acuity. A late return to college in theoretical fields, such as mathematics or astronomy, keeps his mind sharp and immune to Cancer's mood swings. For the Aries who needs physical expression, Cancer's agrarian and husbandry pursuits provide exercise and opportunities to nurture and care for plant life and dependent, domestic animals.

Taurus or the Second House

Taurus begins life at a slow, quiet pace. Personal style and insight are cultivated. Frequently, she begins work or a career early, gaining prowess over personal earnings and developing life-long resources. Just as life seems to be going smoothly, Gemini scatters settled Taurus on the four winds of travel, career changes, and social involvements. Under Cancer's influence, home and family take first place, with Taurus enjoying the role of family matriarch or life's grand master.

As Leo asserts its influence, Taurus returns to a fixed perspective. Long an admirer of beauty, she is now in a position to create it. Simple pastimes of singing or playing an instrument lead to intricate musical work, such as choral or madrigal arrangements or music composition. Taurus is usually blessed with a strong body, and Leo encourages her into more demanding physical expressions, breaking up sedentary life habits.

For the Taurus who enters aged life alone, affairs of the heart will not be denied, with dating or remarriage releasing feelings of love, never before revealed. The new adventure of grandchildren gives opportunities to pass on sage advice and initiate new interests or hobbies for self-fulfillment.

During the Leo phase, Taurus may find herself having problems of the throat, usually arising from cellular toxicities. Because her tastes run to sweets and convenience foods, she must return to fundamentals. Vegetables, fruits, nuts, and berries taken from her lush garden help wash toxicities from her system, provided she uses organic gardening techniques. When her voice is lost to laryngitis or a nervous condition, Taurus needs to examine the use of her words and tendencies to be overbearing. Any negative effect of her words or willful tones indicates the physical reaction of a closed throat.

Gemini or the Third House

Vigor and exploration suit the Gemini child. Without demands of commitment, Gemini discovers life's many avenues, delaying decisions on which will command persistent energy. The Cancer phase brings Gemini in touch with unresolved emotional issues that were unimportant during his initial pursuit of variety. He looks for a permanent home, although this may run no deeper than a long-term rental. With the advent of Leo, Gemini shares his domicile with another. Stabilized emotionally and emboldened to venture into love's domain, he seeks strength in an existing marriage or creates a permanent one if divorce is in his past. A youthful ardor attends his endeavors.

During the fourth life phase, Gemini is touched by his complement sign, Virgo. A return to inquisitiveness is indicated, although Gemini is more inclined to pass on his learning as a teacher. With the Virgo keynote of service, Gemini takes on volunteer programs, teaching those who cannot afford tuition or attend regular school.

Under Virgo, Gemini is prone to nervous problems, usually manifested as intestinal difficulties. Always a picky or sparse eater, he needs to incorporate essential fiber in his diet along with the B-vitamin complex so essential for stabilizing brain operations and repairing various parts of a stressed nervous system.

Virgo causes Gemini to return to writing, although his talents will be considerably more disciplined than previously known. Short articles, critiques, or trade reviews satisfy the need to communicate, as well as returning a good income. Although he never lacked energy, Gemini needs an exercise plan. Walking or biking in fresh air calms his nerves and soothes his digestive system.

Cancer or the Fourth House

Cancer begins life sheltered within the bosom of home and family. Her preferences for weathered and trusted possessions develop during this time. As the Leo phase begins, Cancer seeks fulfillment of her own place as the nurturer, marrying quickly and starting a family. Love is bestowed primarily on the children, who are doted on and well protected from life's onslaughts. Through Virgo, Cancer gains discipline, often turning to business, career, or education, to fulfill inner talents.

As Cancer enters the Libra phase, partnership needs will prevail. If married, she will focus on her spouse. If unmarried, business partnerships or close friendships will become more important as she seeks the close communion she has secretly yearned for all her life.

During the Libra phase, Cancer may experience stomach upsets as she stretches herself into emotional, one-on-one relationships. These upsets are often accompanied by kidney or urinary tract infections. Cancer needs to incorporate foods high in potassium to quell kidney problems. If stomach upsets begin to hamper her efforts in dealing with others, test for high or low hydrochloric acidity in the stomach. Fresh cranberry juice will aide urinary tract infections.

Because Cancer's life phases deal directly with relationships, socializing proves necessary in later years. Group activities lead her into forming close alliances, even seeking a new spouse, if remarriage is a possibility. Group activities raise concern only if Cancer is using them to avoid personal relationships. Late life activities might include certifying as a master gardener, or fund-raising for animal activism.

Leo or the Fifth House

The deep radiant being of Leo nurtures each interest with loving attention. During the Virgo phase, Leo feels a restriction on his normally overflowing heart. He learns to discipline and discriminate the placement of his energies for a more lasting effect. Leo often finds that family duties force him to put aside his own desires. In the Libra phase, he learns to keep love alive, never letting love's embers lose their glow.

In the fourth phase, Leo's generative powers combine with Scorpio's magnetism, and a deep spiritual communion with all life is sought. Containing himself in a faithful relationship, Leo is stunned by the sexual power of Scorpio. Where love had been expressed in words and romantic activities, he learns that true sexual union is in shared love. Leo is amazed that all ages of the opposite sex find him irresistible, Virgo's lessons in discernment prevent him from making inappropriate overtures.

Accustomed to bestowing his power or benevolence through love, Leo is upset by the apparent aloof posture of Scorpio. He may experience heart troubles as he attempts to quell sexual yearnings. Homeopathic remedies or Ayurvedic medicinals to stabilize the heart structure, along with potassium to reduce irregularities and arrhythmias will help. The reproductive organs benefit from supplements of zinc for both sexes, with additional supplements of selenium for men and a calcium/magnesium combination for women.

Volunteer efforts in which he can act as a director or primary contributor, observing the effects of benevolent influence, are a good outlet during this time.

Virgo or the Sixth House

Virgo begins life noticing patterns, rules, and requirements; and learns to operate within many restrictions and personal discipline. In the second phase, Libra introduces the wild-card element of relationship. Here Virgo learns to make accommodations to others by either relaxing their own rules, or understanding that each individual operates with a separate set of personal regulations. Under Scorpio's influence, Virgo runs headlong into the experimental. However, a repressive Virgo is more likely to encounter a compulsion toward demanding perfection. After fixed Scorpio, Virgo is ready for expanding possibilities under Sagittarius. Some Virgos find release in overseas travel, especially lengthy excursions. Others prefer inner pursuits and are inclined to teach spiritual concepts to others.

During the Sagittarius phase, Virgo's health is likely to be very good. Given her normally industrious energy, she is not likely to put on weight. Instead, she feels that she has now energy reserves to persue the demands of Sagittarius. Because indulgence is to be expected, Virgo's delicate digestive system benefits from including more fibrous foods. Virgo's approach to life becomes more relaxed, releasing much of her criticism and turning her fine acuity to the abstract and theoretical.

During this phase, Virgo is in a good position to teach. Sagittarius causes her to appreciate molding young minds, but if children are too much for her, adult students with youthful, fresh perspectives and humorous explanations will benefit from Virgo's experience. Not as strongly inclined under Sagittarius to be the homebody, Virgo needs a variety of good walking or hiking shoes to keep her feet healthy.

Libra or the Seventh House

Libra starts life as the sweet, pretty child with a smile reminiscent of Mona Lisa. Ever conscious of others' feelings, Libra is never smirky, upsetting, or critical. Balanced temperament characterize his approach to life's events, keeping him out of trouble and with time for abstract thinking. Through Scorpio, Libra's balance is assaulted by an intensity that appears in relationships, career, and hobbies and often causes them to turn to psychological studies to understand the basis of intensity. With Sagittarius, Libra again enjoys a relaxed pace and puts his considerable mental talents to work. His observations through the Scorpio period are put in writing, or taught to others. Naturally compassionate, he is neither critical nor imperious in his presentations. Sagittarius bestows high rewards of recognition by others, honors from vocational peers, and general appreciation from his family.

The fourth phase of life, Capricorn, whose ruler Saturn is exalted in Libra, puts him back on the move. His excellent mind and gained honors urge Capricorn recognize his influence on community and region. Libra's end-of-life condition often finds him as the revered and appreciated elder whose experiences and wisdom are sought by many. If involved in a career or business, he continues as a mentor, adopting a calm pace. If he decides to travel, journeys are based on business or benefits to his community.

All in all, Libra's life is about give and take. In health matters, Capricorn tends to lengthen Libra's life. However, if lower back problems have developed over the years, Libra needs to incorporate stretching exercises to maintain mobility, as Capricorn stiffens unused parts. Tendencies to arthritic conditions arise from the kidneys, which may not operate sufficiently. Deposits of uric acid in flexible tissue causes dull pain and inflammations of gout. Sodium foods, primarily fresh vegetables and fruits, and fresh cranberry juice will maintain the kidney's mineral balance.

Scorpio or the Eighth House

Scorpio is the quiet, intense child, who is more comfortable discovering and exploring the environment and making every moment count. During the Sagittarius phase, Scorpio is released from Pluto's intensity, and while there may be a lack of self-confidence in her abilities to pursue goals, opportunities abound. Sagittarius' demand for travel teaches her to compare her opinions about life with those she confronts in other regions and lands. Fixed Scorpio learns that life changes, and no one opinion lasts throughout all conditions. Capricorn brings Scorpio into power over others, but if she has learned to relax under Sagittarius,

she is not inclined to be authoritarian or tyrannical.

During the fourth life phase, opinionated Scorpio encounters Aquarius where rigidity of thinking is the worst of possibilities. However, Scorpio, who has come to appreciate different approaches in life, enjoys the mental inquisitiveness of Aquarius. Through Aquarius, Scorpios take on a more humanitarian view of the world and its problems. Pondering spiritual matters, developing psychic talents, or discussing philosophy at length consume most of Scorpio's time. Turning her opinions into considered perceptions about life, Scorpio finds fulfillment in writing her memoirs or a family history. Aquarius enjoys the physical activity of constructing, which Scorpio may employ in refinishing furniture, interior decorating, or landscaping.

Accustomed to a sedentary lifestyle, Scorpio may encounter lung difficulties while in the Aquarian phase. Shortness of breath is alleviated by controlled breathing exercises. Scorpio's preferences for heavy foods create an acidic condition that forces the lungs to accumulate phlegm. When fluid coats the lung tubes, Scorpio falls heir to phlegmatic illnesses, such as pneumonia or tuberculosis. At the sign of any lung difficulties, Scorpio needs to take a fast from rich or heavy foods, and incorporate more salad vegetables into her diet.

Sagittarius or the Ninth House

As a child, Sagittarius displays a fine mental acuity and innate understanding of the meaning behind events. The sharp mind of youth is equally matched with a capable body. As Sagittarius enters the Capricorn phase, his mind becomes focussed and he is aware of how planning, as well as careful use of his energies and talents, can help him reach his goals. In the Aquarius phase, Sagittarius seeks an equal partnership with others. Preexisting relationships are either modified or ended. From Pisces, Sagittarius experiences a new found compassion that helps him expand his goals to include a benefit for others. Social-mindedness attends his actions, writings, or efforts.

In late life, Sagittarius can develop hip problems. When Sagittarius has failed to relax, reflect on goals, or communicate with his inner spirit, he experiences socket degeneration, arthritic conditions, or sciatica. To prevent these conditions, he needs to restrict rich or starchy foods, and add fresh fruits, vegetables, and lean meats to his diet. Sciatic difficulties are eased by gentle yoga exercises or manipulations through massage or reflexology. Without these preventions, Sagittarius will lose his most honored attribute—freedom of movement.

It is the rare Sagittarian who does not have a life story worth telling. Although he has been frequently glib about his experiences, especially those that were painful, he's in a position to share what he has learned, helping others understand their situations. The sagacious centaur finds fulfillment in volunteer work, teaching others to help themself, writing long fiction, or setting his own memoirs into a perspective history.

Capricorn or the Tenth House

Capricorn is the only sign which starts life old, accepting cares, responsibilities, and burdens the way the rest of us accept candy, play, and naps. Born with a sense of long life, she recognizes time as her ally and willingly receives duties thrust on her in early life. In the Aquarian phase, Capricorn feels uplifted from her previous restrictions. Ever the climber, she builds on her past glories and credentials, finding new avenues and expressions. During the Pisces phase, she relinquishes the boundaries of logic and linear thinking and experiments with her intuition. Her former thoughts about the march of time dissolve as she loses herself in creative pursuits. During the Aries phase, Capricorn is well prepared to venture into a new world of interests and movement.

Capricorn seems to become more physically nimble with age. Few actually end up resembling the old goat, appearing more youthful in temperament and face than at any time in their lives. However, because of burdens carried in early life, Capricorn may experience troubles with her knees. The problem is usually rigidity from too high an intake of calcium, which deposits in cartilage, causing an arthritic condition. Capricorn can remedy this problem by observing a balance of magnesium with calcium. Her ruler Saturn limits her need for calcium; she is wiser to develop her muscles to support bones.

Motivated by the joy of building a lasting empire rather than by making money, Capricorn is likely to continue working late in life.

Whatever her working endeavor, she will only accept a position or start a business that provides plenty of travel and introductions into interests she has never explored.

Aquarius or the Eleventh House

In early life, humane Aquarius is the inventor, whether his inventions are intricate fantasies based on scientific curiosity or amazingly overlooked, but helpful, contraptions that let grandma bake more cookies. Able to see between the lines of life, he perceives more about the world than he ever relates. Within Pisces' influence, Aquarius flounders in emotional depths, usually finding the true love of his life and intensified psychic abilities. In the Aries phase, Aquarius has renewed physical energy. Under the influence of Taurus, Aquarius returns to focus and gains purpose that he applies toward creating lasting foundations for his many ideas and creations. His sense of conviction returns, allowing him to tackle projects that would perplex less experienced people.

Throughout life, Aquarius has had problems with leg cramps, especially the lower leg. For Aquarians who prefer to stand on one foot in the laboratory or the workshop, periodic walking, ascending and descending stairs, and meditations in prone positions relieve the pull of gravity, which causes pooling of blood in the lower legs.

The great satisfaction for Aquarius in late life is developing self-perpetuating programs. Because he is comfortable yoking his energies to others', he seeks to establish foundations, organizations, or fellowships which continue the development of his finest ideas. In the event his finances are inadequate or he cannot raise funds, Aquarius tidies his research notes, possibly in published form, and endows a school or university chair, usually with the condition that eventual proceeds from his research be used to fund scholarships.

Pisces or the Twelfth House

Pisces begins life either in a needy condition or feeling unappreciated which usually forces her into an inner life of hopes and dreams. During the Aries phase, Pisces experiences a rush of physical energy and often indulges in athletic pursuits previously considered risky to undertake. Growing self-confidence marks this period. With the influence of Taurus, Pisces secures her material paradise. Whether the dream has been a lavish estate, a plentiful farm, or a palatial residence, she finds an environment that fulfills the needs of her youth. Armed with material success, she is in a position to help family and children. In the Gemini phase, Pisces feels confident to tackle the challenges of variety, feeling safe to expose herself to diversity, without feeling threatened.

Throughout life, Pisces has problems with her feet. With Gemini's demand for movement, she needs to outfit her feet properly for all types of activities. New shoes usually require a complete change of wardrobe. Cool foot baths, mixed with oil of wintergreen or peppermint, revitalize her tired feet. A gentle massage with a glycerine and water solution regenerates warmth.

Late life finds Pisces on the move. Travel has always brought Pisces joy, but now she ventures into foreign lands. Pisces is unlikely to work in late life. After long struggles with inner or outer adversity, she has come into her own time. Pisces is likely to relate her new experiences through conversations and verbal stories.

After the First Ninety Years

As explained, longevity is a matter of conditioned perspective. Recent studies into the stage of centenarian living yield remarkable, but consistent, qualities among the aged. First, the age of ninety is an important threshold. Most who reach this age experience a resurgence of vitality, restored through reduced food intake, permitting less burden on the body's organs and digestive system.

Second, moderate exercise permits strength training and toning throughout the body's muscular system, now recognized as an important support for the skeletal system. Research applauds full-body activities, particularly walking.

Finally, and perhaps most importantly, those who reach ninety exhibit mental determination, balanced with a strong spiritual belief system. Long-lived individuals expect to reach old age. They don't let other ideas about lifespan subvert their thinking. These advanced seniors are assertive, sometimes described as domineering.

The importance of spiritual beliefs cannot be underestimated. Whether these beliefs are openly communicated or inwardly savored, a spiritual foundation guides judgment during the tests of daily experience and needs. For those willing to prepare for a long life of diverse experiences, cultivate now a warm heart, an open mind, and a strong body. The celebration is just beginning.

Managing Moods with Flower Essences

By Gretchen Lawlor

Flowers delight us with their colors and scents. They evoke memories and lift us out of blue moods. They convey passion, sympathy, or celebration to those we love; they can also heal.

There are a number of healing systems that use the power of flowers to affect moods and heal. Public gardens not only delight the senses, but are architecturally designed to soothe frazzled nerves and allow for pause between commerce or commute, providing an immediate experience of the healing power of nature. Aromatherapy makes use of the essential oils of aromatic plants to enhance the body's immune system, and to restore balance between body, mind, and spirit. Flower essences, which are taken orally in dilute amounts, can affect our attitudes and rebalance emotions. Essences are often used to treat depression and anxiety.

Since ancient times, flower essence theory has been based upon the belief that all health conditions stem from emotional or energetic upset, and to avert a physical crisis or deterioration through sensitive awareness of unbalanced states, balance must be restored. Flower essences are used for many conditions, including physical problems. However, their primary action is upon the emotional nature. Flower essences applied to the body's energy centers help to harmonize the flowing in and out of energy, bringing our energy centers into balance.

Flower essences work particularly well to enhance emotional balance. Medicines made from flower essences are regaining popularity worldwide as a natural alternative to pharmaceutical antidepressants and anti-anxiety medications. These gentler remedies are effective tools for altering our moods, without the frustrating and often debilitating side effects of more powerful medications.

Unlike conventional pharmaceuticals or herbs whose influence is primarily upon the physical body, flower remedies focus their effect upon emotional well-being. Even though many flower essences are made from plants that are also used in herbal medicine, such as comfrey and chamomile, they are very different in their influence. Unlike tinctures

or extracts which can be toxic if taken by the wrong person or at the wrong time, flower essence remedies are self-adjusting in that if the remedy is incorrect it simply has no effect. As well, there are no harmful side effects.

Flower essences are medicines made by extracting the chemical—the plant's life force—from flower petals. This can be accomplished by exposing the freshly picked flowers to sunlight as they lay in a container of spring water. Exposure generally takes several hours, after which the flowers are removed and the liquid, now charged with the flower's energy, is preserved and diluted with alcohol to prevent the essence from spoiling. This parallels to some extent the preparation of homeopathic medications, especially in that both systems use minute amounts of a highly dilute form of the original natural substance to effect healing.

Usually ingested as a liquid, prescribed flower essence treatments can be taken every few minutes for an acute trauma or emergency, or for less acute situations a tonic every four hours or less is frequently recommended. In a crisis, a shift may be experienced within moments, or may take several hours of frequent use to stabilize the emotions. A remedy may be taken for weeks as a tonic to promote slow improvement of a longstanding condition.

Flower essences are safe for everyone. Animals also respond well to them. They can be taken internally or rubbed onto the skin. In hospital settings they can be gently dropped onto the lips, safe even for pre-operative or postoperative patients unable to take anything internally. They can be applied externally in baths, or on compresses, or sipped from a glass of water or juice.

Flower essences work synergistically with other medications, gently supporting the positive effect and assisting in any emotional side effects. They do not antidote any medications, though some flower essence practitioners feel they are of less use when used in conjunction with steroid therapy or the more potent antidepressants. My own experience is that they do work well in conjunction with most antidepressants, with more of a tonic or restorative effect, and are less sedating.

Although flower essences have been used successfully for years by licensed health professionals, no one can explain definitively how they work. The rishis of India (a community of sages who lived in the Himalayas 2–3000 years ago) developed a profound universal theory of unity, which accounted for the universe, the consciousness, the mind and its activities, and the body's energies used flower essences to balance the chakras. Today, Dr. Herbert Fill, M.D., a psychiatrist and former New York City Commissioner for Public Health, uses flower essences almost exclusively over tranquilizers and psychotropic drugs. He believes the essences may act upon the neurotransmitters of the brain. Energetic medicine practitioners feel that the essences work upon dysfunctional patterns within the subtle energetic and physiological mechanisms of the body.

Acupuncture has identified electrical and energetic pathways in the body which seem to act as an interface between the higher frequency energy bodies and the physical body. Many flower essence practitioners actually use their remedies upon acupuncture meridians to quickly impact emotional disturbances.

Essences for Support During Times of Change

Life is a process of continual change, but some periods are more abrupt and traumatic that others. The flower essence Walnut is recommended for the emotional turmoil that is often experience when you are transitioning through any of these major stresses (even though it may be quite a positive change):

Change of job • *Change of home* • *Marriage* • *Divorce* • *New baby* • *Illness* • *Retirement* • *Loss of a loved one* • *Teething* • *Puberty* • *Midlife*

The flower essence Walnut is the largest selling single flower essence in the United States. Used specifically for assistance in times of transition, Walnut breaks links with the past in a gentle way, allowing one to move forward with ease, restoring comfort and equilibrium when shaken by changes. In times of profound change, it also provides protection from outside influences, cocooning one in a safe, protective energy field.

Other flower essences that might be supportive in times of major metamorphosis are: Angel's Trumpet, a remedy to assist in the dying process; Morning Glory, for freeing one from destructive habit patterns; Cayenne, for overcoming inertia; and Scleranthus, to move beyond wavering between alternative paths.

Flowers for Anxiety

Aspen • remedy for fear of the unknown.

Mimulus • remedy for fear related to ordinary events.

Larch • remedy for fear of failure or feeling one is not good enough.

Cerato • remedy for fear of failure remedy, but in this case the afflicted person will lean excessively upon others for support and advice as to how to succeed.

Flowers for Anger and Aggressiveness

Black-eyed Susan • remedy for suppressed anger which needs to be brought to awareness.

Holly • remedy for anger when love is thwarted or denied.

Impatiens • remedy for anger that is quick to flare up.

Snapdragon • aides expression of anger due to verbal abuse for the most minor infraction.

Willow • aides in release of deeply held anger leading to bitterness and resentment.

Flowers for a Broken Heart

Bleeding Heart • remedy for dealing with the ending of love affair, to bring emotional detachment and acceptance.

Borage • brings cheerfulness and an upbeat attitude when the heart feels heavy with grief.

California Wild Rose • helps with painful feelings one is inclined to avoid.

Forget-Me-Not • opens the heart to spiritual realm in order to transcend personal grief for one who has died. It can provide a link to the deceased, like a soul bridge, in those first days to complete unfinished business and allow both parties to move on.

Flowers for Depression and Despair

Baby Blue Eyes • restores trust that stems from a lack of emotional support during childhood. Baby Blue Eyes restores the soul's original innocence and helps one to become more accepting, positive, and open in interactions.

Gentian • for doubt and discouragement from a setback.

Gorse • restores optimism when there is despair with a sense of hopelessness and expectations of ongoing suffering.

Milkweed • for use when alcohol or other mind-and-spirit numbing substances are used to obliterate consciousness of daily problems.

Sagebrush • helps when one has reached rock bottom in an experience of personal devastation. It gives an ability to endure and accept a necessary stage of emptiness.

Flowers in Adolescence

Calla Lily • helps when puberty is delayed, stemming from mixed feelings about sexuality

Goldenrod • is useful for the middle-school ages of the early teens when peer pressure obscures one's ability to be true to oneself.

Holly • helps sibling rivalry and feelings of envy or jealousy about others circumstances.

Willow • clears resentment and bitterness, when the prevailing complaint is that life is not fair, and blame is placed upon parents, authority figures, or society in general.

Flowers for Confidence

Elm • for overwhelm, despair about one's ability to fulfill expectations and responsibilities.

Buttercup • an excellent remedy for people whose gifts are not easily appreciated. It brings a sense of self-worth.

Sunflower • encourages radiant self expression and a positive, balanced ago development.

Mountain Pride • brings a warrior-like courage to challenge or confront adversity.

Aromotherapy

The therapeutic action of volatile oils is the basis of aromatherapy. Essential oils can be taken into the body in a variety of ways. Inhaling the aromas of essential oils can change a stress into contentment, focus, calm, and clarity. They can simply be taken as aromatic herbs in foods or drinks, which many of us do every day. Diluted essential oils can be rubbed onto the skin or inhaled through the nose.

The essential oils of chamomile, clary sage, lavender, lemon balm, and melissa are helpful to treat anxiety. For depression, use geranium, jasmine, rose or thyme essential oils. For general calming, use lavender or chamomile. For heartbreak use sweet marjoram. Hyssop, clary sage, and pine are great stress tonics.

Flowers have always been endowed with magical or divine powers, possessing their own unique natures and temperaments. Each flower seems to have an indwelling spirit or soul which determines its shape or form, habits of growth, and purpose in the world. One has only to look upon a flower in all its exquisite simple beauty and experience its healing presence.

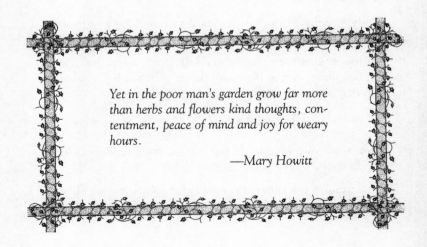

Yet in the poor man's garden grow far more than herbs and flowers kind thoughts, contentment, peace of mind and joy for weary hours.

—Mary Howitt

Choosing Your Pet Companion

Leeda Alleyn Pacotti

You've decided to pamper yourself and give in to some much-needed relaxation. Nestled into a comforter, you drift in and out of your nap, releasing back into the welcoming warmth. Suddenly, you're jarred from tranquility by a nose planted under yours. It doesn't matter whether the nose belongs to your iguana, tuna-breathed cat, shivering chihuahua, or St. Bernard; a memorable time of touching, tenderness, and closeness has come again.

We share a love with our animals that's never really given to another human. Perhaps this bond develops because no matter how familiar we become with our pets, they never progress in expectation or development the way our children do. They frolic forever, surprising us with that occasional posture of compassionate wisdom. We see them delighting in a physical prowess we had to forego, freely giving themselves to experiences we suspect we will never know again.

Ask any person why they have a pet, and you'll hear many reasons. You'll be told the animal needs care. Some elders readily admit that meeting the animal's needs keeps them alive. Children desire the playful companionship of animals. But, there is one commonality—trust with a living being. We're their keepers, their caretakers, their sidekicks; we're their charges for protection.

Stories abound of persons who are certain that animals pick them, and certainly, animals sense our willingness to care for them. All of us have experienced denying the impulse to take an animal, too. Why does the bond between animal and human sometimes happen and sometimes not?

One clue stems from dream interpretation about animal symbols. Generally, animals represent our inhibited traits, whether we are aware of them or not. The type of trait we see in the animal, such as physical strength, mental acuity, or some soulful aspect, pinpoints the trait we hope to bring out in ourselves. Fortunately, what we dream can manifest in the outer world. For example, just as you consider becoming a stronger swimmer, you might acquire a Labrador retriever. Another person decides to increase her economic status and falls in love with a luxuriantly coated Persian cat. Or maybe an individual who feels overly grounded suddenly decides to acquire a brace of birds, or takes up falconry. These examples indicate the preference for a given animal, based on an inner need.

Beyond the dynamic of personal need, however, fall animals which return to us from other lives. Known as familiars, these animals gravitate to us, appearing with us in several lifetimes, or several times in one lifetime. A familiar is exactly what the term implies; these animals know the needs of a particular human soul and have dedicated themselves to return to it as often as possible. When encountering the familiar, human owners usually experience an inescapable demand to own a particular animal. Because of this compelling attraction, the familiar incarnates its soul in any animal species appropriate for the human owner's development. Consequently, the tried and true dog owner inexplicably acquires a cat or snake.

For the hypothetical dog owner, the new cat presents highly developed instincts beyond those seen in dogs. From the cat's perspective, the former dog owner learns to look before leaping, or to remain aloof when urged into unreasonable behaviors. If the animal soul returns as a snake, the former dog owner learns to tread carefully in situations or, from another point of view, to intertwine joyfully in any close relationship.

Although finding an animal companion may appear haphazard, the sign of the Moon in your horoscope describes basic traits you have chosen to acquire in this life. Once you meet this challenge, the progressed Moon, by sign, indicates other traits you hope to exhibit. When considering pet ownership, choosing your animals by your natal or progressed Moon will move you forward in your personal development.

Lunar Pet Choices

Moon in Aries • Pets have physical strength, endurance, and prowess. Because physical needs are reflected between pet and owner, the likely animals will be sporting or fighting dogs. While these animals may not actually be used in sport or game, the owner will be drawn to them in order to feel secure in a neighborhood environment, or to fantasize about participation in aggressive sports.

Moon in Taurus • Pets will reflect luxurious comfort or be an investment. Owners tend to acquire animals that need special diets or grooming. From the standpoint of investment, owners are likely to become patrons for endangered species or rare animals. The desire to conserve and perpetuate runs strong among these owners.

Moon in Gemini • Pets that can be taught to "talk," such as myna birds or parrots, will be popular choices. Song birds, too, will capture the owner's interest, as will any cat or dog which can look them in the eye and respond with murmurs, yodels, or yowls to human speech. The energetic movement of monkeys is also fascinating.

Moon in Cancer • Pets such as turtles and tortoises appeal to the stay-at-home owners, while the more outgoing types are comfortable with responsive herding dogs. When circumstances and real estate permit, Cancer pet owners tend to acquire herds of animals, or to select an animal from a herd or pack for special attention.

Moon in Leo • The outrageous, extraordinary, or coveted are the types of animals Leos will choose. Large African cats would be a first choice, but circumstances or local ordinances usually preempt this choice. Close runners-up are purebred dogs and cats, or thoroughbred horses, especially if they can be displayed in the ring or at competition.

Moon in Virgo • Pets will have a close relationship with the owner. The Virgo owner seeks animals that are sensitive to the sick or can be given responsibility in illness, such as alerting to changes in human body temperature or shifts in illness. Service, healing, and careful attention are mandated in both owner and animal. The Moon in Virgo often indicates that the owner is chosen by pet familiars.

Moon in Libra • Pets with keen mental capabilities, such as terriers, shelties, and chihuahuas, which are bred for highly organized working traits, have special appeal to Libras. Size counts, and Libras prefer miniature animals of all kinds, including ferrets, guinea pigs, and hamsters, or even mice and rats.

Moon in Scorpio • Pets have qualities of strength that are inestimable, and prowess that reveals itself at the last moment. Snakes, especially boa

constrictors and legged reptiles, such as the iguana, fit these special needs of strength and power. As for prowess, Scorpios excel with birds of prey and find a deep satisfaction from falconry.

Moon in Sagittarius • Pet owners seek intelligent, responsive animals who are willing to perform. Horses, preferring those which are sleek and fleet; dogs, especially when they can entertain and provide a humorous release for others; and cats will delight these owners.

Moon in Capricorn • Pets tend to be beasts of burden, possibly draft horses. Capricorns exhibit a strong fondness for powerful sledding dogs, such as the Samoyed and Norwegian elkhound, too. When a country setting is available, herding dogs or goats are often found in small numbers.

Moon in Aquarius • They collect animals in flocks or packs. Unlike the other signs that have designated animals in groups, the Aquarian's group will be an eclectic mix of different breeds and crossbreeds. When space is a problem, expect the Aquarian to have a large aquarium or several small ones, with many varieties of fish.

Moon in Pisces • Pets displaying a strong intuition are favored. Most Pisces pet owners respond better to animals than humans. They are awed by the animal's ability to cope with human emotions that often leave the Pisces feeling alienated. Cats, in particular, are excellent choices for a Pisces. Expect Pisces to rely on the animal's instinctive response to other humans and draw conclusions accordingly.

Owner-Pet Relationships

An interesting perspective of pet ownership ensues from the position, or house placement, of the Moon in your natal and progressed horoscopes. The natal house placement shows the influence from animals throughout your life. As your Moon progresses (taking approximately two-and-one-third years to pass through each house), the area of life influenced by your pet will change. This natural lunar progression makes the owner-pet relationship a dynamic one, as different needs of the owner manifest.

Moon in the First House • The pet will be a constant companion, an extension of the owner who will often mimics the animal's instinctual traits or physical abilities in an effort to strengthen personal development. Frequently, given the highly physical and active nature of the first house, owner and pet will participate together in sport competitions. The First House melds the close cooperation of the equestrian and horse, the hunter and sporting dog, or the rescue team of man and dog.

Moon in the Second House • The owner sees the animal with abilities to create earnings or develop value. Because it's the nature of the Second House to display rather than be involved, the owner is usually removed from directly attending the animal. The Second House shows the owner of racing animals, which earn their way, or the distant owner of herds that are exchanged in commodity trading. As for animals that appreciate in value, owners may invest in genetic research, or acquire prize animals to be sold for stud.

Moon in the Third House • This pet will be seen riding shotgun in the front seat of a vehicle, as a side-by-side passenger. These owners may develop communicative abilities with their animals such as are applicable to television commercials and movies.

Moon in the Fourth House • Animal husbandry is a natural with the owner intimately involved in the day-to-day care of the herd. Owners have nurturing instincts and find deep satisfaction in caring for large numbers of animals. They find it difficult to verbalize the communication that passes between them and their animals. The relationship of individual soul to group soul bespeaks a deep communion of shared sympathetic sentience.

Moon in the Fifth House • Animals will be in displays, shows, and races, but unlike the Second House owner who is removed from animal ownership, the Fifth House owner is directly involved with the animal, enjoying the attention of admirers. These owners are drawn to breeding and see themselves as progenitors of healthier, more appealing animals. Expect any animals to be doted on.

Moon in the Sixth House • These pets frequently enter the relationship specifically to affect the life and health of the owner. Owners often comment that their pets give them a reason to live. Because the Sixth House also denotes employment, owners find ways to bring their pets onto the job site. This may be the dog or cat that travels with a long-distance trucker, or the more committed involvement of owner and dog in the canine corps. The Sixth House preserves human life through animal heroics exemplified by the asphyxiation of a parakeet in mine shafts, which alerted miners to poisonous gases.

Moon in the Seventh House • These pets are frequently gained through marriage or special commitments by individuals who've never owned pets, or had very little involvement with animals. The Seventh House represents an introduction of self-discovery through allowing new owners to discover the mysterious link between animals and humans. When a marriage or partnership dissolves, the Seventh House placement shows a tendency to acquire an animal to avoid a sense of loneliness. Again, the owner is directly challenged to rediscover supportive relationships through animal contact.

Moon in the Eighth House • The pet owner, although deeply fond of the pet, uses the animal as a method for attracting others. A simple illustration drives home this point. Many years ago, this writer encountered a client at a law firm, commanding three magnificent Irish setters. When asked why he brought these animals to the lawyer's meeting, he bluntly said, "Do you have any idea how many beautiful women stop me on the street and ask to pet my dogs?"

Moon in the Ninth House • The animals found here are usually mascots for teams, performing tricks or exhibiting exuberant behavior on command for adoring crowds. In a more personal way, owners involve their pets with long-distance travel.This pet owner plans vacations around activities with the animal, such as hiking trips with dogs, horse treks across country, or sledding excursions with dog teams.

Moon in the Tenth House • This pet owner is deeply committed to the animal as long as public life is not compromised. The Tenth House owner is likely to stay in constant contact with the animal by celebrating its likeness in a business logo. These pets have natural attributes, which evoke a business character through depictions, such as the 20-mule team for reliable borax or the pugnacious bulldog for watchful security. Here, too, fit national emblems, such as the American bald eagle.

Moon in the Eleventh House
• These people may or may not be pet owners, however, they serve as advocates of animal rights, endangered species, and life quality. Those with more direct animal contact involve themselves with no-kill shelters, either as employees or volunteers. When close, personal involvement is preferred, these persons act as pre-adoptive tenders to shelter animals that require special attention because of extremely young age or recuperation after a veterinary procedure.

Moon in the Twelvth House • This owner is chosen by the pet familiar that comes to the owner as a reminder of other lifetime traits or qualities that the owner has either lost sight of or been reticent to actualize. Pets show an unusual patience and diligence toward their owners. The pet's behavior ranges from a quiet acceptance of extreme solitude and seclusion, to the inviting companion who brings the leash for a walk. At some point in the pet/owner relationship, the animal will take the initiative to broaden the owner's scope of human contact.

No Greater Love

Because we humans want to believe we are the highest sentient beings on the planet, we presume our position endows us with a power of life and death over other living beings. As explained before, the choice to have an animal companion arises from mutual will. When we deny this mutual choice, we lose sight of an incredible love sacrifice our animals make.

Besides willing themselves to leave packs and flocks to take up a solitary existence of devotion with a human, animals so love their owners they will die in their place. We have all heard stories from tearful owners of animals who died defending them, or who led them from danger, only to befall the fate intended for the human. But a more compelling trend is starting to emerge.

Strokes, heart attacks, epilepsy, lung disorders, arthritis, AIDS, allergies, and a host of other conditions are befalling our animal companions in numbers never before observed. While some problems may be based in poor diets or pharmaceutical alteratives that can reduce an animal's physical resistance, psychic readings reveal that animals are absorbing the illnesses of their owners specifically to prolong the owner's life.

There is no greater sorrow than knowing we humans, who prize ourselves as the most highly developed life-form on Mother Earth, have little inkling of this magnificent spiritual interplay. Our animals, attuned to the universal life-force and spirit, offer their lives to give us more life. By taking on our illnesses, they give us the time to recognize and act on our special gifts.

As with all revealed truths, knowledge is power. Each pet owner can spare their animal from unnecessary illness or death by simply staying in good health and bravely taking those personal actions that will benefit others. All each of us has to do is overcome our petty fears to act.

Taking responsibility for our life events not only gives our animals the best opportunities for full lives, but eliminates a secondary problem: the continuing reincarnation of the animal's soul as a teacher rather than as a companion. The kindest tribute between owner and pet is knowing they are together again, simply to enjoy each other.

The Magic of Comfrey

Caroline Moss

There has long been a close link between astrology and plants, particularly herbs. Nicholas Culpeper (1616–1654), the distinguished seventeenth-century English herbalist, noted that "physic" (herbal medicine) without astrology was "like a lamp without oil." Culpeper was, in fact, one of the last major practitioners in a field with a long history—the herbalist astrologer. Although different sources ascribe different plants to the various signs of the zodiac, Culpeper placed comfrey firmly under the sign of Capricorn, an earth sign. This seems appropriate for a sign that, in health terms, rules the joints and skin areas where comfrey's medicinal powers are most clearly effective. The herb is also associated with the planet Saturn.

All gardeners, and especially herb gardeners, should be aware of the many uses of this lovely plant. Often found wild by rivers and canals in its native Europe and temperate Asia, comfrey is also naturalized in North America. The botanical name of the plant *Symphytum* comes from the Greek *symphyo* meaning "to unite," and links clearly with the old English country names of knitbone, boneset, and bruisewort. These clearly indicate the valuable properties of comfrey as a healant.

Recent research shows that comfrey contains allantoin and choline—two substances that promote the growth of red blood corpuscles—and makes the advice to apply comfrey to a wound far from an old wives' tale.

Medicinal Comfrey

Today, even those heavily involved in alternative or herbal remedies tend to favor conventional medicine for the treatment of broken bones, however, comfrey's healing properties can be used for the relief of sprains, minor cuts, and grazes. Try warmed leaves bandaged round a sprain, or a compress made with the grated root.

Another way to take advantage of comfrey's healing properties is to take a comfrey bath. Use three or four crushed or bruised whole leaves, which can be removed before getting in the bath, or put chopped leaves in a muslin bag. If you prefer or only have access to dried comfrey from a shop, a strong infusion can be made by pouring boiling water onto about six tablespoons of dried herb, leaving it for ten minutes, and adding the strained liquid to the bath. These baths are healing and soothing after sport for grazes, cuts, and scrapes, or traditionally in the first bath after childbirth.

Cosmetic Uses

The doyenne of herb use, Jeanne Rose, makes multipurpose healing creams and infusions that include comfrey. You should be able to purchase comfrey cream or ointment from your local health shop. They can also be used safely on animals that cannot be prevented from licking their wounds.

Comfrey oil, or "liquid gold", is recommended for eczema and other skin problems. Although it takes some forward planning, you can make your own by cutting leaves (avoiding coarse veins and stems) into roughly one-inch squares; pack cut leaves into a clear, dark, screw-top jar; screw lid on tight; label, and leave for two years without opening. After that time, strain the resulting amber liquid into a small airtight container and apply as needed.

Culinary Comfrey

Current advice is that comfrey should not be taken internally due to possible carcinogenic properties, so steer clear of old recipe books giving medicinal and culinary uses involving the consumption of comfrey. It has been recommended for chest and breathing problems, and those wishing to make use of the doubtless valuable internal medicinal properties should take advice from a qualified herbalist or health shop where capsules and the like are available. Please note that the advice on not taking comfrey internally is conservative and in line with current guidelines. However, do not worry if you have taken the herb recently. It has been in use for hundreds, if not thousands, of years as both a medicine and a vegetable.

Although the leaves have long been used as a green vegetable, as mentioned above, current advice is against consumption. In the nineteenth century, Henry Doubleday (who has an organic and rare species research organization in England named after him) looked at the possibility of using Russian comfrey, with its high protein levels, as a large-scale crop to feed the starving after the Irish potato famines of the 1850s. However, it proved impossible, at that time, to produce enough for large-scale human consumption. A more frivolous use was noted by Geoffrey Grigson in his wonderful A Herbal of All Sorts (out of print since 1959, but scour the secondhand bookshops for this treat). He found a German recipe for comfrey fritters, where leaves were dipped in batter and deep-fried. Comfrey has also, in the past, been grown for animal fodder.

The above roundup of ideas has, hopefully, introduced you to some of the many benefits to be gained from growing and using comfrey. This sometimes neglected plant awaits with rich rewards to all, from the grower who takes pleasure in an interesting plant, to those who explore its many uses in both the home and garden.

Growing Comfrey

Comfrey is not a fussy plant and once happy with its conditions will be prolific. It prefers a moist, fertile position and the more nitrogen rich the soil, the better. If the soil is very poor the plant may succumb to disease, particularly rust (an orange powder on the underside of leaves) that is rather tricky to eradicate. It will take some shade, and the variegated forms need more shelter, as is common with so many of the "fancy" varieties of herbs and flowers. As a member of the Boraginacea family, comfrey often sports several shades of flower on the same plant as do its close family members, borage (Borago officinalis) and lungwort (Pulmonaria officinalis).

The plant propagates well from plant division or from root cuttings at virtually any time of year except winter. Indeed, if one is trying to control the spread of comfrey, especially the taller cultivars, then care must be taken to dig all roots up. Odd pieces chopped off by spade or fork and left in the ground will grow in no time at all! If you should want to get rid of this tenacious plant, dig out the main part and water the soil with a sodium cholorate or ammonium sulphate solution. If this is not done, even the tiniest piece of root left in the ground will shoot up again. The roots go over three feet deep so they're not always easy to get at.

When planning a garden, the standard varieties of comfrey, as has been mentioned, need plenty of room and grow to a good height and thus add form to the back of a wide border. They can also be useful planted in front of a compost heap to keep them at close hand for use, and to block off untidy areas with their height and fullness. Should space be at a premium and you are fearful of how rampant comfrey can become, try the dwarf varieties.

Forms

Although wild comfrey (*Symphytum officinale*) grows to a good four feet tall and spreads impressively, a number of shorter and less invasive cultivated varieties are available for gardens. Wild comfrey is suitable for larger gardens only—probably at the end and the back of a substantial border. The lower leaves, growing in a rosette pattern, are rough and can be over two feet long on heavy, coarse stems. The flowers are not spectacular. However, their little bell-like shape forming clusters of blues, mauves, pinks, or white (depending on the variety of plant and stage of bloom) give a very attractive show throughout the summer. Many books refer to yellow flowers although I have never seen these on the wild plant.

The dwarf cultivars are more suitable for smaller gardens. Try the red flowered dwarf comfrey (*Symphytum grandiflorum*) that grows to around twelve inches tall, the blue flowered (*S. caucasicum*), or the even smaller variegated dwarf variety (*S. caucasicum variegatum*) which reaches six inches high at most. The variegated dwarf is very attractive but does have a marked spreading habit.

For the keen grower there are many other comfreys to search out through the specialist herb nurseries and catalogs. Try Russian comfrey in plain or variegated form (*S. x uplandicum* or *S. x uplandicum variegatum*) both reaching three or four feet. More compact variations include *S. rubrum* with red flowers, the pink flowered *S. sp* "*Langhorns Pink*" (growing to around three feet) or the pink, white and blue flowered version, named for the famed English garden, *S. sp.* "*Hidcote*" (a modest eighteen inches). For white flowers, the *S. orientale* is attractive and has paler leaves than other varieties, and try the bulbous comfrey *S. bulbosum* for narrower leaves with generous bunches of pale yellow flowers. Note that the Russian and variegated Russian forms are just as effective as the standard version for medicinal and fertilizing purposes. The other varieties are primarily for decorative use.

Fertilizer

Generous layers of comfrey leaves, torn up roughly, and added to a compost heap or bin, provide valuable nutrients to the finished product. If you haven't ventured into producing compost, simply dig the leaves into the soil of your vegetable plot in the fall, especially where runner or pole beans are to be grown. You'll reap a rich benefit from your plantings the following spring and summer. Similarly, freshly picked leaves, allowed to wilt for a couple of days, make a fine mulch simply worked into the top layer around flowers and vegetables.

For a highly effective liquid fertilizer, three quarters fill a bucket with torn-up comfrey leaves, add a few common nettles if you have them, and top off with water. After three weeks or so, you will have an excellent, organic garden food. However, beware! This concoction has a powerful smell so it's not suitable for those who cannot store the bucket well away from seating areas, neighbors, and the like. There is a slightly more work and less pungent solution. Cover over one end of a three-or-four-feet-long length of plastic drainpipe and poke a small piece of pipe through the cover to enable liquid to be drawn off. (Try an empty ballpoint pen with its lid, the lid acting as an easily removable cap). Roughly chop or tear comfrey leaves, minus the coarser stalks and veins, into one or two inch squares. Fill the pipe, packing down the leaves as much as possible. Cover. The leaves will break down and the resulting liquid can be drawn off, by removing the ballpoint pen lid, and mixed with water: one part comfrey liquid to forty parts water. This is an excellent all-purpose plant food. The high potash content makes it particularly useful for tomatoes and potatoes.

Vinegar Making

K.D. Spitzer

Homemade vinegars are so simple to make, and are not only more flavorful, but better for you. Cider vinegar can be made from fall and winter apples. The fruit needs to be cleaned, crushed, and the juice strained off.

Fresh, unpasteurized cider can be used, but either way, homemade or store-bought, it's a good idea to activate fermentation yourself.

Sometimes a commercially prepared vinegar will have a cloudy body floating in it. This is a vinegar mother. Vinegar mothers used to be handed down from mother to daughter to keep the taste of a good vinegar.

Unpasturized Cider Vinegar

Pour two-and-one-half gallons of cider into a container (glass, plastic, or stainless steel) that will hold all of it, with a little space left at the top.

Add one-half packet of yeast to one pint of room temperature cider, stir, and let sit for an hour or so until it bubbles. (Use a champagne yeast, not a bread yeast. Check with a wine making supplier for the correct yeast.)

After the cider begins to bubble, add to the large container of cider and stir well. Cover the container with cheesecloth and secure. Stir daily. Keep between 60° and 80°, and out of direct sunlight for three to four weeks until it ferments. Towards the end, taste for the flavor you prefer. It will smell like vinegar.

To prevent further fermentation, strain through a coffee filter to remove the vinegar mother. It is now time to bottle and store the vinegar.

At this point, you may choose to flavor the vinegar. Wrap your seasonings in cheese cloth and toss into the batch of vinegar. It will take five to seven days to flavor the vinegar. Then you can strain, bottle in sterilized bottles and cap. Consider using quart canning jars for the easiest processing.

The vinegar should be brought to a boil before pouring into the bottles. Have a boiling water bath ready for processing the jars of hot vinegar. After placing the jars in the canning kettle, cover and bring the water back to a boil. Process twenty minutes.

Once the vinegar is processed, you can store it indefinitely in a cool, dark place. After it's opened though, you'll want to store it in the refrigerator. This vinegar can't be reliably used for canning as the acidity can't be measured at home and may be less than the safe level of 5 percent. However, it can be used for cooking or in a canning recipe that will be frozen or stored in the fridge.

Wine Vinegar

Wine vinegar can be made using the dregs of an unfinished bottle of wine. Purchase a vinegar mother at a wine or beer supply store. Just add leftover wines to the mother and allow fermentation to convert the wine to wine vinegar. Keep reds separate from whites. This will take about five weeks. If you add only small quantities of wine at a time, you can get fermentation going and convert the alcohol to acetic acid. You must keep feeding it in careful amounts as this is not quite as reliable as buying a vinegar mother. Once you have one established, you can keep it going like a sourdough crock.

Flavored Vinegars

If you want to flavor your vinegars, combining herbs, seeds, and flowers in pretty corked bottles with store-bought vinegars with a 5 percent acidity. Here you are only limited by your imagination. Delicately flavored herbs work best in a white wine vinegar where they are not overwhelmed by the flavor of the vinegar. Tarragon is usually paired with it. Flowers like nasturtiums, or even violets will add a pleasing color as well as flavor to white wine vinegar. Stronger herbs like rosemary, oregano, garlic, and hot peppers do just fine in a red wine vinegar, or malt or cider vinegars. Stone fruits like peaches and apricots can really add drama to a good cider vinegar.

Fresh herbs will take about two weeks to season a vinegar. You can speed up the process by warming the herbs in hot vinegar and using it the same day.

Vinegar is most versatile. It can be used in stews and soups to add piquancy in place of wine. It preserved the vitamin C in pickles and relishes for the long winter months before the availability of year-round produce. We wouldn't have sauerbraten, barbecue sauce, sweet-and-sour-shrimp, potato salad, or sushi without it. It is used as a cleaning product, dissolving soap scum, or mineral deposits in an instant. It has been used as a scented aromatherapy restorative, sniffed by the wealthy from small sterling silver flasks. Both apple cider vinegar as well as balsamic vinegar are taken medicinally as a health preserver. Herbal vinegar is given credit for saving the lives of looters during the chaos generated by the Black Plague in Paris. It is excellent in the bath for dry skin and, of course, used as a rinse, leaves hair lustrous.

The following recipe brings the lovely scent of apples to an unusual and delicious dessert.

Vinegar Pie

9" pie shell

4 egg yolks

2 egg whites

1 cup sugar

¼ cup flour

½ teaspoon nutmeg

½ teaspoon cinnamon

½ teaspoon allspice

½ teaspoon cloves

Pinch of salt

1 cup sour cream

3 tablespoons melted butter

3 tablespoons cider vinegar

1 cup walnuts or pecans

1 cup raisins

Bake the pie crust in a 450° oven 10 minutes. Reduce oven heat to 400°. Beat egg yolks. In a separate bowl, beat the egg whites until stiff. Fold the sugar into the egg whites. Mix in the egg yolks. Stir the flour with the spices and add to the eggs and sugar. Mix the butter and vinegar together and stir in. Then fold in the nuts and raisins. Pour into the pie crust. Bake in the 400° oven for 5 minutes. Reduce heat again to 300° and continue to bake for 15 minutes. When the filling begins to get firm, remove from the oven. Let cool and serve with ice cream or whipped cream. This filling is actually sort of trembly.

Naturopathy

Penny Kelly

Let thy food be thy medicine.

B efore the days of "chemical" doctors, specialists, and surgeons there were doctors who practiced naturopathic medicine. Since before the time of Hippocrates, naturopathy has used the elements of the natural world to strengthen and heal the sick and combat serious diseases.

In earlier times, many people believed that good health was of supreme importance, and great care was taken to eat in ways that had proven to result in excellent bone structure and organ function, good strength and stamina, calm disposition and high intelligence, and reproductive excellence. These qualities and characteristics allowed people to do the physical work required to stay alive. Groups that ignored the rules and principles of good health died out, or disbanded in chaos. Those who honored the laws of nature thrived well.

Until the 1900s, most people lived on and by the land. They grew their own vegetables, fruits, and grains; kept a few chickens or geese for eggs, a cow and her calf for milk, butter, cheese, and meat. They gathered honey from bees, tapped maple trees for syrup, and harvested all sorts of plants, bushes, berries, flowers, and trees for their medicinal properties. As the Industrial Revolution coaxed more and more people off farms and into the cities, those who worked in factories no longer had time to grow their own food. They had to be fed, however, and the result was the rise of the concept of farms-as-industry and commercial food processing.

Today, the processing and manufacturing of food is the biggest industry in the world. The vast majority of Americans no longer grow their own food. In fact, most of us are isolated from the land. We eat manufactured foods which have little or even no nutritional elements to support the constant repair and rebuilding of our body and all its systems. We live in stressful, polluted environments. We drink water with poisonous chemicals in it, get too little exercise, and often end up performing the same dull, routine work day after day. All of this leads to degeneration of the body/mind system. Asthma, arthritis, heart disease, high blood pressure, diabetes, poor eyesight, infertility, premature births, low birth-weight babies, ulcers, poor digestion, colitis, constipation, Alzheimers, multiple sclerosis, osteoporosis, immune system disfunction, hypoglycemia, birth defects, scoliosis, strokes, atherosclerosis, cancers, attention deficit disorders, hyperactivity, and allergies are only some of the ways we are degenerating as a population. Superior, high-quality food can help prevent these diseases, and almost all can be healed.

A Personal Case

One bright spring morning about six years ago, I woke up with a sharp ache in the ring finger of my right hand. The first joint seemed red and swollen and I wondered what I had done to injure it. A few days later, when it was still sore and tender, the thought crossed my mind that it might be arthritis. I tried to dismiss the possibility. After all, I was only forty-six—much too young for such difficulties. The soreness didn't progress beyond an occasional bout in my finger over the next year, so I ignored it.

A year later, after a day of working in the vineyard, my right elbow was throbbing. The next day I couldn't even use my arm, but I thought it was just sore muscles. Things went downhill from there. By May, it was difficult to use the arm at all; in June my shoulder was aching as well; in July, I was wearing a sling for my right arm, and now my other arm was throbbing; by August, I sometimes had to walk with a walking stick to get out to feed the chickens; and by September, my whole body ached. Even sleep was becoming a problem because I had to wake up every time I wanted to turn over. Fatigue was ever present. I could not open jars, and sometimes I would drop things when pain shot up my arms.

My regular medical doctor had told me that I had arthritis, and twice said that nothing could be done for it. She offered me a nonsteroidal, anti-inflammatory drug for the pain. I took the drug for a while, but the side effects bothered me; then I found out that the drug actually added to the destruction of the inflamed joint capsules around fingers, elbows, knees, and other joints, and I decided to abandon the drug in favor of alternative medicines. I tried various herbs, supplements, exercise, and diets, and grew so confused I didn't know what to do or who to believe. Many of the alternatives didn't help at all, and those that did help didn't work for long. My belief in holistic health was deeply shaken. I concluded that it was only helpful for maintaining wellness, but useless when it came to recovering from castastrophic illness. Then I discovered naturopathic medicine.

The few reports I found indicated that naturopathic medicine, a very old tradition, could successfully rebalance the entire metabolism. All sorts of degenerative diseases including cancers, chronic fatigue, asthma, and others were being healed—and I'd never heard of it.

I ended up working with licensed medical doctor who had been practicing naturopathy medicine successfully for a dozen years, but I had to travel out of state to visit him. The healing program he put together for me was comprehensive and demanding, but I stuck to it. Not only did I heal completely, I learned a great deal about how to design a healing program that worked.

The Naturopathic Difference

Naturopathic doctors can help people reverse many kinds of degeneration, but they are licensed in only a handful of states. In 1994, only eight states including Alaska, Arizona, Connecticut, Hawaii, Montana, New Hampshire, Oregon, and Washington State Licensed naturopaths. Although license to practice medicine is denied in those states that do not recognize naturopathy, those who hold degrees in naturopathic medicine are free to work as health consultants and teachers.

As with any professional, each naturopath has their own personal style, specific gifts, and shortcomings. Generally, you would tell the naturopath why you came in and what your physical symptoms were. Where most medical doctors immediately begin scanning the information in their heads for a diagnosis that fits the symptoms you describe, and a prescription drug that will eliminate the symptoms, a naturopath is not allowed to "diagnose"or "prescribe." These two words and their associated practices are part of the dozen or so concepts that are "owned" by the medical profession. Only licensed medical doctors are allowed to use these words when exchanging health services for money. At first, this may seem to be a formidable obstacle to anyone offering alternative healing. However, diagnosis of specific diseases and the power to prescribe drugs are only necessary if you are trying to target and suppress certain symptoms rather than correct the source of the problems.

Naturopathic practitioners are trained to look at the specific symptoms, and then beyond the sympoms to the whole of a client's life. Except for accidents, the huge majority of illness and disease result from our individual choices. Food, stress, meaningful work, personal care, exercise, and relationships all work together to create a totality called lifestyle. And, lifestyle choices do determine individual health or sickness. All of your experiences and choices come together to create the circumstances you must deal with. When good choices are made, things are in balance, and health, joy, and peacefulness are the result. When poor choices are made, life gets out of balance, and sickness or disease, anxiety and frustration are the characteristics of every day.

A major ethical difference between allopathy, which is the term used to identify a typical medical doctor, and naturopathy, is that allopathic doctors usually require you to sign a paper which gives them responsibility for your health, while naturopathic doctors require you to sign a paper indicating that you understand that you are responsible for your own health. Thus, many naturopathic counselors and practitioners spend a lot of time teaching so you will understand exactly what you are doing and why, and can carry on with your own healing in a successful and capable way. There is nothing worse than the feeling of helplessness that accompanies many people to and from the medical doctor's office, and naturopathy seeks to avoid this by making you a principal partner in your own healing processes.

Among the most basic of premises in naturopathy is that each human is a whole being capable of healing themself when factors that support disease are removed. Naturopathic practitioners start by looking deeply at diet. Most people know intuitively when their diet is poor, or the lifestyle needs changing. Some have no idea what to do differently. Others know what to do, but need to be encouraged to make the changes. Some people are willing to make the changes, but stumble over how to find good sources of food, or how to prepare that food once they have it in the kitchen. Food and lifestyle go hand-in-hand, so be aware that changing your diet automatically causes at least a few lifestyle changes.

From food and diet, the naturopath will often move to suggestions regarding which vitamins, minerals, glandulars, and herbal supplements might be taken to improve physical function or resolve problems of various kinds. For instance, a case of irritable bowel syndrome might be eased by aloe vera, lemon balm, chamomile, or peppermint oil. Hypertension needs careful balancing of calcium and magnesium, plus vitamin C, coenzyme Q-10, along with the boost in capillary action given by hawthorn berries. And for many people complaining of problems from arthritis, to prostate trouble, to diabetes, to chronic obstructive pulmonary disease, the addition of specific enzymes and glandulars offers wondrous opportunities for the body to restore function and provide deep healing, or at least ameliorate the more serious complications common to the disease.

If you need to address a serious healing effort but have a poor attitude, are overly skeptical, or just plain terrified into inaction by the power of the disease, a program of flower essence therapy may be started first. This addresses your emotional state in very subtle ways, bringing you into better balance before beginning some of the more vigorous physical therapies. Once you have a more positive attitude, the naturopath may recommend procedures such as packs and poultices, sweat baths, sitz baths, or other water therapies. You may be questioned extensively in terms of your symptoms and then instructed in the use of homeopathic remedies to alleviate some suffering until true healing can be restored.

You may be advised to embark on a detox program ranging from five days to three years, depending on what you are trying to correct. Massage therapy, acupressure, acupuncture, or reflexology may be scheduled either with the naturopathic practitioner, or you may be given referrals to competent professionals in your area. You may be asked to start a juicing program and given advice on investing in a reliable juicer, and buying vegetables or fruits in quantity.

The practitioner may do several tests if they're working in one of the dozen or so states that recognize and license naturopathic medicine. If not, you may be referred to someone who will do the tests. These could be anything from blood tests to hair analysis to tests for food allergies. The naturopath may use iridology which is a close examination of the pupils of the eye since many kinds of disease and degeneration show up in the eye. You may be asked to undergo testing for heavy metals in your system and if the tests come back with high levels of mercury, aluminum, cadmium, or other toxic metals, you may be advised to start chelation therapy to remove these since all healing will be mediocre at

best if you are being poisoned by heavy metals. Naturopaths are familiar with all of these therapies and many more.

Above all, the naturopathic practitioner aims to get to the source of the trouble and help you to heal yourself from that point forward, not just hand out medicines that cover up symptoms and do nothing to correct the source. Naturopaths know what to use, when to use it, how to put together a complete healing program and then move to a maintenance program.

Lifestyle Changes

Naturopathic medicine encourages people to examine the choices they make in life and to make the necessary changes as quickly and smoothly as possible. However, anyone who has looked below the surface of the health problems in America today, runs into the Gordian knot of food, health, agriculture, corporate jobs, and the food processing and manufacturing industry. When a naturopath suggests switching to organic foods, or finding a local farmer who will grow your food, the common response is, "I can't afford it."

Part of the healing program then becomes a little math homework. By adding the cost of your annual grocery bill to the amount you pay for medicines, doctors, various therapies, tests, and health insurance you can get a pretty truthful idea of what you really could afford to spend on good food. All of those sums together are related to keeping you alive and functioning well. If you were supremely healthy, you wouldn't need all the medicines, doctors, therapies, tests, and insurance. You would be able to thrive with superior food and have money left over, even enough to buy catastrophic insurance in the case of an accident.

In a second column of numbers, add the amount you spend on a second car, plus the cost of the gas and insurance to drive to work every day. To this amount add what you spend on eating out, on special clothes for work, for the entertainment you buy in order to keep yourself distracted from the dissatisfactions of your lifestyle, and you'll have a pretty good idea of how much you could actually cut your expenses if you just stayed home and produced your own food. Add in the joys of a less frenetic home, the ability to raise your own children, the possibilities of earning a few extra dollars from the sale of your vegetables or perhaps a favorite hobby, and you might just decide you really can't afford to work in the corporate world.

Of course, it takes a lot of physical work to turn over soil, get seeds planted, get the transplants in the ground, weed, water, side-dress with compost or a compost tea, harvest, perhaps freeze or can the extra produce, build the compost pile for next season, and make your lunch and supper "from scratch" every day. It seems so much easier to run to the grocery store, grab something for lunch at the closest fast-food place, and go out to dinner regularly. It's so much faster to heat up something for dinner rather than assemble ingredients and spend an hour, probably more, cooking, eating, and cleaning up. The part that is not easier occurs when your heart beats unevenly and hurts with every hurried step, or asthma attacks cut off your supply of oxygen. It is not faster when your joints refuse to move without excruciating pain, when high blood pressure begins bursting small blood vessels in the brain and suddenly you can't remember certain things. Nor is it cheaper when your eyes refuse to focus and you need a couple pairs of glasses, when infertility sends you to a special clinic for fertility treatments, or when cancer appears and you don't have the time or energy to do your life's work because every moment goes into the effort and expense of healing.

Getting people to look at the food problem in order to resolve a health problem often brings up career problems. People feel trapped by the need to make money and the schedules that money-making creates. If you are jumping out of bed at the break of day to the shrill crow of the alarm clock, hurrying out the door to join the local A.M. traffic jam, spending all day in an office handing paper back and forth just to collect your paycheck at the end of the pay period, you may be asking, "Is this all there is?"

Those who are unsatisfied with their career often end up projecting this dissatisfaction into their relationships. Sometimes relationships themselves are the source of the ill health.

If you hardly ever have time for your spouse, are sending your children away to day care centers, schools, and latch key programs or trying to find time to visit aging parent and grandparents, you may be wondering regularly what the meaning of it all is. Realistically, the "meaning" may come down to the debts you are trying to pay off for things like food, shelter, and clothing, the vacation you took last summer, Christmas, entertainment, or new furniture.

Discussion and examination of all of this brings most clients face-to-face with the fact that they have lost touch with who they are, what they love to do, and how they want to be. The desperately ill often do or try almost anything to return to good health, but those who are just "not feeling well" have a more difficult time justifying lifestyle changes until they come face-to-face with, and answer, these questions.

In the end, when the naturopathic practitioner has done a good job, people heal because they understand their own wholeness and their connections to nature and each other. They easily grasp and nurture responsibility for their own health and become avid learners who keenly understand the effects of poor foods, limited diets, toxic agriculture, high stress, incompatible relationships, and unhappy careers. They quickly take up an interest in detoxifying their bodies, learn how to use herbs, educate themselves about various alternative therapies, and shift their approach to life from one of keeping themselves distracted with entertainment to keeping themselves balanced well in body and mind, and in pursuit of an authentic life. To a naturopath, this is true healing.

Be Free of Emotional Buttons

Maritha Pottenger

The Moon reflects our most basic emotions. It symbolizes our need for emotional security and the paths that we take to find it. The Moon reveals aspects of our childhood, when we first learned about life and how to cope with feelings. Because much of what the Moon represents is nonverbal and preverbal (infancy experiences), the issues relating to the Moon are often difficult to articulate, deeply buried, and ultra-sensitive.

Your Moon sign gives you important clues about the best way to cope with the emotional storms of life. It shows what nurtures you, and helps you to feel warm, safe, protected, and secure. It reveals individual strengths and the kind of support systems needed to survive and surmount the trials and tribulations of life. It reveals your weaknesses and the emotional buttons that get you into trouble. Examining each Moon sign in turn, will reveal patterns from your earliest years and ways to reassure them.

One warning before you dash off to read your own Moon sign. Every horoscope has a mixture of factors. Your Moon sign is only part of the picture, and what is written here should (ideally) be balanced with other factors. Each reader should read the Moon in Cancer section as well as your own Moon sign. If your personal horoscope provides more reinforcement for the Moon itself than for the sign of your Moon, you'll experience many of the Moon in Cancer motifs. And, it doesn't hurt to check out other Moon signs. Any planet making a strong aspect (connection) to the Moon in your chart will manifest somewhat like the Moon in the sign that planet rules. For example, if Pluto is connected to the Moon in your horoscope, you'll be dealing with some Moon in Scorpio issues.

Moon in Aries or Aspecting Mars

These eager, independent parents, nurtured the Moon in Aries child- with action, excitement, and strong personal focus. These individuals expect an emotional life that is vibrant, ever-fresh-and new.

In a dysfunctional family, the parent(s) could have been angry and too self-centered to pay attention to their child. Sometimes a parent felt

trapped and may have turned distant or abusive. As a result, the child associates emotional safety with being separate, free, and independent. Taking care of oneself is a major script within the home.

Aries Moon people can "fly off the handle" easily if tempers are to close to the surface, and those close to them might say they react to emotional stress like a "brat." It's hard for the Moon in Aries person to ask for help or show vulnerability. They may be equally resistant to providing emotional sustenance and support to others. (Remember: The family script is "Everyone is on their own.")

One of the strengths of Moon in Aries is encouraging people to find a balance between dependency and independence; between caring for family and looking after one's own interests. Moon in Aries people will take the initiative and can help others to develop more emotional self-reliance.

Button Releasing Tools

Movement • Any physical motion. Take a walk while discussing highly emotional matters, or work out to dissipate some feelings.

Ask for what you need • Even though you believe you can "do it yourself," ask (occasionally) for reassurance and assistance. And, even though the initial reaction from a loved one often is "do it yourself," they can practice taking an extra moment and become willing to help out—at least somewhat.

Mantra • I can be both strong and nurturing.

Moon in Taurus or Aspecting Venus

In a functional home, children were fed, held, caressed and touched, providing the child comfort and stability. The parent(s) felt safe, affectionate, and reliable. The Moon in Taurus child knew what to expect in emotional relationships; life was generally predictable. These adults have a strong, inner security. They take care of others by helping them to get comfortable and to feel good. Very in tune with their senses, they can be somewhat hedonistic, enjoying all the material pleasures (eating, drinking, making love, making money, and/or collecting beautiful things).

In a dysfunctional family, the parents could have been excessively materialistic, perhaps valuing "things" more than people, or they were too indulgent toward the child. Perhaps the parents were stubborn and resistant to change. These children developed an emotional habit of seeking safety through the senses, or of keeping their emotional (and domestic) life as fixed as possible.

This is one of the Moon signs that can "stuff" feelings by eating, or indulging in other physically gratifying pursuits that can complicate the emotional tensions. The biggest threat to the Moon in Taurus individual is unpredictability, as it arouses the frightened inner child.

Moon in Taurus people can excel at repetition. Once a routine is established, they feel safe. And, once they make a commitment, they have good stamina for carrying through.

Button Releasing Tools

Establish a safe, comfortable space • Create a sensually pleasing "nest" with soft cushy chairs, pretty surroundings, and favorite foods.

Contact a loved one • Touching and being touched often helps when feeling threatened. A massage or back-rub can lower the panic level.

Look for familiar patterns • Find an element in the current situation that reflects back to an earlier experience when you handled the situation successfully.

Mantra • I enjoy bringing pleasure to myself and others.

Moon in Gemini or Aspecting Mercury

Conversation, variety, communication, and change were important in this family. In healthy families, the child is often talked to, read to, and encouraged to develop intellectually. Activities such as, music lessons, dancing, and youth groups were probably important. Games and recreation are highlighted.

In dysfunctional families, too much is going on. Even meals may be haphazard affairs. The parent(s) may talk too much, have trouble focusing, rationalize away emotions, or can be too flippant. Some parents will try to act like a sibling rather than a parent to their child, or try to capture lost youth through inappropriate behavior. Priorities may be unclear. A script of "No feelings are really important," could have been adopted.

Button Releasing Tools

Think • Emotions, for a Moon in Gemini person, are best understood through reading about them, thinking about them, and talking about them. Objective feedback is very valuable.

Say what's important • Being understood is really important. Finding the right labels, descriptions, and definitions is important. Use puns, word play, jokes, or humor to help defuse an uncomfortably intense situation.

Take a drive • A little distance is often a wise move.

Keep a diary or a journal • Looking back over what was written can reveal important patterns that can help or hinder you.

Develop your emotional priorities • Learn to feel more deeply, to give more weight to some emotions. As your understanding grows, you can help to explain emotional exchanges and be an objective eye into the world of the heart for other people.

Mantra • I can use the right ideas and words to heal and protect.

Moon in Cancer

In functional families, the Moon in Cancer child is loved unconditionally in a safe environment. These individuals grow into adults who are comfortable both giving nurturing support, love and caring, and being vulnerable enought to receive from others.

In dysfunctional families, something is out of balance. The family that may have encouraged a child to stay immature and needy because the parents needed to have someone to take care for. The other extreme is the individual who is literally or emotionally abandoned. The Moon in Cancer child can also be expected to parent their own parents, siblings, or other family members. In such cases, trust is a major issue. The threat of abandonment tends to trigger a "helpless" child response.

Button Releasing Tools

Establish boundaries • Since Moon in Cancer people are extra intuitive and empathic toward loved ones, it can be difficult to sort out their feelings from the emotions of those around them.

Develop an active inner life • Privacy is vital. Keep some time for yourself every day.

Vent • Express feelings through journal writing, pounding pillows, talking with friends, artistic expression, or screaming (in privacy).

Develop a good support system • Having friends that one can truly rely on is necessary, but even pets can offer positive support. The first step to emotional health for caregivers is developing relationships with people on whom you can lean rather than always being depended upon.

Get in contact with water • Take a bath before discussing a difficult subject, walk near a body of water, or visit a fountain.

Mantra • True security lies within me.

Moon in Leo or Aspecting the Sun

In functional families, children were encouraged to express themselves, develop healthy self-esteem and gain love and thrills through doing more than they had done before. Praise and positive strokes were common. As adults, these individuals are excellent teachers, trainers, and motivators. They have mastered the art of the sincere, well-timed compliment, and their enthusiasm is contagious.

In dysfunctional families, the child may have had to compete with a parent for the limelight—a no-win situation when a parent is bigger, stronger, more experienced, etc. Extravagant emotions could have been standard operating procedure within the home. The Moon in Leo child may have felt that the only way to receive any notice was to become more dramatic than everyone else. Pressures to perform or amount to something could have been excessive. Gambling or other forms of risk-taking might have been inculcated along with the daily bread. Security needs became tied to the rush of adrenaline. In an odd twist, a sense of safety is experienced through thrill-seeking.

Button Releasing Tools

Seek positive excitement • This can come through playful physical activities, physically active vocations, or hobbies and interests that allow for constructive forms of an adrenaline rush.

Cultivate positive friendships • Choose friends and colleagues who are generous with positive feedback and will provide valuable support.

Focus on creative outlets • Do something fresh and exciting. A little romance and flirtation can pick up the mood of a Leo Moon.

Treat yourself like royalty • Do some pampering. Cater to yourself.

Mantra • Love keeps me feeling vital and alive.

Moon in Virgo Moon or Aspecting Vesta

The family usually emphasized work, service, and doing things well. Often, the Moon in Virgo child works from a younger age than their peers. Sometimes the family just has a strong work ethic, and sometimes there is an ill or incompetent parent. Occasionally, the Moon in Virgo child learns the unconscious lesson that being ill is the way to be taken care of.

In a dysfunctional family, the Moon in Virgo child may feel their value comes from what they do. Children in such circumstances may feel worthless except when they are doing the tasks that the parents define as correct. There may be excessive criticism and rigidity in the home. Cleanliness, or other Virgo fetishes, could be taken to extremes. Common responses in these situations are to work harder, to be of more service, or to strive to increase efficiency and productivity.

Button Releasing Tools

Learn to share the load • Just because you can do something does not mean that you should do it! Practice letting other people do some of the work (even when they are not as efficient). Learn not to step in immediately when something needs fixing.

Analyze • Make a list of pros and cons and think in terms of the bottom line.

Get organized • Straighten drawers, closets, bookshelves, or the filing cabinet.

Mantra • I am dedicated to personal well being and helping others develop competence.

Moon is in Libra or Aspecting Venus

These are sweet, diplomatic, and charming individuals with good instincts for pleasing people. In a functional home, the Moon in Libra child was a valued part of the team. The parents were encouraged cooperation and open communication; art, beauty, balance, and harmony were valued.

In a dysfunctional home, style may have been valued over substance. "Keeping up with Jones" and saving face with the neighbors could have been too important. These children may have learned that compliance was the only road likely to lead to safety and security. If someone didn't like you, then danger was in the air!

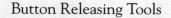

Button Releasing Tools

Create an attractive environment • A messy or ugly nest can literally throw Moon in Libra individuals off balance.

Seek out beauty • Do something to make the milieu more attractive when your upset.

Focus on justice and equality • Comparing and contrasting different ideas and the perspectives of various people can be helpful for spotting win/win solutions.

Mantra • I share easily and comfortably with others.

Moon in Scorpio or Aspecting Pluto

In a functional home, the Moon-in-Scorpio child is encouraged to look within, to know and understand the self. Loyalty and perseverance are usually highlighted.

In dysfunctional homes, the Moon in Scorpio infant and child may be exposed to tears, threats, emotional blackmail, passive-aggressive behavior, and invasion of privacy. In extremes, physical or sexual abuse is possible. The child learns that safety rests in revealing as little as possible, and being as invulnerable as possible. In very negative circumstances, the child may learn to bide their time until revenge can be had. They may become the family scapegoat.

Button Releasing Tools

Forgiveness (of self as well as others) • This is a vital skill to learn.

Learn to let go • Letting go of emotional issues will ease your mind.

Therapy, journal keeping, occult studies • Tools that allow one to contact and make friends with the unconscious are very useful.

Establish a position of power • Choose the territory for discussions; limit the confrontation to certain issues; set standards of how long people talk, who gets to rebut whom, etc. Arranging a therapeutic setting is an excellent move for people with Moon in Scorpio. One of the greatest strengths of Moon in Scorpio people is that they can go through difficult, painful emotional times that would wipe out other people. Seek out essential information. Make sure that all the relevant facts are clear. Moon in Scorpio types can turn liabilities into assets.

Mantra • I am transforming negative emotions into positive ones.

Moon in Sagittarius or Aspecting Jupiter

Such individuals are often buoyant and upbeat. In functional homes, they may have traveled, been exposed to a cosmopolitan atmosphere, had parents that were literary, witty, independent, or idealistic. The children probably developed a firm faith, a positive attitude, an eagerness to try for more and to "go for the gusto" in life.

In dysfunctional families, freedom-loving parents condition children to look after themselves and not to "want" much from family. Perhaps the parents had very high standards due to religion or moral principles, so the child learned to give everything no matter how hopeless it looked. If the parents were very restless and easily bored, the child may have learned that any emotional attachments led to losses when you had to move on again or the parents developed new interests.

Button Releasing Tools

Get some space • Literally. Tough discussions can be held outdoors. Psychologically, an open door must be available.

Be true to your highest values • Doing so will give you the strength to surmount just about anything.

Look for the silver lining • Optimism applied to any situation can only improve things.

Mantra • I feel at home (secure) anywhere in the world.

The Moon in Capricorn or Aspecting Saturn

The impact of the parents on the childs emotional life was very strong.

In functional families, the parents were hardworking, reliable, dedi-cated, responsible, and utterly dependable. They provided rock-solid stability for the child. They encouraged the child to develop strength, competence and coping skills.

In dysfunctional families, the child often felt overwhelmed. There may have been excessive discipline, criticism, or other harsh conditions that undermined the child's strength and confidence. In extreme cases, the child may be afraid to try anything convinced they would fail. In some cases, the child's script was "If you work really hard, maybe you won't be hurt as much." In other homes, even very young children were expected to be ultraresponsible, some even parenting their own parents or laboring arduously to look after family members.

When emotional stress rears its head, the Moon in Capricorn indi-vidual tends to either do nothing (if the inner feeling is one of worth-lessness), or to take on too much responsibility. Overcoming these but-tons means taking a realistic look at the situation.

Button Releasing Tools

Write issues down on paper • It can help. Moon in Capricorn people can benefit from exercises to raise self-esteem.

Learn to let go and delegate • Ask yourself: "Is this really my job?"

Seeking out positive, affirming authority figures • You can benefit much from a mentor. Their best resource is common sense and pragmatism.

Mantra • I am clear about what is my responsibility and what is not.

Moon is in Aquarius or Aspecting Uranus

In a functional family, the parents encouraged the child's individuality. Freedom, open communication, a fascination with the future, and lots of tolerance were likely qualities within the home. An attraction to the new and different could lead to quite a bit of change and intellectual stimulation.

In dysfunctional families, the emotional life was very uncertain. The parents could have been erratic, perhaps they felt trapped by par-enthood and kept pulling away (or even ran away from home literally or figuratively). Perhaps a parent was cold, aloof and emotionally unavail-able, or moved often, or other aspects of the home were constantly shift-ing. Emotions might have been rationalized away. Dependency could have been anathema. The child may have learned a script of "Safety lies

in one's intellect and in being independent."

Button Releasing Tools

Survey your options • When emotional stress strikes, look for additional possibilities. Sometimes adopting a radically different perspective will resolve a problem.

Listen to head and heart • Practice the fine art of enough (but not too much!) detachment.

Learn tolerance • Being able to withhold judgment on the other person's concerns and complaints is often the first step to resolving disagreements.

Remember your feelings • Mental skills can help to help solve emotional challenges as long as they remember to pay homage to feelings as much as to thinking.

Mantra • I can find emotional safety within an atmosphere of flux and change.

Moon in Pisces or Aspecting Neptune

These families tend to be ultrasensitive and easily hurt. These "psychic sponges" pick up the moods and emotions from people around them. In functional families, they learn to use their intuition, further develop their feeling for beauty, and find ways to enhance the magic, mysticism, and inspiration within their nests.

In dysfunctional families, the Moon in Pisces child may end up wanting to run away from the world. Drugs, alcohol, fantasy, or other escapist temptations could be used within the family of origin. Confusion, lies, deception, misdirection, and evasion are apt to be used against the child, who then learns to exercise these ploys themself. Sometimes, they become the family victim and are conditioned to a pattern of self-sacrifice.

Button Releasing Tools

Learn when to stand your ground • When emotional stress strikes, the immediate impulse is to hide or run away. Although, running away and "living to fight another day" can be a wise move, holding firm is often necessary.

Choose a setting that is serene and lovely • Water close by would be a bonus.

Make a brief exit • Take a break, let your imagination soar, then come back to deal with the real world. These escapes are on your terms and in your control.

Tune into the other person • Understanding how others feel is a great resource for resolving many conflicts and solving many problems!

Mantra • The Divine Source provides all the protection that I need.

As each of us understands the strengths (and weaknesses) indicated by our Moon sign, we can move beyond old insecurities and create more fulfilling lives. May the Goddess (Selene, Luna) be with you!

The Alchemist's Moon

Ken Johnson

More than most other occult sciences, alchemy remains mysterious. Some have believed that the obscure language of the alchemists, founded in the lore of metals and natural substances, was purely symbolic, and that the quest for the philosopher's stone, the great elixir of life, was an inner quest. And yet we know that some alchemists were indeed involved in laboratory experiments, for their researches gave birth to the science of chemistry as we know it.

But if in fact they strove to transmute base metals into gold, or to achieve physical immortality, we must still wonder—were they successful? Is there any truth to the legends of mysterious adepts such as Nicholas Flamel and Paracelsus, who reportedly achieved eternal life?

We shall probably never know. But at the very least, we may unravel some of the threads of their mystical teachings, for they expressed themselves in the language of symbolism—a universal language. And at least part of the alchemical mystery is expressed in the symbolism of astrology.

The alchemists recognized two essential principles, sometimes called gold and silver, but just as often referred to as Sun and Moon. Here are some of their metaphors for the Sun: it is red in color and sometimes called "the red tincture"; it is hot and dry; it is of the essence of fire; and it is related to heaven, the "world above." In chemical terms, it is sometimes referred to as sulphur.

The Moon is described in opposite terms. It is white in color; it is cool and moist; and it is often associated with the essence of water. It is related to the earth rather than the heavens, and in chemical terms it is often linked with salt.

Those with a background in astrology or any other branch of magical studies will easily recognize that the Sun represents the masculine principle while the Moon represents the feminine principle. Another way of saying it is that the Sun represents spirit, while the Moon represents soul.

Some people seem to use the terms "spirit" and "soul" interchangeably, while in reality they are two very different things. Unfortunately, they are defined differently by various and sundry writers on metaphysics. It is worth taking a few moments here to see how the alchemists defined these terms.

To the alchemists, "Spirit" was that divine spark within us which is truly immortal. It is envisioned as something "above," like a mountain peak, so that taking the "spiritual" path may be seen as an ascent to the heights, climbing a mountain. Spirit makes us contemplative, unconcerned with the mere "things of this world"; it can also make us extremely detached, perhaps even aloof. The primary symbols of Spirit, or the masculine principle, are gold and the Sun.

Soul, on the other hand, is something deep, and in that sense it lies below us rather than above. If Spirit is a mountain peak, Soul is a valley—soft and moist, flowing with streams, calmed with green trees. If Spirit makes us detached, Soul keeps us connected, binding us to people, places and things with the bonds of love. The primary symbols of the Soul, or feminine principle, are silver and the Moon.

While both principles are necessary for life to exist, one should not be allowed to predominate at the expense of the other. Too much Spirit may leave us burning with a fire that is ultimately cold, for it disconnects us from concern for humanity and the earth. Too much Soul leaves us mired in the swamp of shifting moods and emotions, unable to take action or make clear decisions. In alchemy, the ultimate balance between Spirit and Soul is perceived as a marriage. And this all-important marriage is symbolized in astrological terms as the New Moon.

The imagery of this "mystical marriage" between the Sun and Moon is beautiful and powerful. In the old alchemical texts, the two luminaries are depicted as King Sol and Queen Luna, and the illustrations which chronicle their marriage are often graphically erotic. The result of their union is the production of the philosopher's stone or the elixir of eternal life. This final goal is usually shown as a new creature, Mercurius, both male and female, born from the mystic marriage of Sol and Luna, although sometimes the Sun and Moon themselves are shown uniting as one being, male and female together.

This has caused some investigators to wonder whether the alchemists actually practiced a form of sexual yoga similar to the Tantric rituals of India. There are, in fact, curious echoes from the alchemical texts which suggest that rituals of this sort were indeed being practiced in the Western world during the Renaissance or shortly thereafter. It is known that alchemists frequently did their work in concert with a female partner, called a *soror mystica* or "mystical sister." The journals of Thomas Vaughan, which chronicle his discovery of the philosopher's stone along with his wife Rebecca, are tantalizing in their suggestions of sexual yoga. A letter from the British alchemist John Pordage to his soror mystica, Jane Leade, actually identifies the alchemical fire as being located "in the belly"; in his letter, Pordage instructs Leade on how to raise this fire up the spinal column.

Others have theorized that the "mystical union" between the Sun and Moon was an internal psycho-spiritual process, and here again, the analogies between alchemy and yoga are quite detailed. Many schools of yoga postulate two *nadis* or "channels" running up the axis of the spinal cord. These two nadis are perceived as male and female, and thus as solar and lunar respectively. As the yogi or yogini meditates and practices techniques of breathing, his or her vital energies are raised through these two channels and through the seven chakras (which some say correspond to the seven metals of alchemy or the seven astrological planets). In the sixth chakra, or "third eye," the two nadis fuse together into one, and the yogi escapes duality, becoming a unified being. This is the mystic marriage which produces Mercurius, the opening of the crown chakra or thousand-petaled lotus.

Alchemy was practiced in China and India as well as in the West, and the astrological symbolism runs like a common thread between all these cultures. In India, it is acknowledged by scholars and mystics alike that alchemy and tantra were once part of a single great discipline. There are even hints that elements of this great discipline are inconceivably ancient, stretching back to prehistoric horizons when the mystical polarities so familiar to us were reversed: a time when the Sun was a goddess and the Moon was a god.

A familiar Hindu story tells us of Chandra the Moon King, who, in his monthly sky journey, lingered too long at the mansion of his most erotic bride, Rohini (the star Aldebaran). Chandra's other wives cursed him to waste away unto death, but then took pity on his illness. The curse was altered so that he would alternately waste away and then wax full again during the course of every month. But there are other versions of the same story, more relevant to our exploration of the Moon in alchemy. An old Sanskrit alchemical text tells us of how Chandra, the Moon King, became sick and started to waste away; this represents the lunar orb as it begins to wane, just past the Full Moon. But just as Chandra was about to disappear altogether, he was united with his bride Rohini in a mystic marriage. This, according to the interpretation, represents the rebirth of the nocturnal luminary during the time of the New Moon, and Rohini is therefore the Sun. Restored by his union with the goddess, Chandra re-emerges from her shadow to wax large and full again in the night sky.

In conclusion, we may say that there is not just one alchemical Moon, but many. There is an almost infinite variety in the way the alchemists imagined the Moon's function in terms of symbolism, but there are common themes among them all. The Moon always represents our soul, our inner emotional nature, waxing and waning upon the tides of feeling. Considered alone, it cannot bring us to a realization of our own completeness. For that, it needs to be united with spirit, with that shining, powerful sense of selfhood or inner direction which moves us and impels us onward, and which is symbolized by the Sun. Whether we perceive the Sun as a king and the Moon as a queen whose union gives birth to Mercurius, the "Self," or whether we see the Moon as an ailing monarch and the Sun as an all-powerful erotic goddess who renews him, the drama of death and rebirth remains the same.

Whenever you watch the Moon wane in the sky, and then see it disappear altogether, it is a time to meditate on renewal and rebirth. The moment of darkness when the night is moonless is a moment when something new is being born. Rest within your own inner darkness—the stillness at the center of your being. There, each month, you will discover what it is in your own inner nature that is being renewed and reborn—the key to your own inner alchemy.

2001

LLEWELLYN'S

Leisure &
Recreation

Leisure & Recreation

How to Choose the Best Dates

E veryone is affected by the lunar cycle. Your lunar high occurs when the Moon is in your Sun sign, and your lunar low occurs when the Moon is in the sign opposite your Sun sign. The handy Favorable and Unfavorable Dates Tables on pages 29-51 give the lunar highs and lows for each Sun sign for every day of the year. This lunar cycle influences all your activities: your physical strength, mental alertness, and manual dexterity are all affected.

By combing the Favorable and Unfavorable Dates Tables and the Lunar Aspectarian Tables with the information given in the list of astrological rulerships, you can choose the best time to begin many activites.

The best time to perform an activity is when its ruling planet is in favorable aspect to the Moon—that is, when its ruling planet is trine, sextile, or conjunct the Moon (marked T, X, or C in the Lunar Aspectarian), or when its ruling sign is marked F in the Favorable and Unfavorable Days Tables. Another option is when the Moon is in the activity's ruling sign.

For example, if you wanted to find a good day to train your dog, you would look under animals, and find that the sign corresponding to animal training is Taurus, and that the planet that rules this activity is Venus. Then, you would consult the Favorable and Unfavorable Days Tables to find a day when Venus (the ruling planet) is trine, sextile, or conjunct (T, X, or C) the Moon; or when Taurus (the ruling sign) is marked F in the Favorable and Unfavorable Days Table; or when the Moon is in Taurus.

Animals and Hunting

Animals in general: Mercury, Jupiter, Virgo, Pisces
Animal training: Mercury, Virgo
Cats: Leo, Sun, Virgo, Venus
Dogs: Mercury, Virgo
Fish: Neptune, Pisces, Moon, Cancer
Birds: Mercury, Venus

Game animals: Sagittarius
Horses, trainers, riders: Jupiter, Sagittarius
Hunters: Jupiter, Sagittarius

Arts

Acting, actors: Neptune, Pisces, Sun, Leo
Art in general: Venus, Libra
Ballet: Neptune, Venus
Ceramics: Saturn
Crafts: Mercury, Venus
Dancing: Venus, Taurus, Neptune, Pisces
Drama: Venus, Neptune
Embroidery: Venus
Etching: Mars
Films, filmmaking: Neptune, Leo, Uranus, Aquarius
Literature: Mercury, Gemini
Music: Venus, Libra, Taurus, Neptune
Painting: Venus, Libra
Photography: Neptune, Pisces, Uranus, Aquarius
Printing: Mercury, Gemini
Theaters: Sun, Leo, Venus

Fishing

During the summer months the best time of the day to fish is from sunrise to three hours after, and from two hours before sunset till one hour after. In cooler months, fish do not bite until the air is warm, from noon to 3 pm. Warm, cloudy days are good. The most favorable winds are from the south and southwest. Easterly winds are unfavorable. The best days of the month for fishing are when the Moon changes quarters, especially if the change occurs on a day when the Moon is in a watery sign (Cancer, Scorpio, Pisces). The best period in any month is the day after the Full Moon.

Friends

The need for friendship is greater when Uranus aspects the Moon, or the Moon is in Aquarius. Friendship prospers when Venus or Uranus is trine, sextile, or conjunct the Moon. The chance meeting of acquaintances and friends is facilitated by the Moon in Gemini.

Parties (Hosting or Attending)

The best time for parties is when the Moon is in Gemini, Leo, Libra, or Sagittarius with good aspects to Venus and Jupiter. There should be no aspects to Mars or Saturn.

Barbecues: Moon, Mars

Casinos: Venus, Sun, Jupiter

Festivals: Venus

Parades: Jupiter, Venus

Sports

Acrobatics: Mars, Aries

Archery: Jupiter, Sagittarius

Ball games in general: Venus

Baseball: Mars

Bicycling: Uranus, Mercury, Gemini

Boxing: Mars

Calisthenics: Mars, Neptune

Chess: Mercury, Mars

Competitive sports: Mars

Coordination: Mars

Deep-sea diving: Neptune, Pisces

Exercising: Sun

Football: Mars

Horse racing: Jupiter, Sagittarius

Jogging: Mercury, Gemini

Physical vitality: Sun

Polo: Uranus, Jupiter, Venus, Saturn

Racing (other than horse): Sun, Uranus

Ice skating: Neptune

Roller skating: Mercury

Sporting equipment: Jupiter, Sagittarius

Sports in general: Sun, Leo
Strategy: Saturn
Swimming: Neptune, Pisces, Moon, Cancer
Tennis: Mercury, Venus, Uranus, Mars
Wrestling: Mars

Travel

Long trips which threaten to exhaust the traveler are best begun when the Sun is well aspected to the Moon and the date is favorable for the traveler. If traveling with others, good aspects from Venus are desirable. For enjoyment, aspects to Jupiter are preferable; for visiting, aspects to Mercury. To prevent accidents, avoid squares or oppositions to Mars, Saturn, Uranus, or Pluto.

For air travel, choose a day when the Moon is in Gemini or Libra, and well aspected by Mercury and/or Jupiter. Avoid adverse aspects of Mars, Saturn, or Uranus.

Air travel: Mercury, Sagittarius, Uranus
Automobile travel: Mercury, Gemini
Boating: Moon, Cancer, Neptune
Camping: Leo
Helicopters: Uranus
Hotels: Cancer, Venus
Journeys in general: Sun
Long journeys: Jupiter, Sagittarius
Motorcycle travel: Uranus, Aquarius
Parks: Sun, Leo
Picnics: Venus, Leo
Rail travel: Uranus, Mercury, Gemini
Restaurants: Moon, Cancer, Virgo, Jupiter
Short journeys: Mercury, Gemini
Vacations, holidays: Venus, Neptune

Writing

Write for pleasure or publication when the Moon is in Gemini. Mercury should be direct. Favorable aspects to Mercury, Uranus, and Neptune promote ingenuity.

Hunting & Fishing Dates

From/To	Quarter	Sign
January 8, 8:09 am - January 10, 7:44 am	2nd	Cancer
January 16, 2:02 pm - January 18, 10:35 pm	4th	Scorpio
January 26, 11:39 am - January 28, 11:35 pm	1st	Pisces
February 4, 7:00 pm - February 6, 7:21 pm	2nd	Cancer
February 12, 9:51 pm - February 15, 5:02 am	3rd	Scorpio
February 22, 5:45 pm - February 25, 5:20 am	4th	Pisces
March 4, 3:24 am - March 6, 5:30 am	2nd	Cancer
March 12, 7:43 am - March 14, 1:17 pm	3rd	Scorpio
March 22, 12:28 am - March 24, 11:43 am	4th	Pisces
March 31, 9:23 am - April 2, 12:54 pm	1st	Cancer
April 8, 6:01 pm - April 10, 10:47 pm	3rd	Scorpio
April 18, 8:00 am - April 20, 7:18 pm	4th	Pisces
April 27, 2:49 pm - April 29, 6:25 pm	1st	Cancer
May 6, 3:00 am - May 8, 8:05 am	2nd	Scorpio
May 15, 4:01 pm - May 18, 3:41 am	4th	Pisces
May 24, 9:42 pm - May 27, 12:12 am	1st	Cancer
June 2, 9:56 am - June 4, 3:58 pm	2nd	Scorpio
June 11, 11:53 pm - June 14, 12:03 pm	3rd	Pisces
June 21, 6:40 am - June 23, 7:55 am	4th	Cancer
June 29, 3:28 pm - July 1, 10:13 pm	2nd	Scorpio
July 9, 7:05 am - July 11, 7:36 pm	3rd	Pisces
July 18, 4:56 pm - July 20, 5:43 pm	4th	Cancer
July 26, 9:17 pm - July 29, 3:44 am	1st	Scorpio
August 5, 1:30 pm - August 8, 2:05 am	3rd	Pisces
August 15, 2:55 am - August 17, 4:25 am	4th	Cancer
August 23, 4:50 am - August 25, 9:59 am	1st	Scorpio
September 1, 7:32 pm - September 4, 7:58 am	2nd	Pisces
September 11, 11:09 am - September 13, 2:16 pm	4th	Cancer
September 19, 2:27 pm - September 21, 6:02 pm	1st	Scorpio
September 29, 1:50 am - October 1, 2:08 pm	2nd	Pisces

Hunting & Fishing Dates

October 8, 5:19 pm - October 10, 9:54 pm	3rd	Cancer
October 17, 1:03 am - October 19, 3:47 am	1st	Scorpio
October 26, 8:56 am - October 28, 9:15 pm	2nd	Pisces
November 4, 10:44 pm - November 7, 3:34 am	3rd	Cancer
November 13, 10:44 am - November 15, 1:51 pm	4th	Scorpio
November 22, 4:52 pm - November 25, 5:21 am	1st	Pisces
December 2, 5:30 am - December 4, 9:15 am	3rd	Cancer
December 10, 6:09 pm - December 12, 10:30 pm	4th	Scorpio
December 20, 1:09 am - December 22, 1:45 pm	1st	Pisces
December 29, 2:40 pm - December 31, 5:09 pm	2nd	Cancer

Editor's note: This chart lists the best hunting and fishing dates for the year 2001, but not the only possible dates. To accommodate your own schedule, you may wish to try dates other than those listed above. To learn more about choosing good fishing dates, see the fishing information on page 146. To learn more about hunting dates, see the animal and hunting information on page 145.

The Goddess in Your Moon

Dorothy Oja

We are multifaceted beings composed of many traits and archetypes blended together in a mix that is unique to each of us. Each horoscope (planetary pattern) comprised of planets, signs, houses, and aspects is complex; the array of expression is infinite. Some of these expressions are latent within us, but we can access that latency to enrich our lives, and those of others, with a fresh nuance of personality. Discovering the goddess energies in your Moon can serve you well in identifying with aspects of yourself that you may be using now, as well as those not fully realized.

The Goddess was there in the very beginnings of time, and very culture has a storehouse of facinating goddess tales. As you read these goddess stories, you may be surprised to discover the wealth of unused feminine expression encoded in your cellular being. Although I associate two goddesses with each Moon sign, all goddesses are universal, appearing in different cultures and easily emboding more than the one sign. They are all facets of the one great goddess archetype, The GreatMother. Take time to ponder the magical stories of the goddesses associated with your Moon; draw nourishment and inspiration; identify with the goddess energy in yourself, and honor the goddesses you draw to you in the women you love as mates, friends, acquaintances, or coworkers.

Have fun with this journey. May you feel enhanced and enriched from deeper research into the roots of the feminine archetypes. It is up to us to keep these myths and symbolic stories alive and well in ourselves, as we merge them into our daily lives, and carry their legends into a new millennium. We must never forget them.

Moon in Aries

Pele

The Hawaiian goddess Pele, associated with eruptions and volcanic activity, can be seen as the epitome of a vibrant, creative, expressive woman with an Aries Moon, or any woman who holds a great deal of fire energy in her astrological chart. She is passionate, sensual, and unafraid of the chaos caused by fire because, like ardent, active Aries, she realizes that

it is through cycles of passionate activity that we evolve. Pele is said to have fancied handsome young chiefs and enjoyed participating in sports. She is also impatient and jealous.

The story goes that Pele fell in love with Lohiau, a talented flute player, and made him her lover. After three days she returned to her mountain promising him that she would return. But busy Pele longed for Lohiau and decided her sister Hiiaka should go fetch him. Impatient for their return, she feared Hiiaka would steal her lover away even though the sister had no such designs. Pele's jealousy consumed her. She destroyed Hiiaka's gardens and killed her poet friend. Hiiaka took revenge by making love to Lohiau on the edge of Pele's crater. In a fury, Pele burned Lohiau in the crater but could not destroy her immortal sister.

Pele teaches us that fire energy can be a double-edged sword. It can warm the earth and create life, or be jealous, impatience, or angry, and bring great destruction

Kore

Kore is actually a triple goddess (maiden, mother, crone). As maiden, she is the unexpressed nature of woman and suited to the fresh, springtime energy of Aries. It was Kore (Persephone) who was abducted by Hades (Pluto) from her mother Demeter (Ceres) and taken to the Underworld where she become his queen. Although she was allowed to return to her mother, it was ordained that Kore would spend three months every year in the Underworld and nine upon earth as she was still the dark lord's queen.

In the myth she was taken against her will, and this is indeed what happens to some women. But, what counts is how we transform our experiences, those that we have willingly chosen, and those that were forced upon us. Kore is the spirit of youthfulness and the potential for new growth.

Moon in Taurus

The Black Madonna

The Black Madonna was revered in the first millennium when black was associated with wisdom, and the so-called "black arts" were rituals to attain wisdom. Then, in the twelfth century (and especially after the Black Plague of the 1400s) she was replaced with the archetype of the Christian Virgin Mary who was touted as the perfect representation of a reverent woman. The natural qualities associated with the Black Madonna fell from favor and began to be suppressed. Taurus possesses the energy of Mother Earth herself. The earth is a rich black loam, fertile and luscious. The Black Madonna as an emblem of fertility fits earthy, sensuous Taurus well. The primal darkness is feminine, that of the womb. In ancient cultures black was considered transformative, and white or bone was the color of death. It wasn't until later that light became reason and black was seen as evil to be transcended. Contemplating and meditating on the Black Madonna allows us to return to the deep mysteries held in the earth, and in the dark, rich loam of our beginning. Moon in Taurus contains the strength and unyielding security of that which is permanent, of the primal energies that are irrefutable.

Gaia

Gaia, the oldest and most primeval of the Greek goddesses, is said to have existed in the endless span before creation. Eventually, Gaia desiring love, created the heavens and took Uranus for her lover. Subsequently, she bore the deities of heaven. Then she created the sea, named it Pontus, and took the sea as a lover. She bore the deities of the sea. When chaos settled into form, that form was Gaia, the full-breasted earth. She was the essence of fertility and creation. Gaia was revered at shrines across ancient Greece, on mountaintops and in deep, sacred oracular caves. Offerings to Gaia were placed at the sacred openings and fissures of her surface.

She was a prophetess who spoke of what was to come, inspiring the oracles at Delphi, Dodoan, and elsewhere to tell the will of Gaia. Even after the male gods came to power, the Greeks swore their most sacred oaths to Gaia, thereby recognizing her superior position. She was called the "oldest of the holy ones." For us today—Gaia reminds us to revere the ancient Earth, honoring it and our bodies as the holy shrines they are, and to remember where we came from and what nurtures us.

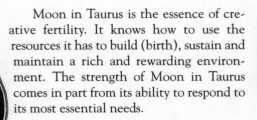

Moon in Taurus is the essence of creative fertility. It knows how to use the resources it has to build (birth), sustain and maintain a rich and rewarding environment. The strength of Moon in Taurus comes in part from its ability to respond to its most essential needs.

Moon in Gemini

Gum Lin and Loy Hi Lung

Gum Lin and Loy Hi Lung are Chinese folklore heroines. Gum Lin is a poor peasant girl, a weaver of mats and brooms. When a drought threatens their lives, she goes in search of reeds for weaving, and a solution for the water problem. She finds and gathers a cluster of reeds by a clear, blue lake and returns home. During the night, she dreams of forging a channel to connect the lake water with her thirsty village. The next day she leaves with her pickaxe and shovel with the intention of carving a lip at the lake's edge for water to spill toward the village. At the lake, the most easily accessible spot to dig is confined by a stone gate that will not open. A mysterious voice tells her, "These waters are yours if you find the key to the gate." Pondering the puzzle, Gum Lin hears a peacock say, "The daughter of the dragon." As the birds fly away, she hears, "Go to the lake and sing the song of your people." She obeys and the daughter of the dragon, Loy Hi Lung, hearing her song emerges from the lake. Gum Lin asks Loy Hi Lung for the key. Loy Hi Lung says that the key is deep beneath the lake in her father's lair, but if Gum Lin will sing for the dragon, Loy Hi Lung would slip into the dragon's cave and get the key. Their plan works and Gum Lin unlocks the gate. The water carves its own path and soon reaches the parched village saving the people.

Thirst can be a metaphor for the thirst for knowledge, which is always of interest to the Gemini. The mysterious voice is reminiscent of Gemini telling stories and sharing experiences.

Spider Woman

Spider Woman comes from of the native Pueblo people of the American Southwest. Her story tells of how in the beginning, there was no living creature, nothing but Spider Woman. In the dark purple light glowing at the Dawn of Being, Spider Woman spun a line from East to West and from North to South. Then she sat by her threads that stretched to the four horizons and sang in a deep, sweet voice. Her singing brought forth two daughters; one who became the mother of the Pueblo people, and one who became the mother of all others. She and her daughters created the heavens. When that was in place, Spider Woman used the red, yellow, black, white, and red clays of the earth to make people. After creating people, Spider Woman placed upon them a covering of creative wisdom which she'd spun from her own being.

Spider Woman is clever like Gemini, and she loves and appreciates variety. She has the tolerance necessary for living among others, and honoring and finding value in cultural differences. This charming story reminds us to remain open to learning and information for it is this openness and curiosity that will guide their way.

Moon in Cancer

Ix Chel

Ix Chel, the sacred silver disc of the dark heavens and first woman of the world, is a Mayan goddess. As the tale goes, in the beginning, the Moon and the Sun were equally bright. The Sun grew enamored of the luminous Ix Chel but her grandfather guarded her. The Sun transformed himself into a hummingbird to woo Ix Chel, but the grandfather suspected the bird and wounded him with a clay pellet. While caring for the wounded hummingbird, she grew tender, and they decided to run away together. They took off in a boat but grandfather sent lightning bolts after them and killed Ix Chel who had transformed herself into a crab. Heavenly dragonflies ministered to her for thirteen days and Ix Chile emerged whole and brilliant once again. She married the Sun but things did not go well. The Sun grew jealous and accused Ix Chel of being unfaithful with his brother, the morning star. Refusing to listen to her denials, he threw Ix Chel down to Earth. Although they reconciled, the Sun grew jealous again and beat Ix Chel. At this point Ix Chel flew into the night never to return. She remained married but always disappeared when her husband came near.

One of the greatest gifts that Ix Chel gave was her example that a woman must be able to come and go as she pleases. This story tells us about the constancy yet changeability of the Moon's cycle, of woman's cycles, of the tides. We are also reminded of the sensitivity of women's emotions especially when they are mistreated, and that it is in their nature to withdraw in one form or another. The Moon in Cancer is both glorious and sensitive, its emotions are easily engaged and its caring is healing. The story reminds the Moon in Cancer that it can be independent when necessary.

Cerridwen

Cerridwen, an ancient Celtic goddess whose name means "Cauldron of Wisdom," had a son who was quite ugly. She, like any mother, wanted the best for her child, so she concocted a special brew that would give her child foresight and the magical abilities that she herself possessed. Observing the movements of the Sun, Moon, and stars, she added ingredients at the proper planetary moments. It is unclear how the young lad, Gwion, who stirred the cauldron, came to drink the precious drops intended for Cerridwen's son Morfran, but that is what happened. The remainder of the brew split the cauldron apart and poured onto the ground. With his newfound powers, Gwion changed himself into various animals, seeking to escape the wrath of Cerridwen. But when Gwion became a grain of wheat, Cerridwen, as a hen, ate him. Gwion grew in her womb for nine months. After his birth, Cerridwen threw the baby into a raging river. It is told he was rescued and became a great poet.

Cerridwen's tale mirrors the Moon in Cancer's expression of a mother's love, devotion, and willingness to go to great lengths for her child. Cerridwen also points to the part of the Cancer principle that becomes wrathful toward anyone who would harm the interests of her child. Moon in Cancer, with its natural caring and nurturing abilities, holds the space real or symbolic (womb, home, environment) wherein the seed can transform into its inherent ability.

Moon in Leo

Sekmet (Bast)

Sekmet, an Egyptian goddess whose name means "The Powerful," is said to have come from the eye of her father Ra, the leader of the Egyptian gods. She is typically depicted as a woman with the head of a lion and carrying a torch. A solar disc representing the might of the Sun sits on her head. A warrior maiden, she represents the fierce, scorching, and destroying rays of the Sun, and personifies the fire element, courage, physical prowess, and the color red.

The story goes that she became disgusted with humanity and tried to destroy them. Her rage was so devastating that Ra stepped in to stop the carnage. He mixed vats of beer and pomegranate juice to replicate the blood that Sekmet longed for. The ruse succeeded and intoxicated Sekmet fell into a drunken stupor. Upon awakening, she had spent her anger. Bast is an alternative identity of Sekmet and expresses the fertilizing force of the Sun's rays. Bast later transformed into a cat-headed woman carrying a breastplate with a lion's image. She ruled pleasure, joy in life, and dancing.

This dual goddess symbolizes the expansive nature of Leo—the fierce lion protectress who can rage with anger, as well as the playful cat who loves to celebrate and enjoy life. The Moon in Leo is proud and fierce and often surprises by exhibiting strong masculine qualities, and she understands the nature and personalities of men.

Bridget

Bridget, a Celtic goddess, was born at sunrise with a flame shooting from her forehead. She is a firepower goddess, in touch with both fire and water energies. Kildare, a region in Ireland, is the center of Bridget's worship and the place of her shrine. The site held a sacred fire that was attended by nineteen virgin priestesses until it was extinquished by soldiers of Henry the VIII. It was reignited in 1996 and remains a perpetual flame.

The priestesses who tended the flame spread the lore of Bridget's wisdom and healing to the women of the village who came and brought food for them. Bridget's wells sprang up throughout the countryside and became sources for healing diseases, even leprosy. The story of Bridget and the archetype of Moon in Leo teach us that no matter what happens never allow your inner sacred fire to die, and know that you can always revive the flame. Bridget also speaks of the personal integrity of Moon in Leo and that this strong energy must be honored and tended.

Moon in Virgo

Hestia

The Greek goddess Hestia was a virgin goddess and keeper of the hearth flame. There are no statues of her because she took no human form, but rather was seen only in the hearth fire. Her attributes are purity, attentiveness, and devotion to preserving tradition. Eventually, six vestal virgins were put in charge of the flame at Vesta's shrine. Their tour of duty was thirty years and they had to remain virgins during their service or else be buried alive.

The vestal priestesses spent ten years learning, ten years practicing their duties, and ten years teaching. Virgo works consistently toward a greater level of skill, not unlike the dedication of the vestal priestesses. Hestia also ruled the eternal city flame that was carried by torch to colonies to indicate their acquisition and create cohesion. Tradition has it that a new home was not established until a woman brought fire from her mother's hearth to ignite her own. The images of Hestia become richer upon contemplation and the duty and service inherent in the myth is sustaining and comforting.

Moon in Virgo places a high value on skillfulness, order, and consistency. We can relate this to a sense of community and service to the greater good that is very much a part of the Virgo archetype. This is a humble sign that rarely blows its own horn, preferring instead to be dutiful and fulfill its commitment, although sometimes it's critical of those who do not.

Demeter

Demeter, the Greek harvest goddess, suits Moon in Virgo because Virgo is the time when the fruits of the harvest are gathered, stored and distributed. Demeter was worshiped in fireless sacrifices, preferring all offerings in their natural state. Demeter was also Persephone's mother, and when Persephone was abducted by Hades and taken to the Underworld, Demeter disregarded her duties and withdrew her energies until the plants wilted and shriveled. It is said that the green earth changed for the first time into the yellow-gold autumnal shades. After much pleading with Zeus, Persephone was allowed to return to her mother with the understanding that she go back to the Underworld every year for three months. Demeter's joy brought the earth into bloomed again.

Virgo has an innate gift for the rituals and processes of daily life, accepting the gradual shifts and changes of nature instead of fighting changes as so many other signs do. Moon in Virgo has a refreshing naturalness that is calming and caring. It also has the capability of shifting between innocence and wisdom, and yielding and withholding. Through this process, the Moon in Virgo learns adaptability to ever changing circumstances and environments.

Moon in Libra

Aphrodite

Aphrodite, the Greek goddess associated with love, was a seductive, desirable goddess who gave life and youthful vigor, took her pleasure from deities and mortals alike, and ruled sexual love, passion, desire, marriage, and beauty. At her festivals, the sexes often exchanged roles and dressed in each other's clothing. While Aphrodite was said to have been born from the foam of the sea, and is depicted in a famous painting by Boticelli as sailing on a seashell in all her radiant beauty, her early origin is eastern Mediterranean. Eventually, her cultural roots and indiscriminate lust clashed with those of her adopted country's more intellectual sensibilities. Her sacramental promiscuity deteriorated in the patriarchal culture and became prostitution. The Moon in Libra woman is ever in conflict with the more wanton elements of the female. Her strong desires are often held in check by a veneer of social propriety.

Aphrodite urges us to become aware of the choices we make in the name of love, as well as understanding how we view our own attractiveness. She also teaches us about being unashamed of how we express love and affection, and she asks us to be the only judge of where we choose to place our affections. Aphrodite threatens patriarchal rules governing women's behavior. Charming, beautiful, seductive Moon in Libra has all the qualities inherent in the goddess Aphrodite, including the struggle of how to use them.

Ishtar

Ishtar is found as far back as 5000 BCE in ancient Sumerian culture and the eastern Mediterranean. She was called "Queen of Heaven," and is thought to have descended from the planet Venus. Early statuettes of Ishtar show her in a welcoming pose of holding out her breasts. In this way she is honoring (as women should) the beauty, healing energy, and

promise of womanhood. Ishtar expresses the complexity of femininity just as Libra wants to balance the forces of value and desire. She was the ever-virgin warrior, never giving her essence to anyone, warring with any who tried to take it. She is also the wanton woman, constantly plotting to find a new lover. She is judge and counselor, the old wise one whom women emulated in the courts. Ishtar encourages full expressions of feminine nature versus the overly restrictive socially correct ones. These are also some of the qualities of Libra.

Moon in Libra has a sweet side, but the wise warrior, the one who understand the nature of social interaction is also represented. Like Ishtar, Moon in Libra seeks to balance the alternately warlike and lustful energies of the feminine.

Moon in Scorpio

Kali

Kali is the Hindu goddess responsible for all life from birth to death. She is the beginning and the end, the sum of the cycle. In this sense, she represents the full diversity of life experience including drama, humor, tragedy, sorrow, and as such, she is the ultimate expression of Scorpio. Kali is a rich interpretation of our potential, hopes, and resourcefulness in the everyday living of our lives. Her statuettes are typically colored blue-black, and she has four arms and a third eye. Her eyes are bloodshot and her red bloody tongue sticks out.

The Kali energy, once summoned, is uncontrollable, very much like the engaged passions of Scorpio. A story is told that once Kali dared to dance with Shiva, the Lord of the Dance. She was celebrating the slaughter of several demons by drinking their blood and dancing her victory on their corpses. In her drunken state, Kali's dance became increasingly wild, until she realized that Shiva was underneath her and she was dancing him to death. She slowed, but only momentarily. It is said one day she will resume her wild, abandoned, uncontrollable dancing and end the world. Kali represents an absolute and all-pervasive energy. She is beyond fear and seeks to teach us to move beyond our fears of annihilation. Kali expresses both the powerful and vulnerable qualities of Moon in Scorpio and the fact that they need to be blended into one deep understanding. Moon in Scorpio also reflects the obsessiveness of Kali and her intent focus once she is involved.

Shakti

Shakti is a manifestation of the Hindu goddess Devi, which literally translated means "power." Indian Tantric texts describe Shakti as pure or primal energy. She is known as the goddess of lust and destruction who causes all action to occur. She embodies tremendous transformative power just as the sign Scorpio does, and is related to the serpent of Kundalini Yoga. One of the symbolic images of Scorpio is the serpent and its relationship to raw power and sexuality, the animating life force. Although each male god has a Shakti to stimulate his creative force, Shakti power is believed to be dynamic while the male deities are passive.

Moon in Scorpio teaches women to accept our powerful nature, our ability to influence, our strength, prowess, genius, and potential to express fully whatever we deeply desire. The archetype of Scorpio has a natural understanding of the strong sexual desire that needs a full sexual expression. Moon in Scorpio understands the deep passions that drive human beings and gravitates naturally to the deepest mysteries of life.

Moon in Sagittarius

Rhiannon

Rhiannon is a Welsh goddess most often spoken of riding a white horse that none could catch and carrying a pouch of abundance. Rhiannon loved to roam the forest and woods for pleasure, and she was adept at changing herself into any animal she desired. As the story goes, one day while Rhiannon played in the forest in the guise of a hare, a hunter's dogs frightened her. The hunter Cian took pity on her and because of his display of kindness, Rhiannon transformed back into her beautiful self and invited Cian to stay on the island that was her home. One day while Rhiannon was bathing, Cian surprised her and sought to force his body on hers. Outraged, Rhiannon turned herself into a mare and brought her hoof down on Cian's thigh splintering it. Cian limped for the rest of his days, remembering both the kindness and fury of the goddess.

Rhiannon was also said to have an assertive wit, tinged with a bit of sarcasm. This last description fits with Sagittarius, typically a very direct personality. Rhiannon exemplifies a love of nature and animals as well as a need for some solitude. Sagittarius rules the thighs, and being a mutable sign, can certainly shift and change its moods.

The Moon in Sagittarius woman loves to run free like Rhiannon and has a strong sense of outrage at injustice. Meditating on Rhiannon can help us determine which battles are worth fighting. Rhiannon's pouch of abundance fits the sign Sagittarius, for on many levels this sign embodies abundance and certainly opportunity. Sagittarius gathers a wide array of experiences, not all of them joyful but in the final analysis, this sign overcomes adversity and finds "abundance" or wisdom within a host of challenging experiences.

Maat

Maat was an Egyptian goddess of physical and moral law, justice, and truth. She is depicted most often with an ostrich feather in her hair and the ankh, the symbol of life, in her hand. Sometimes she is seen with wings on her arms. In the Judgment Hall of the Tuat, the heart of a dead person was weighed against Maat, transformed into a feather and representing the truth. If the heart was light with justice, the soul could wander freely among the gods. If the heart was heavy with evil, it was instantly destroyed. Maat suits the judicial symbolism and the court system typically associated with Sagittarius. Sometimes Maat is described as "The Eye," but she is really concerned with the heart, where moral judgments are made. Again, this fits the fiery Sagittarius, always seeking the wisdom of the heart and the generosity of right. Maat encourages living consciously according to universal law so as to insure the soul's place in the afterlife. One of the roles of Maat was to guide the Sun god Ra as he made his journey across the skies. Journeying is certainly part of the Sagittarius archetype as is the continual quest for wisdom and understanding. Contemplating the story of Maat can bring forth the natural Moon in Sagittarian instincts of generosity and good will leading to good deeds, in the name of being human out of warmth of the heart.

Moon in Capricorn
Morrigan

The Celtic goddess Morrigan was a battle queen who used her magic to aid her favorite warriors, and as a hag or crone was capable of shape shifting into her favorite bird, the crow. Crows pick the bones of the dead, symbolism for Capricorn, who experiences and the reveres the simple essentials or "bare bones" of life and existence. The crone aspect of Morrigan reminds us of the fears associated with aging and loss of power. Her messages to us is: Honorable endings are part of the natural cycle of life. There is a frightening aspect to Morrigan but she teaches a code of magical behavior. For instance, her story states that the one who did the wounding must nurse the victim. She makes connections of responsibility for proper conduct. She is a guardian of death of old energy patterns, worn-out ideas, and anything that will no longer further life's process.

Although the woman with a Capricorn Moon is a great mother, she has a different quality than Moon in Cancer. Capricorn is more stringent and concerned with procedures, rules, and the necessity of habit, ritual, and history. Remember, Capricorn is involved with progress and achievement. Morrigan teaches that once the natural cycles are accepted and you are free of fear, you are then free to live fully.

Ashera

Ashera, whose name means "straight," was a Canaanite goddess. In her temples, Ashera was never depicted in a human form, but rather as an unshaped piece of wood. However, in private devotions she was sometimes represented as a simple clay figurine without legs which was inserted in the soft earthen floor of the home. These images of Ashera express the simplicity of the Moon in Capricorn—essential without frills, and the adherence to a personal code of behavior. The quality of "straight" can also be aligned with Capricorn's upstanding qualities and sometimes inability to relax from the many duties and responsibilities it shoulders. In her sacred groves, Asherah was known as "She Who Builds," providing the clay of the earth, teaching her people brick making. Ashera taught those who revered her how to build shelters from the heat and cold, and how to build her sacred shrines. These again are wonderfully accurate images of Moon in Capricorn: one who seeks to build all sorts of structures and finds security in shelter; one who is disciplined enough to teach others, and whom others can count on to be reliable.

Moon in Aquarius

Oya

Oya is a goddess of the Yoruba region in western Africa. She is known as the goddess of storms on the Niger River. This is fitting with Aquarius—always willing to make a storm, or create disturbances or unexpected awakenings wherever it goes. The name Oya means "she tore," because her winds tear up the river's otherwise placid surface. She is a warrior goddess and a patron of female leadership. It is told that when Oya enters a dancer, the dance become wild and Oya swings her sword—symbols for the element air and Aquarius. She often dances with her arms outstretched to ward off ghosts. She is the only goddess who is able to control ghosts. Oya emigrated to new lands (Aquarians are often transplanted to lands far from the place of their birth) with her children in tow, changing her form to suit her new surroundings. She is also a patron of justice and memory. Here again is a connection to the Moon in Aquarius ideal of truthfulness and the development of mind, mental faculties, reason, and logic. The Aquarian Moon is never conventional and typically a woman holding this Moon position is deeply concerned with human rights, in general, but particularly of women.

Nut

Nut is the Egyptian sky goddess most often depicted floating high over a semicircle that represents the sky. Her legs and arms symbolize the four pillars on which the sky supposedly rested. Nut was the personification of the heavens and the sky and the place where the clouds formed. In fact, she ruled over every region where the Sun rose and traveled from east to west. Representations of Nut picture her entire body and limbs bespangled with stars. Sometimes she is seen painted with protecting wings stretched out over the deceased and with the emblems of celestial water and air in her hands. This last depiction is a wonderful reminder of Aquarius holding the urn and allowing the waters of consciousness to flow down into humanity. Nut helped and protected the dead who appealed to her for food and other needs. It is Nut who reaches down from the heavens to take the hand of each who dies, taking them in her arms to place them as stars of the universe. Aquarius is more concerned with the larger social fabric and less with individual ego-consciousness. The goddess Nut contains the wide and far-reaching perspective that is associated with Moon in Aquarius and the protection of human rights.

Moon in Pisces

Kuan Yin

Kuan Yin is a Chinese goddess whose name translates to "earth" and "woman." Kuan Yin is best known as the holy mother of compassion. It is said that she achieved ultimate enlightenment, but chose to return to the peoples of the earth in moments of deepest need. Kuan Yin's name is also translated as "she who hears the weeping world." She is a goddess of mercy and prayerfulness. Simply saying her name in prayer is said to ensure salvation from physical and spiritual harm. Peace, mercy, and nonviolence to other beings are also her testimony. This description of Kuan Yin fits the energy of Moon in Pisces—the deep need for connection, the reverence for and the feeling of connectedness to all other human beings. Moon in Pisces does best in life when it maintains a connection with a spiritual truth and seeks to live that truth. This highly sensitive Moon, with soft boundaries and fine antennae to pick up the subtlest energies, often hears or feels too much. Moon in Pisces needs the solace of a spiritual practice to alleviate the confusion of overstimulation. Piscean types who follow careers involving health and healing often chose more subtle ways of healing, such as through music, art, or writing. Kuan Yin is often depicted as riding on a swift dolphin.

Morgan Le Fay

Morgan Le Fay is known as a Celtic sea goddess, and to this day in Brittany sea sprites are called morgans. Le Fay is translated as "the fairy" or "the fate." In Italy there are tales of a Fata Morgana who lived beneath the waters of a lake. There is also a link to the Etruscan goddess Fortuna at whose shrines omens of the future bubbled forth from underground springs. In the Arthurian legends, she is Morgan, the Lady of the Lake.

It was she who tricked the wizard Merlin into teaching her his magic. In Welch myth, Morgan is said to be a queen of Avalon, the underworld fairyland where King Arthur was carried when he disappeared from the world. In other tales she was an immortal artist and healer who lived with her eight sisters in Avalon. Morgan is mysterious, just as the energy of Pisces is mysterious, and contains within it all the best memories of when women were revered in the world. Pisces is open to the magical aspects of life. In Piscean sensibilities there is always something bubbling forth—images, thoughts, and messages drawn forth almost mystically, magically from who knows where. Pisces has a seductive and glamorous side. It can inspire and uplift the surrounding energies, and in turn it is easily affected by the mood or tone of its environment. Moon in Pisces must know that reverence, love, and respect can only begin with oneself and a deep sense of dignity.

These myths are rich with symbolism and evoke a wealth of illustrious images. There are innumerable goddess myths contained in all the cultures of history that await your perusal and internalization. Their universal intent is always to allow your special gifts and powers to influence and flow into the world thereby enriching the evolution of consciousness. Goddess bless your journey.

Moon Lore

Verna Gates

While the garish Sun pierces our eyes with its fierce glare, the gentle Moon lights the night for lovers and poets and planters.

Throughout the centuries, the gentle beacon of the night has served as a heavenly reminder of life as it is lived on this earthly plane. It is the Moon that carries us through the cycle of life—growth, change, death, and rebirth. In the past, babies were carried outside and shown the waxing Moon to promote growth and health. Lovers have rejoiced in her round, full fertility and dreamed of children to come. Around the world, couples were advised to marry under a Full Moon for maximum fertility in the formation of the family to come. The dying have looked to her rebirth as comfort from the finality of death. With its cyclic nature, the Moon was seen as the weaver of fate and the controller of destinies.

Many believed the Moon served as a way station for departed souls on route to paradise. People in India, Alaska, Persia, and Greece watched the Moon fill up with souls as it increased in size. When these seekers moved on to their final resting place, the Moon waned, awaiting more spiritual travelers. In India, these souls are said to return to the earth for reincarnation with the falling rain.

Because the lunar crescent resembles the shape of a boat, it came to be associated with the journey across the sky into the realm of the dead. For the Egyptians especially, it represents the ship of moonlight bearing the newly departed soul through the darkness into the new dawn of a glorious afterlife. The afterlife was of vital importance to the ancient Egyptians, who enjoyed the highest quality of earthly life known in antiquity.

For most of the great religions, the Moon has represented death and resurrection, a vital component for Christians and Muslims, as well as the ancients. The Moon also dictated the religious calendar and presided over sacred rites. Easter, the holiest of Christian celebrations, moves around the calendar looking for the first Full Moon following the Vernal Equinox.

For Greeks, the second century writer, Plutarch wrote the *De Facie Lunae* to explain the process: First the fleshy body was consumed by Demeter, who represented the earth's natural decomposition. Once the

earth completes its purification of the body, the soul floats above the Earth on its way to the Moon. If any sins need to be purged from the soul, purification occurs during the rising upward, letting the pains of Earth stay weighted down. Some souls remain in spirit form to guide humanity while others seek the final destination to the faraway isles of the dead.

At one time, the conquering Roman Empire took in so many cultures and had so many new gods, there was a constant round of festivals and appeasement. So packed was the Roman religious calendar that a Moon watcher was employed to witness the exact time of the New Moon rising so that a precise schedule of events could be organized for the coming month.

Those excellent astronomers, the Druids, reckoned their days by the Moon with the day even starting the night before. A Celtic week had nine nights, with the ninth night of the month a night of completion. Three weeks of nine nights equals twenty-seven days, a lunar month. The sixth day of the Moon was the time when the Druids cut the sacred mistletoe. This plant was noted for its ability to heal, especially infertility and exposure to poison. It also protected against all things brought by fire or water.

The Virgin Mary is often pictured seated or standing on a lunar crescent in contrast to the brighter light of her son. Another reference to Mary in association with Moon is "a woman clothed with the Sun and the Moon under her feet," found in Revelation 12:1.

In the Islamic religion, the lunar crescent is a powerful symbol of the faith. This emblem of rebirth is seen on the tops of the towers calling the pious to pray. The Moon was first honored by Mohammed when he started the lunar calendar in 631 A.D. To this day, the twelve lunar months officially begin when two honest men first see the New Moon rise from a mountain top. The flags of thirteen countries, including Turkey, Algeria, and Pakistan display the crescent Moon as a symbol of national Islamic devotion. The lunar crescent also appears in the coats of arms in many a devout Muslim family.

Lunar Lunacy

The Moon gives her Latin name, *Luna*, (the Roman goddess), to the word "lunatic." As late as 1940 a defendant used Moon madness as an excuse for murder in England. Police officers and emergency room workers across the world swear by the effects of the Moon on those weak of mind or morals.

There was also the fear of wantonness in even the finest people. In 1688, an author wrote that the "double conjunction of Venus and the Moon produces extreme lubricity and brings venereal disease and causes women of quality to become enamored of manservants," and "For those who have maidservants, do not left them wash the dishes during the Full Moon as they will break them up."

Magical Moonbeams

For many centuries, maidens were discouraged from lying in the moonlight because they could fall prey to the lustful advances of the Moon man who could descend upon them, and even a glance at the Full Moon could risk the conception of a Moon-child. And the womanly cycle was the result of Moon man's visits to the Earth every month during the dark of the Moon. Once his mission was complete, he emerged reborn as the New Moon. His special Moon herbs—those that bloomed at night— were most effective for curing female troubles.

Many cultures honored lunar fertility cults, a vital function in the days of low population and high mortality. The priestesses of these cults were powerful forces who could stop the course of rushing rivers, reverse the wheel that spun the stars, and call the trees to pull up their roots and lumber down from the forest. Their magic could chart the course of human life and determine the reins of political power. Those who crossed these leaders could be doomed to a life of barrenness, separated from the fertile Moon's blessings.

In Polynesia, the Moon was female and shared the wealth of her vast fertility with all women. They called her "first woman" and all things sprang from her womb. Women desirous of children could call upon her for aid and she would share her fecundity.

In China, young couples lie together under the moonbeams for a blessed conception during the Harvest Moon in the autumn. During this fifteenth month of their lunar calendar, the Moon is celebrated with festivals and the eating of moon-cakes.

Moon beams are so filled with potency that a protective circle must be drawn around the magic practitioner before lunar spells are invoked. Traditional practitioners of lunar magic, from Egyptian Moon priestesses to the Druids, wore white robes the color of moonbeams. One ancient practice called "drawing down the moon" is captured on Greek vases from antiquity and is still used today to capture lunar forces. First a circle is drawn by the leader's knife. A ceremony for purification follows with chants and dances accompanied by burning incense. Once the ritual is complete and the Moon is drawn, three spells may be cast. The magician must be careful with words, for the wishes made will return threefold to their creator, be they for good or ill.

Collect the dew during a lunar eclipse for the most magical of powers. This captured lunar energy can heal the sick and bring luck and love.

In the famous Witches' brew from Shakespeare's Scottish play, *Macbeth*, the three Witches add "slips of yew sliver'd in the moon's eclipse," to their concoction. The words to this speech are attributed to an ancient curse that still sends shivers down the spines of superstitious thespians. Many will not quote the play off the stage as it portends ill luck.

For assured good fortune, carry a rabbit's foot that was collected by moonlight. In many cultures, instead of a man's face, they see the big ears and fuzzy tail of a rabbit living on the Moon, especially in India, where the hare was sent to the Moon by the god Indra as a reward. Since the fertile hare is associated with the fecund Moon, it is one of her creatures and brings moonbeam magic to the carrier of its foot.

There has not been a time when this mysterious orb has not fascinated us. As early as 7000 B.C., cave dwellers in Spain drew symbols of her on their stony walls. Even though we have studied her and landed on her surface, still she turns on some ancient light that draws us to her magic.

Moon Folktales

Verna Gates

The Worm and the Flea

The animals laughed when the worm and flea clan stepped forward with their offer to force Sun and Moon out of their house. The world had been in darkness for days while this sullen pair of sky orbs refused to exit their windowless home made of thick stones. The larger animals had tried coercion, then threats, attempting to pry them from their home. All was to no avail.

Things were growing desperate on Earth. The trees were dying. The tides couldn't decide whether to ebb or flow without Moon's guidance. The honeybees couldn't see the flowers to make their honey. And the world was growing cold. Undaunted by the other's skepticism, the angleworms and the fleas made good on their offer to save the world. They traveled far to the home of Sun and Moon with the fleas riding on a gopher's back.

When they arrived, the angleworms immediately went to work drilling tiny holes into the stone house. Gopher crept near to the holes so that the fleas could jump into the house. The fleas headed straight for Sun and Moon and tore into their skin with a terrible determination. The two orbs were soon itching and scratching faster than a hummingbird can flap its wings. To escape the fleas' torturous attack, the Sun and Moon fled into the sky. The other animals looked heavenward in amazement. Since they discovered their great power, the fleas now keep the other animals humble with their itchy bites, although, you rarely see the gopher scratch. For the animals, fleas are no longer a laughing matter.

The Moon Escapes the Underworld

This story begins beside the Nunbirdu Canal in ancient Mesopotamia. Ninlil, lady of the wind, couldn't resist the cool, fresh water and dove in. She was spied by Enlil, god of the spring rain, who was smitten by the sight of her. Ninlil refused Enlil's advances, but he wasn't deterred, and grabbing a boat he proceeded with his seductive pleas from the top of the

water. By the time he arrived at Ninlil, she was willing to share his love and she was made pregnant. Unfortunately, Ninlil's parents were not pleased. Enlil was acused of rape, arrested, and banished to the Underworld. The lovestruck Ninlil followed.

When Ninlil came through the city gate, Enlil, knowing it would be the Moon's destiny to live in the Underworld forever and not wanting that to be the Moon's destiny, disguised himself as the gatekeeper and convinced Ninlil to sleep with him in order to offer another child to the place of shadows. The result was Nergal, king of the Underworld.

At the river to the Underworld, Enlil disguised himself again, this time as the river god. When Ninlil asked if he had seen Enlil, he noted her pregnanacy with the Moon. He seduced her again saying the Underworld needed another substitute. That coupling conceived the Underworld god Ninazu.

At the last stop in this world, the ferryman to the Underworld recognized the woman who searched for Enlil. Again, it was Enlil in disguise. He begged to create yet another being to substitute for his son the Moon in the Underworld. That union conceived Enbilulu, the god of the river running into the afterlife.

When the Moon Suen was born, he was able to take his honored place in the pantheon of the sky. His loving parents had provided three brothers to rule over the Underworld while he rode across the sky. However, he still spends three days a month with his brothers in the Underworld. Once his visit is complete, the New Moon rises.

Where God Was Created

The word *Teotihuacan* in the Aztec tongue means "Place where God was created." The ancient city of Teotihuacan was already in ruins when the Aztecs arrived. These bold warriors were awed at the sight of the great pyramids and palaces that once were. At the city's Pyramid of the Sun and the Pyramid of the Moon, the great sky entities themselves had been born.

After the destruction of the Earth and the fourth Sun, four powerful gods met at Teotihuacan to bring light into the darkness. In order to create a new Sun, the gods knew that of one them would have to be sacrificed by fire. The handsome and narcissistic Tecuciztecatl volunteered in a swaggering boast to become the new Sun. In their wisdom, the gods decided that Tecuciztecatl should compete against the modest Nanahuatzin to decide who would fire the sky as the Sun or calm it with lunar light as the Moon.

It took four days to build the great sacrificial fire. Meanwhile both competitors purified themselves with prayer on the two pyramids. When the fire was boiling hot, the two gods were called upon to throw themselves into the flames. The vain Tecuciztecatl brought gold for sacrifice, and wore the finest robes. Nanahuatzin wore paper, and offered cactus spines dipped in the holy water of his own blood.

Tecuciztecatl took the first dash toward the blazing flames but faltered. Four times he approached the heat with great ceremony, but little determination. Finally, Nanahuatzin was brought forward. He walked slowly into the flames with closed eyes and the steady gait of the hero. His bravery shamed Tecuciztecatl to finally toss his own body into the fire.

The gods waited in the darkness for the Sun to rise. Instead, the garish Tecuciztecatl rose as the Moon with the Sun's brightness. Insulted, the gods sought a way to tame his light. Spying a rabbit, one of the gods hurled him into the air, striking the face of Tecuciztecatl. The rabbit can be seen there still. Soon after, Nanahuatzin broke the horizon in the east as the fifth Sun, and a new dawn arrived.

Watcher of the Herds

In the Alaskan village of the Gwich'in, a boy was born to a loving mother. This destitute but deserving mother was blessed by the boy, not

only for his health and strength, but also because the boy was a magician. He held the secret of the caribou and from the time he could tod-
dle, he could call in the herd and provide all the villagers with meat for
the winter.

Soon, his mother was one of the most honored women of the tribe
and had accumulated many riches. Suitors came for the hand of a woman
who could produce such a shaman.

Meanwhile, the son selected the best hunters and taught them the
secrets of hunting an animal with sacred intent. He showed them how to
call to the animal's spirit, and how to honor the animal's sacrifice. When
his mother's future and his village secured, the boy vanished. His parting
words revealed his destination to his beloved mother. He told her to look
for him on the Moon, holding a caribou, fresh from the hunt. He warned
her saying, "If he stands and hunts, game will be plentiful and the village
will prosper. However, if the light of the Moon captures him resting on
his side, food will be scarce and preparations will need to be made." His
mother has gone on, but the boy on the Moon still warns us of the times
ahead on Earth.

Electional Astrology

Estelle Daniels

When people went to an astrologer years ago, they seldom knew their actual date of birth. Instead they would ask the astrologer a question or deliver a token from a sick person, and the astrologer would cast a chart using that information as a starting point. The astrologer would use horary astrology (the art of astrological divination) to determine the nature of the problem, the answer to the question, or what was causing the illness and if the person would get well or die. If a person wanted to plan an event in the future, the astrologer would use electional astrology, and applying the rules for horary, would look ahead for a time which would maximize their chances for success. This article will detail a few simple techniques you can use to help you time important activities.

It can get very difficult and frustrating to try to live your life totally in accordance with these techniques, not to mention it can drive you crazy. But if you save these techniques for the important things you can increase your chances for success.

The Moon is the main timer in electional astrology. It's the fastest moving planet, staying in each sign between two and three days, and traveling through the entire zodiac each month, so if you are waiting for a certain Moon sign, the most you will have to wait is a month. The Moon is the initiator of action in horary and electional astrology, so working with the Moon in a particular sign or house can be quite effective.

These techniques are best used when you have some time and can make a choice about when you will act. If you want to buy a car, waiting for a Gemini or Virgo Moon or the Moon in your Third House can increase your chances for getting the best car at the best price. You can certainly look, test, and do research before the Gemini or Virgo Moon, but if you wait to sign or buy until that optimum time, you can probably make yourself a better deal. Looking for a place to live is best done when the Moon is in Cancer or your Fourth House. Again, you have decided on a general neighborhood, price range, and style. I've found that if you use those specific days, you may find something quicker, and at a better price.

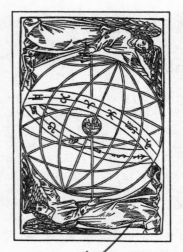

You have two to three days when the Moon is in the sign or house you want to work with. Sometimes it falls on a weekend, which can limit your options if you are looking for a job, but you could use that day to mail out a bunch of resumes. Just do the best you can. Even if you try and the timing doesn't work, you are no worse off than before. If you simply cannot wait, electional astology offers insight into the cosmic influences at work, giving you advance notice of pitfalls you might avoid.

Cosmic Power Times

If you know your own Sun, Moon, and Ascendant signs, you can determine when the cosmic energies will enhance yours. For example, if the Moon for the day is in the same sign as your Sun, Moon or Ascendant the power is with you. You'll be more effective, have stronger will power, more sales resistance, and receive better reactions to you and your endeavors. But if the Moon for the day is in the sign opposite that of your Sun, Moon, or Ascendant, it is a cosmic nonpower time for you because the power is being divided between you and something or someone else. If you are working on behalf of someone else, though, you can be an effective advocate during this time because your natural tendency is to put the other guy's interests first. It is also a good time to be invisible, you can blend in with the crowd.

You can add another level of effectiveness to your life by tying the use of cosmic-power days to your birth chart. If you know your Ascendant, then each astrological sign corresponds to a certain house in your personal chart, and the signs naturally correspond to specific houses. Aries is the natural First House, Virgo to the natural Sixth House, and so on. If you are using the Moon in conjunction with your natal chart, use the table below to fine-tune each astrological sign corresponding to each house in your chart. There may not be a 100 percent correlation because of the table of houses used, or if you were born far north or south of the equator, but there will be enough correlation for these energies to work pretty well.

If your ascendant is:

Aries	Taurus	Gemini	Cancer
1-Aries	1-Taurus	1-Gemini	1-Cancer
2-Taurus	2-Gemini	2-Cancer	2-Leo
3-Gemini	3-Cancer	3-Leo	3-Virgo
4-Cancer	4-Leo	4-Virgo	4-Libra
5-Leo	5-Virgo	5-Libra	5-Scorpio
6-Virgo	6-Libra	6-Scorpio	6-Sagittarius
7-Libra	7-Scorpio	7-Sagittarius	7-Capricorn
8-Scorpio	8-Sagittarius	8-Capricorn	8-Aquarius
9-Sagittarius	9-Capricorn	9-Aquarius	9-Pisces
10-Capricorn	10-Aquarius	10-Pisces	10-Aries
11-Aquarius	11-Pisces	11-Aries	11-Taurus
12-Pisces	12-Aries	12-Taurus	12-Gemini

Leo	Virgo	Libra	Scorpio
1-Leo	1-Virgo	1-Libra	1-Scorpio
2-Virgo	2-Libra	2-Scorpio	2-Sagittarius
3-Libra	3-Scorpio	3-Sagittarius	3-Capricorn
4-Scorpio	4-Sagittarius	4-Capricorn	4-Aquarius
5-Sagittarius	5-Capricorn	5-Aquarius	5-Pisces
6- Capricorn	6-Aquarius	6-Pisces	6-Aries
7-Aquarius	7-Pisces	7-Aries	7-Taurus
8-Pisces	8-Aries	8-Taurus	8-Gemini
9-Aries	9-Taurus	9-Gemini	9-Cancer
10-Taurus	10-Gemini	10-Cancer	10-Leo
11-Gemini	11-Cancer	11-Leo	11-Virgo
12-Cancer	12-Leo	12-Virgo	12-Libra

Sagittarius	Capricorn	Aquarius	Pisces
1-Sagittarius	1-Capricorn	1-Aquarius	1-Pisces
2-Capricorn	2-Aquarius	2-Pisces	2-Aries
3-Aquarius	3-Pisces	3-Aries	3-Taurus
4-Pisces	4-Aries	4-Taurus	4-Gemini
5-Aries	5-Taurus	5-Gemini	5-Cancer
6-Taurus	6-Gemini	6-Cancer	6-Leo
7-Gemini	7-Cancer	7-Leo	7-Virgo
8-Cancer	8-Leo	8-Virgo	8-Libra
9-Leo	9-Virgo	9-Libra	9-Scorpio
10-Virgo	10-Libra	10-Scorpio	10-Sagittarius
11-Libra	11-Scorpio	11-Sagittarius	11-Capricorn
12-Scorpio	12-Sagittarius	12-Capricorn	12-Aquarius

Another cosmic power time is when the Moon is in the same sign as your Tenth House, which gives you a burst of public energy. This works irregardless of where other placements might be (like a natal Sun in the Fourth, which might make the Moon going through your Tenth House a nonpower time. It still gives you a boost of public energy, though you will be less comfortable with it than others without that Fourth House Sun). The Moon in your Tenth House is less powerful than the other cosmic power times, but it can be another energy boost.

During the times the Moon is not in the same sign as your Ascendant, Sun or Moon, nor is it in the sign opposite that of your Ascendant, Sun, or Moon, nor is it in the same sign as your Tenth House, you are neither helped or hindered by the Moon's sign. However, the Moon is still in some sign and house, and those energies will be prominent for you.

Although the Moon's sign is experienced by everyone in the whole world simultaneously, each person has their own Ascendant which adds another layer of complexity to how people deal with the universal energies. If the Moon is in Cancer, it may mean Eleventh House energies for a person with a Virgo Ascendant, but a person with an Aries Ascendant will be experiencing Fourth House energies. So the Cancer influence is the same, but the house influence will be different for each Ascendant. And whether that Cancer Moon is a cosmic power time for you or cosmic nonpower time depends upon your personal chart. But it is still a Cancer Moon for everyone.

The techniques of using just the Moon sign or house of the Moon are fairly basic to electional astrology. While doing a full electional chart takes additional factors into account, using the Moon only can add effectiveness to important events in your life.

Here is a list of the Moon signs and the houses they correspond to in the natural chart. This sign-house correlation is not exact, but close enough for the purposes we use it for here. Some Moons are naturally better for certain activities. Some activities are more effective under two or more Moons. This list is intended to be as broad as possible to maximize activities, and opportunities for success.

Aries or First House

This is a Moon of awakenings and beginnings, for starting new things, for optimism, or just enjoying life. It's a "me-first" Moon, so if you want to work on being more self-assertive, use this Moon time. It's a time for developing your ego and strengthening your will, for exploration, pioneering, daredevil stunts, and confrontations. Physical activities, sports, and workouts are enhanced. This Moon deals with your outer appearance and how you present yourself to people one-on-one. Use this Moon if you want to develop warmth, ambition, passion, zeal, energy, optimism, a never-say-die spirit, spontaneity, quick recovery from setback or defeat, and  courage. Get a makeover, get your hair done, get your colors tested, get a new wardrobe. Things to watch out for: impulsiveness, anger, arguments, combativeness, violence, inflated egos, leaving others behind, lack of consideration for those less fit, and immaturity.

Taurus or Second House

This is the time to deal with money, possessions, movable property; to address what has value for you. Use this Moon sign when asking for a raise; for paying bills, loans, or debts of any kind; for determining what makes you feel important or valued. It's also a good sign for gardening, music, and marriage. If you want something in your life to be permanent, use Taurus, for it is the most fixed of all the signs. Faithfulness and reliability are emphasized. Habit and routine can be easily established, but you can also get into a rut. Now is the time to showcase your personal talents. Taurus rules anything having to do with comfort and material security. This is a good sign to buy tangible art that is practical or will increase in value. Use this Moon to develop patience, tenacity, self-worth, networth, aesthetics, music, silence, will power, comfort, security, and financial skills. Things to watch out for: laziness, indolence, stubbornness, greed, placing value on money and material possessions over intangibles, judging only by net worth, silence in the face of needing to address wrongs, unwillingness to leave the nest, and inertia.

Gemini or Third House

Traveling, communications, good common sense, and the ability to test the popular pulse are in Gemini's realm, as is anything having to do with communication, computers, speaking, or writing. A Gemini Moon

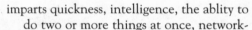

imparts quickness, intelligence, the ability to do two or more things at once, networking, and quick thinking that enables you to talk your way out of situations. Short trips are emphasized, as is anything having to do with transportation: cars, bikes, trains, or planes. This is a good time for fixing, buying, or selling a car. Trade and commerce are under the Taurus Moon's influence, as do dealings with siblings, basic education or a weekend seminar. This Moon enhances eye-hand coordination, manual dexterity, speech and diction, common sense, ability to read people, and teaching skills. Things to watch out for: inconstancy, too much talking and not enough listening, incessant talk, lying, gossip, thievery, inability to concentrate or to sit still, unwillingness to be alone, fickleness, vacillation, boredom, games playing, fast talking con men, and scams.

Cancer or Fourth House

This is the Moon of home, hearth, and mother. Food and eating issues are addressed here. This is a good Moon for marriage, asking for a raise, or anything having to do with a place to live—finding, buying, or selling a home, moving, or redecorating. This is also the Moon which deals with the past, in general, and your past in particular. It's good for genealogy work, or family reunions. This is a good Moon for divination and psychic matters. If you want to develop intuition, emotional depth, or work with the spirit world use this Moon phase. Your tenacity, ambition, helpfulness, patience, sense of humor, teaching, financial skills, imagination, patriotism, and traditions can all be enhanced under this Moon. Things to watch out for: excessive emotions, maudlin sentimentality, moodiness, inconsistancy, irritability, crabbiness, clinging to people and problems, emotional dependence, hoarding, being stuck in a rut of routine or habit, whining, shyness, worrying about what others think of you, projecting your feelings onto others.

Leo or Fifth House

This is a joyous Moon with a grand zest for life, love, romance, fun, amusements, vacations, games, pastimes, hobbies, and enjoyment of the good life, children and anything to do with children, selling a home if you want to maximize profit, speculation, investments and gambling. Acting and the theater are emphasized here. If you want to make a grand and/or generous gesture, this Moon will assure you get the recognition you crave. This Moon is good for organizing large- scale projects, planning on a grand scale, and for making big decisions; for developing pride, joy, self-confidence, artistic skills, acting ability, will power, investment skills, rapport with children, sense of humor, generosity, and the ability to let go and have fun. Things to watch out for: excessive ego, hogging the spotlight, ego overruling common sense, putting play before work, compulsive actions (drinking, gambling, sex), stubbornness, pride, being overbearing, pomposity, or games playing.

Virgo or Sixth House

Work, the workplace, coworkers, employees, looking for a job, changing jobs, but not necessarily for changing careers are emphasized under this Moon. As are health and wellness, illness and disease, food, nutrition, vitamins, diets, cleanliness, and hygiene. This is a good time to get a physical, have tests run, or to develop healing abilities. This is an excellent Moon for cleaning your house, doing small chores; for buying, selling, or fixing your car; for organizing and budgeting, or for meeting your obligations and paying back debts. This Moon deals with relatives in general, but especially aunts and uncles, cousins, etc. This is a good Moon for writing, especially of detail or technical kinds. Things to watch out for: all work and no play, excessive obligations, overextending resources, over commitment, being nitpicky, being bogged down in the details, excessive or petty bureaucrats, hypochondria, malingering, exaggerating symptoms, cheapness, skimping on necessities, or martyrdom.

Libra or Seventh House

This is the classic Moon for marriage or partnerships of any kind—business, personal, and romantic. Diplomacy and negotiation are emphasized here, so if you want to be an advocate, counselor, advisor, or hire someone for professional services, use this Moon. If you have to deal with an open enemy or find a thief, this is the Moon. Buy art which makes you feel good, makes your surroundings more beautiful, and enhances your decor. Use this Moon to develop grace, charm, manners, partnership skills, diplomacy, aesthetics, harmony, peacefulness, or business skills. Things to watch out for: indecisiveness, needing the approval of others, unwillingness to be alone, neediness, constant deferral to another against your needs or wants, laziness, arguments, unwillingness to compromise, inability to forge a separate identity, getting stuck in either/or situations without looking at other alternatives, lose/lose situations, win/lose situations, superficiality, judging by appearances, social one-upmanship, being wishy-washy.

Scorpio or Eighth House

This Moon deals with sex, death, dying, inheritance, legacies, wills, taxes, paying debts, making loans, borrowing money, dealing with mortgages, insurance, credit, shared resources, of any type, the profits of a partnership, sexual dysfunction or disease, sexual satisfaction and pleasure, for dealing with occult, psychic matters, exorcisms, communicating with the spirit world, divination and scrying. This is a good time for finishing up uncompleted projects. Use this Moon to develop intensity, will power, deep understanding, occult abilities, courage, sharing skills, budgeting, financial skills, ability to take the bad with the good, healing abilities, tenacity, and sexuality. Things to watch out for: moodiness, morbid thoughts, dwelling on evil, obsession, stubbornness, emotional brinkmanship, ultimatums, seeing everything as life or death, suspicion, paranoia, inability to open up to another, snooping, digging up skeletons, airing the dirty laundry, betrayal, or intimidation.

Sagittarius or Ninth House

This Moon deals with long-distance travel, all forms of travel and transportation with emphasis on air or sea travel, religion, faith, devotion, religious institutions and experiences, religious people, and higher education. Use this Moon to develop hope, faith, understanding of complex issues and thoughts, wisdom, sense of justice, *joie de vivre*, the mind and learning, far-reaching goals, freedom, political instincts, and understanding. If you want things to be happy and go well, this is a good luck time. This is a good Moon for big partys or events, sports and athletics, politics, and dream work. Things to watch out for: pompousness, arrogance, one-upmanship, being a bore, unintentional insults, going overboard, intolerance, fanaticism, incessant talk, inability to settle in one place, unwillingness to commit, unfaithfulness, proselytizing, extravagance, unrealistic expectations, or overblown promises.

Capricorn or Tenth House

This is the Moon of career, profession, honor, reputation, public standing, public speaking, and work. If you want to change careers or ask for a promotion or raise, make sure you have solid accomplishments behind you to show your value and worth. This can also be a good Moon for starting a business, but make sure you are well funded and have a solid business plan. This Moon also has to do with your father and other authority figures. If you have to deal with a boss or other person in power, or if you have to go over someone's head, this is a good time for it. This is a Moon for success. Use this Moon to develop ambition, public standing, reputation, honor, courage, business skills, executive skills, patience, planning, respect for authority, understanding of power used correctly, frugality, financial skills, organizing ability, career, and wisdom. Things to watch out for: social climbing, ruthlessness, miserliness, nose to the grindstone, inability to empathize, business over anything else, cheapness, skimping on necessities, poverty, exploiting the masses, old-fashioned attitudes, facism, being a control freak, aspiring to unrealistic expectations, hiding from society or obligations, or being a hermit.

Aquarius or Eleventh House

This is the best Moon to ask for a raise. Emphasis is on teamwork and friendliness—groups, clubs, fraternities, friends, and friendships. This is also a good luck time, use it for things you want and may not have to work for: lotteries, games of chance, etc. This is a political Moon. Issues are prominent, matters dealing with social issues, public well-being, elected officials, political parties and functions are prominent. This Moon is good for working out your hopes, aspirations, and ambitions—things that will make you happy in life. Use this Moon to develop a social sense, freedom, group identity, friendship, originality, uniqueness, utopia, new values and ideas, independence, objectivity, rationality, innovation. Things to watch out for: unexpected, weird happenings or people, inability to connect on a personal level, superficial charity, letting outside groups or friends get in the way of personal or family needs, pie-in-the-sky unrealistic expectations, overblown promises, stubbornness, fixed ideologies, unbridled change for changes sake, extremism, anarchy, fascism, unwillingness to conform, refusal to listen to others.

Pisces or Twelfth House

This is the Moon of secret, hidden, unknown things. Occult and psychic matters are emphasized here, as are exorcisms, dealing with the spirit world, divination, magic, work with perfumes, oils, incense and potions, dealing with massive bureaucracy, hospital stays, medical treatments or having medical tests run, spying and covert activities to discover who your secret enemies are. This is a good time for charitable giving and volunteering. This is a spiritual Moon, but not necessarily religious. Use this Moon to develop spirituality, psychic abilities, sympathy, empathy, ability to let go, healing abilities, faith, charity, sacrifice, imagination, visualization, dealing with your fears and phobias, confronting the unknown. Dealing with past matters and things which you thought were long resolved but pop up unexpectedly are in tune with this Moon. Large animals come under this Moon. This is a good Moon for endings and finishing anything. Things to watch out for: making people feel sorry for you, inability to face your faults or shortcomings, blaming, feeling overwhelmed, being too sensitive, taking on the sorrows of others, inability to draw boundaries, poison, spying and espionage, secrets, covert actions, hypochondria, projecting your feelings onto others, martyrdom, inability to relate to reality, getting caught up in fantasy and illusion, getting conned, shooting yourself in the foot, self-undoing, imprisonment, being wishy-washy.

Happy Halloween

Louise Riotti

Halloween is one of the oldest festivals reflecting traditions and revelries that evolved over 2,000 years and through many cultures. Many of its customary rites can be traced to ancient Greece, and the familiar symbols and activities associated with the holidays have their roots firmly established in Celtic and Roman practices. Halloween means "hallowed" or "holy evening" because it takes place the day before All Saints' Day.

The Druids, an order of priests in ancient Gaul and Britain, believed that ghosts, spirits, fairies, goblins, Witches, and elves came out to harm people on Halloween. We know little about Druid rites because their doctrines were passed on orally and members were sworn to secrecy. They considered the cat sacred and believed that cats had once been human beings but were changed into animal form as a punishment for evil deeds. From these Druidic beliefs comes the present-day use of Witches, ghosts, and cats in Halloween festivities.

The Symbols of Halloween

Pumpkins

The word "pumpkin" dates back to the seventeenth century and is derived from the Old French, *pompion*, which in turn was derived from the Greek word for melon, *pepon*, meaning "cooked by the sun," or "ripe."

The original jack-o'-lanterns were made by the Celts. Irish children carved grotesque faces on hollowed-out turnips, large potatoes, or rutabagas and placed lighted candles inside. The frightening faces were meant to scare away Witches and goblins who were thought to wander on Halloween night. After the festivities, the jack-o'-lanterns were placed in their cottage windows to protect their homes. The custom was brought to America by Irish immigrants in the nineteenth century where pumpkins eventually replaced the turnips.

Carving jack-o'-lanterns has become a fine art, and while the holiday is celebrated all over the world in many ways, nowhere does it enjoy more enthusiastic and imaginative expression than in the United States.

Many superstitions and symbols are connected with Halloween. The Irish have a tale about the origin of jack-o'-lanterns. They say that a man named Jack was unable to enter heaven because of his miserliness and he could not enter hell because he had played practical jokes on the devil. So he had to walk the earth with his lantern until Judgment Day.

Witches, Goblins, and Fairies

A Witch riding on a broomstick is one of the most popular Halloween symbols. The word "Witch" comes from the old English word, *wicca,* which means "sorceror or sorceress." Halloween's association with Witchcraft dates back to both Pagan and Christian times.

October 31 was the traditional night when devils, goblins, and Witches gathered to mock the festival of the church on the eve of All Saints' Day by holding unholy revels of their own. Organized Paganism continued even after the Church prevailed over its pageantry and superstition and many still believe in spirits and magical rites. Halloween continued to be the great Witches night, and one of the four principle Witches seasonal sabbats was celebrated on this night.

The English, Scots, and Irish believed Halloween was the time for the gathering of fairies, ghosts, goblins, elves, and trolls. It was believed that some of these spirits played pranks on Halloween night's end, and good fairies also came to confuse them and protect humans. Ghosts were thought to visit homes during the Pagan New Year's feast. They were treated to elaborate banquets and then led away by masked and costumed villagers who, representing the souls of the dead, led the ghosts out of the village.

Black Cats

The concept of a black cat as a magical and sinister object is old indeed. It is often depicted today riding with a Witch on a broomstick, but it was once worshipped as a deity. In the legends of Greece and Rome, Hecate, goddess of sorcery and patron of Witches, chose a women who had been changed into a cat as her priestess. Traditionally the black cat has been the Witch's most frequent companion and help-mate in mischief. The stealthy grace of the cat, along with its demonic glare and fiendish whiskers, made it quite naturally a symbol of Halloween. At one time it was believed that Witches could change themselves into cats at will.

We've all heard it said that it is bad luck to have a black cat cross your path. This superstition stems from an old Irish belief that meeting with a cat while on a journey will lead to a Witch appearing and causing you bad luck.

Halloween Colors

Have you ever wondered why orange and black seem to be the most frequently displayed colors for Halloween? This, too, is rooted in tradition and reflects the twin origins of the ancient holiday. Orange, being suggestive of ripened fruits, vegetables, and grains reminds us that Halloween was originally a festival of the harvest. Black, on the other hand, evokes fantasies of black magic, Witches, cats, and the mysteries of Halloween. This is a direct link to the time when Halloween was celebrated as a festival for the dead, and a night for the gathering of evil spirits.

Skeletons

Skeletons are still a favorite Halloween symbol and are often depicted on costumes. In addition to holding an attraction for children on Halloween because they are gruesome and terrifying, their association with grave-yards and the dead evokes a fear of the unknown. The Celts believed Halloween to be the night when dead souls visited their homes. As mentioned before, children love to be scared if an adult is near.

Dressing in costumes dates back to the Middle Ages when the costumes were representations of well-known saints, biblical characters, and local legends. Costumes today still reflect this idea, and while Witches and skeletons are still popular choices, many of today's favorite costumes reflect the fantasy of popular TV, movie, and storybook characters.

In neighborhoods throughout the country, children and adults can be seen outfitted as their favorite "monster" or their most fanciful dream come true. Halloween is the most widely celebrated holiday that officially sanctions using the disguises, costumes, and masks that enable children of all ages to continue an activity that begins in early childhood.

Trick or Treating

In ancient Britain, one Druid custom involved going from home to home begging for firewood and food to complete the celebration of their New Year. Another custom, in medieval times, was for the poor to go "a souling" which was the exchanging of prayers for dead souls and promising to lure bad spirits away from town in return for gifts of food. Today, most of us look forward to the sight and sound of children dressed in fanciful costumes tricking and treating through the neighborhood.

After the parade through the neighborhood is over it adds to the fun of the evening to have the children gather—outdoors if the weather permits—to build a bonfire. It is nice to have plenty of marshmallows for toasting, peanut butter or jelly sandwiches, and warm apple juice or cocoa. As the children settle down, the stage is set for story telling.

Whether there is a Full Moon or no Moon, Halloween is unquestionably a celebration of the night. It is the time when a storyteller can recount scary tales of Witches, goblins, or haunted houses with all moans, groans, and flourishes suitable to the story. Even the bravest start peeking over their shoulders.

Have A Haunted Party

Our imaginations have been haunted by Witches, ghosts, and goblins for thousands of years during Halloween, and a trip through a haunted house at this time is always scary (delightfully so), thrilling, dramatic, and magical. The haunted house, as an organized Halloween activity, has become very popular in recent years. In our own community, the Kiwanis Club has taken over the holiday under the name of "Sinawik" (the letters of their name in reverse). And they have, of course, provided the haunted house with suitable mirrors and monsters. If your community doesn't sponsor a haunted house, consider getting together with your neighbors and having a Haunted Halloween Party.

Competing in a contest is always fun and something everybody can take part in. Spreading out winners as much as possible adds to the fun.

Halloween is a perfect time for giving a reward for great costumes. The prizes should be in keeping with the spirit of the night—funny or symbolic. Prizes could be coloring books, comics, story-books, jump ropes, crayons, pencils, pens, instant photos of the children (or adults) in costume, or snack coupons to a local fast food shop or ice cream parlor. If the contest party is for children,  make sure each one gets a prize, treat, or favor of some kind. Medals made of cardboard and ribbon can be given for first, second, or third prize to be pinned on the winning costumes.

Many children of today (and quite a few adults as well) have never ridden in a horse-drawn vehicle. No matter where you live, the end of October certainly brings the end of the harvest season and the beginning of winter, and the hayride is traditional for this season. With the costumes and decorations of Halloween you have the perfect outdoor celebration for children and adults—and to many, something very different.

If you want to include a hayride for your guests, inquire among local farmers or horse stables in advance of the holiday to find out if have horses, wagons, and drivers for a weekend night near October 31. It's not quite the same, but if no horses and wagons are available, a generous splashing of hay on a flatbed truck could be used.

Some kind of entertainment during the ride is essential. A sing-a-long with guitar accompaniment, storytelling during the ride, or a square-dance, or dinner party at the end of the ride work well. If the ride is to be extensive, plan to have simple, easy-to-transport refreshments along on the ride, or prepared at the hayride site. Fruits and nuts, popcorn, doughnuts, or cookies are favorite portable foods. If older children are to participate in the hayride, be sure to get parental consent.

Halloween Dinner Party

Halloween is the perfect time to entertain a small dinner party. If you want to serve something really different to family and friends, try a "Meal-In-A-Moon." Pumpkins are ruled by the Moon and should be planted in Cancer, Scorpio, Pisces, or Libra. If you don't happen to have one of your own, buy a four to six pound pumpkin and cut off the top about one-fourth of the way down. Clean the pumpkin out, saving the seeds to be toasted later. Cut out most of the pumpkin flesh and cube it, but leave about a half-inch-thick shell. Here is the recipe for:

Meal-in-A-Moon

1 medium pumpkin, 4 to 6 ½ cups cubed

1 cup bread crumbs

2 pounds lean ground beef

2 tablespoons chopped pecans

1 cup water

2 medium onions chopped

¼ pound melted butter

Salt and pepper

1 tsp. oregano

Parsley for garnish

Cut off the top of the pumpkin about one-fourth of the way down and reserve. Place both pieces of the pumpkin, prepared as above, in a large pot of salted boiling water and parboil for 15 to 20 minutes, depending on size. Meanwhile, mix beef, onion, bread crumbs, oregano, pumpkin cubes, pecans, and salt and pepper to taste. Drain pumpkin by placing upside down on paper towels. Fill cavity with the meat mixture. Add top as a cover. Place in a buttered baking dish, brush outside with melted butter, adding one cup of water to bottom of dish. Bake 45 minutes to an hour at 350° in a preheated oven. Test for doneness by removing top of pumpkin and piercing the inside flesh with a knife to check for tenderness. Remove pumpkin carefully with two wide spatulas, place on a serving dish and garnish with parsley. Serves 4 to 8.

Various additions may be made to mixture such as cooked broccoli or green peas.

Cheese Corn Sticks

Corn is so much a part of the harvest, dating back to the days that the Native Americans brought it as a gift to the early settlers, that it seems appropriate to accompany the "Meal-In-A-Moon" with these delicious corn sticks:

1 cup sifted flour

2 teaspoons baking powder

½ cup grated cheese

1 teaspoon sugar

1 egg

½ cup butter, melted

1 ½ teaspoon salt

2 ½ cups whole kernel corn

Stir together flour, sugar, salt, and baking powder. Add corn, cheese, and butter to well-beaten egg. Combine with dry ingredients. Spoon batter into hot, greased, cornstick pan sections. Bake at 425° 10 to 15 minutes. Makes 12 sticks.

Chocolate Popcorn Balls

2 cups sugar

1 teaspoon vanilla extract

8 cups popcorn

½ cup water

Melted coating chocolate

Pinch cream of tartar

½ teaspoon almond extract

Cook the sugar, water, and cream of tartar to the hardball stage; then add the flavors. Pour a portion of the syrup over the popcorn and let the remainder stand in a warm place. Form into small popcorn balls, then dip them into the remaining syrup, one at a time. Lay on waxed paper to become firm, then dip into melted chocolate. Wrap in waxed paper. Store in a cool place.

Relationships and the Moon

David Pond

The Moon pulls at the oceans and gives them their tides. So too it pulls at your emotional nature and represents how you adapt to the ever changing tides of your emotions. The Moon represents what you need from life to feel comfortable, supported, and nurtured. It also represents how you nurture yourself and others. Your Moon sign governs much of your instinctual and habitual way of being—the pull of the past. Representing where your habits are at, it thus finds expression in your habitat. By following its lead, you are led to the type of home and environment you would thrive in. Your comfort zone is described by your Moon, and last, but certainly not least, your Moon sign describes how you most naturally express your emotions.

All these issues are important in a relationship and the importance of compatible Moons in a relationship can't be overstated. I once overheard a conversation between one of my astrology students and her friend who was asking her about the important clues to look for in assessing birth charts as to their compatibility. Her response was eloquent in its simplicity: "Make sure the Moons are happy." Her reply points to the importance of the Moon in relationships—it must be considered just as important as the Sun for compatibility. Before we explore the Moon through each of the signs, let's explore the Moon and the emotional needs of life.

If you are a Moon watcher, you've noticed that it rises at a different time each night and appears a slightly different shape as well. The Moon is the most changeable of all the heavenly bodies—every twenty-eight days it goes through its complete cycle, from the New Moon to Full Moon and back again. This changeability of the Moon is an important aspect of understanding its relationship to the human psyche as well. It represents how you respond to the ever-changing panorama of life.

Our Western culture has not prepared us for this side of our character. Even our language betrays us with labels for our moods as "up" and "down." The obvious problem with this labeling is the assumption that half the cycle is considered not favorable. If you ask me how I am feeling and I respond with, "I'm feeling down today," that might put pressure on you to somehow cheer me up and get me out of my bad mood. This starts early in life whenever we say to a child, "What's wrong?" or tell them to smile for mommy, and so on.

I prefer the Eastern labels of yin and yang, or even "inward" and "outward" for giving a healthier understanding of this cyclic nature of our being. Be mindful of these culturally ingrained attitudes when dealing with the emotional cycles of your relationship partner. Try to avoid asking what's wrong, implying it is not good to be withdrawn, or asking why they feel that certain way, implying it was a decision to feel a particular way. A more helpful line of questioning might be to ask how they are feeling, or asking what they are going through as these are open questions and do not carry implied judgments.

We have been raised in a culture that believes everything stacks up neatly under intellect. It is not true. Our intellect (Mercury) and our emotions (Moon) operate autonomously of each other, and we don't decide to feel, we simply do.

Although we all respond in various ways to these Moon cycles, we all experience them. I suspect the moodiness that many people experience is simply a noncreative way of aligning with these cycles and rhythms. When you are feeling low, can you go with the energy and cultivate enriching inward experiences? All spiritual activity—prayer, meditation, worship, etc., is inward turning, but it is also enriching. Creative experiences, walking alone in nature and contemplating life, reading certain books, and listening to certain music can put us in touch with this inward turning tide in proactive ways altogether different than simply being in a bad mood. Then, when the tide of your emotional character shifts and you come out of the inward phase, you are refreshed from your experience and ready to project your energy outward again.

Chart Your Cycles

It could be helpful to familiarize yourself with the natural rhythm of your emotions by charting your cycles on a calendar. (An astrological calendar with the Moon signs would be best.) When you first wake up in the morning, before you involve yourself with the day, assess your emotional state. Use a scale of +3 to –3 to rate your general mood. Ecstatic would be +3, neutral would be 0, and –3 would be the blues. Just take stock of your emotional nature before the day starts providing "reasons" for your moods. Write your assessment on the calendar. After a few months, notice if there are cycles that can be discerned. Are there patterns with your moods and signs of the Moon?

The Moon Through the Signs

As you read the Moon through each of the signs, consider the people you know with this placement to see if this helps you better understand their emotional style. When reading about your own placement, consider creative, proactive methods for allowing for your natural emotional needs.

Moon in Aries

The fiery nature of your Moon in Aries animates your emotional nature with pure energy. Your emotions are intense and spontaneous, and you need a relationship that allows for this exuberance. If blocked, this fiery energy turns feisty and relationships can become a battleground. Your emotional nature requires excitement. Since you act in the moment on your emotional feelings, you keep the air clear in a relationship. If you are feeling something, whatever it is, it gets expressed. Fortunately, once expressed, you are done with it and typically carry no grudges. You love surprises and need a relationship that keeps this part of you happy. You seem to be like an emotional cheerleader, always inspiring and motivating others to take action in their lives. At best, you provide an eternal spark that keeps your relationships dynamic and alive.

Areas to work on: impatience, intolerance, and wanting every experience to be the best one ever can make it difficult for others to relax in your presence. Without stepping out of yourself and becoming aware of other people's needs, you run the risk of becoming insensitive without even knowing it. Aries understands life by direct experiences; this is appropriate, but also makes it difficult to develop the empathy necessary for close emotional relationships. There is nothing wrong with your intensity, you are born with it, but your energy can simply be too much for certain individuals. You tend to run at high all the time, but you'll need to learn to allow others their down time. Believe it or not, not everyone wants to be up all the time!

Moon in Taurus

The Moon is very much at home in earthy Taurus and your emotional nature is rooted in the natural world. You have deep appreciation for what is real and genuine, and these are certainly qualities you will look for in others. Sensual and affectionate, you need a "hands on" relationship that is not always sexual—simple human touch is very gratifying for you, especially around the neck and shoulders. You have enduring emotions and want a relationship that can build on what is real. You tend to shy away from excessively complex relationships and flighty individuals. Security, stability, and continuity are important for your emotional well-being and you thrive in relationships that offer these qualities. Your love is long lasting and you want to be with someone you can depend on. Taurus is the connoisseur of the zodiac, and you have an eye for quality, whether concerning possessions or people. Although you like nice things, you also appreciate life's simple pleasures and want a relationship with a partner to share life's uncomplicated joys.

Areas to work on: your great strength is to hold your ground in the face of change, but this is also your weakness when life presents situations that you must adapt to. You can be stubborn, rigid, and inflexible and these tendencies will certainly cause problems in your love life. When you find yourself resisting change, ask yourself if it's really in your best interest to make a stand in this situation. If change and adaptation is really what is being called for, get out of your own way and seek to find security in the new situation. You are vulnerable to any perceived threats (real or imagined) to your security. This can block growth by inhibiting the desire to try new experiences. Stretch your comfort zone every once in awhile to allow opportunities for growth in your relationship

Moon in Gemini

With your Moon in Gemini, you have a lively, engaging emotional nature. Gemini relates to life through the mind, and this blending of the mental realm with the Moon's emotional nature leads to a very intellectual approach to emotions. You need to be with a partner who can talk with you through emotional issues. Gemini likes the comfort of words to distance themselves from the raw emotions. This need for mental stimulation leads to a busy life with variety. The wrong partner would consider your emotional nature flighty and fickle, yet the right partner finds your variety of interests stimulating and exciting. Too much routine in a relationship bogs you down and is tiresome; you want to be with a partner who is open to explore the many fascinating interests that life affords. Your childlike openness and curiosity would thrive in a relationship that allowed you room to express your naturally flirtatious character with people you meet throughout the day. You would not do well with the strong silent type.

Areas to work on: Your emotional agility can mask a discomfort with sinking into the emotional experience that others experience as extremely difficult to pin down. You can always adapt and head off in a new direction, but can you stick with an encounter to experience the fullness of the moment? If you constantly change directions, you miss much of the depth of your relationships. This same changeability can cause you to constantly second-guess yourself. This can also make it difficult to sink into the depth of the moment by always staying on the lookout in case something better comes along.

Moon in Cancer

The Moon is said to rule the sign of Cancer and is at its strongest here. You are a nurturer and caregiver and need to be needed. Home and family issues are the strength of Cancer, and you need to be able to share this most intimate side of life with your partner. It might take you time to allow another into your inner most world, but once you establish this closeness, you are the most loyal of all. You need to be involved in your partner's personal life, and you need to be able to feel his or her emotions. It is intolerable when others close off this part of who they are to you. Cancer is meant to take everything personally and you would need a partner who understands that your emotional nature is not a bad thing that should be fixed! Once you learn that it is safe to feel your emotions, you help others access this same depth of meaning in their lives as well. You are deeply sentimental and value an attentive partner.

Areas to work on: Cancer attaches with great tenacity to whatever, or whomever, they bond with. This attachment can turn into clinging when it goes too far, then others can feel your love as smothering rather than mothering. Remember, when you identify another person as the source of your needs being met, you essentially become a drain to that person; you always need something. When this is the case, you would be advised to work on filling your own cup with life throughout the day. Then, when you bond with your partner, you will be sharing your fullness instead of your emptiness. Cancer can become overly attached to the past; so another issue to work on would be learning to allow new growth in your relationships.

Moon in Leo

Leo is the star of the zodiac and you like to express your emotions with dramatic flair. You have a radiant personality and a big heart. Generally playful, you prefer to celebrate life rather than just trudge along, and feel comfortable with love expressed in a big way. You like to have fun and seek out ways to make a relationship entertaining. With your winning personality, you are used to getting your way. Your fiery nature is best suited for an action-oriented relationship that stresses the personal aspect of life. You are very loyal to those you love, demanding an up-close and personal relationships. Actually, you demand a lot out of others, but you offer just as much. You simply will not tolerate being on the back burner in your partner's life. You believe life is meant to be lived with gusto and you don't want a partner who will hold you back. Fun, play, romance, recreation, children, and creativity; not such bad homework, and these are the aspects of life that you want to share with your partner.

Areas to work on: Pride is a wonderful emotion when you've done something well, but this same pride all too easily gets in the way when you are at odds with others. The fire signs are naturally defensive, and Leo is chief among them in this regard. The tendency to defend first and consider the other person's view points later must be overcome to establish a healthy rapport with others. Your will power is admirable and will serve you well in many a life test, but it also makes you stubborn and resistant to change even when change is in your best interest.

Moon in Virgo

Your emotional expression is most often sincere and genuine, and you certainly value these qualities in others. Virgo is uncomfortable with the highs and lows of intense emotions, preferring to steer a steady, level course. When you are in the throes of deep emotion, your style is to work through it by finding some task or chore to throw yourself into until the mood passes. Virgos lives by the adage "A friend in need is a friend indeed." When you care for someone, you express your feelings by being helpful.

Your fastidious nature will play out in relationships. You would appreciate a partner who has a good wardrobe, who is well groomed, and

who would enjoy sharing simple daily tasks together. Health related activities, including trying new diets and forms of exercise, would also be favorite shared activities, as well as involvement with nature. You prefer to keep your life simple and uncluttered, and are most comfortable with a partner who also enjoys the beauty of simplicity.

Areas to work on: The perfectionistic tendencies of Virgo, when applied to the emotional nature of the Moon, show you to be way too hard on yourself, and at times, others. You tend to analyze your emotions and try to figure them out, instead of simply feeling them. To expect perfection with some type of craft or skill is one thing, but is out of place with emotions. You need to cut yourself, and others, a little slack to broaden your range of what is acceptable in a relationship. Your task-oriented approach to life can squeeze out the needed time to cultivate the fun and romance of a relationship. If your schedule is the problem, it can also be the solution—schedule a weekly "date night" and other nurturing activities for your relationships as well.

Moon in Libra

Libra is said to rule relationships, and with the Moon here, your emotional nature is fed by relating to others. Your emotional nature is quite refined, so style, eloquence, and class are important to you in a partner. For you, a romantic evening might be to get all dressed up and attend a culural event. Ambience is everything. No one has more natural grace and charm than those with Moon in Libra. You abhor the rude and crude elements of life. In relationships, you feel most comfortable in a relationship where major decisions are shared; you want to hear your partner's opinions before making up your own mind, and you're more willing than most to make concessions for your partner's emotional needs

Areas to work on: You tend to avoid unpleasant issues as if they were the plague! On the one hand, if you avoid an unpleasant encounter with your partner and the issue truly goes away, that's great. But if you sidestep an important issue and it doesn't really go away, it becomes like the elephant in the living room that nobody is talking about. This wouldn't be the high road at all—it is simply denial and avoidance. Every relationship does have its share of unpleasantries to deal with and you must learn to stand up and negotiate the situation in a way that is in everyone's best interest.

Moon in Scorpio

You have a deeply passionate, intense emotional nature, which thrives in relationships that allow for this. Casual and easy love is not your style. You need to feel your partner's emotions and passions, not just know they are there. You get the hidden meaning beneath the words being spoken and can feel the intentions of others, so no one can pull the wool over your eyes nor deceive you. However, like a moth to the flame, your early relationships are often stormy, passionate, almost desperate, as all those with Moon in Scorpio seem to have to work through abandonment and betrayal issues of one type or another. Eventually, you learn that trust must be impeccable in your primary relationships, otherwise it brings out parts of your character that you don't even like. With trust, the beauty of Scorpio is entered into transformational intimacy. You are also very good with handling money, even shrewd, and are most comfortable managing shared resources in a relationship. You also come up with good ideas for you and your partner to invest your resources (time, money, and energy) together.

Areas to work on: Mistrust and buried resentments are the chief culprits that can interfere with healthy relationships for Scorpio. Jealousy and possessiveness can also block the flow of love in your life. Realize the absolute futility of resentments that get pushed beneath the surface where they cannot be dealt with. Resentments will happen, but make a vow not to let them carry over to the following day. Make a vow to process the issues, learn the lessons and let go of it, before you go to sleep. Otherwise these untended to issues will accumulate and you will start the next day in the hole.

Moon in Sagittarius

With the Moon in fiery Sagittarius, you have an exciting, enthusiastic, and upbeat emotional nature that thrives on action, exploration of life and the mind, and traveling. A companion who would travel with you, as Sagittarius is most at home on the road, and who appreciates a good philosophical debate (not arguments), would be perfect as you need a partner who can engage you on that level. Honesty is a must; dishonesty might be the only transgression you can't forgive. You are high-minded and even religious, and need to believe in the morals and ethics of your partner to sustain your love. Your positive outlook and generally upbeat emotional nature requires a relationship that doesn't have a lot of down time.

Areas to work on: The downfall of Sagittarius can be a dogmatic, evangelical, "holier than thou" attitude that can be a real put-off to others. Make sure that you have expanded your own perspective on life before you encourage others to do the same. Look into the various religions, philosophies, and political views that are expressed on our planet. Then, when you attempt to inspire others to a larger view, you won't be simply proselytizing your own narrow perspective. Another area that can be a difficult is dealing with the downside of emotional cycles. It can feel as if you are drowning or being suffocated when you experience other people's deep emotions. Your tendency is to immediately rise up and frame it in a positive light. This is natural for you, but can leave others feeling unsupported in their experience.

Moon in Capricorn

Capricorn, ruled by Saturn, gives you a rather serious and controlled emotional nature. You pride yourself in being competent and resourceful and this will certainly have an impact on your relationships. You are not a person that presents your needs easily, often leading others to feel as if you do not need them. Look for a commitment-based relationship with another task-oriented person that is willing to build a life together, shoulder to shoulder, pitching in and getting the work done of creating a successful life together. You are responsible, accountable, and punctual and would value these qualities in another. Most comfortable in the role of being a provider, you need a relationship with someone who respects your ambitions and need to achieve. Mutual respect is ultimately quite important to you, and you are much more attracted to sincerity and genuineness than the "song and dance" type of person. Your ideal partner would be able to get underneath all of this protocol to the soft spot within you that only mates and children ever reach into and bring into the light. With those closest, you can be wonderfully gentle and affectionate.

Areas to work on: "Work" is your default setting, so you tend to get an "A" in task-oriented activities, and fail miserably when it comes to play. True, you need a partner that supports your career ambitions, but you would benefit by someone who reminds you when life is becoming imbalanced and some play is in order. You always seem granite strong to others and professionally, this is an advantage, but in your personal relationships, this will be a handicap. You need to learn how to reveal your vulnerabilities and sensitivities to those closest to you, or your relationships can suffer a lack of intimacy.

Moon in Aquarius

Intellectual Aquarius tends to approach emotions through the mind. You are more comfortable talking about your emotions than actually feeling them, so this mental realm will need to be a strong area of sharing in a relationship. You value those who stand for their own thoughts rather than simply accepting the values of others. Your emotional nature requires independence and freedom, so you will need a partner that does not hold on too tightly. You are just as willing to grant a great deal of freedom to your partner, but if you feel too reined in, trouble begins. Friendships are a source of strength for you, thus you want a partner who can be a best friend and is secure enough to allow you enough freedom to pursue your friendships outside of your main relationship. Although unconventional, you are undoubtedly loyal to the max in all your friendships. You value that which is most unique in others and seem to live by the adage "Don't judge me, I won't judge you." To be with a partner who dwells too much on personal emotional feelings is restrictive to your nature—you prefer to rise above this personal level and see things from the big picture. Your beauty is that you constantly challenge a relationship to grow beyond conventions.

Areas to work on: Others can translate your natural aloofness as insensitivity unless you cultivate empathy and patience with your partner's emotional issues. Aquarius is naturally uncomfortable in the deep waters of emotion and seeks to rise up out of it to get some air. Your partner can feel totally invalidated at the emotional level unless you cultivate simple listening skills. If you are still at the stage of Aquarius where you need to "prove" your freedom, you'll spend more time dodging emotional commitments than actually settling into the relationship. When you get on to "expressing your right to be free," the edge is gone in your emotional nature and you simply act on your uniqueness and individuality, thus attracting support, rather than conflict.

Moon in Pisces

Pisces is the most sensitive of all the signs and, since the Moon rules your emotional nature, your sensitivity will certainly affect your relationships. You are compassionate and supportive of others, making it important for you to choose a partner who would not take advantage of you. Pisces is an incurable romantic and with your Moon here, you thrive in a relationship that is rich in emotional content—you need to be able to feel what is going on with your partner. You are quite comfortable in a supportive role and most often choose a partner who is strong and assertive in the world, but benefits from your emotional support. However, you can go the opposite direction and fall in love with a person who is not making it at all in the world, but whom you believe in. Your inner world is immense and you need some quality alone time everyday to drop into your comfort zone, so ideally your partner would give you space in your relationship to allow for this. Your emotional capacity is expansive enough to totally engulf your partner with your love, but you will likely have to watch for codependency tendencies, as you will carry your partner's emotional issues as if they were your own. You can be sweet, kind, and gentle and would benefit from a relationship in which you can be devotional.

Areas to work on: Martyring, self-denial and self-pity are the downside of Moon in Pisces. It is too easy to put yourself last in your relationships, and then indulge a "woe is me" attitude. There can be a difficulty in separating your emotions from those of others with this placement. It is likely that you get caught up in worrying too much about those you care for, essentially smothering others with your fears. Your natural compassionate nature can easily turn to pitying others, or feeling the pain of others and not being able to free yourself. You cannot turn a deaf ear to the suffering in the world; that is simply not going to happen. But you could learn to "lay other people's problems on the lap of God" so you are not carrying this heaviness in your heart.

Hesiod's Ancient Almanac and Days of the Month

Bruce Schofield

Roughly 2,700 years ago in ancient Greece, writing began to be used to record the stories that had formerly been kept in the memories of professional storytellers. This was the time of the transition between the oral tradition and the written tradition, an event perhaps not unlike the transition from print to digital media that is taking place today. The first two Greek writers, Homer and Hesiod, are still read by students, classicists, and historians today. Their "books" were the epic poems of Homer, *The Iliad* and *The Odyssey*, and a collection of long poems attributed to Hesiod (Hee'-see-odd) that include the *Works and Days* and the *Theogony*. All of Hesiod's works, and those of Homer as well, were written in dactylic hexameter meter, probably because that was the easiest way for these carriers of the oral tradition to keep them memorized.

Not much is known about Hesiod. From his writings we are able to glean bits and pieces, but there is much uncertainty and scholars will likely debate the details of his life for centuries to come. It does appear that Hesiod's father was a sailor and farmer, and due to financial problems, moved from Asia Minor to mainland Greece. He had two sons, Perses and Hesiod, to whom he left his land. Hesiod's brother Perses managed to get the larger share of the inheritance, by bribing a corrupt local ruler. He then proceeded to run his farm into the ground. In his book *Works and Days*, Hesiod portrays his brother as greedy, a spendthrift, and an idler, and he directs most of his advice on how to live the good life to Perses.

Hesiod became a farmer, and if his writings are any indication of how he operated his farm, he was like a Boy Scout, doing everything properly and honestly. He believed passionately in two things, justice and hard work. As for why he was motivated to put his knowledge about farming in writing, Hesiod tells us that one day, while tending sheep on Mt. Helicon, he actually met the Muses. They taught him a glorious song which eventually became the text of *Works and Days*. Another reference to Hesiod's life mentions an important poet's contest, which he won. Hesiod apparently died violently, murdered while traveling home

after winning the poetry contest. He was staying at a family's house and was killed by two sons who suspected him of seducing their sister. They threw his body into the ocean, but it was brought ashore by dolphins and later buried.

Portions of poems attributed to Hesiod, and references to Hesiod's writings that appear in later Greek writings, indicate that he wrote on many subjects, including topics like astrology and divination by birds. In some cases, the fragments of these writings that have survived the ages are questioned by scholars as to their authenticity. The authenticity of his book the *Theogony*, a work on the Greek gods and their origins, is not in doubt and it remains an indispensable reference to this subject. Hesiod's *Works and Days* is of special interest to readers of the *Moon Sign Book* because it is essentially an almanac that guides one through the cycle of the year and the cycle of the month.

The first, and larger, portion of *Works and Days* describes the cycle of the year and how a resourceful and honest person should live it. This section begins with a lengthy introduction devoted to the gods intermixed with Hesiod's opinions on justice and what is right and what is wrong. It immediately becomes apparent to the reader that his brother Perses clearly falls into the later category.

Throughout *Works and Days* Hesiod offered advice, much of which is relevant today. For example, Hesiod said, "He does mischief to himself who does mischief to another, and evil planned harms the plotter most." This notion, that negative thoughts can implode within oneself and cause all sorts of mental and physical problems is a tenet of today's New Age philosophy. Throughout his poem, Hesiod relentlessly promoted honesty and hard work as exemplified in the line "If your heart within you desires wealth, do these things [the practical advice he gave out] and work with work upon work." Hesiod believed that the right way to satisfy desire was to work for it. What this line also tells me is that Hesiod's world was probably far from idyllic, it was filled with rotten people—or why would he have made these points over and over again. What's very interesting about Hesiod is that, unlike Homer, he was addressing the common man. While Homer told tales of heroes, Hesiod told of farmers and woodsmen who cut the wood for the ships that Homer's heroes sailed to glory on.

Still, Hesiod was far from the world of today. Like the larger society that he belonged to, Hesiod drew sharp lines between women and men. "Do not let a flaunting woman coax and cozen and deceive you: she is after your barn. The man who trusts womankind trusts deceivers." Hesiod also offered men some advice about marriage. He recommended that a man should marry around the age of thirty, preferably to a younger woman grown up five years (about age eighteen to twenty). In Hesiod's times, this was probably very good advice for bachelors.

Astronomical references abound in the text of the *Works and Days* and inform the reader as to when specific agricultural activities should be commenced. Ploughing should begin at the Winter Solstice, and vines should be pruned sixty days after this event. Grain should be winnowed when Orion rises just before dawn, which is in July, but when Orion is at the Midheaven just before dawn, in September, it's time to pick the grapes. Having outlined the cycle of the year, which is based on the movement of the Sun and its relationships to the prominent constellations, Hesiod then addressed the cycle of the Moon. This later section of *Works and Days* is pure astrology.

The Moon's cycle of about twenty-nine days was counted by the ancient Greeks in several ways. First, there was the basic cycle itself, which varied between twenty-nine or thirty whole days (days don't come in fractions—this is the origin of our months of varying days). The cycle of the Moon, or month, traditionally began at sunset with the first appearance of the crescent Moon just after the New Moon. It ended with the Moon's disappearance into the early morning rays of the Sun just before the next New Moon. The second way the cycle was counted was by dividing it into waxing and waning halves. The fourteen or fifteen days before the Full Moon, days when the illuminated portion of the Moon gradually extends to fullness, are the waxing days. As the Moon moves in its cycle from Full to New Moon, the illuminated portion declines. This is the waning half of the cycle. The third way of counting the cycle of the Moon was by dividing it into thirds of ten days each. The first third Hesiod called the waxing month, the middle third was called the midmonth, and the final third the waning month.

In *Works and Days*, Hesiod uses all three counting traditions to describe the various points in the Moon's cycle that are good or bad for one thing or another. He first counts the entire cycle, referring to the positive qualities of the first, fourth, and seventh days of the Moon (the first day being the day on which the crescent appears after the New Moon, about one to one-and-a-half days after the New Moon). He then shifts into another way of counting the cycle and says the sixth day of the midmonth is bad for plants. This day, six days into the second third of the cycle, is also day sixteen of the Moon, the day after the Full Moon. (I'm pointing this out because I want to let readers understand how Hesiod wrote and how I arranged the list below should they look up the original text).

Hesiod's "good" and "bad" days of the lunar month, all the days that are noted in his *Works and Days*, are organized below in a form easier to read than the original poem. I've added a few comments in parentheses. Here is the scheme of the world's first lunar almanac, one that predates this *Moon Sign Book* by 2,700 years!

Starting from the crescent one day after New Moon:

1   A holy day.

4   A holy day, and a day for bringing home a bride. A good day to open a jar. (By opening a jar, Hesiod probably means a jar of food or perhaps wine. I would think this day, which is the favorable sextile between the Sun and Moon, is a good one for new beginnings of almost any kind.)

5   A holy day, but also potentially bad.

6   Unfavorable for female births, but good for gelding goats and sheep, and for building a fenced-in pen. More favorable for the birth of a boy, though he will be sharp-tongued, cunning, and stealthful. (This is the day leading up the square between the Sun and Moon at the first quarter, which according to traditional astrology, is a time of stress, though favorable for doing construction work.)

7   First Quarter.

8   Good for getting work done, and for gelding boars and bulls.

9   Good for getting work done. A good day to be born,

whether male or female. Never a totally evil day. (Both this day and the previous day follow the stressful first quarter but are within the period of the waxing Moon. In traditional astrology, the period of the waxing Moon is the time to move things along toward fruition at the Full Moon.)

10 Favorable for the birth of males. (This is the first trine between the Moon and the Sun, a time long considered by astrologers as favorable for doing most things.)

11 Excellent for shearing sheep and picking fruits. (Obviously, this means a good time for harvesting).

12 Even better for shearing sheep and picking fruits, a good day for a woman to work on her loom and get on with her work. A good day for gelding hard-working mules. (Notice that this day and the previous, days that occur just before the climax of the Full Moon, are days for harvesting. This makes perfect sense if one sees the Full Moon as the point of "ripeness" in the total lunar cycle.)

13 Don't sow seeds now. Favorable for nurturing plants. (This is too close to the Full Moon for starting plants, or other things as well.)

14 The holiest of days. Favorable for the birth of females. Favorable for taming sheep and oxen, dogs, and mules. Favorable to begin building narrow ships. (This and the next day are the Full Moon, a time of spiritual climax that may have been reflected in religious rituals of Hesiod's time. It is also a time of decisiveness, which is needed to tame animals or to make fast ships. It is also the time when the Moon is a rival to the Sun, and perhaps this is the reason for it being a favorable day for female births.)

15 Full Moon.

16 Unfavorable for plants, but good for the birth of males. Not favorable for female births or for weddings.

17 Thresh grain, cut beams for building. (Notice that this day, near the beginning of the waning portion of the lunar cycle, is favorable for threshing or processing grain, not for harvesting

it. It follows that this point of the lunar cycle is good for continuing work on activities that were begun during a waxing Moon.

19 Conditions improve toward evening. (On this day the Moon is moving toward the favorable trine aspect to the Sun.)

20 A day on which wise men are born. (This day is when the favorable trine between Sun and Moon form, and right before the third quarter of the Moon, which is a square between Sun and Moon. According to Dane Rudhyar, one of the most important astrologers of the twentieth-century, the third quarter represents a "crisis of consciousness" in the unfolding of human life. In other words, this quarter differs from the first quarter, considered a "crisis in action," by being a time that produces challenges of the mind. It follows then that intelligent people might be born just before or near this part of the lunar cycle.)

22 Third Quarter.

24 Avoid troubles. A fateful day, worse in evening.

27 Favorable for opening wine jars, for yoking oxen and mules, and launching a ship. (Why this day, so near to the end of the cycle, should be good for such things is not clear to me.)

29 New Moon.

30 New Moon. The best day for supervising work done and giving out rations. (This makes sense as one cycle is closing while another is coming into being. It's a time for evaluating things.)

You've no doubt noticed that Hesiod left out many days. Of these he says, "The other days are meaningless, untouched by fortune. Men have days they favor, but few really know." What I think Hesiod means by this statement is that other traditions may have something to say about these other days, but he doesn't recognize them as important.

Do the astrological fortunes of the days really work? In general, you'll notice that the delineations for the waxing (first half) of the lunar cycle are both more positive and plentiful than those of the waning half. There is also the testimony of traditional Western astrology to consider.

Notice that the day before the first quarter is considered bad. This is in keeping with the astrological notion that the square between the Sun and Moon, which forms at the first and third quarters, is stressful, and that activities should not be commenced just before it becomes exact. Theoretically, the fortune of the 21st day should also be bad. Also notice that the day before the Full Moon is very fa-

vorable, but the day after unfavorable. Astrology points to the Full Moon as being the climax of the lunar cycle, decline sets in just after the alignment between the Sun and Moon become exact. Days 10 and 20, the days near the trine aspect between Sun and Moon, are days of good fortune, again consistent with the astrological doctrine of the essential positiveness of the trine aspect.

Hesiod's *Works and Days* is a fascinating almanac, and also a window through which we can see what life was like in ancient Greece. His account of the lunar cycle recounted here is a record of a kind of "living" astrology that was deeply integrated into the lives of these early hardworking farmers, except for Hesiod's lazy brother Perses, of course.

LLEWELLYN'S

Business
& Legal
Ventures

Business & Legal Ventures

How to Choose the Best Dates

When starting a new business or any type of new venture, check to make sure that the Moon is in the first or second quarter. This will help it get off to a better start. If there is a deadlock, it will often be broken during the Full Moon. You should also check the aspects of the Moon to the planet that rules the type of venture with which you are becoming involved. Look for positive aspects to the planet that rules the activity in the Lunar Aspectarian (pages 28–51), and avoid any dates marked Q or O.

Planetary Business Rulerships

Listed below are the planets and the business activities that they rule. If you follow the guidelines given above and apply them to the occupations or activities listed for each planet, you should have excellent results in your new business ventures. Even if it is not a new venture, check the aspects to the ruler of the activity before making moves in your business.

Sun: Advertising, executive positions, acting, finance, government, jewelry, law, and public relations

Mercury: Accounting, brokerage, clerical, disc jockey, doctor, editor, inspector, librarian, linguist, medical technician, scientist, teacher, writer, publishing, communication, and mass media

Venus: Architect, art and artist, beautician, dancer, designer, fashion and marketing, musician, poet, and chiropractor

Mars: Barber, butcher, carpenter, chemist, construction, dentist, metal worker, surgeon, and soldier

Jupiter: Counseling, horse training, judge, lawyer, legislator, minister, pharmacist, psychologist, public analyst, social clubs, research, and self-improvement

Saturn: Agronomy, math, mining, plumbing, real estate, repairperson, printer, papermaking, and working with older people

Uranus: Aeronautics, broadcasting, electrician, inventing, lecturing, radiology, and computers

Neptune: Photography, investigator, institutions, shipping, pets, movies, wine merchant, health foods, resorts, travel by water, and welfare

Pluto: Acrobatics, athletic manager, atomic energy, research, speculation, sports, stockbroker, and any purely personal endeavors

Business Activities

Advertising, General

Write ads on a favorable Sun sign day while Mercury or Jupiter is conjunct, sextile, or trine the Moon. Mars and Saturn should not be aspecting the Moon by square, opposition, or conjunction. Ad campaigns are best when the Moon is well aspected in Taurus, Cancer, Sagittarius, or Aquarius.

Advertising, Newspaper

The Moon should be conjunct, sextile, or trine Mercury or Jupiter.

Advertising, Television, Radio, or Internet

The Moon should be in the first or second quarter in the signs of Gemini, Sagittarius, or Aquarius. The Moon should be conjunct, sextile, or trine (C, X, or T) Uranus, and Uranus should be sextile or trine (X or T) Jupiter.

Business, Education

When you begin training, see that your lunar cycle is favorable that day and that the planet ruling your occupation is marked C or T.

Business, Opening

The Moon should be in Taurus, Virgo, or Capricorn and in the first or second quarter. It should also be sextile or trine (X or T) Jupiter or Saturn.

Business, Remodeling

The Moon should be trine or sextile Jupiter, Saturn, or Pluto, or conjunct Jupiter.

Business, Starting

In starting a business of your own, see that the Moon is free of afflictions and that the planet ruling the business is marked C or T.

Buying

Buy during the third quarter, when the Moon is in Taurus for quality, or in a mutable sign (Gemini, Virgo, Sagittarius, or Pisces) for savings. Good aspects from Venus or the Sun are desirable. If you are buying for yourself, it is good if the day is favorable to your Sun sign.

Buying Clothing

See that the Moon is sextile or trine to the Sun during the first or second quarters. During Moon in Taurus, buying clothes will bring satisfaction. Do not buy clothing or jewelry when the Moon is in Scorpio or Aries. Buying clothes is best on a favorable day for your Sun sign and when Venus or Mercury is well aspected, but avoid aspects to Mars and Saturn.

Buying Furniture

Follow the rules for machinery and appliances but buy when the Moon is in Libra too. Buy antiques when the Moon is in Cancer, Scorpio, or Capricorn.

Buying Machinery, Appliances, or Tools

Tools, machinery, and other implements should be bought on days when your lunar cycle is favorable and when Mars and Uranus are trine (T), sextile (X), or conjunct (C) the Moon. Any quarter of the Moon is suitable. When buying gas or electrical appliances, the Moon should be in Aquarius.

Buying Stock

The Moon should be in Taurus or Capricorn, and should be sextile or trine (X or T) Jupiter and Saturn.

Collections

Try to make collections on days when your Sun is well aspected. Avoid days when Mars or Saturn are aspected. If possible, the Moon should be in a cardinal sign: Aries, Cancer, Libra, or Capricorn. It is more difficult to collect when the Moon is in Taurus or Scorpio.

Consultants, Work With

The Moon should be conjunct, sextile, or trine Mercury or Jupiter.

Contracts

The Moon should be in a fixed sign and sextile, trine, or conjunct Mercury.

Contracts, Bid on

The Moon should be in the sign of Libra, and either the Moon or Mercury should be conjunct, sextile, or trine (C, X, or T) Jupiter.

Copyrights/Patents, Apply for

The Moon should be conjunct, trine, or sextile Mercury or Jupiter.

Electronics, Buying

When buying electronics, choose a day when the Moon is in an air sign (Gemini, Libra, or Aquarius) and well aspected by Mercury and/or Uranus.

Electronics, Repair

The Moon should be sextile or trine Mars or Uranus in one of the following signs: Taurus, Leo, Scorpio, or Aquarius.

Legal Matters

A good aspect between the Moon and Jupiter is best for a favorable legal decision. To gain damages in a lawsuit, begin during the increase of the Moon. In seeking to avoid payment, set a court date when the Moon is decreasing. A good Moon-Sun aspect strengthens your chance of success. In divorce cases, a favorable Moon-Venus aspect is best. Moon in Cancer or Leo and well aspected by the Sun brings the best results in custody cases.

Loans

Moon in the first and second quarters favors the lender, in the third and fourth favors the borrower. Good aspects of Jupiter and Venus to the Moon are favorable to both, as is the Moon in Leo, Sagittarius, Aquarius, or Pisces.

Mailing

For best results, send mail on favorable days for your Sun sign. The Moon in Gemini is good, as are Virgo, Sagittarius, and Pisces.

Mining

Saturn rules mining. Begin work when Saturn is marked C, T, or X. Mine for gold when the Sun is marked C, T, or X. Mercury rules quicksilver, Venus rules copper, Jupiter rules tin, Saturn rules lead and coal, Uranus rules radioactive elements, Neptune rules oil, the Moon rules water— mine for these items when the ruling planet is marked C, T, or X.

New Job, Beginning

Jupiter and Venus should be sextile, trine, or conjunct the Moon.

News

The handling of news is related to Uranus, Mercury, and the air signs. An increase in spectacular news occurs when Uranus is aspected.

Photography, Radio, TV, Film, and Video

Neptune, Venus, and Mercury should be well aspected. The act of photographing does not depend on particular Moon phase, but Neptune rules photography, and Venus rules beauty in line, form, and color.

Promotions

Choose a day when your Sun sign is favorable. Mercury should be marked C, T, or X. Avoid days when Mars or Saturn is aspected.

Selling or Canvassing

Begin these activities during a favorable Sun sign day. Otherwise, sell on days when Jupiter, Mercury, or Mars is trine, sextile, or conjunct the Moon. Avoid days when Saturn is square or opposite the Moon.

Signing Papers

Sign contracts or agreements when the Moon is increasing in a fruitful sign, and on a day when Moon-Mercury aspects are operating. Avoid days when Mars, Saturn, or Neptune are square or opposite the Moon.

Staff, Fire

The Moon should be in the third or fourth quarter, but not Full. There should be no squares (Q) to the Moon.

Staff, Hire

The Moon should be in the first or second quarter and should be conjunct, trine, or sextile (C, T, or X) Mercury or Jupiter.

Travel

See the travel listing in the Leisure & Recreation section.

Writing

Writing for pleasure or publication is best done when the Moon is in Gemini. Mercury should be direct. Favorable aspects to Mercury, Uranus, and Neptune promote ingenuity.

Economic Forecasts for the Year 2001

Kaye Shinker

Since ancient times astrologers have looked at a select number of charts set for the capital of their country to determine the future economic picture. Financial astrologers look at the same charts, studying the position of the Sun, Jupiter, and Saturn specifically. First they look at the position of these planets in the solstice and equinox charts when the Sun reaches zero degrees of the cardinal signs Capricorn, Aries, Cancer, and Libra. Next they look at the solar eclipses. There will be two in 2001. However, there was one on December 25, 2000, right after the Winter Solstice, therefore, we will include it in this forecast. In other words, there are three solar eclipses between December 21, 2000, and December 21, 2001.

This promises to be an extremely busy year with full employment and associated wage inflation as one theme. Consumer spending on durable goods will continue to push up earnings of most corporations. Throughout the year there is a trine between Jupiter and Uranus, then a trine between Saturn and Neptune. These two aspects will expose deceptions and accounting irregularities. The result is publicly held corporations will need astute public relations personnel.

Winter Solstice and Capricorn Ingress

The Capricorn ingress for 2001 occurred December 21, 2000, at 8:37 am EST. Never have Americans had so many new toys. From the baby boomers and down, each generation loves toys with wheels, batteries, and dialogue. If it's small it's good. The theme of this year is to downsize every mechanical gadget we possess. This is a whole new economy and start-up companies dot the landscape. It's as though everything is being reinvented. The holiday season isn't long enough to try all of them.

The focus of attention for the year ahead will be on institutions and in particular government. Treaties will present all sorts of opportunities with the power of the Internet forcing new agreements between nations. Fluctuating international currency is increasingly a problem.

Intellectual property is a huge issue. Lots of methods are proposed to protect it as well as ways to compensate the authors and inventors. North Americans hold most of the patents and copyrights that keep the world wide web up and running. They have a lot of control and probably are not willing to give it away. Protecting their intellectual property is a priority.

So the new administration will have some interesting challenges, but keeping the economy rolling isn't one of them. Once again there just is not enough labor to get the work done. The Mexican and Canadian borders must allow free flowing immigration no matter what organized labor proclaims as unfair.

During 1999–2000, there was a lot of chicanery as various financial institutions were deceived by their customers or employees. These boring scandals will make headlines. The price of financial stocks will remain low until April.

Zero year elections are difficult for vice presidents. (To those of you who bought this before the election, choose wisely.) Somehow the new vice president will need to take over the job. But for now the new president is quietly taking over the reigns of power. He is arranging to cut taxes, eliminate government red tape, and figure out what to do about the huge number of civil service employees who have chosen to retire. "Help Wanted" ads litter the Washington, D.C., newspapers.

Jupiter in Gemini

Jupiter starts the year retrograde in Gemini, then goes direct on January 25, quickly transiting through Gemini until he reaches Cancer on July 13. Jupiter will remain in Cancer until August 2, 2002.

The inauguration of the new president is the first major event of the new year. Who's who in the computer industry will be in conspicuous attendance. The deal makers will wear tuxedos with jogging shoes and pocket protectors instead of handkerchiefs. The ladies will opt for denim.

The financial markets will be quiet until after the inauguration, but then the bull markets shoves up. Business writers call it the "Honeymoon" between the new president and Congress. Astrologers say, "Jupiter has gone direct."

The sign Jupiter transits indicates the commodities you can expect to see in abundance. A bountiful supply means a lower price, while items in short supply tend to be expensive. For example, Gemini rules automobiles, and cars are relatively cheap until August 2001. With Jupiter's transit of Gemini, an abundance of cars, trucks, cabs, and bikes are jamming highways. Cellular phones, calculators, and computing devises will be stuffed in briefcases or even hanging off of the now fashionable telephone lineman's belt. Begging for a corner in your home will be an abundant supply of all kinds of telecommunications—satellite dishes, cable boxes, VCRs, radios, and skinny television sets. Office supply stores will be overwhelmed with merchandise. Expect price wars.

There is an abundance of books, newspapers, and magazines. These will fill the mail box creating an annoying oversupply of paper for the recycling bin. Recycling all the excesses will become start-up businesses for entrepreneurial types. Inexpensive vehicles suggests all sorts of new business opportunities. At-home workers need supplies delivered to the door. Local package services will jam their trucks with stuff ordered on the Internet.

On the other hand, industries that produce chemicals, drugs, perfume, and plastics will find their raw materials, which are imported from foreign countries, in short supply. Oil and fish will be expensive. Food processors will find their supply lines difficult and their labor very expensive. These industries are not shy about increasing their prices and profit margins.

Jupiter in Cancer

When Jupiter moves to Cancer on July 13, the supply of houses will be abundant and, therefore, less expensive. Suddenly there are too many houses on the market, a result of overbuilding and high interest rates. There is also a glut of appliances, furniture, and building supplies. In addition to too many homes, retail establishments built to keep pace with urban sprawl are becoming a liability. Competitive discounting means eventually quite a few of these businesses fail to pay the rent.

Those large shopping malls that evolved into an array of clothing and shoe shops are beginning to lose their customers as people shift their purchasing style. Many become the ghost towns of the twentieth century, providing local authorities with new headaches.

There will be shortages in gems, handcrafted fine furniture, designer clothing, eyeglasses, dental supplies, and medical equipment. Other arenas to look to for shortages are entertainment, recreational vehicles, casinos, software games, and toys.

Hotels, restaurants, cruise ship holidays are in oversupply and they are cheap. Those who schedule a vacation for August or September will be able to purchase excellent values with their vacation dollar.

The focus of Jupiter's transit through Cancer will be adjusting the family to the technology of the twenty-first century. In the nineteenth century, genteel ladies gave their friends calling cards that stated which day they would be home and available to entertain visitors. The twenty-first century version will be communicated via e-mail to plumbers, carpenters, electricians, repair folks, and delivery services.

In the first part of the twentieth century, groceries, merchandise, and services were delivered to homes because shoppers lacked transportation. Twenty-first century shoppers, starved for time and working nontraditional hours, will increase their demands for home deliveries even as the supply of low-wage laborers dwindles.

Movies and television have created a pent-up demand worldwide for North American memorabilia. The order fulfillment capabilities of the Internet make it possible for international customers to purchase everything, and Internet auctions will add to the flow of goods. The world economy is booming. People no longer depend on their local wholesalers and retailers for merchandise.

Saturn in Taurus

Saturn has been in Taurus since June 10, 1998, placing strong emphasis on acquisitions, organizing, and streamlining. We've seen a rash of smaller banks being acquired by larger banks, but it's been a catch-22. Every time they achieve organization their personnel quits or retires leaving even the best-organized financial institutions dealing with personnel problems. The larger banks have too many services, and none are done well. The financial news headlines criticize banks for being financial warehouses with too many irons in the fire. Around April 15, the largest banks complete some strategic divestitures which will help them focus their attention back on the banking business. There is plenty of restructuring and a few more strategic mergers. Their shareholders finally get a good return on their investments.

Rising interest rates are advantageous to the boutique-style banks. These neighborhood banks realize there is no such thing as a small account, and their mini-accounts offered to young customers will begin pay off. This is a bull market for the average consumer as the various financial institutions beg for business.

Speaking of April, the Internal Revenue Service and its penchant for paper work continues to frustrate the public. The government has collected plenty of tax money, but the money hasn't been spent, nor have taxes been reduced. Both the new president and his opponent promised tax cuts, but Congress continues fighting along party lines until around May 1 when they finally get the job done.

Saturn in Gemini

The mood changes when Saturn finally moves into Gemini. He made a brief appearance in Gemini during the late summer of 2000. (Remember the tiny preelection tax cut?) Fortunately, wages increased and everyone spent the extra dollars getting organized by having two of everything. The major topic of conversation is traffic and how to avoid it. Freeways are jammed twenty-four hours a day, prompting some folks to move away from it, creating a housing glut in the most congested areas. Others are arranging flex hours, or computer commuting. Public transportation is the issue on the agenda of every local government.

Qualified commercial drivers are scarce. Vehicle repair folks have their appointment books filled. Repair technicians for communications equipment are nonexistent. Skilled labor is undereducated. Senior citizens are finding themselves teaching basic mechanics at night school.

Rich and healthy, the baby boomers are retiring from the work force creating even more of a labor shortage. Employers offer consulting fees, stock options, and travel perks.

The Internet and other communications devices have empowered second and third world citizens to stay home and work for higher wages instead of immigrating to wealthier countries. But English is the language of technology, and retired U.S. citizens with a sense of adventure or teaching skills have found employment abroad. Retired teachers or civil servants are in demand in every emerging economy.

Basic education has a very real shortage of teachers. This is especially true in grammar schools. Both private and public schools have huge retirement woes as neither pays enough to encourage recent college graduates to seek employment with them. Parents who demand a quality education for their children are finding that they have to do it themselves.

Publishers of educational software and books need to develop new products, and improve selling strategies to accommodate Internet-savvy youngsters. Computers are cheap enough for each child to have their own, but blocking software is in high demand from parents of these little geniuses.

Shareholders are unhappy that their corporations are spending so much money on public relations due to products winding up in court, poor quality control, and other public relations difficulties. This is especially true of vehicles and various communication devices. Litigation seems to be fashionable, and the Internet has made researching liability law a new game for the ordinary citizen.

Earned income continues to fuel the markets. Investor's portfolios are trending away from mutual funds, and teams of investors are having fun doing their own research. Technology gives them equal footing with the brokers and online trading is how portfolios are managed. There are a lot of millionaires making very creative use of their electronic gadgets.

Uranus, Neptune in Aquarius

Uranus entered Aquarius on January 13, 1996, and will depart December 31, 2003. Aquarius, the sign of invention, is ruled by Uranus, the planet that travels through space sideways.

Mall owners find they need to be creative with live entertainment, events, and demonstrations similar to a state fair. Kiosks proliferate with sampling booths and customers ordering on line. Customers with notebook computers will enter their own ordering data. Retailers who relied on their giant warehouse boxes to attract customers will convert them into shipping centers. Commercial drivers will earn good money.

Since 1996, casual Fridays have taken over the entire week and office hours are when the professional's converted bus shows up in your neighborhood. Work time is when you do it, dissolving yet another business tradition.

The stock exchanges and other financial venues operate around the clock. The twenty-four hour clock set for Greenwich Mean Time will be a favorite gift. Education is in the midst of a revolution. Parents need their older children at home and are willing to take time to instruct the younger ones. Public schools will offer local tax credits for various home-school classes.

Uranus, Jupiter, Neptune Trine

Jupiter will be trine Neptune and Uranus throughout the year. This means that the news media will have lots of fun with some interesting shenanigans exposed during late 1999 and 2000. Financial institutions are the most vulnerable since their employees are followed by trails of paperwork. Deceptions by various market-makers will also be exposed. Recently deregulated utilities and transportation systems are also vulnerable to scandals.

The Internet has been sneaking into our lives through the telephone and cable wires for a while now. We've been buying a few things, sending jokes on the e-mail, and checking out our stocks. By 2001, the Internet is part of our lives and we run to the computer every morning to check our e-mail and the weather report.

Neptune in Aquarius

Inventions usually have a number of applications other than their original purpose, and an incredible number of inventions have appeared since November 28, 1998, when Neptune entered Aquarius. New applications will continue to appear throughout the Aquarius transit that ends February 4, 2012. Creativity with electronics is the major objective.

Imagine a journalist sharing an interesting story with several thousand folks via an e-zine that pays by percentage of subscriber hits. As a consumer, imagine fewer trips to the recycling bin. These changes will, of course, create more demand for bright young students to work with various electronic venues. Creative management techniques will provide answers. One possibility is to divide work into take-home projects. Business will take advantage of their bright young employees, and be able to offer post high school education via Internet classrooms as an employment perk.

Time is a precious commodity and students are anxious to use theirs efficiently. Technical students and writers are the first choice of corporate recruiters who could make football recruiters look like rookies.

The traditional ivy-covered university will need to recreate itself. For example, English and philosophy classes are best taught online. Accounting and sociology are also easy to translate to the electronic medium. Lab classes in the sciences might reduce time on campus to several weeks. Alumni associations and supporters of brick-and-mortar universities don't know what to think as students and their parents find creative ways to use their time and money. For example, attending classes via the computer, and showing up in the classroom only when hands-on learning is required.

Fashion, drama, music, painting, and literature have made a quantum leap. If it's outrageous it will sell. Three-dimensional art is favored, especially if light and shadow change the painting. Sort of like getting two for the price of one. In drama, expect characters with a definitive philosophy expressed in the story line. Commercial music will combine electronic and acoustic instruments to create preposterous sounds.

The new art does not appeal to the usual establishment agencies for distribution. All of these innovations in the arts will require expensive risk-taking by the artists. This suggests penny stocks will be available to investors willing to back entertainers.

Pluto in Sagittarius

Pluto has been in Sagittarius since November 11, 1995, and will it leave that sign on Thanksgiving eve in 2008. While Pluto is in the middle degrees of Sagittarius trains, planes, and automobiles continue to be full of passengers seeking beautiful vistas and exciting adventures. Countries with exotic parks and attractions will benefit from tourism dollars, but visitors should beware of safety issues. Making sure the visitors have a safe, unique experience with all the local cultural entertainment will provide third world entrepreneurs with plenty of extra dollars to spend. Festivals and local sporting events will find their venues crowded, and local restaurants and craftsmen will have a new audience.

While business travelers have cut back on overnight stays, the hospitality industry will revise their marketing strategy to attract extended- stay visitors. Leisure travelers tend to be longer and make extensive use of the facilities. The result is abundant economic opportunities.

December Eclipse

The Christmas Eclipse occurred December 25, 2000, at 12:22 pm EST. This eclipse, at 4° ♑ 17', promised improved international trade and the expansion of telecommunications. The whole change in international commerce is fated and little can be done to change the trend. The crisis centering on intellectual property is just one of the many issues; exchanging currencies is another. There is talk that a currency similar to the Euro is being negotiated by international banks.

Throughout the holiday season various religious groups found young people joining their celebrations. Yes, it is a form of youthful rebellion, and suspicious parents who have avoided church are watching their young folks. The need for social activity and some relief from the inherent sterility of the computer seems to be responsible for their choices.

Throughout January 2001, money will pour into the stock exchanges, with February seeing new highs for all exchanges. Communications are overcoming language and cultural barriers, and everyone refuses to miss the opportunity to invest. The climb is steady with an emphasis on various international funds and durable goods manufacturers.

Weather is normal for your area.

Spring Equinox

The first day of spring occurs March 20 at 8:31 am EST, and predicts the year ahead for agriculture. It will be a beautiful spring with a wide variety of crops planted by farmers and gardeners. Normal weather will aid in production of abundant crops and lead to a healthy economy. Farmers foresee fair prices, but the real profits will go to organic farmers who will have more orders than they can handle. People are willing to pay for quality food that was organically grown. This trend will continue to reward the upscale grocers with higher profits. Of course, organically grown products require intense labor and therefore a new type of sharecropping will find the rural land owner's visiting their contract lawyers.

There is a demand for new harvesting equipment and marketing techniques. Unhappy past experience with government controls finds the agriculture community seeking new ways to share their surplus. Trucks are hauling all sorts of machinery to their rural customers.

In May there is a chance that the United States will have to deal with the aggressive military of another country. It's difficult to determine, but either the Internet or the Air Force wins.

Summer Solstice and June Eclipse

The first solar eclipse of 2001 occurs four-and-a-third hours after the Cancer ingress June 21 at 6:58 am EDT at 0° ♋ 10'. The eclipse quickly modifies the forecast.

The housing boom is coming to a conclusion. Increasing prices have met resistance from new group of buyers unwilling to spending half their income on shelter. They consider their money better spent on the kids education, entertainment, and recreation. Therefore, real estate prices are on hold and some are actually going down.

Tight labor forces the minimum wages to inflate, which in turn will force the Federal Reserve to push up interest rates.

Family income is the issue of the Summer Solstice. Small home computer businesses are keeping everyone in the family employed, and the extra dollars find their way into new savings accounts as banks begin to make special offers to attract customers.

Online and banking with their credit and debit cards is making a cashless society more of a reality. Fewer people are willing to spend one Saturday a month on bills.

The government is making another go-around to tax the Internet. Another concern is fielding complaints about aggressive offshore gambling. International law is designed for fishing, shipping, drugs, and wars, not casinos. Taxing would provide some controls, but congressional committees determine that enforcement is impossible. Little Internet machines are difficult to regulate.

Big business and families of soldiers are insisting that the government return soldiers to their homes. The e-mail from the troops indicates they are playing not soldiering, and there's plenty of work to be done at home.

A great deal of aggressive male energy is concentrated on uncovering international money scams. In 1999 and 2000, a lot of people were deprived of their hard-won savings by con artists. Summer 2001 will find all sorts of news headlines exposing dreams and screams of these swindlers.

Summer sports teams struggle between teams and their owners makes headlines. The bottom line is earned income from the media just can't match the salary expectations of the talented employees. This is a power struggle with a lots of pubic controversy.

The June eclipse shows that the encryption software is finally sophisticated enough to solve security problems and cheap enough for the artistic community to purchase it.

The weather in your area will be cool, smoking volcanoes will take the blame. Beautiful for touring the National Parks.

The Fall Equinox and Libra Ingress

The Fall Equinox occurs September 22 at 6:04 pm EDT. It describes trade both national and international. This is the time of year we weigh in the crops, count the money and go shopping. It is also the time of year when folks weigh and measure their holdings in the stock market. Usually they sell a few of their winning purchases to pay the bills left over from summer. Stockholders are promised dividend increases as the market falls into it's October doldrums. Movement in price by years end will be minimal thus little money is made. Equity shares are still in short supply but prices have remained lackluster. The Dow has taken to hovering around 15,000, Standard & Poor's at about 2,200, and the NASDAQ at 4,000.

However, around November 12, there is volatility in real estate investment trusts (REIT's). The problem is the auto market—no one needs a new car. Easy maintenance and fewer miles means that there aren't many reasons to trade the old one. Auto stocks have been the least-favored equities most of the year because the new models are ugly and the sturdy SUV's and light trucks are still running very nicely.

Hiring bonuses, stock options, higher hourly wages, and guaranteed overtime are being offered by employers to woo skilled workers into the companies. The high school graduating class of 2000 will be prized employees since they have been trained to work by their self-employed parents, work on any task assigned, and need very little management.

The Internet is completing its consolidation phase. Popular sites collect a lot of revenue from advertising and also a lot of criticism from subscribers. Cultural misspeaks bring floods of e-mail and the international quality of the Internet gives the service providers some real headaches.

Shareholders meetings are starting to appear on the integrated versions of the net where it is possible to vote in real time as the corporate officers bring up the pros and cons of various issues. Local and state governments might decide that elections will be possible through the Internet. However you look at it, the computer hardware companies will find a way for all of us to have a computer (color coordinated) in our homes, and perhaps one in the car. They're working on one for jogging around the park. Weather is going to be very wet.

December Eclipse

The December 14 eclipse will occur at 3:27 pm EST at 22° ♐ 56'. Corporate merger's are all the rage and international unions are common, especially the Internets. Again corporations are trying to succeed with old leadership. Marketing and sales are intertwined and difficult to distinguish. On the home front, everyone is getting married. Finding a reception hall is turning into a problem though. Online gift registration works, thankfully.

Presenting a sales pitch is very difficult without voice and follow through. Price has to be everything. Public relations writers are in demand. Those who can write with a flare are the new darlings of the Internet, and are in huge demand. Earned income is fairly high. Folks are saving for special events. Luxury travel is the most favored way to spend this discretionary income. Health issues are making headlines. Drug stores and vitamin companies will have even higher profits. This winter season brings some pretty irascible flu germs. A healthy lifestyle and diet will help keep the sniffles away.

Your favorite retail store is definitely a different place. Malls are becoming demonstrations centers—something like a continuous state fair. If you like something you put your card in a terminal and it's delivered to your house or office. Wow! That's easy. Of course, a new market will open up for returned merchandise.

Creative advertising will be required to realize sales. Media outlets will include public transportation. There will be "www.com's" on all those give away coffee cups, ball point pens, and key chains.

International sales will be the focus of managers as the world economy finishes its Internet connections. From abroad, the emerging middle class will focus on purchases for their homes. Customer demand will be high for beautiful furniture and electronic gadgets for their homes and offices.

The winter ahead will experience mild weather.

Winter Solstice and Capricorn Ingress

The Winter Solstice begins at 2:21 pm EST on December 21, 2001. The household budget for 2002 includes that new fuel cell. The commercials equate it to the invention of the internal combustion engine. The fuel cell promises to revolutionize the way we get around. Farmers and small businessmen are particularly enchanted with its possibilities. The rest of us are trying to picture it in the garage providing electricity for all of the gadgets in our homes. Most of us are waiting for the price to drop.

Change is the key word for 2002, especially in the corporate officers of publicly held companies. Many are retiring to become involved in new types of businesses. The new economy has created splendid partnership opportunities for management. There is a plethora of new businesses. Large corporations, where mentoring has been neglected, will find new managers impossible to hire.

The twenty-first century is about partnerships. Equal is the keyword. The new economy will force management and their operations staff into a new style of leadership that will use two people with equal powers and responsibilities. The paradigm has changed and everywhere management is forced to try new ideas.

Congress has given up trying to please the public with tax policy. Now they are asking business. Every news program and chat network during the year ahead will have taxes as a topic. We are amazed how the new administration, which promised to simplify and rewrite the tax code, has managed to make it more complicated. The public begins to wonder if their home computer is smart enough to sort out all of the complicated rules.

Work Place Politics

Alice DeVille

People spend a lot of time engaged in the ritual of work. Making the right career choice and finding an employer who appreciates your talents are important considerations, but that's only the beginning. It is up to you to sustain an interest in the mission and to make continuous improvements within the organization. Harmony flows when you take the time to build rapport and strengthen relationships with peers, subordinates, and the people in charge. It takes skill to turn challenging situations into consensus-building opportunities, and to acquire the socialization skills so important in the work place.

Naturally, there will be days when misunderstandings and problems abound; days when you must call on your wisdom to clarify problems and solve misunderstandings, or simply bite your tongue. The world of work is ever changing and each employment arena must be ready to respond to the signals of trouble brewing.

Because the Moon changes signs approximately every two-and-one-half days, traveling through the entire zodiac in a month, she plays a part in establishing the mood and dynamics in the work place. The Moon's sign and house in your natal chart relates to your attitudes and behaviors, and often depicts the type of people you'll meet on the job—coworkers, colleagues, employers, and customers. If she's placed in your natal Second House of income, Sixth House of work, or Tenth House of career and authority figures, you may change jobs often if you don't feel connected to your work or the company's prevailing philosophy. Other interpretations suggest you may work predominately with women, desire a position of public prominence, or want a vehicle to promote your creative ideas. These house placements are not the only way the Moon affects your career. If you are curious about how your Moon's sign and house position can influence your work, order a chart from Llewellyn's Computerized Services (see coupon in the back of this book), or seek the advice of an astrologer who specializes in work place management.

The Moon's emotional vibes influence the climate and conditions in the work place. Lunar cycles affect the ebb and flow of communications, including travel and contract negotiations. When the Moon is at

the peak of her receptivity, you feel
nurtured and secure. You connect to
your role and stay confident about the
contribution you make in carrying out
the mission. At other times the Moon
seems fickle and moody, her effect on
daily routines coming in the form of
problems that need solving by individuals who must find a way to get
the work done.

The focus of this article is the
Moon's influence on promoting a harmonious work environment. Take a
look at the types of issues the Moon
inspires as she transits through the
signs and your work environment. The
Moon serenely reminds you that you will be valued for your work if you
place a high priority on understanding work place politics. Learn the ropes
and integrate strategies that work successfully for a variety of circumstances. Let the Moon be your messenger, helping you build the skills that
make you an outstanding communicator and an effective problem solver.

♈ Aries

When the Moon transits the competitive sign of Aries, the themes of
adventure, action, initiative, and forcefulness come up. Conversations
range from strongly animated to downright boisterous. An air of urgency
invades offices and boardrooms as leaders meet to close the loop, tighten
deadlines, and demand performance levels that tend to leave less
assertive workers exhausted. Someone could pose a "take it or leave it"
ultimatum over the deadline, and the only face-saving response is to start
negotiating. Begin with a well-posed question that shows your interest
and concern: "When is the latest date you need this work?" Then get
busy!

Under this Moon, you'll also hear about job opportunities. If you are in
the market for a change, you will want to get a jump on rivals by submitting
your resume early. If you are thinking about promotion potential and a long-
term career ladder, read the organization's promotional literature, check out
the informal networks, and express your interest in employment by checking in with the human resources department that received your resume.

Taurus

When the Taurus Moon rises, talk turns to money—fiscal accountability, contract negotiation, budget planning, raises, promotions, and development opportunities. Since the Taurus Moon sets a conservative tone, the decision making team will give the okay when a convincing presentation shows that productivity goals can be met with the targeted dollars. Savvy financial officers gain advantage when they come to the table with ball park estimates of the dollars they need to run an effective operation. Available resources are evaluated, and approval for how many get promoted, and how much of the pot goes into investing in human resources is determined. Although a Taurus Moon identifies with promoting job security, today's companies seldom promise lifetime employment and predictable merit increases. In truth, methods of promotion and raises are as varied as the managers who negotiate them. You would be surprised at how many people forego raises because they are afraid to ask for what they deserve. Be sure you don't lose out! Build value that can be perceived by others. Devote energy to maintaining a good relationship with your boss. Then learn how to showcase your contributions and be assertive when it comes to asking for what you need.

Under a Taurus Moon you aren't the only one asking for a raise, applying for jobs, or competing for training opportunities. Support your negotiating power by assessing where you want to be in the advancement loop in the next five years. Spend time analyzing your accomplishments. Then make an appointment to see your employer and ask for that 10 percent raise you've earned.

Gemini

One of the greatest challenges you face at work is bringing other people around to your way of thinking. When the Moon travels through Gemini, selling ideas is a dominant theme. If you have meeting or conference planning responsibilities, select dates with this Moon prominent and you will maximize your chances for success. People want to talk, discussion is lively, questions come freely. Participants often show up wearing their yellow power ties or blue business skirts symbolizing their desire to communicate and network.

A Gemini Moon promises debates and a lively atmosphere in which to present new concepts. Be aware that many voices may want to share an opinion though; have a facilitator present to track decisions and keep talkative people from monopolizing the floor. Plan a follow-up social event to keep discussions going and stimulate congeniality among participants.

An ideas success depends on getting it accepted. Decision makers want to know that you have ideas for improving the service your company gives. Be enthusiastic and prepared to convince management that your idea is worth implementing. Don't be surprised if a bonus appears in your paycheck to reward your effort. You deserve it! If you are the one listening to new proposals, be sure to ask questions of colleagues or subordinates without sounding critical, or giving the premature impression that you have rejected an idea. Respond to insightful proposals by asking for supporting data. Avoid superficial Gemini Moon game playing that could give the impression you like the idea when you really can't stand it.

✓Cancer

If you're in direct contact with the public, or you run your own business, a recurring challenge is pleasing customers. When the Moon is in Cancer, customer sensitivities seem heightened. Under stressful aspects, they can be picky, petulant, or aloof—making an encounter difficult. You could say they are getting under your skin—but say it only to yourself! It's tempting to tell someone off, but it could hurt your pocketbook. Be tactfully assertive with customers, employees, coworkers, or even your boss. You can be sure customers are watching and may be affected by the outbursts or demands.

Cancer Moon brings out the desire to show the mutual benefits obtained from an exchange. You intuitively realize that you need to ask diplomatic questions when turmoil exists, information is missing, or clients have unreasonable expectations. Difficult encounters will heighten your appreciation of negotiating skills and inspire you to place a high priority on working out difficulties without alienating a needy customer. The energy of the Cancer Moon is ideal for solving quirky dilemmas such as disruptive children and lost orders. Your goal is to encourage clients to come back and to share with others how well their needs were met. Convince your customers that you appreciate the cooperative relationship that allows you to give them service with a smile.

Leo

The Moon in Leo provides an opportunity for you to showcase your talents and accomplishments. If you have an important meeting, try to get it with the highest ranking official possible. Take the challenge to ask questions yourself to determine if you and the company are suited to each other. If you want the position, assure your interviewer that you have what it takes to be part of the corporate culture. Enthusiasm counts!

Leo is known for displaying poise and elegance. It's up to you to demonstrate that you have it. Find out how your new boss' peers support the department where you will work. Is there respect or alienation? What is the team spirit like? How does the division fund projects? Once you determine that your prospective employer has the budget and clout to support your desired career ladder, ask how long people generally stay in the company and what benefits and incentives the firm offers.

The Leo Moon offers a favorable time for the interviewer, too. Interviewing can be frustrating because each candidate has different motives for wanting the position. Your job is to put the applicant at ease. Then go to work finding out what the interviewee can do for your company, how the individual has performed past assignments, the candidate's salary needs, and the probable date of availability. When the Moon is in Leo, individuals forge solid employment relationships.

Virgo

Organizations thrive on ideas, on creative solutions to old problems, and on new strategies for growing the business. Use the analytical qualities of a Virgo Moon to assess what is working in an organization, and what is not. Virgo's presence is sure to evoke productive thought from employees. Even though the company may never implement the suggestion, the ideas generated represent creativity.

Under a Virgo Moon, ideas get a critical look from analysts, inventor, subject matter specialists, ad hoc teams, or decision makers who have a vested interest in product integrity and concept workability. Whatever the case, the organizationally correct way to give feedback should never be one that deflates an employee's ego or discourages future input. Yes, there is constructive criticism, but recipients seldom see it that way. Never imply that ideas won't work, cost too much, or must have been developed when the employee came to work after a bout with insomnia. The discerning critic will ask for help in identifying aspects of the idea that may not work, or are in conflict with ideas already in place. When you involve to solve, it becomes apparent to each party that the idea has flaws and both of you have a hand in looking for a sensible alternative.

The Virgo Moon can bring out the "know-it-alls" offering unsolicited advice that's often tinged with warnings about the awful things that will happen if conditions—the budget, deadlines, or the quality of equipment—don't change. Another variation of this Moon is "the snoop" who makes it a point of catching his peers goofing off, coming in late, or making personal telephone calls. Use the positive energy of the Virgo Moon to deliberate on the childish messages. In your most matter-of-fact tone, ask your informants how they think you should use this information, and watch them blink. Before long you will have them thinking twice before they swear by indiscriminate statements, and you will be known for your problem-solving skills.

Libra

A Libra Moon is perfect for resolving conflicts. We're not talking here about routine differences of opinion, but rather about hard clashes and behaviors that make it difficult for employees to perform their jobs. Situations where employees are not speaking to key personnel whose input is vital to getting the work out on time. Your gift is seeing both sides of issues.

The core issues do not necessarily surface during the Libra Moon, but conflicts seem to have better chances for settlement at this time. You will be more successful in implementing a strategy for breaking the deadlock in a disagreement if both parties admit the role they play in causing the dispute. Avoid any diversions that make upper managers the villains when you need to carry out your responsibility in explaining unpopular policies. You may cite the policy, but don't hide behind it and act like you don't really support it. You will lose credibility. If you have responsibilities for mediation or have a particular situation that needs attention, look at your calendar to plug in the favorable Libra Moon phase. The players will seem less contentious and your expertise will enhance harmonious work relations.

Scorpio

Under the clever, intense Scorpio Moon, you can expect an unwillingness from people to share if pressed for details in public. And, if you're confronted with volatile customers threatening to have you fired because they received poor service, check your ephemeris for a Scorpio Moon. but even if you're right, don't bother arguing. Instead, do everything you

can to defuse the tension. This option will show that you are not intimidated by the hothead. A small percentage of customers actually complain to the offending company, but they do complain to others and they will take their business elsewhere. If the customer takes you up on the offer to speak to your boss, protect your credibility and your paycheck, and state that you are sorry the customer would not allow you to help solve the complaint.

Another example of Scorpio politics is the experience of a coworker who hides behind inadequate performance and missed deadlines by blaming the errors on you. You have damage control to do with your boss who may believe your coworker's lies and accuse you of something where you share no blame. Be patient. Listen to your boss's complaint so that you understand the gist of it, but then instead of accusing your criticizer of lying, report on the situation as objectively as you can. Describe what you know and correct misinformation. Let your boss be the one to figure out who embellished the truth. Like the Scorpio-affiliated Phoenix, you will arise from the ashes of discredit to the higher elevations of truth.

Sagittarius

Ethical dilemmas are the specialty of truth-seeking Sagittarius. Under this Moon transit moral challenges—bribery to win contracts, breaking promises, falsifying reports, showing favoritism, stealing, or other deceptive practices—are spotlighted. You may be asked to act hastily or injudiciously for the sake of producing larger company profits; your performance may be under par; or your company may give only lip-service to ethical behavior, and the Sagittarius Moon reminds you to deliberate with your higher mind. If you see someone stealing company equipment or cash, you have an obligation to familiarize yourself with the organization's policies regarding internal theft, as well as your own state's laws. (You could be prosecuted for failure to report what you have witnessed.) Unless you feel you could be in physical danger, you may thwart the act of theft by saying to the perpetrator in a nonthreatening manner: "I see that you have loaded up your briefcase again, you must be burning the midnight oil." In your own subtle way you have alerted the thief that the act has not gone unnoticed, and given them a second chance to change their mind before leaving the premises. By simply raising doubt about why your colleague may be filling a briefcase with company goods, you may prevent further acts of larceny from occurring. Internal theft sabotages company morale and stability.

Situations that create shadowy undertones in the work environment, such as falsifying the contents of a report, affect trust and create insecurity. If you raise the possibility of attracting unfavorable publicity when your facts and figures come under scrutiny, you may force your employer to think about the inevitable baggage that comes with false claims. Instead, opt for writing a report that highlights the strengths of the operation or product, and rely on the clear-thinking intelligence of the Sagittarius Moon to guide you when such moral challenges arise. Sagittarius enjoys the adventure of learning all facets of the dilemma. The truthful Archer sends flaming arrows to pinpoint questionable behavior and address the philosophical perspective. Ride the wave of integrity and the universe is yours.

Capricorn

The sign of power and authority, Capricorn themes relate to bosses and authority figures. It's normal for employees to devote considerable time to understanding the boss's psyche and seeking ways to win that coveted approval. (If you are interested in learning more about the unique characteristics of bosses, see my article in the Llewellyn's *2000 Sun Sign Book* titled "You and Your Boss.") In some cases, bosses are demanding and difficult to work with, requiring special handling techniques to prevent alienation. Typical Capricorn Moon tension could revolve around having your authority circumvented, being told your performance is not as good as a peer's, dealing with a perfectionist boss, or being blamed for you boss's mistakes.

No one wants to work in an "or else" environment, but the Capricorn Moon often brings to light behaviors that give such an impression. When this Moon transits on a work day, it is not unusual for the "top dogs" to exercise their authority, and you can expect the best and the worst behaviors to surface. Under positive conditions, important decisions, or approval of plans occur suggesting achievement of milestones. All too often, though, this difficult Moon placement highlights preexisting tension or situations of conflict that you have ignored.

Bosses want you to know they have the power. Many employees fear their superiors and settle for artificial relationships instead of challenging the boss's position, even though disagreement might help the mission. Withholding their opinions is more the norm than providing a truthful analysis of assigned work. Remember not to let fear of your boss hurt your career. If you tiptoe around, they will forget you exist because you have nothing to contribute. The meek do not get promoted.

With the Capricorn Moon influence you may experience micro-management, a style that clashes with those employees who look for empowerment opportunities that give them greater ownership in decision making. If you are a subordinate manager, it soon becomes the norm to keep your finger on the pulse beat, a time-consuming task, because the boss wants a read on the status quo at any given moment. If you are ready for a boss with a more participative management style, your wishes could be granted under a Capricorn Moon transit as this period frequently brings in a changing of the guard. Take the opportunity to delegate to other members of your team.

Aquarius

The goal-oriented Aquarius Moon transit highlights management; how to make the work place more humanitarian; or how to know who's playing on your team. When members cooperate, your efforts succeed; if they undermine your contributions, you may fail or experience frustration. Personality differences and diverse work styles add complexity to gaining the support you need.

For some individuals, working together means putting on a united front. Others would say "teamwork" means finding ways to get along with coworkers whose habits and attitudes clash with their own. The Aquarian Moon calls for using finesse in identifying motivators for staying on top of the workload. During this transit, wise managers look for innovative ways to distribute work, and credit noteworthy team effort. Without demeaning the less ambitious, they acknowledge the extraordinary effort of disgruntled people who feel they do too much. Harmonious messages soften the edge. Who could argue against creating a win-win work environment?

Networking is synonymous with Aquarius Moon rising—perhaps in the organization's Third, Seventh, or Eleventh Houses. If you like being among the movers and shakers, take advantage of this lunar transit to attend meetings, workshops, and conferences; have lunch with colleagues from different companies; meet your favorite mentor to get the inside track on industry updates; join Toastmasters, an organization that helps you gain poise as well as public speaking skills. Once you feel secure, look for show-and-tell opportunities— sign up as a keynote speaker at one of the monthly luncheons, or sponsor an informal brown bag luncheon at your work site and encourage colleagues to develop their speaking skills by presenting their own media show featuring leading edge topics or hobbies. After you have given everyone a fair shot at publicizing their uniqueness, ask how you might tap those resources for the next major project. Brainstorm

to strengthen the vision and use Aquarius' democratic approach to foster healthy competition. Don't forget the applause and your wacky sense of humor.

Pisces

The Moon in Pisces accents sensitive handling to maintain equilibrium in the workplace. Since Neptune rules Pisces, you won't always have a clear picture of the real issues unless you ask some well executed questions. You'll find supervisory personnel dealing with orders that are ignored, performance that is subpar, ill-timed requests for leave, and employees who are having personal problems. The magnitude of the "messes" varies with the situation, yet the chaos or miscommunication is unmistakable. Feelings are on the table because parties are not satisfied with the status quo. The solution is to intensify power, demonstrate assertiveness, and increase employee respect without getting testy. If you follow the intuitive drift of the Pisces Moon, the message you hear would be: Wear kid gloves.

Victims, hypochondriacs, and substance abusers make their appearances under this transit. If you are a supervisor, I'm sure you've noticed when employees seem to have it in for each other. Although you may prefer to stay clear of the conflict, it is sure to affect their productivity and that of others who witness their recurring bickering. Forget about formal settings across the conference table. Offer a distressed employee the couch or a comfy chair in a private office, or suggest a cup of coffee or tea while you're sifting through fragile work place energy

You're not going to psychoanalyze anyone, but you are going to pay attention to body language, eye contact, and passionate words. Ask both parties what is straining the relationship—then listen carefully. Facilitate the discussion so there are no interruptions while one or the other is speaking. Help them hear each other, and define specific needs they believe the other is sabotaging. Ask for their ideas on how both sets of needs may be met. Their differences may not seem as far apart as they perceived. If you sense these employees may continue to dwell on their past disagreements, remind them that only the present and the future count. Suggest they "erase" the unpleasant tapes that bring up offenses which occurred more than a few hours ago. Using the intuitive faculties of the Moon in Pisces, you have tempered a sensitive issue. When the dust settles, congratulate yourself on your fair and compassionate resolution.

Void-of-Course Moons in Business

Madeline Gerwick-Brodeur

We've all encountered time-outs from teachers, parents, or sports, so it's not really surprising that there are cosmic time-outs; times when we're not supposed to take important actions, make decisions or purchases, or start new projects. After watching void-of-course Moons in business for many years, I am convinced that we would be much more successful in business, and make better use of our time and resources, if only we observed them.

What are Void Moons?

A void-of-course Moon occurs between two and four times per week, and can last from a few minutes to more than two days. The Moon is considered void-of-course from the time it makes its last major aspect to a planet in a sign (for example, Scorpio) until it has passed into the next house (Sagittarius). An important point to remember is that the last aspect must still be applying in order for the Moon not to be void. Once the last major aspect of the Moon becomes exact, the aspect is considered to be over and the Moon is considered to be "void." There are other definitions of void Moons that could create exception to this definition, but we'll start with this one and discuss the other definitions later in the article. Fortunately, there are several astrological calendars, including Llewellyn's *Astrological Calendar*, that tell us when void Moons occur.

Astrologically, the cycles occurring overhead indicate the universe's plan for each day. If you observe the energies and aspects daily, you'll soon notice that your projects or work activities tend to reflect the energies shown by the planets. So just as awareness of our own cycles and transits tell us what is happening to us on a personal level, the planet transits indicate the type of universal energy that will be reflected in decisions, new projects, contracts, purchases, and new businesses.

In more distant times, the astrological aspects happening overhead were considered to be the "Divine Plan" of the day. Understanding this allowed one to make the best use of each day. Although this information is now largely ignored, primarily because we've convinced ourselves that we are in control, the "Divine Plan" is still there. All we need to do is heed it and take action accordingly.

Part of this plan includes a rhythm of increase and decrease—times to take action and times to wait. We can see this with the monthly cycle of the Moon as it increases from a New Moon to a Full Moon, then decreases to a Dark Moon, which is then followed by a New Moon again. We also see this rhythm in the cycle of the seasons. There are times to plant crops, times to harvest, and times to let the soil rest in preparation for a new planting season. From the universe's example, constant forward progress is not only impossible, but undesirable.

The void Moon is a signal to pause within these larger cycles; to observe regular "down" times, when we stop long enough to take a breath and gain perspective. We're not robots, even though our bosses may wish we were, but part of the living universe with the same needs for cosmic time-outs as all other organic processes. Void Moons are part of this cycle of life.

Does this mean that progress stops altogether during void Moons? Not at all! Just because a baby or project isn't ready to be birthed yet doesn't mean it isn't growing and developing. We're just supposed to take different types of action instead. It's an excellent time to reflect on what you've learned and what you might still need to learn, for reading, reviewing, considering options, researching, and brainstorming. They're also ideal for doing paperwork, writing reports, filing, cleaning the office, or finishing anything.

When you find yourself ready to launch something new, or make decisions—even about purchases—during a void Moon, this should be a red flag to you. You're either missing critical information or you misunderstand something vital. Stop yourself and try to discover what it is, instead of pushing forward. You'll be glad you did. Best of all, when you observe void Moons and don't push forward with decisions, new starts, important actions, or purchases, you save time, money, and regrets.

Nothing Positive Will Come of It

There is some interesting history concerning presidents inaugurated under a void Moon. Nearly all the presidents that were inaugurated under a void Moon have died in office. The only exception to that was President Ford, who replaced President Nixon, but nothing came of his presidency. He had no agenda and no mandate to accomplish. In essence, President Ford was a placeholder for the office of the President.

President Nixon was elected the second time under a void Moon, just prior to the Watergate scandal. In fact, the Watergate break-in itself occurred during a void Moon, suggesting that the correct interpretation is "nothing positive will come of it."

In my years of observing void Moons in business, I have found that to be most accurate explanation. Frequently plenty of things "came" of our decisions and important new starts during void Moons, just nothing we ever wanted. Instead of the success we'd hoped for, we were rewarded with dead ends, obstacles, frustration, endless hassles, wasted resources and no progress. Then we got failure! Only when we were lucky did nothing come of it first.

Several years ago the *Wall Street Journal* printed an article about astrological research that was conducted on 1,400 randomly selected bankrupt businesses. An amazing 100 percent of them were started during a void Moon! So it would seem, the best prevention would be not to start new businesses during a void Moon. If you do though, the only known way to counter this is to reincorporate the company during a better date and time. Doing so has turned businesses around almost instantly.

Following are some examples in several areas. The following examples of how void Moons affect business is based on more than fifteen years of personal observation.

In every case that management decided to fund and/or approve new product development during void Moons, NONE of them ever made it to market. It wasn't uncommon for us to have spent $500,000 before management finally reconsidered their original decision and pulled the plug. All of these decisions had the same thing in common—critical information was either misunderstood or missing.

Retail promotions that start during void Moons fail badly. One retailer spent $1,400 on ads for a major promotion. The day he selected for his event had a void Moon the entire day, and not one person showed up! When customers do show up for sales events during void Moons, they either fail to buy or return their purchases later. Most purchases made during these times tend not to work out for various reasons.

Ads placed during void Moons also yield little or no results, even when the magazine or trade journal is considered excellent and has done well with other ads in the past. This can be disastrous when ads for several months are placed at the same time to get better pricing, since none of the ads will bring in much revenue. Sometimes there won't even be inquiries for ads placed during a void Moon, making it a total failure.

Trade shows that open under void Moons have dismal attendance, even in very large cities like New York. I have worked as an exhibitor at some trade shows during void Moons, and they had so few attendees, that the majority of the people walking down the aisles were exhibitors.

During a void Moons is the worst time for making sales calls, unless it's to finalize details on an order that's already been placed. Trying to see new prospects, start new business with existing customers, or get an order is not only wasted time, but damaging as well. If you try to close a sale during a void Moon, you have a very high chance of losing the order. If you're really lucky, your customer will be sick, have an emergency, or otherwise be unable to see you. Or you may be told that no decision has been made yet. Telephone sales also yield much lower results. People don't answer the phone, even if they're available; they're not in the mood to buy, often because they don't have enough information about what they need yet; or if they do buy, they may decide to return it.

Manufacturing

Manufacturing changes made to products during void Moons also bring losses. Although the international company I worked for tested all their product changes prior to implementing them, the ones that led to worldwide product recalls were implemented during void Moons. The savings the company had hoped to realize from these product changes turned into serious losses instead. Testing products during a void Moon can either give a false sense of security. If nothing goes wrong, it may be that the test was done incorrectly or the product's failure point wasn't tested appropriately. That's what usually happened when a product change was tested and implemented before the failure mode was discovered. What you will get is plenty of information about what needs to be fixed. Save yourself time and money by not testing and implementing product changes during void Moons.

Printing

After several years of watching print jobs started during void Moons turn into printing nightmares, I knew better than to ever take anything to the printers during a void Moon. But we sometimes have serious deadlines to meet, and occasionally I've been tempted to ignore the void Moon. One time, I was quite late getting a newsletter written and ready for printing. By the time it was ready to go, the Moon was void for an entire day. After much frustration, I decided not to take the newsletter to the printers until the void Moon was over.

What a surprise! By the time it was over, I had found five errors that were previously unnoticed and received some very critical information that I needed to add to it. I thanked myself repeatedly for not taking it in during the time-out. Now, no matter how late I am getting something out, I'm never tempted to ignore a void Moon.

Purchasing

It's best to delay purchases during void Moons because making a purchase is a decision—something not favored during these times. If you buy a personal item during a void Moon, you will normally discover something wrong with the item after you buy it. The color won't be right, or the style is wrong for the rest of your wardrobe. Even worse, it may have a quality issue, or be missing parts. For this reason, the purchasing department may have the strongest need to observe void Moons of all the departments in a company. Just placing one-time orders for parts, maintenance, or repair items during void Moons commonly results in quality problems with the parts; parts not shipping on time or shipping via the wrong carrier; receiving the wrong parts or missing some parts. In some cases, the products had to be returned or reworked to make them usable.

Now imagine what happened when long-term contracts for parts were signed during void Moons. In some cases, the supplier was unable to meet the purchasing requirements. They may have bid the contract too low just to get the business, but then failed to perform. Sometimes a supplier didn't want to expand, but they couldn't keep up with our orders either. In other cases, the company signed contracts for quantities that were never needed (the product wasn't as successful as it was forecast to be) and the supplier lost money. Regrettably, since our purchasing contracts typically extended over a year, the problems lasted that long, too. Sometimes these contracts had to be cancelled and reassigned to other suppliers, but often we endured a year's worth of hassles.

In one case, a manufacturer of fancy metal tins could not get a good set of colors from the computer file for color separations. After five attempts and spending $10,000, he looked at the date of the purchase order and realized it had been placed during a void Moon. He cancelled the purchase order immediately and reordered it at a better date and time. The problem with the computer file was discovered almost immediately, and a simple press of one button saturated the colors. He had no further problems with his order.

Computers

Strange things have happened with computers during void Moons. The most amazing story concerned the main computer system for a video production company that failed miserably at the beginning of a void Moon and no one could fix it, no matter what they tried. Even stranger though, the system started working again as soon as the void Moon was over. No one was able to explain this!

Some computer consultants have reported that jobs started during void Moons often take considerably longer than anticipated. There can be unexpected compatibility issues with upgrades or adding new software, or a hardware part breaks. Sometimes the computer won't restart or the network server breaks down. Of course, if you're a consultant and doing a job on an hourly basis, delays are probably good news. But if your fee is a fixed amount for the job, then you're losing!

Meetings

In general, unless the purpose of a meeting is to monitor the status of a project, brainstorm, or to obtain or provide information, the meeting will be a waste of time. In every case when we held meetings during void Moons to make important decisions, we failed. Sometimes the person who understood the most about the situation got called away, leaving the rest of us without answers to our questions. Sometimes we were missing key information needed to make the best decision. Sometimes we misunderstood the information presented. In all cases, whenever we pushed ahead to make a decision in spite of our ignorance, we had to scrap our misguided efforts and begin again. Sometimes we paid dearly!

Scheduling for Professional Services

If you schedule clients or patients for professional services, it's a good idea to pay attention to void Moons. A first-time client or patient should not be scheduled during a void Moon. They will either get lost or stuck in traffic and never arrive, or they don't finish their treatment. It's best to schedule repeat clients or patients during void Moons.

If you're a lawyer, don't take a case when the Moon is void, or ask the client to sign an agreement for you. These are the worst cases you'll ever encounter, and you'll wish you had never seen this client before it's all over.

Travel

Business trips started under void Moons often encounter very difficult experiences and frequently are unsuccessful for the intended purpose of the trip. Negotiations often fail, or one of the parties isn't able to meet their obligations. The hotel, car rental, or airline may not be able to find your reservation. The airplane may not take off on time, or you may be stuck in traffic and unable to get to your flight.

It's not uncommon for a person to get sick, be attacked or mugged, or be involved in an accident if a trip is started under a void Moon. One fellow was riding in a cab that was involved in an accident with another taxi; to make matters worse, the cabbies got out and started fistfighting. If you must take a trip during a void Moon, go someplace to rest and relax—a getaway vacation—but be aware even those can be tough experiences, so do your best to avoid them.

Legal Issues

If you are planning to sue someone, don't file the papers during a void Moon. Heartache and lost money will likely come of it, because you are not likely to win. If you plan to settle a suit, it will be a waste of time to meet during a void Moon, as nothing will come of it. And to top it off, if you go to court, you must hope that you won't be assigned a court date and time during a void Moon. The Paula Jones trial against President Clinton was set to start during a void Moon, and as we all know, the case was thrown out before it ever got started.

When a Void Moon is Not Void

Some people have noticed that void Moons don't always have negative consequences, and there are various reasons for this. First of all, if the Moon is applying in a major aspect (conjunction, sextile, square, trine, or opposition) to either the Part of Fortune and/or one of the angles of the chart (Ascendant, Midheaven, Immum Coeli, or Descendant), then the Moon is not void. To use this great exception, you must have an actual location and with which to work. This definition of void Moons is used extensively by modern horary (the branch of astrology that answers people's questions) astrologers, but not by classical horary astrologers. Astrological calendars cannot show this information, since they are not specific to one location.

If this exception is true, even when the Moon is void for an entire day, according to the traditional definition, there are several times when it isn't. These mini-times don't last long, but they do work and they can be used for finding the emergency "out" in a tough situation. I have not seen extensive data or quantitative research into this question, but I have observed situations where these conditions exist during a void Moon and something good does come of the situation.

One of my clients works in an organization that often applies for grants. Once they worked until the deadline was upon them, and had to use overnight delivery to get their application submitted on time. However, the Moon was void the entire day. My client called in a panic because it was very important to get this grant and he couldn't see how it could be done. I found a time for him that had both an applying aspect to an angle and an aspect with the Part of Fortune, and he shipped the grant via Fed Ex. A few weeks later, he got the grant.

Another client reported that he had expected very few people to show up for a lecture during a void Moon, but to his surprise, about seventy people attended. When I checked the date, time, and location for the event, the Moon was conjuncting the cusp of the Tenth House (the Midheaven).

Another dimension of Void Moons is the use of parallels and contraparallels to determine the last aspect in a sign. Based on experience, parallel and contraparallel aspects of the Moon appear to be valid last aspects. What is a parallel or contraparallel aspect? A parallel occurs when two planets are the same number of degrees north or south of the ecliptic path. In an ephemeris, this information is shown under declinations. For example if one planet is 4 degrees north and the Moon is also 4 degrees north, they are parallel.

To imagine what this looks like in space, picture a line in space (known as the ecliptic) passing around the Earth, much like the imaginary line of the equator does. The ecliptic marks the Sun's apparent path around the Earth, as seen from Earth. The planets revolve around the Sun on the same plane as Earth at about 7 degrees from the ecliptic, except Pluto which is at 17 degrees. Now, visualize two planets above or below the line by the same number of degrees. Essentially they are conjunct in a different dimension, conjunct by declination, instead of longitude. The two planets can be in any signs, and as long as they are the same number of degrees above or below the ecliptic, they are parallel.

A contraparallel is similar, but in this case, one planet is the same number of degrees north of the ecliptic as another planet is south. For example, if one planet is 7 degrees south and the Moon is 7 degrees north of the ecliptic, then they are considered contraparallel. Or the Moon may be 12 degrees south when another planet is 12 degrees north.

Although most of the literature shows parallels are similar to conjunctions, and contraparallels to be similar to oppositions, they are both positive last aspects when used for electional or timing purposes. A parallel of the Moon as a last aspect shows a long-term alliance and a contraparallel shows a temporary alliance. Although I have not yet found sufficient studies with objective data available on this, to put this question to rest once and for all, I have found them to be valuable. In my experience, the Moon doesn't behave like it's void when it will still make a parallel or contraparallel after it's last longitudinal aspect.

During the impeachment process for President Clinton, the Senate Republicans and Democrats formed a temporary alliance about how their proceedings would be managed. The final aspect of the Moon for the sign it was in was a contraparallel to Jupiter and there was unanimous agreement by all the senators about how to proceed.

There are months when no parallels or contraparallels make a final aspect of the Moon, and other months may have up to six of them. So it's hard to give an actual estimate of how often parallels and contraparallels occur as the last aspect. Over a year though, about 25 percent of the time, parallels and contraparallels are the final aspect of the Moon. If it's true that the Moon is not void when there is still a parallel or contraparallel to be made, then about 25 percent of the time, the void Moon occurs later than the times shown in most astrological calendars.

I'm aware of only two calendars that include parallels and contra-parallels as a final aspect of the Moon. They are *Mary Shea's Good Day' Action Planning Guide* (self-published), and my *Good Timing Guide: Better Business Through Better Timing*. Everyone must decide for themselves whether they find the Moon to be void, or not, when there is still a parallel or contraparallel to be made. I encourage you to test it and decide for yourself.

There are other timing tips that can also increase our productivity and assist us in cocreating harmoniously with the universe. However none of them are as important as observing void Moons and using them appropriately. I've seen millions of dollars lost in just one company from pushing forward during these times. Just imagine the billions of dollars wasted each year by companies all around the world for the same reason.

Now visualize a work world that understands time is different each day, and that makes use of time appropriately. Imagine a world in which we no longer waste billions each year chasing mistakes due to misunderstandings or missing vital information. Asian companies have used astrological timing in business, with considerable success, for centuries. Perhaps the West is now ready to awaken to this incredible tool and join them!

How Your Moon Sign Affects Your Career

Stephanie Clement

Your astrological Sun sign is the primary indicator of your vitality, individuality, and confidence. The Moon sign is the secondary influence, offering assistance when the primary psychological approach to life is not broad enough to cover the demands we face. Jungian psychology teaches that there are four basic functions of consciousness that are related in pairs: Thinking vs. Feeling and Sensation vs. Intuition. We all have these four components, but one or two of them predominate, becoming consciously preferred much like right or left handedness. As a result, pair opposites often develop as secondary and even subliminal support functions.

Your Sun sign generally reflects the most conscious capacity, and the Moon sign indicates a second function that serves as an ally and friend, bolstering your habitual approach to the world. When the Sun and Moon are in the same element, this means that your conscious style is aided very directly by your less conscious style. If the Sun and Moon are in opposite elements—air and water, or earth and fire—you are uniquely equipped to meet the world with the broadest range of conscious skills. Astrologically, the elements of the Sun and Moon describe your most likely ways of relating to others and for understanding yourself.

As a career ally, the Moon reflects the skills that come into play when you have gone as far as you can with your direct efforts. It also indicates how you can modify your efforts or make subtle changes in direction to accomplish your goals more easily; and it shows how your deep capacity to learn from your personal unconscious information pool, as well as the Collective Mind, engage to help you along life's path.

The following table shows the signs, their elements, and the psychological function associated with the element.

Sign	Element	Psychological Type
Aries, Leo, Sagittarius	Fire	Intuition
Taurus, Virgo, Capricorn	Earth	Sensation
Gemini, Libra, Aquarius	Air	Thinking
Cancer, Scorpio, Pisces	Water	Feeling

While the three signs of each elemental set share many qualities, each sign has qualities unique to itself as well. Thus Aries, Leo, and Sagittarius all think somewhat alike in terms of broad psychological processes, but each sign also has its own focus.

Sometimes people don't conform to their Sun or Moon type. They may have been raised in an atmosphere where a different type was encouraged, for example. Still, the Sun indicates your strongest tendency, and the Moon shows the support system you have available to you. Any profound exertion to suppress either would ultimately prove to be detrimental to the psyche.

Elements: Support Functions of the Moon

Fire—Intuitive

Intuition offers you strong support if you have the Moon in a fire sign. This can be very useful no matter what the Sun sign element. You have the gift of being able to see into the future to determine where your career activities are taking you. You are able to perceive the future outcome of your current activities in ways that other people admire but probably don't understand. The gift of intuition helps you to relate your perceived goal, your present actions, and the probable outcome of those actions as a system. You may know someone whose work not only doesn't promise career advancement, but also fails to even meet requirements. This person seems to have no clue about the future. You also know people who do the work they are given, have an eye on the future, and act as though there is a direct connection between the two. Even when their actions seem inconsistent with the present needs of their job, you can see that there is a method to their madness, and that eventually, everything moves toward future success. The latter is demonstrating an intuitive awareness.

Intuitive Moons are inventive in their work, able to find new ways to accomplish old tasks in ways that not only work in the present, but will continue to work in the future. They sense the possibilities in a situation, and then find the means of developing it. The Moon in fire signs, nevertheless, serves a supportive role. Whatever the primary choices of the Sun, the Moon takes action in support of those decisions, and does not go against the grain. Where career is concerned the fire Moon can be used to broaden the technique of a sensation type, partner with the logical process of the

thinking type, or comple-
ment the sound judgment
of the feeling type.

Aries

Your eagerness and drive at
work may sometimes be
mistaken for a desire to
gain control by others. On
the other hand you do
want to be in control—if
not now, then later. Your
efforts all serve to move
you toward a leadership
position where your strong personality can have its way. You are a good
decision maker because you look into the future and have a sense of what
needs to happen to achieve your goals.

You can be very impulsive, a quality that sometimes lands you in the
middle of cutting edge activities. The key here is to avoid the bleeding
edge of recklessness. Don't gamble all your money on an untested venture unless you are willing to lose it all.

One drawback of the Aries Moon is your hastiness. In your rush to
get on to the next enterprise, you sometimes fail to complete the previous one, and are prone to act without thinking. You find that your feelings have pushed you to action, and that the results are not what you
expected or wanted. Experience will teach you to think ahead, but
remain focused on the task at hand until it is finished. You are able to
adapt to circumstances without giving up your sense of self or personal
goals; to direct yourself wholeheartedly toward a goal; and you don't see
anything inconsistent about changing direction if it promises better
results. Any setbacks are seen as temporary, or even necessary sidesteps
on your path to success.

Leo

Intuitive, creative Leos know that, just as bread requires a certain amount
of baking, career moves demand proper timing to achieve the proper result.
Capable of waiting for the right moment to take action, you seek a comfortable setting to wait in, and you spend your money carefully to achieve
that comfort, but without wasting your hard-earned cash on temporary
pleasures. At the same time, you enjoy a good time and are the life of the

office. Your inner sense of how to make others comfortable—an intuitive connection—is part of what moves you forward on the career track, for it is precisely because other people are comfortable around you that they trust you and are willing to call you their leader.

One drawback of the Moon in Leo is the tendency to work too hard, pressing forward to reach goals as soon as humanly possible. You may overestimate your own capacity for work, accepting greater and greater responsibility, which is okay on a personal level, but when it comes to your employees, you have to cut some slack. Not everyone shares your vision, and not everyone has the same work capacity. It's important to engage your generous nature when you are evaluating the performance of others.

Above all, you love the game itself and you're a good player because you can see ahead many steps. You also can plan your strategy around your sense of what other people are most likely to attempt. Thus you are rarely caught completely off guard by their actions.

Sagittarius

You have an active interior life, vivid night dreams, and vivid waking visions of where you are headed and how to get there. Your dreams inform you in an almost conversational manner of what you need to do to make progress. Because you see and then communicate a bit of the future, you're an inspiration to others who may feel but cannot yet articulate their visions. You love the planning phase of any venture.

Your mood can change easily. Not attached to a specific worldview, or personal view for that matter, you are subject to the psychic currents flowing around you. This sensitivity can be a drawback if you allow yourself to be caught up in a flow that becomes a side trip. Now, an eddy that allows time for a situation to develop is another thing altogether, and you seem to know the difference almost every time. You are willing to invest significant effort and capital in a developmental process that has the promise of success. If it doesn't work out, you are willing to scrap it and try something different. You recognize that any idea is only as good as the people who implement it, and you learn not to think of their limitations as your personal failures.

Generally an idealist, you know that thoughts are as potent as actions. Thus you encourage optimism in yourself and others. Life is a matter of constant change for you, but the changes carry you in an ever more creative direction.

Earth—Sensation

Regardless of your career field and the skills necessary for it, you have a complementary set of practical skills that help you analyze a situation and figure out what to do. You are the person who can find a way to fix something even without the proper tools; who can look at a set of facts and come to unusual conclusions—finding solutions where other people only see difficulty; and having the inner capacity to provide practical insight for yourself, you can be a very good assistant.

On-the-job training can jump-start you into a new career because you learn best from actual hands on experience. You are also a good trainer, as you know the steps in a process and are able to approach the training in a logical way.

Once you are into a task, it's not easy to distract you from your goal. You have the ability to stick to a project, return to it after an interruption, and follow it through over a long period of time. Part of your comfort level at work is tied to this persistence—you are less comfortable with constant interruptions, and like to work steadily at a task. You also like to have intermediate milestones so you can check how well you are doing. These could include in between deadlines, quality checks, etc.

Carl Jung has the Sun in Leo and Moon in Taurus. The thrust of his analytical psychology was to reach deep into human experience with his intuition (Leo Sun). He then applied practical methods (Taurus Moon) to build a model of the patient's psyche. His psychology has given us a practical framework for understanding ourselves.

Taurus

Above all, you seek to be comfortable. This may not sound like a helpful trait where career is concerned, but it actually is. You seek to create a work environment in which the work can proceed without a lot of fanfare. You also respect the needs of your peers and employees, and seek to provide a place where they can each maximize their own potential. For yourself, this means having comfortable shoes if you must stand for long periods of time, and a comfortable chair if you are seated at a desk throughout the day.

In order to have the same level of comfort at home, you are willing to spend a little extra to get just the right furniture, carpets, or kitchenware. In order to have the extra money, you seek a career with an above-average pay rate. The practical inner voice applauds small sacrifices at work in order to achieve the comfortable lifestyle you want.

Virgo

The Virgo Moon reflects the capacity to methodically examine information and seek the best solution. Successful career development depends on your ability to consider what is best for the product, the company, or your client, and then seek to find it, without letting your personal opinions dominate the process. You could have a very successful real estate career if you are able to accomplish this one thing. You listen to the client, find out what they can afford and what they want. You then seek the property that matches both criteria. It may be that you don't sell a family the most expensive house they can afford, but you do explain the value of a home slightly larger than the one they first describe. You listen to their priorities and meet them with the best offerings on the market, or you inform them of the market conditions that prevent getting some of the things on their list.

The same skill will be valuable in any career. As you develop a work "personality," you will take the edge off being overly precise and "correct" in your efforts, and learn to relax into the practical process of completing your work. You have the capacity to be organized without being a nitpicker, diligent without becoming obsessive. Whatever your Sun sign, you have a practical foundation for all your efforts.

Capricorn

You are intensely interested in your work, and while some jobs will keep your attention longer, you will put your whole effort into the job. You sometimes feel discomfort in emotional situations, and while you may feel you must offer some help to those in trouble, you really don't want to, or even know how. It is important to recognize where your responsibilities begin and end with your coworkers. You can learn how to offer appropriate support in the form of smaller tasks that show you care, yet you don't offer to shoulder the entire responsibility for the other person. What you have is endurance and patience.

You are able to come up with an idea, and then patiently work with it to manifest results. In doing so, you tend to run ahead of others, and they may think you are a flash that happens to be successful a lot of the time. They never seem to see the bumps in your path and the effort it takes to be the lead climber. Yet they often expect you to pull them up to your level. Learning to balance responsibility for others and responsibility for yourself is essential to your career success.

Air—Thinking

The Moon in air indicates a typical process of assimilating information until the solution to a problem becomes evident. You are able to seek out the historical or factual data you need, and then to sort it in a logical, rational manner. You have the capacity for objective examination of all the material you discover, and you can argue more than one side as you come to a decision. Often you are able to go through this process one time and make a firm decision. This is because you have paid attention to everything along the way. Generally people cannot fault you for ignoring obvious possibilities.

The best style of education for Moon in air signs is to pursue challenges that require exploration, thereby developing logical procedures. At the same time, you need experiences that put you in touch with other people, particularly in groups. Otherwise, your methods may become too subjective to be translated into the practical environment of the workplace.

The best careers for you are those that focus on the organization and manipulation of data that call for logical and rational focus. You could be a programmer, surveying the needs of the big picture and then writing detailed units of code to achieve it. Another example is legal or technical writing, where the data is clear and you draw the logical conclusions, or simply describe the process so other people can use the equipment or program. In the former, you seek to convince a judge or jury of a particular interpretation. In the latter, you provide practical rather than theoretical instruction.

Gemini

Your Gemini Moon reflects your vivid imagination and the ability to express it to others. You are a natural writer, teacher, and communicator with the capacity for logical thinking, as well as communicating your emotions. At first you may not be fully aware of the difference, but training and experience provide an unsurpassed combination.

With your capacity to see all sides of a question, and to pick up nuances of culture and language, you would make a good mediator or diplomat. Training in one or more foreign languages will be a big advantage later. You may find that even though your job description does not call for it, you tend troubleshooting problems on a day-to-day basis. You know who to call to get a specific answer, and how to expedite projects. Your generally cheerful attitude encourages others to follow your lead.

Conversely, you tend to be somewhat scattered. This ranges from a messy desk to losing track of important details. You also tend to skim over the top of a subject, remaining unaware of the depth of material you could be analyzing. Even though your personal interest does not take you into the details, you need to develop the capacity to go there, as many work situations require that you know as much as possible about what you are doing.

Alexander the Great had the Moon in Gemini. His conquests were based on desire (Sun in Cancer), but his methods were anchored in the logical decision-making and strategic planning of his Gemini Moon.

Libra

Your inner desire to maintain balance guides everything you do. The Libra Moon reflects your capacity to express feelings, and your need to find affection. Nevertheless, pursuing love interests at work is generally not a good idea. Your company may even have rules concerning dating coworkers, making it a good idea to establish and adhering to strict boundaries.

You dependence on partnership helps you to form strong work relationships, and by being dependable yourself, you attract people to work with you. You can teach this quality to your employees (and even your boss) by example. The team work environment is becoming more functional each year, with different team members taking the lead role in different circumstances. You have the capacity to function both as leader and follower.

Sometimes you tend to place the emphasis on unimportant details. Within a group, have your say, but then listen to others and go with the consensus. Holding out for your own position should be reserved for moments when you feel ethical issues are at stake, or when you see into a situation and perceive a problem others are not aware of. Then it is essential to have developed your powers of persuasion, as well as the ability to organize information and present it effectively. Remember, often is isn't about being right, it's about being present and contributing to the mix of ideas.

Aquarius

The Aquarius Moon reflects the richness of your ideas and the mental power you bring to your career. You are able to examine situations, consider the individuals involved, and draw conclusions about the most effective course of action. This results in your achieving supervisory positions early in your career. Whether this is the direction you want to go remains open to question. At heart, you are a dyed in the wool individualist and may not want to be running the show.

You are strongly independent, yet you are able to change when the need arises. This cannot be said for the majority of people, so you should value this capacity within yourself. Don't fault others for being less flexible. Instead, develop a communication style that helps them to change while making them feel it was their idea, or at least an acceptable one.

You have a wealth of ideas for your career future; ideas that can support the direction your Sun sign while adding depth to your mix of skills. By considering where you and the world are going in the future, you can adjust today's work to lead subtly into the future you have planned for yourself. Use your sympathetic nature to help others, but also help yourself along the way.

Water—Feeling

Water sign Moons embody the feeling function that uses rational mental processes to make judgments about the world and their place in it. The feeling function, despite its name, is not about emotions as much as it is about decision-making—using the faculty of judging the available evidence. This is not logical like the thinking process, but it is considered to be rational—that is, it is a mental process that you choose to engage. Nonrational processes (sensation and intuition) are generally processes of apprehension of events and input, and are much less dependent on personal decision. They just happen, whereas thinking and feeling processes are self-initiated.

The Moon's element is water, and in careers where sensitivity is involved, water Moons thrive because they understand the emotions underlying other people's actions. They are able to judge the level of emotion, the power behind it, and the best way to direct it. Thus, water Moons may choose counseling, sales, or other jobs where interpersonal relationships form the basis of the career. The Moon in water would be a strong arbitrator. They can determine what is most important to each side, and make decisions that reveal their understanding of both positions.

Water sign Moons often have a psychic awareness of the world, sensing changes in people's mood and compensating for them almost without thinking. You can smooth ruffle feathers before they look mussed by simply indicating that you are aware of the feelings involved.

Cancer

The Moon in Cancer reflects a strong "felt" sense of what is right. Judgment is often based on a gut feeling that a certain direction is best. You understand the relationship between your emotional state at a given moment and other information that is coming in. You tend to flow with situations, waiting for the proper time to inject your view. Because of this style, your opinion carries more weight.

You are an astute judge of a person's place in a group, giving you an advantage, but don't overdo it—others will resent your ability to manipulate people and situations. You also want to attend to each individual's sense of themselves, making everyone happy. This ability serves you well in a career like convention management or administrative planning, where sensitivity to each individual is as important as the overall goal.

You have the ability to actively follow a path while fitting into the predefined processes. Like water running down hill, you "go with the flow" and at the same time bring in your own ideas. Your sensitivity to the flow—its rate of speed, the bumpiness, or other qualities—makes you a valued commodity. You sense a shift in the practical or emotional tide before others and are able to recommend adaptations to a plan already in motion, thus redirecting work to suit the new demands.

Scorpio

Regardless of your Sun sign, you have an fighting spirit that keeps you in the game when others give up and go home. This tenacity helps you achieve your own goals, and can be a huge asset if you avoid the temptation to steamroll others in your path. People will admire your ambition only if you acknowledge theirs.

Your tendency is to overdo from time to time, and then attempt to compensate by working extra hard to accomplish your goals. This can lead to mental burnout and physical exhaustion. It would be better for you to speculate on what is 80 percent of your capacity, for example, keeping 20 percent in reserve for if the going gets tough. In this way you can consistently perform at your best, and in the process you avoid offending others by appearing to be trying to outdo them and forcing them to keep up an unreasonable pace.

You love the truth. In fact, you require the truth from your boss, your peers, and your employees. Because of this, you must always stick to the truth in your dealings. Don't be seduced into shady deals where you must sacrifice this ideal. Over time you will develop ways to be more tactful while still being truthful. If you follow this path, when the going is really tough your peers will look to you for guidance. You are not afraid to be on the edge of disaster, pulling projects out of the "fire" and setting them on a new, more effective course.

Pisces

Your openness to mental and emotional influences from others is both a valuable career asset and a near curse. The downside is that you will feel every current of mental and emotional energy around you until you learn to filter it. This means you must make a distinction between what is around you and how it affects you. Otherwise your recognition of a situation may become indistinguishable from your relationship to it, much as a child watching a horror movie becomes its victim. Such filtering becomes an unconscious process, rather like walking—you may remember input, but at the moment you don't let it bother you. Then you process it later. The filtering skill places you in a valuable career position, as you get to the heart of a problem quickly and don't get caught up in side issues.

Your moodiness can be a career deficit. You will want to have a reversible filter that also works from the inside out, allowing you to have your feelings without broadcasting them to everyone around you. This can be tough, as you want to be true to yourself but still moderate your emotionalism at work.

Another side of your sensitivity is the potential to drift, following the lead of others, without strong personal goals. By yielding, you create two possible difficulties: You don't achieve the goals reflected by your Sun sign because you are busy helping other people to achieve theirs, and you may yield to less than ethical suggestions that get you into serious trouble. Remember that your Sun sign shows the nature of the boat you travel in and the direction in which you sail. The Moon reflects the method of propulsion and how you steer around obstacles. You sense the obstacles on the psychic level and learn to ease around them without having to take a solid stand.

The Current Mode of Thinking

We notice changes in our thinking as the Moon moves through the signs. Although I won't need to define those differences here, I do feel it is important is to see such alterations of mood as learning experiences. All too often we find our selves stuck in a rut of thinking and acting the same way we've always done. By being aware of the shifting lunar energy, we get a glimpse of other modes of thinking, and learn to appreciate them and use them in our own lives.

Practical Timing Tips for Business People

Maria K. Simms

Small entrepreneurial businesses, a great many of them owned by women, are making their mark in the business world. Creative people tired of corporate life have found a myriad of ways to make it on their own. Women have found that the varied skills learned through home-making and child-rearing serve them quite well in business. Naturally multitask oriented, women find they are well suited to handling or overseeing the various phases of managing a small business, and find it much more satisfying than being a salaried employee. This article is aimed at the business decision-maker—the entrepreneur, freelancer, small business-owner, executive of a larger business—anyone who works independently and has the power, the responsibility and assumes the risk of "calling the shots."

You're a person who sometimes must make potentially critical decisions quickly. You know that being in the right place at the right time can be critical to your success, and astrology can help give you that timing "edge." In the hands of a person who understands a particular business—its products, markets, cycles, opportunities, and pitfalls—and who has a honest self-awareness of his or her own strengths and weaknesses, astrological knowledge provides a powerful added leverage for success. If, however, you think that astrology can make decisions for you and ensure your "luck," you are using it superstitiously and would be better off to stay away from it. Astrology is only a tool. The power is not with the planets, it is within you! You must direct the use of the tool just as you might use market trend cycles for guidance. When your instincts and your knowledge of your particular business tell you otherwise—pay attention.

The late Neil F. Michelsen, founder of the highly successful astrological business, Astro Communications Services, Inc., in San Diego, used to say, "If it comes to a contest between astrological indicators and a strong gut-level feeling, I trust my gut." He knew his business (I'm speaking here of his market, his staff, his customers, and his computers, rather than astrology), and he had a considerable amount of common sense.

The really important decisions regarding your business, such as when to officially start it, how to choose a partner, or when to sign that make-or-break contract deserve a more complex astrology than is within the scope of this article. For major decisions, a full Election Chart that's cast for a time and place when the planets are judged to be in very favorable positions for the type of event that one wants to begin is recommended. Just as the occasion of a birth has a natal chart, a chart can be cast for exact date, time, and place can be read for information about basic character, current patterns, growth potential and all the various ups and downs of cyclical change.

I highly recommend an astrological consultation with an astrologer who can interpret your birth chart, and perhaps give you annual update on your current cycles. No form of astrological timing will work well for you unless you also know yourself and how you act and react in certain situations. Self-knowledge plus timing knowledge will give you a major edge in learning how to handle problems and make successful choices. Select an astrologer who can also interpret the chart of when your business began and the current cycles of that chart. You may also want to have an Election Chart made for important events or life choices.

A word about the chart of when your business began: It's best to elect that time in advance. If you've already started your business, you may or may not have recorded the actual time it started, but you surely remember the day. Even that much information will be useful to an astrologer, because for a business, a chart set for noon gives worthwhile information; though not as good as exact time, it's useful. In my experience, the instinctive time the owner of a business takes the first tangible step to bring the business into being is the most accurate business chart. A later chart of incorporation or grand opening day may be, but it won't tell the story quite as well as the original chart.

Most people are far too busy to afford the time to run to an astrologer, or even to be constantly checking every table in this book. Remember, your knowledge of your business is of priority importance, and the future is largely what you make of it. Even I, as a businesswoman for many years and also a trained astrologer, have done full Election Charts only for very major events, plus taking a good annual look at the upcoming cycles of my own and the business' chart. For day-to-day business, I use very much the same techniques as I'll telling you about in this article, usually taking no more time for them than a quick glance at the astrological calendar hanging near my desk. For those of you who do not read aspects, the Moon Tables in this book will be useful, for they give quick at-a-glance keys to consult for which days have easy flow aspects and which ones are potentially challenging.

In regard to aspects, I don't quite agree with the Moon Tables on one point. They give the impression that square aspects are always unfavorable. That does not correspond to my experience. To be sure, squares often represent something challenging about the situation or the time period, but challenge is not necessarily a bad thing. If you were one who avoided challenge, you wouldn't be in business in the first place. So long as you handle the challenge well, you're actually more likely to see tangible action with squares than with an easy flow day of trines that are often lacking in energy and just drift by. I remember learning that lesson after planning an open house event on a day in which the only aspects were a couple of trines. Not all that many people came and business was lackadaisical. Next time I picked a day with squares and there was a lot more action, and sales! We worked quite a bit harder, of course, but that was part of the challenge.

I could say somewhat the same thing about oppositions. They generally mean that something needs balance, and often there's some aspect of relationship opposition. Again, challenging, but if handled well, it can turn out for the best.

So, look at the Moon Tables, but if you see a day that's marked "U" or "u" meaning "unfavorable for your Sun sign," take a harder look before you decide to do nothing on that day. Your Sun sign is only one among several other astrological factors to take into consideration when deciding whether to accept the challenge of a "U" or "u" day.

Here are the most significant techniques any layperson can learn to use with minimal effort-and also the ones that I have used most reliably for day-to-day business decisions.

The Phases of the Moon

I consider Moon phases the easiest and most useful of astrological timing techniques.

From New Moon to first quarter is the time to start something new. At New Moon ideas emerge; hunches can be especially valuable. As you move toward first quarter, plans take shape; projects get off the drawing board and begin to manifest.

First Quarter to Full Moon is the time to take decisive action, move forward, revise and develop, evaluate and learn.

At Full Moon, results are evident. If ideas that emerged at New Moon look like winners—even if you're not all that sure, don't give up. Keep working. This is a high time for accomplishment.

Full Moon to last quarter is a time to effectively consolidate your gains on that "winner." If more development time seems to be needed, you'll wind down a bit, reevaluate, and tie up loose ends. Hey, this is only a one month cycle. This project may just take more time and thought.

Last quarter to New Moon is a time for reflection and revision. If something isn't working out, it may be time to let it go, and begin to dream up possible new plans. On the other hand, the project that had potential may yet be reincarnated with some introspection and revised plans.

The monthly Moon Tables in this book give you the phases and other valuable information. It's also useful to have an astrological wall calendar, such as Llewellyn's *Astrological Calendar*, hanging near your desk and phone for quick reference. Some calendars show the symbols which also look like the actual Moon phase observed in the sky. The four primary phases are clearly shown. Llewellyn's calendar shows them in words. I'll mention here that the New Moon is dark (not visible in the night sky) at the actual clock time given in this book and on calendar, and the thin crescent doesn't appear until about the third day after New Moon.

If there's no possible way you can postpone the needed action until the "right" phase, sometimes you can still be in the flow by changing the nature of your intent. For example, you want to hire a new employee, but it is the last quarter phase, and the book says that you should hire within first or second quarter. You know that by the time New Moon goes by, this person will most like have another job and your opportunity will be gone. Your instinct and knowledge of your business tell you this person's presence will enable you to revise a project, delegate more, and eliminate a problem within your business. All those things fit right in with the symbolism of last quarter Moon. It would be appropriate to take action and hire the person.

Knowing the sign of the Moon will give you an edge on understanding what to expect from the general mood of people around you on a given day. People vary in their individual moods, of course, but everyone responds, to some degree, to the moods around them. Understanding the signs may help you understand some of the frequently shifting moods, the ups and downs, of the general public. Consider, in this case, that the Moon sign of the day represents your business public—customers, vendors, staff, and business colleagues—anyone you encounter throughout the course of your business day might be expressing the mood of the Moon, or interests that are associated with its sign. Notice how very different adjacent signs are from one another. Moods can change drastically from sign to sign, from one day to the next—an excellent reason why you should be aware of them

Moon in Aries

Activity is more likely motivated by impulse than by well-thought-through plans. Slowness or resistance may cause temperaments to flare. Be prepared to handle "me first" attitudes, assertive energies, and impatience. Resist tendencies toward impulse buying; emphasize the exciting, innovative qualities of your products or services; and direct upbeat, individual attention toward customers.

Moon in Taurus

Energy mellows and slows as the prevailing attitudes shift toward resistance to change, caution, and even stubbornness. Security needs predominate. People care more about comfort and positive sensual experience—the feel, texture, taste, and smell of things, as well as appearance—are enhanced. Take your time with people, be patient. Emphasize quality and reliability.

Moon in Gemini

The phone rings constantly, and although interruptions abound, it's a good time to push forward with communication activities. It's also a potentially scattered, restless time when people flit here and there, talk a lot, but are unable to make up their minds. They'll want to look at and try everything. Variety and novelty appeal. Thinking prevails over feeling. Be ready to chat with people and answer questions. Keep communications clear, and curb your tendency to be distracted.

Moon in Cancer

Reason and rationale lose out to subconscious responses as feeling now prevails over thinking. People tend to respond emotionally rather than through logic, even when they're not aware they are doing so. They may be more vulnerable than usual, taking offense when none was intended. Caution and sensitivity is recommended in dealing with others, and also in monitoring how you, yourself, react to them. Make people comfortable in your homey atmosphere, and feed them.

Moon in Leo

Energies run toward spontaneity, upbeat spirit, generosity, and fun. People are extra susceptible to complements, so long as they are sincerely given. Treat customers like royalty; even more than you usually do. Point with pride to the creative aspects of your business, but curb any tendencies toward arrogance, or to overt reaction on your part to arrogance expressed by others.

Moon in Virgo

This is a good time to handle tasks that require great attention to detail. Clear your desk, and tackle those clean-up or reorganization projects you've been putting off. The mood around you is likely to be more discriminating than usual, with greater concern for cleanliness, exactness, efficiency. Emphasize quality control, technical support, follow-up service. Appeal to the intellect and to technical skills. Moods become more subdued, and critical tendencies are emphasized.

Moon in Libra

Expect increase in any tendencies toward indecision in yourself or others. Patience, friendliness, and tolerance help. Balance, harmony and aesthetic appeal are important. Take stock of the appearance of your place of business for possible improvements. Emphasize teamwork, and appreciation for the contributions of each to the whole. Be friendly, sociable, and be absolutely fair in all your dealings.

Moon in Scorpio

Moods tend to become more intense, which may be noticed as a general impatience, or in overreactions to perceived offenses. Be aware, so you can avoid walking into it, or can maintain calm and tactful if you do. Expect people to be dissatisfied with superficial answers. They'll probe, possibly even express suspicion. Analysis and scrutiny are emphasized. Go into depth when you are asked to explain your product or services. Show attention and respect for your customer's knowledge and perceptions.

Moon in Sagittarius

Restlessness, a sense of adventure, idealism, and strong opinions that may be expressed freely and sometimes dogmatically should be expected. Here, superficiality and faith rather than probing for hidden flaws may prevail. The urge to stretch increases as independence, freedom, options, opportunity, idealistic faith, or a touch of the exotic motivate people.

Moon in Capricorn

The prevailing mood becomes practical and considerably more serious. Shoppers take a more no-nonsense, business-like approach. Status-conscious Capricorns look for dependability, workmanship, and quality in a good buy. Pessimism may seem more prevalent, requiring extra reassurance and patience. Establish your integrity to earn credibility with customers. Guarantees of consistency and the reliability of your service will impress.

Moon in Aquarius

The mood turns more gregarious, but don't take that as an invitation to get too chummy, or people will back off. The mood is detached, intellectual, curious, and not particularly serious. Humor will be appreciated; innovation will impress; as will the unique, unconventional, or perhaps even the eccentric, or weird. Show off the latest developments in your product line or service—especially if they serve humanitarian needs.

Moon in Pisces

The mood is likely to be rather passive, perhaps on the quiet side. People are more gentle and kind, more impressionable and vulnerable than usual, and may become too easily discouraged. If you play music in your place of business, keep it calm and soothing now. Compassion for others is heightened, as is interest in all humanitarian services. You may feel like daydreaming, or imagination may inspire.

Moon Void-of-Course

From the time the Moon makes its final aspect to any planet before leaving a sign, until it enters into the next sign, it is said to be "void-of-course" and not recommended for accomplishing much other than very routine work, or the continuation of projects already begun. The traditional interpretations of void Moon say that "nothing happens," or that things began, decisions made, or objects purchased just don't fulfill expectations.

I'm one who always test and retests such "rules," figuring that one ought to be able to get around them one way or another. This one, however, seems determined to thwart most attempts at strategically disregarding its symbolism. I've often discovered that sad fact both when I knew the Moon was void in advance, and also when I hadn't noticed until after the fact. I'd been determined to get some calls made but could get nothing but voice mail machines, or no answer at all. I've tried to start projects and found I didn't have what I needed, went out to find it and the store was out of it, or closed; or I'd find it, and find out later that it didn't work right.

When you see that the Moon is void, it's generally best to kick back and reflect on your business and yourself, and let what's been going on around you sink in and assimilate. Ideas may emerge that you can develop later. Every business person needs time for reflection. Don't push what can't be pushed.

On the other hand, one can sometimes take advantage of a void Moon to do things where you don't want anything other than routine results, or no results at all. For example, you could make that appointment with the person who's been after you, but with whom you don't really want to do business. They'll be glad that at least you were willing to talk. Or you could file routine papers that won't be subject to further scrutiny or revision.

You can find a Void Moon Table on page 56 of this book, or if you have that astrological calendar, you can also glance at it. The Moon "v/c" symbol with the time will appear on the date where it occurs, and you'll also see "Moon enters," the name of sign, and the time on the date where that occurs.

Retrogrades, especially Mercury

The retrograde periods of the planets, shown for this year in a table toward the beginning of this book, are said to be times when the energy of the planet that is retrograde turns inward, is delayed, or is somehow out-of-kilter. Matters ruled by that planet are said to be prone to delays.

Mercury, ruler of all matters of communication, is retrograde for several weeks an average of three times a year. Often portrayed as the villain of retrograde tradition (threatening, in my observation, to verge on an almost superstitious dread among some astrologically knowledgeable people), this planet retrograde is much maligned. I've mused on this tradition often during my eight-plus years of heading a company with Communication as part of its name. Obviously, my business couldn't close down, or even cease its normal, daily communication activities, at any of the times when Mercury was retrograde. The mail still has to go out, contracts often have to be signed, books need to go to the printer, and so on. It's not unusual for Customer Service personnel to be confronted with a few astrologically knowledgeable customers who insist on delaying their much wanted purchases until Mercury goes direct, which may be one of our prime actual "effects" of the phenomenon. One, I believe, that needs to be considered, for it seems to me that there is no significant difference in frequency.

Of course, the natal chart of my business had Mercury retrograde, as did my own natal chart and that of the founder of the business. That may make some difference. I've heard astrologers speculate that when one has retrograde planets, one tends to handle the retrograde transits better.

But every so often, a Mercury retrograde period really seems to live up to all of its bad press. When I've checked, it's usually been a time when the "station" (the exact degree of the zodiac on which Mercury turns retrograde or direct) was in close, challenging aspect to something important in my chart or the business chart.

In any case, I think it is wiser to consider the period of Mercury retrograde as one of a flashing yellow light to be interpreted as caution in all communication activities, not a stop sign. My list of cautions you should take are things you should take care about anyway, but especially during Mercury retrograde. Carefully check any papers you have to sign. Take extra care to keep copies, receipts and tracking notices. Purchase and use back-up software for your computer files. Sleep on important, potentially controversial letters (and e-mails) before you send them. Repeat back what you think you heard somebody say before you over-react to it. Be sure you've thought through what you are communicating and state it clearly. Be alert to how you are being received, so potential misunderstandings can be properly clarified.

Venus and Mars retrograde periods may be perceived as times of delay, especially if your business involves the areas ruled by the planets. Such periods are infrequent—some years don't have either of these two planets retrograde.

In 2001, Venus will be retrograde in March and April. Financial matters may be delayed during Venus' retrograde period. If your business deals in finance, luxury items, or anything to do with beauty or art, you have reasons to be more alert during this time. Mars is retrograde in May, June, and July. You may experience slowdowns or delays in businesses that have to do with metals, engineering, carpentry, the military, fire, or sports equipment and supplies.

Jupiter, Saturn, Uranus, Neptune, and Pluto will always be retrograde for a few months out of every year, and because of that, will probably not be of major notice to you most of the time. If you experience a significant delay, you might look toward the end of the retrograde period of whatever planet or planets are retrograde, for a time when things can move forward more easily.

A Concluding Note on Astrological Timing

The rules of timing are useful to note, but don't be a slave to them. It can be a highly useful tool that can be used to help you make decisions, just as analysis of other types of cyclical activity can be useful. Never forget, though, that you are the power. The planets should be taken as signposts to guide you along a possibly easier route. The best of things can sometimes happen at the worst of times. At the same time, choosing to move with the flow of our planetary cycles is generally easier than fighting against the current. Your best decisions may be guided by astrology, but must be placed in context of your knowledge of your business, your instincts and your own good common sense.

Moon Sign Shopping

Heyde Class-Garney

Attention shoppers! Have you ever wondered if there was a "better" time to buy things? Well, though elective astrology—timing events based on astrological signs and aspects—you can select the best time to buy most things.

Elective astrology will help you to avoid buying thoughtlessly, and may help you keep a close tab on your purse strings. Based on the theory that each sign rules over particular items, and that the Moon transiting over the various houses creates more favorable or less favorable times to make purchases, it's to your benefit to familiarize yourself with each house, and with each changing face and mood of the Moon. By choosing advantageous times to make you buys, you can ensure yourself a quality purchase, along with peace of mind.

When the Moon is void-of-course (check an astrological calendar or the Void-of-Course Table in this book), purchases may not function correctly, may be of a poorer quality, or may not ever be used. Mercury retrograde is another time to avoid shopping. You may pick the wrong size, shape, or color, or end up with an item that doesn't function and has to be returned. Since Mercury retrogrades three times a year for three weeks at a time, shopping during this transit may be impossible to avoid. Just pay attention. Keep your eyes open to possible quality problems, and by all means, keep the receipt. Venus goes retrograde about every eighteen months for six weeks, so Venus ruled items such as clothes, jewelry, art, music, and cosmetics should not be purchased during those times. Other considerations to factor are the current aspects and the quarters of the Moon. These will vary according to the Moon sign and also the item being purchased. Be sure to check both the Astro-Almanac on page 12, and the Business & Legal Section starting on page —for favorable dates and further guidelines.

Aries Moon

Shopaholics beware! Impulsive Mars rules this Moon sign. Saying "no" is not on the agenda, so don't be surprised to find yourself cruising down the store aisles, spending with wild abandon. Part of this craze is due to the action-oriented nature of Aries, but it doesn't stop there. Burn-out is another factor to consider with fiery Aries. That fancy gadget or trendy item that just caught your eye may soon lose its appeal after you've used it with enthusiasm at every opportunity. If you want to stay on good terms with your spouse, leave your credit cards at home, or forego shopping all together today. But if you must shop, purchase sporting equipment, tools, machinery, and building materials. Clothing and jewelry should be avoided if possible, along with those little trivial items that you really don't need or want. Be sure to check for sextiles and trines to both Mars and Uranus, along with a favorable lunar cycle for yourself in The Moon Tables beginning on page 28. All quarters of the Moon are appropriate. But try to keep a tight grip on your wallet.

Taurus Moon

This is a prime shopping day for just about anything. You may be attracted to expensive, higher quality items though. Due to the conservative, fixed nature of this Moon sign, you may tend to be practical, and not overspend. In this Venus ruled sign items such as clothing, jewelry, cosmetics, art, music, and even concert tickets are favored. Try to buy them in the first and second quarters with positive aspects to the Sun and Venus. Since Taurus is associated with the earth, buying plants, shrubs, flowers, and seeds is also appropriate. Domestic matters will take precedence, so furniture and home furnishings, or even a new home or car is in order. Check for sextiles and trines to Saturn for long-lasting wear. Taurus is well known for its prudence and resourcefulness, so investing in stocks, annuities, retirement funds, or any speculation that has a long-term benefit will pan out well. First and second quarter Moon phases with positive aspects to Jupiter and Saturn will aid investments. A trip to the grocery store should be high on your to-do list. All and all, Taurus will prove to be a superior buying time.

Gemini Moon

Expect the shopping malls to be packed as this Mercury ruled Moon sign has people on the go. Gemini and the media are synonymous, so books, magazines, newspapers, and writing items are favorable purchases. Buying a different or new car may satisfy you, or a weekend trip might be in order. But keep in mind that with such a hefty purchase its essential to have positive aspects to both Mercury and Uranus, and by all means be sure Mercury is direct before venturing onto the car lots. Purchasing a lemon is more likely during a Mercury retrograde period. Negotiating the ticket price can work in your favor as you may be more versatile now. Arranging travel plans and buying tickets can prove to be a bonus, along with items relating to travel such as cameras, film, and luggage. The restless nature of Gemini can cause people to shop just for the curiosity factor, however. An interest in gadgets could dominate your mood, making electronics a positive buy. Check for favorable aspects to both Mercury and Uranus and avoid Mercury retrogrades. One more thing to avoid during a Gemini Moon is impatience There is always another day to spend your money if you find you can't get your act together.

Cancer Moon

If there every was a time tailor-made for window shopping, the Cancer Moon is it. You will most likely dismiss nonessential spending all together. Cancer is the quintessential wheeler-dealer type, so utilize this skill and negotiate the price of your new home. Try to purchase your home in the New Moon if possible. The mood to purchase other home-related items such as rugs, lamps, pictures, along with yard and gardening supplies, may surface. Every Moon sign has its weakness, and food is it for this nurturing Moon sign. So, a trip to the grocery store or to the nearest bakery or deli is appropriate. Expect to emerge with a passel of food. Since Cancer is associated with things from yester-year, a trip to the local flea market or antique mall can produce positive and valuable discoveries. Remember to have fun spending as you may cling to your money like bees to honey.

Leo Moon

This is a fabulous day to shop, especially for clothes and jewelry. Be sure to take into consideration that you will be buying the most expensive "everything" and experience not a care in the world. When you finally reach the limit on your Visa card (extravagance and overindulgence are key words for this fire ruled Moon sign) there's no need to beat yourself up, but do pick only the items you want most. If that's out of your price range, use common sense and wait until it goes on sale. Now is the time to watch the aspects carefully. For clothes buying, check for favorable aspects to the Sun, Venus, and Mercury, preferably in a first or second quarter Moon. Avoid all aspects to Mars and Saturn. Squares and oppositions to both Venus and Jupiter should be avoided as they will only enhance your urge to overspend. And in lieu of the fact that you may have the attitude that you are the king or queen of the entire world, you may opt to use all available resources to get what you want. Being overly generous is another pitfall. Attempt to restrain yourself and shop until you find the most for your money.

Virgo Moon

Shopping may be rather exhausting during this discriminating Moon sign. This is a superior time to purchase anything health related—vitamins, herbs, supplements, and medicines—and have no fear of junk food mysteriously appearing in your cart either, as you will be more likely to choose health conscious foods instead. Economical Virgo has a knack for saving money, so by all means, bring the coupons along. Mercury, ruler of communication, music, and travel rules over Virgo as well. So dash on down to the book store, or choose to arrange a nice get away for two or the whole family. Its essential that there are positive aspects to Mercury, and that you avoid Mercury retrograde. Be sure to check this book's Leisure & Recreation section for more details on specific types of travel.

Libra Moon

Expect to shop till you drop because Libra and shopping literally go hand-in-hand, and you will buy just about anything your little heart desires. Libra is a lover of beauty, so head out to the mall, beginning your day in style, with a trip to your favorite cosmetic counter. Along the way, you can indulge your passion for clothing, lingerie, and even shoes. You may also find yourself attracted to trivial trinkets, home furnishings of any kind, art work, music, electronics, flowers, and even candy. But realize that no wallet is safe today, so if you are experiencing a temporary lack of cash, opt to postpone shopping for a more sensible day. About the only real trouble you will run into, besides spending all your money, is making up your mind.

Scorpio Moon

The Scorpio Moon will help you focus on ways to increase your net worth. This complex Moon sign can help you turn over a new leaf, creating some much-needed cash. Scorpio's ruling planet, Pluto, is associated with speculation among other things, so get cracking and buy up those stocks you have been deliberating over. Don't forget to check the Business & Legal section of this book to assure the outcome of your purchase. You may also choose to invest in a savings plan, retirement fund or certificate of deposits. The fixed (stable) quality of Scorpio will help you money or investments stay where its suppose to. Buying a home is a good bet today—especially if you don't want to move again. You may even consider buying a car. Trust that your intuition will be sharp and you can see right though the car-dealers "sell." And if it's a fourth quarter Moon, you may get an even better bargain. Avoid buying clothes and jewelry as you may never wear them.

Sagittarius Moon

Be ready to kick up your heels and head for the shopping mall. This Jupiter-ruled sign screams "if one is good, ten is better," and the word "no" doesn't seem to exist in this Moon's vocabulary. Attempt to heed the advice—buyer beware! Car buying can be very joyfully, but you may end with a vehicle ten times bigger than what your family really needs. The Moon should be in favorable aspect to Mercury and Uranus when you purchase a car. You may get a touch of the travel bug. Foreign travel will give you that taste of adventure that you are seeking now. And if there are negative aspects to Jupiter, alter your decision to buy until a more favorable time. Attempt to keep a firm handle on your wallet and you should come home with a little extra cash.

Capricorn Moon

Sensible and practical, a Capricorn Moon is great for things like clothes, shoes, and school supplies. Financial matters—long-term investments, on-line trading, stocks and bonds—are all favored here. It is essential to check for sextiles and trines to both Jupiter and Saturn to assure longevity and receiving a good return on your stocks though. Favorable aspects to Venus won't hurt either as Venus is associated with both attraction and money. This responsible, organized Saturn ruled sign governs real estate. This should put you in the right frame of mind to invest, giving you that little push you may need to go ahead and purchase that hefty chunk of real estate you have been eyeing for some time now. Or better yet, you might choose to build yourself a new home, which means you will need tools and lumber.

Aquarius Moon

Anything that is unusual, bizarre, or just down right weird is what you will most likely be attracted to with Uranus-ruled Aquarius. Buying a black Victorian chair with leopard spots would be a normal occurrence now. But besides the oddities, this is your best day to buy any major appliances (either gas and electric powered), or electronic items. After all, Uranus rules over electricity, computers, broadcasting, and even inventing. When purchasing appliances, be sure to check your own personal lunar cycle for favorable times, as well as the aspects of Mars and Uranus to the Moon. If Mercury, Uranus, or Mars are retrograde, stay out of the appliance store, unless of course you are ready to make several trips back and forth returning the same item as it just doesn't seem to function correctly. For computers, stereo components, and even radios, follow previously stated rules for electronics.

Pisces Moon

You feet may hurt and your wallet may be empty, but don't despair—use that vivid imagination Pisces is famous for to your advantage, and conjuring up some cash to indulge all your shopping fantasies. One fantasy may include buying that expensive perfume or jewelry that you've daydreamed about. Since Pisces rules over the feet, you will want to buy all your shoes today, particularly the comfy kind. While cruising on your shopping spree, be on the look out for your favorite video tapes or photography equipment as both are associated with Neptune, Pisces' ruling planet. The major factor to keep in mind now is that you may end up deluding yourself into many unneeded purchases. So stop and think before spending your money.

Farm,

Garden,

& Weather

Farm, Garden, & Weather

How to Choose the Best Dates

Animals and Animal Breeding

Animals are easiest to handle when the Moon is in Taurus, Cancer, Libra, or Pisces. Avoid the Full Moon. Buy animals during the first quarter in all signs except Scorpio or Pisces. Castrate animals in Gemini, Cancer, Capricorn, or Aquarius. Slaughter for food in the first three days after the Full Moon in any sign except Leo.

To encourage healthy births, eggs should be set and animals mated so births occur when the Moon is increasing in Taurus, Cancer, Pisces, or Libra. Those born during a semifruitful sign (Taurus and Capricorn) will produce leaner meat. Libra yields beautiful animals for showing and racing. To determine the best date to mate animals or set eggs, subtract the number of days given for incubation or gestation from the fruitful dates given in the following tables. For example, cats and dogs are mated sixty-three days previous to the desired birth date. See tables on pages 317–318.

Garden Activities
Cultivating

Cultivate when the Moon is in a barren sign and waning, ideally the fourth quarter in Aries, Gemini, Leo, Virgo, or Aquarius. Third quarter in the sign of Sagittarius will also work.

Cutting Timber

Cut timber during the waning Moon in an air, earth, or fire sign.

Fertilizing and Composting

Fertilize when the Moon is in a fruitful sign (Cancer, Scorpio, Pisces). Organic fertilizers are best when the Moon is waning, chemical fertilizers when the Moon is waxing. Start compost when the Moon is in the fourth quarter in a water sign.

Grafting

Graft during first or second quarter Capricorn, Cancer, or Scorpio.

Harvesting and Drying Crops

Harvest root crops when the Moon is in a dry sign (Aries, Leo, Sagittarius, Gemini, or Aquarius) and waning. Harvest grain for storage just after Full Moon, avoiding water signs (Cancer, Scorpio, Pisces). Harvest in the third and fourth quarters in dry signs. Dry in the third quarter in fire signs.

Irrigation

Irrigate when the Moon is in a water sign.

Lawn Mowing

Mow in the first and second quarters to increase growth and lushness, and in the third and fourth quarters to decrease growth.

Picking Mushrooms

Gather mushrooms at the Full Moon.

Planting

For complete instructions on planting by the Moon, see Gardening by the Moon on page 285, A Guide to Planting Using Sign and Phase Rulerships on page 291, and Companion Planting on page 309.

Pruning

Prune during the third and fourth quarters in Scorpio to retard growth and to promote better fruit, and in Capricorn to promote better healing.

Spraying and Weeding

Destroy pests and weeds during the fourth quarter when the Moon is in Aries, Gemini, Leo, Virgo, Sagittarius, or Aquarius. Weed during a waning Moon in a barren sign. For the best days to kill weeds and pests, see pages 305 and 306.

Transplanting

Transplant when the Moon is increasing and preferably in Cancer, Scorpio, or Pisces.

Gardening by the Moon

Today, people often reject the notion of Moon gardening. The usual nonbeliever is not a scientist, but the city dweller who has never had any real contact with nature and no experience of natural rhythms.

Camille Flammarian, the French astronomer, testifies to Moon planting: "Cucumbers increase at Full Moon, as well as radishes, turnips, leeks, lilies, horseradish, and saffron; onions, on the contrary, are much larger and better nourished during the decline and old age of the Moon than at its increase, during its youth and fullness, which is the reason the Egyptians abstained from onions, on account of their antipathy to the Moon. Herbs gathered while the Moon increases are of great efficiency. If the vines are trimmed at night when the Moon is in the sign of the Lion, Sagittarius, the Scorpion, or the Bull, it will save them from field rats, moles, snails, flies, and other animals."

Dr. Clark Timmins is one of the few modern scientists to have conducted tests in Moon planting. Following is a summary of his experiments:

Beets: When sown with the Moon in Scorpio, the germination rate was 71 percent; when sown in Sagittarius, the germination rate was 58 percent.

Scotch marigold: When sown with the Moon in Cancer, the germination rate was 90 percent; when sown in Leo, the rate was 32 percent.

Carrots: When sown with the Moon in Scorpio, the germination rate was 64 percent; when sown in Sagittarius, the germination rate was 47 percent.

Tomatoes: When sown with the Moon in Cancer, the germination rate was 90 percent; when sown in Leo, the germination rate was 58 percent.

Two things should be emphasized. First, remember that this is only a summary of the results of the experiments; the experiments themselves were conducted in a scientific manner to eliminate any variation in soil, temperature, moisture, and so on, so that only the Moon sign is varied. Also, note that these astonishing results were obtained without regard to the phase of the Moon—the other factor we use in Moon planting, and which presumably would have increased the differential in germination rates.

Further experiments by Dr. Timmins involved transplanting Cancer and Leo-planted tomato seedlings while the Moon was increasing and in Cancer. The result was 100 percent survival. When transplanting was done with the Moon decreasing and in Sagittarius, there was 0 percent survival. The results of Dr. Timmins' tests show that the Cancer-planted tomatoes had blossoms twelve days earlier than those planted under Leo; the Cancer-planted tomatoes had an average height of twenty inches at that time compare to fifteen inches for the Leo-planted; the first ripe tomatoes were gathered from the Cancer plantings eleven days ahead of the Leo plantings; and a count of the hanging fruit and its size and weight shows an advantage to the Cancer plants over the Leo plants of 45 percent.

Dr. Timmins also observed that there have been similar tests that did not indicate results favorable to the Moon planting theory. As a scientist, he asked why one set of experiments indicated a positive verification of Moon planting, and others did not. He checked these other tests and found that the experimenters had not followed the geocentric system for determining the Moon sign positions, but the heliocentric. When the times used in these other tests were converted to the geocentric system, the dates chosen often were found to be in barren, rather than fertile, signs. Without going into a technical explanation, it is sufficient to point out that geocentric and heliocentric positions often vary by as much as four days. This is a large enough differential to place the Moon in Cancer, for example, in the heliocentric system, and at the same time in Leo by the geocentric system.

Most almanacs and calendars show the Moon's signs heliocentrically—and thus incorrectly for Moon planting—while the *Moon Sign Book* is calculated correctly for planting purposes, using the geocentric system. Some readers are also confused because the *Moon Sign Book* talks of first, second, third, and fourth quarters, while some almanacs refer to these same divisions as New Moon, first quarter, Full Moon, and last quarter. Thus, the almanacs say first quarter when the *Moon Sign Book* says second quarter. (Refer to "A Note about Almanacs," page 10.)

There is nothing complicated about using astrology in agriculture and horticulture in order to increase both pleasure and profit, but there is one very important rule that is often neglected—use common sense! Of course this is one rule that should be remembered in every activity we undertake, but in the case of gardening and farming by the Moon it is not possible to use the best dates for planting or harvesting, and we must select the next best and just try to do the best we can.

This brings up the matter of the other factors to consider in your gardening work. The dates we give as best for a certain activity apply to the entire country (with slight time correction), but in your section of the country you may be buried under three feet of snow on a date we say is good to plant your flowers. So we have factors of weather, season, temperature and moisture variations, soil conditions, your own available time and opportunity, and so forth. Some astrologers like to think it is all a matter of science, but gardening is also an art. In art, you develop an instinctive identification with your work and influence it with your feelings and wishes.

The *Moon Sign Book* gives you the place of the Moon for every day of the year so that you can select the best times once you have become familiar with the rules and practices of lunar agriculture. We give you specific, easy-to-follow directions so that you can get right down to work.

We give you the best dates for planting, and also for various related activities, including cultivation, fertilizing, harvesting, irrigation, and getting rid of weeds and pests. But we cannot tell you exactly when it's good to plant. Many of these rules were learned by observation and experience; as the body of experience grew we could see various patterns emerging that allowed us to make judgments about new things. That's what you should do, too. After you have worked with lunar agriculture for a while and have gained a working knowledge, you will probably begin to try new things—and we hope you will share your experiments and findings with us. That's how the science grows.

Here's an example of what we mean. Years ago, Llewellyn George suggested that we try to combine our bits of knowledge about what to expect in planting under each of the Moon signs in order to gain benefit from several lunar factors in one plant. From this came our rule for developing "thoroughbred seed." To develop thoroughbred seed, save the seed for three successive years from plants grown by the correct Moon sign and phase. You can plant in the first quarter phase and in the sign of Cancer for fruitfulness; the second year, plant seeds from the first year plants in Libra for beauty; and in the third year, plant the seeds from the second year plants in Taurus to produce hardiness. In a similar manner you can combine the fruitfulness of Cancer, the good root growth of Pisces, and the sturdiness and good vine growth of Scorpio. And don't forget the characteristics of Capricorn: hardy like Taurus, but drier and perhaps more resistant to drought and disease.

Unlike common almanacs, we consider both the Moon's phase and the Moon's sign in making our calculations for the proper timing of our work. It is perhaps a little easier to understand this if we remind you that we are all living in the center of a vast electromagnetic field that is the Earth and its environment in space. Everything that occurs within this electromagnetic field has an effect on everything else within the field. The Moon and the Sun are the most important of the factors affecting the life of the Earth, and it is their relative positions to the Earth that we project for each day of the year.

Many people claim that not only do they achieve larger crops gardening by the Moon, but that their fruits and vegetables are much tastier. A number of organic gardeners have also become lunar gardeners using the natural rhythm of life forces that we experience through the relative movements of the Sun and Moon. We provide a few basic rules and then give you day-by-day guidance for your gardening work. You will be able to choose the best dates to meet your own needs and opportunities.

Planting by the Moon's Phases

During the increasing or waxing light—from New Moon to Full Moon—plant annuals that produce their yield above the ground. An annual is a plant that completes its entire life cycle within one growing season and has to be seeded each year. During the decreasing or waning light (from Full Moon to New Moon), plant biennials, perennials, and bulb and root plants. Biennials include crops that are planted one season to winter over and produce crops the next, such as winter wheat. Perennials and bulb and root plants include all plants that grow from the same root each year.

A simpler, less accurate rule is to plant crops that produce above the ground during the waxing Moon, and to plant crops that produce below the ground during the waning Moon. Thus the old adage, "Plant potatoes during the dark of the Moon." Llewellyn George's system divided the lunar month into quarters. The first two from New Moon to Full Moon are the first and second quarters, and the last two from Full Moon to New Moon the third and fourth quarters. Using these divisions, we can increase our accuracy in timing our efforts to coincide with natural forces.

First Quarter (Increasing)

Plant annuals producing their yield above the ground, which are generally of the leafy kind that produce their seed outside the fruit. Examples are asparagus, broccoli, Brussels sprouts, cabbage, cauliflower, celery, cress, endive, kohlrabi, lettuce, parsley, spinach, etc. Cucumbers are an exception, as they do best in the first quarter rather than the second, even though the seeds are inside the fruit. Also plant cereals and grains.

Second Quarter (Increasing)

Plant annuals producing their yield above the ground, which are generally of the viney kind that produce their seed inside the fruit. Examples include beans, eggplant, melons, peas, peppers, pumpkins, squash, tomatoes, etc. These are not hard and fast divisions. If you can't plant during the first quarter, plant during the second, and vice versa. There are many plants that seem to do equally well planted in either quarter, such as watermelon, hay, and cereals and grains.

Third Quarter (Decreasing)

Plant biennials, perennials, and bulb and root plants. Also plant trees, shrubs, berries, beets, carrots, onions, parsnips, peanuts, potatoes, radishes, rhubarb, rutabagas, strawberries, turnips, winter wheat, grapes, etc.

Fourth Quarter (Decreasing)

This is the best time to cultivate, turn sod, pull weeds, and destroy pests of all kinds, especially when the Moon is in the barren signs of Aries, Leo, Virgo, Gemini, Aquarius, and Sagittarius.

Moon in Aries

Barren and dry, fiery and masculine. Used for destroying noxious

Moon in Taurus

Productive and moist, earthy and feminine. Used for planting many crops, particularly potatoes and root crops, and when hardiness is important. Also used for lettuce, cabbage, and similar leafy vegetables.

Moon in Gemini

Barren and dry, airy and masculine. Used for destroying noxious growths, weeds and pests, and for cultivation.

Moon in Cancer

Very fruitful and moist, watery and feminine. This is the most productive sign, used extensively for planting and irrigation.

Moon in Leo

Barren and dry, fiery and masculine. This is the most barren sign, used only for killing weeds and for cultivation.

Moon in Virgo

Barren and moist, earthy and feminine. Good for cultivation and destroying weeds and pests.

Moon in Libra

Semifruitful and moist, airy and masculine. Used for planting many crops and producing good pulp growth and roots. A very good sign for flowers and vines. Also used for seeding hay, corn fodder, and the like.

Moon in Scorpio

Very fruitful and moist, watery and feminine. Nearly as productive as Cancer; used for the same purposes. Especially good for vine growth and sturdiness.

Moon in Sagittarius

Barren and dry, fiery and masculine. Used for planting onions, seeding hay, and for cultivation.

Moon in Capricorn

Productive and dry, earthy and feminine. Used for planting potatoes and other tubers.

Moon in Aquarius

Barren and dry, airy and masculine. Used for cultivation and destroying noxious growths, weeds, and pests.

Moon in Pisces

Very fruitful and moist, watery and feminine. Used along with Cancer and Scorpio, especially good for root growth.

A Guide to Planting

Using Phase & Sign Rulerships

Plant	Phase/Quarter	Sign
Annuals	1st or 2nd	
Apple trees	2nd or 3rd	Cancer, Pisces, Taurus, Virgo
Artichokes	1st	Cancer, Pisces
Asparagus	1st	Cancer, Scorpio, Pisces
Asters	1st or 2nd	Virgo, Libra
Barley	1st or 2nd	Cancer, Pisces, Libra, Capricorn, Virgo
Beans (bush & pole)	2nd	Cancer, Taurus, Pisces, Libra
Beans (kidney, white, & navy)	1st or 2nd	Cancer, Pisces
Beech Trees	2nd or 3rd	Virgo, Taurus
Beets	3rd	Cancer, Capricorn, Pisces, Libra
Biennials	3rd or 4th	
Broccoli	1st	Cancer, Pisces, Libra, Scorpio
Brussels Sprouts	1st	Cancer, Scorpio, Pisces, Libra
Buckwheat	1st or 2nd	Capricorn
Bulbs	3rd	Cancer, Scorpio, Pisces
Bulbs for Seed	2nd or 3rd	
Cabbage	1st	Cancer, Scorpio, Pisces, Libra, Taurus

Plant	Phase/Quarter	Sign
Cactus		Taurus, Capricorn
Canes (raspberries, black-berries, and gooseberries)	2nd	Cancer, Scorpio, Pisces
Cantaloupes	1st or 2nd	Cancer, Scorpio, Pisces, Libra, Taurus
Carrots	3rd	Taurus, Cancer, Scorpio, Pisces, Libra
Cauliflower	1st	Cancer, Scorpio, Pisces, Libra
Celeriac	3rd	Cancer, Scorpio, Pisces
Celery	1st	Cancer, Scorpio, Pisces
Cereals	1st or 2nd	Cancer, Scorpio, Pisces, Libra
Chard	1st or 2nd	Cancer, Scorpio, Pisces
Chicory	2nd or 3rd	Cancer, Scorpio, Pisces
Chrysanthemums	1st or 2nd	Virgo
Clover	1st or 2nd	Cancer, Scorpio, Pisces
Corn	1st	Cancer, Scorpio, Pisces
Corn for Fodder	1st or 2nd	Libra
Coryopsis	2nd or 3rd	Libra
Cosmos	2nd or 3rd	Libra
Cress	1st	Cancer, Scorpio, Pisces
Crocus	1st or 2nd	Virgo
Cucumbers	1st	Cancer, Scorpio, Pisces

Plant	Phase/Quarter	Sign
Daffodils	1st or 2nd	Libra, Virgo
Dahlias	1st or 2nd	Libra, Virgo
Deciduous Trees	2nd or 3rd	Cancer, Scorpio, Pisces, Virgo, Taurus
Eggplant	2nd	Cancer, Scorpio, Pisces, Libra
Endive	1st	Cancer, Scorpio, Pisces, Libra
Flowers	1st	Libra, Cancer, Pisces, Virgo, Scorpio, Taurus
Garlic	3rd	Libra, Taurus, Pisces
Gladiola	1st or 2nd	Libra, Virgo
Gourds	1st or 2nd	Cancer, Scorpio, Pisces, Libra
Grapes	2nd or 3rd	Cancer, Scorpio, Pisces, Virgo
Hay	1st or 2nd	Cancer, Scorpio, Pisces, Libra, Taurus
Herbs	1st or 2nd	Cancer, Scorpio, Pisces
Honeysuckle	1st or 2nd	Scorpio, Virgo
Hops	1st or 2nd	Scorpio, Libra
Horseradish	1st or 2nd	Cancer, Scorpio, Pisces
Houseplants	1st	Libra, Cancer, Scorpio, Pisces
Hyacinths	3rd	Cancer, Scorpio, Pisces
Irises	1st or 2nd	Cancer, Virgo
Kohlrabi	1st or 2nd	Cancer, Scorpio, Pisces, Libra

Plant	Phase/Quarter	Sign
Leeks	1st or 2nd	Cancer, Pisces
Lettuce	1st	Cancer, Scorpio, Pisces, Libra, Taurus
Lilies	1st or 2nd	Cancer, Scorpio, Pisces
Maple Trees	2nd or 3rd	Virgo, Taurus, Cancer, Pisces
Melons	2nd	Cancer, Scorpio, Pisces
Moon Vines	1st or 2nd	Virgo
Morning Glories	1st or 2nd	Cancer, Scorpio, Pisces, Virgo
Oak Trees	2nd or 3rd	Virgo, Taurus, Cancer, Pisces
Oats	1st or 2nd	Cancer, Scorpio, Pisces, Libra
Okra	1st	Cancer, Scorpio, Pisces, Libra
Onion Seeds	2nd	Scorpio, Cancer, Sagittarius
Onion Sets	3rd or 4th	Libra, Taurus, Pisces, Cancer
Pansies	1st or 2nd	Cancer, Scorpio, Pisces
Parsley	1st	Cancer, Scorpio, Pisces, Libra
Parsnips	3rd	Taurus, Capricorn, Cancer, Scorpio, Capricorn
Peach Trees	2nd or 3rd	Taurus, Libra, Virgo, Cancer
Peanuts	3rd	Cancer, Scorpio, Pisces
Pear Trees	2nd or 3rd	Taurus, Libra, Virgo, Cancer
Peas	2nd	Cancer, Scorpio, Pisces, Libra

Plant	Phase/Quarter	Sign
Peonies	1st or 2nd	Virgo
Peppers	2nd	Cancer, Pisces, Scorpio
Perennials	3rd	
Petunias	1st or 2nd	Libra, Virgo
Plum Trees	2nd or 3rd	Taurus, Virgo, Cancer, Pisces
Poppies	1st or 2nd	Virgo
Portulaca	1st or 2nd	Virgo
Potatoes	3rd	Cancer, Scorpio, Taurus, Libra, Capricorn
Privet	1st or 2nd	Taurus, Libra
Pumpkins	2nd	Cancer, Scorpio, Pisces, Libra
Quinces	1st or 2nd	Capricorn
Radishes	3rd	Cancer, Libra, Taurus, Pisces, Capricorn
Rhubarb	3rd	Cancer, Pisces
Rice	1st or 2nd	Scorpio
Roses	1st or 2nd	Cancer, Virgo
Rutabagas	3rd	Cancer, Scorpio, Pisces, Taurus
Saffron	1st or 2nd	Cancer, Scorpio, Pisces
Sage	3rd	Cancer, Scorpio, Pisces
Salsify	1st or 2nd	Cancer, Scorpio, Pisces

Plant	Phase/Quarter	Sign
Shallots	2nd	Scorpio
Spinach	1st	Cancer, Scorpio, Pisces
Squash	2nd	Cancer, Scorpio, Pisces, Libra
Strawberries	3rd	Cancer, Scorpio, Pisces
String Beans	1st or 2nd	Taurus
Sunflowers	1st or 2nd	Libra, Cancer
Sweet Peas	1st or 2nd	Cancer, Scorpio, Pisces
Tomatoes	2nd	Cancer, Scorpio, Pisces, Capricorn
Shade Trees	3rd	Taurus, Capricorn
Ornamental Trees	2nd	Libra, Taurus
Trumpet Vines	1st or 2nd	Cancer, Scorpio, Pisces
Tubers for Seed	3rd	Cancer, Scorpio, Pisces, Libra
Tulips	1st or 2nd	Libra, Virgo
Turnips	3rd	Cancer, Scorpio, Pisces, Taurus, Capricorn, Libra
Valerian	1st or 2nd	Virgo, Gemini
Watermelons	1st or 2nd	Cancer, Scorpio, Pisces, Libra
Wheat	1st or 2nd	Cancer, Scorpio, Pisces, Libra

2001 Gardening Dates

Dates	Qtr	Sign	Activity
Jan. 4, 1:57 am-Jan. 6, 6:44 am	2nd	Taurus	Plant annuals for hardiness. Trim to increase growth.
Jan. 8, 8:09 am-Jan. 9, 3:24 pm	2nd	Cancer	Plant grains, leafy annuals. Fertilize (chemical). Graft or bud plants. Irrigate. Trim to increase
Jan. 9, 3:24 pm-Jan. 10, 7:44 am	3rd	Cancer	Plant biennials, perennials, bulbs and roots. Prune. Irrigate. Fertilize (organic).
Jan. 10, 7:44 am-Jan. 12, 7:26 am	3rd	Leo	Cultivate. Destroy weeds and pests. Harvest fruits and root crops for food. Trim to retard growth.
Jan. 12, 7:26 am-Jan. 14, 9:05 am	3rd	Virgo	Cultivate, especially medicinal plants. Destroy weeds and pests. Trim to retard growth.
Jan. 16, 2:02 pm-Jan. 18, 10:35 pm	4th	Scorpio	Plant biennials, perennials, bulbs and roots. Prune. Irrigate. Fertilize (organic).
Jan. 18, 10:35 pm-Jan. 21, 9:57 am	4th	Sagittarius	Cultivate. Destroy weeds and pests. Harvest fruits and root crops for food. Trim to retard growth.
Jan. 21, 9:57 am-Jan. 23, 10:43 pm	4th	Capricorn	Plant potatoes and tubers. Trim to retard growth.
Jan. 23, 10:43 pm-Jan. 24, 8:07 am	4th	Aquarius	Cultivate. Destroy weeds and pests. Harvest fruits and root crops for food. Trim to retard growth.
Jan. 26, 11:39 am-Jan. 28, 11:35 pm	1st	Pisces	Plant grains, leafy annuals. Fertilize (chemical). Graft or bud plants. Irrigate. Trim to increase growth.
Feb. 31, 9:21 am-Feb. 1, 9:02 am	1st	Taurus	Plant annuals for hardiness. Trim to increase growth.
Feb. 1, 9:02 am-Feb. 2, 3:56 pm	2nd	Taurus	Plant annuals for hardiness. Trim to increase growth.
Feb. 4, 7:00 pm-Feb. 6, 7:21 pm	2nd	Cancer	Plant grains, leafy annuals. Fertilize (chemical). Graft or bud plants. Irrigate. Trim to increase growth.
Feb. 8, 2:12 am-Feb. 8, 6:35 pm	3rd	Leo	Cultivate. Destroy weeds and pests. Harvest fruits and root crops for food. Trim to retard growth.
Feb. 8, 6:35 pm-Feb. 10, 6:46 pm	3rd	Virgo	Cultivate, especially medicinal plants. Destroy weeds and pests. Trim to retard growth.
Feb. 12, 9:51 pm-Feb. 14, 10:23 pm	3rd	Scorpio	Plant biennials, perennials, bulbs and roots. Prune. Irrigate. Fertilize (organic).
Feb. 14, 10:23 pm-Feb. 15, 5:02 am	4th	Scorpio	Plant biennials, perennials, bulbs and roots. Prune. Irrigate. Fertilize (organic).
Feb. 15, 5:02 am-Feb. 17, 3:59 pm	4th	Sagittarius	Cultivate. Destroy weeds and pests. Harvest fruits and root crops for food. Trim to retard growth.
Feb. 17, 3:59 pm-Feb. 20, 4:53 am	4th	Capricorn	Plant potatoes and tubers. Trim to retard growth.

2001 Gardening Dates

Dates	Qtr	Sign	Activity
Feb. 20, 4:53 am-Feb. 22, 5:45 pm	4th	Aquarius	Cultivate. Destroy weeds and pests. Harvest fruits and root crops for food. Trim to retard growth.
Feb. 22, 5:45 pm-Feb. 23, 3:21 am	4th	Pisces	Plant biennials, perennials, bulbs and roots. Prune. Irrigate. Fertilize (organic).
Feb. 23, 3:21 am-Feb. 25, 5:20 am	1st	Pisces	Plant grains, leafy annuals. Fertilize (chemical). Graft or bud plants. Irrigate. Trim to increase growth.
Mar. 27, 3:06 pm-Mar. 1, 10:36 pm	1st	Taurus	Plant annuals for hardiness. Trim to increase growth.
Mar. 4, 3:24 am-Mar. 6, 5:30 am	2nd	Cancer	Plant grains, leafy annuals. Fertilize (chemical). Graft or bud plants. Irrigate. Trim to increase growth.
Mar. 9, 12:23 pm-Mar. 10, 5:47 am	3rd	Virgo	Cultivate, especially medicinal plants. Destroy weeds and pests. Trim to retard growth.
Mar. 12, 7:43 am-Mar. 14, 1:17 pm	3rd	Scorpio	Plant biennials, perennials, bulbs and roots. Prune. Irrigate. Fertilize (organic).
Mar. 14, 1:17 pm-Mar. 16, 3:45 pm	3rd	Sagittarius	Cultivate. Destroy weeds and pests. Harvest fruits and root crops for food. Trim to retard growth.
Mar. 16, 3:45 pm-Mar. 16, 11:02 pm	4th	Sagittarius	Cultivate. Destroy weeds and pests. Harvest fruits and root crops for food. Trim to retard growth.
Mar. 16, 11:02 pm-Mar. 19, 11:36 am	4th	Capricorn	Plant potatoes and tubers. Trim to retard growth.
Mar. 19, 11:36 am-Mar. 22, 12:28 am	4th	Aquarius	Cultivate. Destroy weeds and pests. Harvest fruits and root crops for food. Trim to retard growth.
Mar. 22, 12:28 am-Mar. 24, 11:43 am	4th	Pisces	Plant biennials, perennials, bulbs and roots. Prune. Irrigate. Fertilize (organic).
Mar. 24, 11:43 am-Mar. 24, 8:21 pm	4th	Aries	Cultivate. Destroy weeds and pests. Harvest fruits and root crops for food. Trim to retard growth.
Mar. 26, 8:50 pm-Mar. 29, 4:01 am	1st	Taurus	Plant annuals for hardiness. Trim to increase growth.
Apr. 31, 9:23 am-Apr. 1, 5:49 am	1st	Cancer	Plant grains, leafy annuals. Fertilize (chemical). Graft or bud plants Irrigate. Trim to increase growth.
Apr. 1, 5:49 am-Apr. 2, 12:54 pm	2nd	Cancer	Plant grains, leafy annuals. Fertilize (chemical). Graft or bud plants. irrigate. Trim to increase growth.
Apr. 6, 3:57 pm-Apr. 7, 0:22 pm	2nd	Libra	Plant annuals for fragrance and beauty. Trim to increase growth.
Apr. 8, 6:01 pm-Apr. 10, 10:47 pm	3rd	Scorpio	Plant biennials, perennials, bulbs and roots. Prune. Irrigate. Fertilize (organic).
Apr. 10, 10:47 pm-Apr. 13, 7:21 am	3rd	Sagittarius	Cultivate. Destroy weeds and pests. Harvest fruits and root crops for food. Trim to retard growth.

2001 Gardening Dates

Dates	Qtr	Sign	Activity
Apr. 13, 7:21 am-Apr. 15, 10:31 am	3rd	Capricorn	Plant potatoes and tubers. Trim to retard growth.
Apr. 15, 10:31 am-Apr. 15, 7:11 pm	4th	Capricorn	Plant potatoes and tubers. Trim to retard growth.
Apr. 15, 7:11 pm-Apr. 18, 8:00 am	4th	Aquarius	Cultivate. Destroy weeds and pests. Harvest fruits and root crops for food. Trim to retard growth.
Apr. 18, 8:00 am-Apr. 20, 7:18 pm	4th	Pisces	Plant biennials, perennials, bulbs and roots. Prune. Irrigate. Fertilize (organic).
Apr. 20, 7:18 pm-Apr. 23, 3:56 am	4th	Aries	Cultivate. Destroy weeds and pests. Harvest fruits and root crops for food. Trim to retard growth.
Apr. 23, 3:56 am-Apr. 23, 10:26 am	4th	Taurus	Plant potatoes and tubers. Trim to retard growth.
Apr. 23, 10:26 am-Apr. 25, 10:11 am	1st	Taurus	Plant annuals for hardiness. Trim to increase growth.
Apr. 27, 2:49 pm-Apr. 29, 6:25 pm	1st	Cancer	Plant grains, leafy annuals. Fertilize (chemical). Graft or bud plants. Irrigate. Trim to increase growth.
May 3, 11:50 pm-May 6, 3:00 am	2nd	Libra	Plant annuals for fragrance and beauty. Trim to increase growth.
May 6, 3:00 am-May 7, 8:53 am	2nd	Scorpio	Plant grains, leafy annuals. Fertilize (chemical). Graft or bud plants. Irrigate. Trim to increase growth.
May 7, 8:53 am-May 8, 8:05 am	3rd	Scorpio	Plant biennials, perennials, bulbs and roots. Prune. Irrigate. Fertilize (organic).
May 8, 8:05 am-May 10, 4:10 pm	3rd	Sagittarius	Cultivate. Destroy weeds and pests. Harvest fruits and root crops for food. Trim to retard growth.
May 10, 4:10 pm-May 13, 3:20 am	3rd	Capricorn	Plant potatoes and tubers. Trim to retard growth.
May 13, 3:20 am-May 15, 5:11 am	3rd	Aquarius	Cultivate. Destroy weeds and pests. Harvest fruits and root crops for food. Trim to retard growth.
May 15, 5:11 am-May 15, 4:01 pm	4th	Aquarius	Cultivate. Destroy weeds and pests. Harvest fruits and root crops for food. Trim to retard growth.
May 15, 4:01 pm-May 18, 3:41 am	4th	Pisces	Plant biennials, perennials, bulbs and roots. Prune. Irrigate. Fertilize (organic).
May 18, 3:41 am-May 20, 12:29 pm	4th	Aries	Cultivate. Destroy weeds and pests. Harvest fruits and root crops for food. Trim to retard growth.
May 20, 12:29 pm-May 22, 6:12 pm	4th	Taurus	Plant potatoes and tubers. Trim to retard growth.
May 22, 6:12 pm-May 22, 9:46 pm	4th	Gemini	Cultivate. Destroy weeds and pests. Harvest fruits and root crops for food. Trim to retard growth.

2001 Gardening Dates

Dates	Qtr	Sign	Activity
May 24, 9:42 pm-May 27, 12:12 am	1st	Cancer	Plant grains, leafy annuals. Fertilize (chemical). Graft or bud plants. Irrigate. Trim to increase growth.
Jun. 31, 5:41 am-Jun. 2, 9:56 am	2nd	Libra	Plant annuals for fragrance and beauty. Trim to increase growth.
Jun. 2, 9:56 am-Jun. 4, 3:58 pm	2nd	Scorpio	Plant grains, leafy annuals. Fertilize (chemical). Graft or bud plants. Irrigate. Trim to increase growth.
Jun. 5, 8:39 pm-Jun. 7, 12:23 am	3rd	Sagittarius	Cultivate. Destroy weeds and pests. Harvest fruits and root crops for food. Trim to retard growth.
Jun. 7, 12:23 am-Jun. 9, 11:20 am	3rd	Capricorn	Plant potatoes and tubers. Trim to retard growth.
Jun. 9, 11:20 am-Jun. 11, 11:53 pm	3rd	Aquarius	Cultivate. Destroy weeds and pests. Harvest fruits and root crops for food. Trim to retard growth.
Jun. 11, 11:53 pm-Jun. 13, 10:28 pm	3rd	Pisces	Plant biennials, perennials, bulbs and roots. Prune. Irrigate. Fertilize (organic).
Jun. 13, 10:28 pm-Jun. 14, 12:03 pm	4th	Pisces	Plant biennials, perennials, bulbs and roots. Prune. Irrigate. Fertilize (organic).
Jun. 14, 12:03 pm-Jun. 16, 9:39 pm	4th	Aries	Cultivate. Destroy weeds and pests. Harvest fruits and root crops for food. Trim to retard growth.
Jun. 16, 9:39 pm-Jun. 19, 3:42 am	4th	Taurus	Plant potatoes and tubers. Trim to retard growth.
Jun. 19, 3:42 am-Jun. 21, 6:40 am	4th	Gemini	Cultivate. Destroy weeds and pests. Harvest fruits and root crops for food. Trim to retard growth.
Jun. 21, 6:40 am-Jun. 21, 6:58 am	4th	Cancer	Plant biennials, perennials, bulbs and roots. Prune. Irrigate. Fertilize (organic).
Jun. 21, 6:58 am-Jun. 23, 7:55 am	1st	Cancer	Plant grains, leafy annuals. Fertilize (chemical). Graft or bud plants. Irrigate. Trim to increase growth.
Jun. 27, 11:11 am-Jun. 27, 10:19 pm	1st	Libra	Plant annuals for fragrance and beauty. Trim to increase growth.
Jun. 27, 10:19 pm-Jun. 29, 3:28 pm	2nd	Libra	Plant annuals for fragrance and beauty. Trim to increase growth.
Jul. 29, 3:28 pm-Jul. 1, 10:13 pm	2nd	Scorpio	Plant grains, leafy annuals. Fertilize (chemical). Graft or bud plants. Irrigate. Trim to increase growth.
Jul. 4, 7:21 am-Jul. 5, 10:04 am	2nd	Capricorn	Graft or bud plants. Trim to increase growth.
Jul. 5, 10:04 am-Jul. 6, 6:33 pm	3rd	Capricorn	Plant potatoes and tubers. Trim to retard growth.
Jul. 6, 6:33 pm-Jul. 9, 7:05 am	3rd	Aquarius	Cultivate. Destroy weeds and pests. Harvest fruits and root crops for food. Trim to retard growth.

2001 Gardening Dates

Dates	Qtr	Sign	Activity
Jul. 9, 7:05 am-Jul. 11, 7:36 pm	3rd	Pisces	Plant biennials, perennials, bulbs and roots. Prune. Irrigate. Fertilize (organic).
Jul. 11, 7:36 pm-Jul. 13, 1:45 pm	3rd	Aries	Cultivate. Destroy weeds and pests. Harvest fruits and root crops for food. Trim to retard growth.
Jul. 13, 1:45 pm-Jul. 14, 6:13 am	4th	Aries	Cultivate. Destroy weeds and pests. Harvest fruits and root crops for food. Trim to retard growth.
Jul. 14, 6:13 am-Jul. 16, 1:26 pm	4th	Taurus	Plant potatoes and tubers. Trim to retard growth.
Jul. 16, 1:26 pm-Jul. 18, 4:56 pm	4th	Gemini	Cultivate. Destroy weeds and pests. Harvest fruits and root crops for food. Trim to retard growth.
Jul. 18, 4:56 pm-Jul. 20, 2:44 pm	4th	Cancer	Plant biennials, perennials, bulbs and roots. Prune. Irrigate. Fertilize (organic).
Jul. 20, 2:44 pm-Jul. 20, 5:43 pm	1st	Cancer	Plant grains, leafy annuals. Fertilize (chemical). Graft or bud plants. Irrigate. Trim to increase growth.
Jul. 24, 6:08 pm-Jul. 26, 9:17 pm	1st	Libra	Plant annuals for fragrance and beauty. Trim to increase growth.
Jul. 26, 9:17 pm-Jul. 27, 5:08 am	1st	Scorpio	Plant grains, leafy annuals. Fertilize (chemical). Graft or bud plants. Irrigate. Trim to increase growth.
Jul. 27, 5:08 am-Jul. 29, 3:44 am	2nd	Scorpio	Plant grains, leafy annuals. Fertilize (chemical). Graft or bud plants. Irrigate. Trim to increase growth.
Aug. 31, 1:16 pm-Aug. 3, 12:53 am	2nd	Capricorn	Graft or bud plants. Trim to increase growth.
Aug. 4, 12:56 am-Aug. 5, 1:30 pm	3rd	Aquarius	Cultivate. Destroy weeds and pests. Harvest fruits and root crops for food. Trim to retard growth.
Aug. 5, 1:30 pm-Aug. 8, 2:05 am	3rd	Pisces	Plant biennials, perennials, bulbs and roots. Prune. Irrigate. Fertilize (organic).
Aug. 8, 2:05 am-Aug. 10, 1:23 pm	3rd	Aries	Cultivate. Destroy weeds and pests. Harvest fruits and root crops for food. Trim to retard growth.
Aug. 10, 1:23 pm-Aug. 12, 2:53 am	3rd	Taurus	Plant potatoes and tubers. Trim to retard growth.
Aug. 12, 2:53 am-Aug. 12, 9:59 pm	4th	Taurus	Plant potatoes and tubers. Trim to retard growth.
Aug. 12, 9:59 pm-Aug. 15, 2:55 am	4th	Gemini	Cultivate. Destroy weeds and pests. Harvest fruits and root crops for food. Trim to retard growth.
Aug. 15, 2:55 am-Aug. 17, 4:25 am	4th	Cancer	Plant biennials, perennials, bulbs and roots. Prune. Irrigate. Fertilize (organic).
Aug. 17, 4:25 am-Aug. 18, 9:55 pm	4th	Leo	Cultivate. Destroy weeds and pests. Harvest fruits and root crops for food. Trim to retard growth.

2001 Gardening Dates

Dates	Qtr	Sign	Activity
Aug. 21, 3:19 am-Aug. 23, 4:50 am	1st	Libra	Plant annuals for fragrance and beauty. Trim to increase growth.
Aug. 23, 4:50 am-Aug. 25, 9:59 am	1st	Scorpio	Plant grains, leafy annuals. Fertilize (chemical). Graft or bud plants. Irrigate. Trim to increase growth.
Aug. 27, 7:02 pm-Aug. 30, 6:47 am	2nd	Capricorn	Graft or bud plants. Trim to increase growth.
Sep. 1, 7:32 pm-Sep. 2, 4:43 pm	2nd	Pisces	Plant grains, leafy annuals. Fertilize (chemical). Graft or bud plants. Irrigate. Trim to increase growth.
Sep. 2, 4:43 pm-Sep. 4, 7:58 am	3rd	Pisces	Plant biennials, perennials, bulbs and roots. Prune. Irrigate. Fertilize (organic).
Sep. 4, 7:58 am-Sep. 6, 7:18 pm	3rd	Aries	Cultivate. Destroy weeds and pests. Harvest fruits and root crops for food. Trim to retard growth.
Sep. 6, 7:18 pm-Sep. 9, 4:41 am	3rd	Taurus	Plant potatoes and tubers. Trim to retard growth.
Sep. 9, 4:41 am-Sep. 10, 1:59 pm	3rd	Gemini	Cultivate. Destroy weeds and pests. Harvest fruits and root crops for food. Trim to retard growth.
Sep. 10, 1:59 pm-Sep. 11, 11:09 am	4th	Gemini	Cultivate. Destroy weeds and pests. Harvest fruits and root crops for food. Trim to retard growth.
Sep. 11, 11:09 am-Sep. 13, 2:16 pm	4th	Cancer	Plant biennials, perennials, bulbs and roots. Prune. Irrigate. Fertilize (organic).
Sep. 13, 2:16 pm-Sep. 15, 2:39 pm	4th	Leo	Cultivate. Destroy weeds and pests. Harvest fruits and root crops for food. Trim to retard growth.
Sep. 15, 2:39 pm-Sep. 17, 5:27 am	4th	Virgo	Cultivate, especially medicinal plants. Destroy weeds and pests. Trim to retard growth.
Sep. 17, 2:00 pm-Sep. 19, 2:27 pm	1st	Libra	Plant annuals for fragrance and beauty. Trim to increase growth.
Sep. 19, 2:27 pm-Sep. 21, 6:02 pm	1st	Scorpio	Plant grains, leafy annuals. Fertilize (chemical). Graft or bud plants. Irrigate. Trim to increase growth
Sep. 24, 1:48 am-Sep. 24, 4:31 am	1st	Capricorn	Graft or bud plants. Trim to increase growth.
Sep. 24, 4:31 am-Sep. 26, 1:05 pm	2nd	Capricorn	Graft or bud plants. Trim to increase growth.
Oct. 29, 1:50 am-Oct. 1, 2:08 pm	2nd	Pisces	Plant grains, leafy annuals. Fertilize (chemical). Graft or bud plants. Irrigate. Trim to increase growth.
Oct. 2, 8:49 am-Oct. 4, 1:01 am	3rd	Aries	Cultivate. Destroy weeds and pests. Harvest fruits and root crops for food. Trim to retard growth.
Oct. 4, 1:01 am-Oct. 6, 10:12 am	3rd	Taurus	Plant potatoes and tubers. Trim to retard growth.

2001 Gardening Dates

Dates	Qtr	Sign	Activity
Oct. 6, 10:12 am-Oct. 8, 5:19 pm	3rd	Gemini	Cultivate. Destroy weeds and pests. Harvest fruits and root crops for food. Trim to retard growth.
Oct. 8, 5:19 pm-Oct. 9, 11:20 pm	3rd	Cancer	Plant biennials, perennials, bulbs and roots. Prune. Irrigate. Fertilize (organic).
Oct. 9, 11:20 pm-Oct. 10, 9:54 pm	4th	Cancer	Plant biennials, perennials, bulbs and roots. Prune. Irrigate. Fertilize (organic).
Oct. 10, 9:54 pm-Oct. 12, 11:58 pm	4th	Leo	Cultivate. Destroy weeds and pests. Harvest fruits and root crops for food. Trim to retard growth.
Oct. 12, 11:58 pm-Oct. 15, 12:26 am	4th	Virgo	Cultivate, especially medicinal plants. Destroy weeds and pests. Trim to retard growth.
Oct. 16, 2:23 am-Oct. 17, 1:03 am	1st	Libra	Plant annuals for fragrance and beauty. Trim to in- crease growth.
Oct. 17, 1:03 am-Oct. 19, 3:47 am	1st	Scorpio	Plant grains, leafy annuals. Fertilize (chemical). Graft or bud plants. Irrigate. Trim to increase growth.
Oct. 21, 10:11 am-Oct. 23, 8:26 pm	1st	Capricorn	Graft or bud plants. Trim to increase growth.
Oct. 26, 8:56 am-Oct. 28, 9:15 pm	2nd	Pisces	Plant grains, leafy annuals. Fertilize (chemical). Graft or bud plants. Irrigate. Trim to increase growth.
Nov. 31, 7:48 am-Nov. 1, 12:41 am	2nd	Taurus	Plant annuals for hardiness. Trim to increase growth.
Nov. 1, 12:41 am-Nov. 2, 4:12 pm	3rd	Taurus	Plant potatoes and tubers. Trim to retard growth.
Nov. 2, 4:12 pm-Nov. 4, 10:44 pm	3rd	Gemini	Cultivate. Destroy weeds and pests. Harvest fruits and root crops for food. Trim to retard growth.
Nov. 4, 10:44 pm-Nov. 7, 3:34 am	3rd	Cancer	Plant biennials, perennials, bulbs and roots. Prune. Irrigate. Fertilize (organic).
Nov. 7, 3:34 am-Nov. 8, 7:21 am	3rd	Leo	Cultivate. Destroy weeds and pests. Harvest fruits and root crops for food. Trim to retard growth.
Nov. 8, 7:21 am-Nov. 9, 6:49 am	4th	Leo	Cultivate. Destroy weeds and pests. Harvest fruits and root crops for food. Trim to retard growth.
Nov. 9, 6:49 am-Nov. 11, 8:53 am	4th	Virgo	Cultivate, especially medicinal plants. Destroy weeds and pests. Trim to retard growth.
Nov. 13, 10:44 am-Nov. 15, 1:40 am	4th	Scorpio	Plant biennials, perennials, bulbs and roots. Prune. Irrigate. Fertilize (organic).
Nov. 15, 1:40 am-Nov. 15, 1:51 pm	1st	Scorpio	Plant grains, leafy annuals. Fertilize (chemical). Graft or bud plants. Irrigate. Trim to increase growth.
Nov. 17, 7:40 pm-Nov. 20, 4:55 am	1st	Capricorn	Graft or bud plants. Trim to increase growth.

2001 Gardening Dates

Dates	Qtr	Sign	Activity
Nov. 22, 4:52 pm-Nov. 22, 6:21 pm	1st	Pisces	Plant grains, leafy annuals. Fertilize (chemical). Graft or bud plants. Irrigate. Trim to increase growth.
Nov. 22, 6:21 pm-Nov. 25, 5:21 am	2nd	Pisces	Plant grains, leafy annuals. Fertilize (chemical). Graft or bud plants. Irrigate. Trim to increase growth.
Nov. 27, 4:06 pm-Nov. 30, 12:04 am	2nd	Taurus	Plant annuals for hardiness. Trim to increase growth.
Dec. 30, 3:49 pm-Dec. 2, 5:30 am	3rd	Gemini	Cultivate. Destroy weeds and pests. Harvest fruits and root crops for food. Trim to retard growth.
Dec. 2, 5:30 am-Dec. 4, 9:15 am	3rd	Cancer	Plant biennials, perennials, bulbs and roots. Prune. Irrigate. Fertilize (organic).
Dec. 4, 9:15 am-Dec. 6, 12:11 pm	3rd	Leo	Cultivate. Destroy weeds and pests. Harvest fruits and root crops for food. Trim to retard growth.
Dec. 6, 12:11 pm-Dec. 7, 2:52 pm	3rd	Virgo	Cultivate, especially medicinal plants. Destroy weeds and pests. Trim to retard growth.
Dec. 7, 2:52 pm-Dec. 8, 2:57 pm	4th	Virgo	Cultivate, especially medicinal plants. Destroy weeds and pests. Trim to retard growth.
Dec. 10, 6:09 pm-Dec. 12, 10:30 pm	4th	Scorpio	Plant biennials, perennials, bulbs and roots. Prune. Irrigate. Fertilize (organic).
Dec. 12, 10:30 pm-Dec. 14, 3:47 pm	4th	Sagittarius	Cultivate. Destroy weeds and pests. Harvest fruits and root crops for food. Trim to retard growth.
Dec. 15, 4:48 am-Dec. 17, 1:43 pm	1st	Capricorn	Graft or bud plants. Trim to increase growth.
Dec. 20, 1:09 am-Dec. 22, 1:45 pm	1st	Pisces	Plant grains, leafy annuals. Fertilize (chemical). Graft or bud plants. Irrigate. Trim to increase growth.
Dec. 25, 1:12 am-Dec. 27, 9:39 am	2nd	Taurus	Plant annuals for hardiness. Trim to increase growth.
Dec. 29, 2:40 pm-Dec. 30, 5:40 am	2nd	Cancer	Plant grains, leafy annuals. Fertilize (chemical). Graft or bud plants. Irrigate. Trim to increase growth.
Dec. 30, 5:40 am-Dec. 31, 5:09 pm	3rd	Cancer	Plant biennials, perennials, bulbs and roots. Prune. Irrigate. Fertilize (organic).

Dates to Destroy Weeds & Pests

From		To		Sign	Quarter
Jan. 10	7:44 am	Jan. 12	7:26 am	Leo	3rd
Jan. 12	7:26 am	Jan. 14	9:05 am	Virgo	3rd
Jan. 18	10:35 pm	Jan. 21	9:57 am	Sagittarius	4th
Jan. 23	10:43 pm	Jan. 24	8:07 am	Aquarius	4th
Feb. 8	2:12 am	Feb. 8	6:35 pm	Leo	3rd
Feb. 8	6:35 pm	Feb. 10	6:46 pm	Virgo	3rd
Feb. 15	5:02 am	Feb. 17	3:59 pm	Sagittarius	4th
Feb. 20	4:53 am	Feb. 22	5:45 pm	Aquarius	4th
Mar. 9	12:23 pm	Mar. 10	5:47 am	Virgo	3rd
Mar. 14	1:17 pm	Mar. 16	3:45 pm	Sagittarius	3rd
Mar. 16	3:45 pm	Mar. 16	11:02 pm	Sagittarius	4th
Mar. 19	11:36 am	Mar. 22	12:28 am	Aquarius	4th
Mar. 24	11:43 am	Mar. 24	8:21 pm	Aries	4th
Apr. 10	10:47 pm	Apr. 13	7:21 am	Sagittarius	3rd
Apr. 15	7:11 pm	Apr. 18	8:00 am	Aquarius	4th
Apr. 20	7:18 pm	Apr. 23	3:56 am	Aries	4th
May 8	8:05 am	May 10	4:10 pm	Sagittarius	3rd
May 13	3:20 am	May 15	5:11 am	Aquarius	3rd
May 15	5:11 am	May 15	4:01 pm	Aquarius	4th
May 18	3:41 am	May 20	12:29 pm	Aries	4th
May 22	6:12 pm	May 22	9:42 pm	Gemini	4th
Jun. 5	8:39 pm	Jun. 7	12:23 am	Sagittarius	3rd
Jun. 9	11:20 am	Jun. 11	11:53 pm	Aquarius	3rd
Jun. 14	12:03 pm	Jun. 16	9:39 pm	Aries	4th
Jun. 19	3:42 am	Jun. 21	6:40 am	Gemini	4th
Jul. 6	6:33 pm	Jul. 9	7:05 am	Aquarius	3rd
Jul. 11	7:36 pm	Jul. 13	1:45 pm	Aries	3rd

Dates to Destroy Weeds & Pests

Jul. 13	1:45 pm	Jul. 14	6:13 am	Aries	4th
Jul. 16	1:26 pm	Jul. 18	4:56 pm	Gemini	4th
Aug. 4	12:56 am	Aug. 5	1:30 pm	Aquarius	3rd
Aug. 8	2:05 am	Aug. 10	1:23 pm	Aries	3rd
Aug. 12	9:59 pm	Aug. 15	2:55 am	Gemini	4th
Aug. 17	4:25 am	Aug. 18	9:55 pm	Leo	4th
Sep. 4	7:58 am	Sep. 6	7:18 pm	Aries	3rd
Sep. 9	4:41 am	Sep. 10	1:59 pm	Gemini	3rd
Sep. 10	1:59 pm	Sep. 11	11:09 am	Gemini	4th
Sep. 13	2:16 pm	Sep. 15	2:39 pm	Leo	4th
Sep. 15	2:39 pm	Sep. 17	5:27 am	Virgo	4th
Oct. 2	8:49 am	Oct. 4	1:01 am	Aries	3rd
Oct. 6	10:12 am	Oct. 8	5:19 pm	Gemini	3rd
Oct. 10	9:54 pm	Oct. 12	11:58 pm	Leo	4th
Oct. 12	11:58 pm	Oct. 15	12:26 am	Virgo	4th
Nov. 2	4:12 pm	Nov. 4	10:44 pm	Gemini	3rd
Nov. 7	3:34 am	Nov. 8	7:21 am	Leo	3rd
Nov. 8	7:21 am	Nov. 9	6:49 am	Leo	4th
Nov. 9	6:49 am	Nov. 11	8:53 am	Virgo	4th
Nov. 30	3:49 pm	Dec. 2	5:30 am	Gemini	3rd
Dec. 4	9:15 am	Dec. 6	12:11 pm	Leo	3rd
Dec. 6	12:11 pm	Dec. 7	12.52 pm	Virgo	3rd
Dec. 7	2:52 pm	Dec. 8	2:57 pm	Virgo	4th
Dec. 12	10:30 pm	Dec 14	3:47 pm	Sagittarius	4th

Gestation & Incubation

Animal	Young/Eggs	Gestation/Incubation
Horse	1	346 days
Cow	1	283 days
Monkey	1	164 days
Goat	1–2	151 days
Sheep	1–2	150 days
Pig	10	112 days
Chinchilla	2	110 days
Fox	5–8	63 days
Dog	6–8	63 days
Cat	4–6	63 days
Guinea Pig	2–6	62 days
Ferret	6–9	40 days
Rabbit	4–8	30 days
Rat	10	22 days
Mouse	10	22 days
Turkey	1–15	26-30 days
Guinea Hen	15–18	25-26 days
Pea Hen	10	28-30 days
Duck	9–12	25-32 days
Goose	15–18	27-33 days
Hen	12–15	19-24 days
Pigeon	2	16-20 days
Canary	3–4	13-14 days

Egg Setting Dates

Dates to be Born	Sign	Qtr.	Set Eggs
Jan. 4 1:57 am-Jan. 6 6:44 am	Taurus	2nd	Dec. 14-16 2000
Jan. 8 8:09 am-Jan. 9 3:24 pm	Cancer	2nd	Dec. 18-19 2000
Jan. 26 11:39 am-Jan. 28 11:35 pm	Pisces	1st	Jan. 5-7
Jan. 31 9:21 am-Feb. 1 9:02 am	Taurus	1st	Jan. 10-11
Feb. 4 7:00 pm-Feb. 6 7:21 pm	Cancer	2nd	Jan. 14-16
Feb. 23 3:21 am-Feb. 25 5:20 am	Pisces	1st	Feb. 2-4
Feb. 27 3:06 pm-Mar. 1 10:36 pm	Taurus	1st	Feb 6-8
Mar. 4 3:24 am-Mar. 6 5:30 am	Cancer	2nd	Feb. 11-13
Mar. 26 8:50 pm-Mar. 29 4:01 am	Taurus	1st	Mar. 5-8
Mar. 31 9:23 am-Apr. 1 5:49 am	Cancer	1st	Mar. 10-11
Apr. 6 3:57 pm-Apr. 7 0:22 pm	Libra	2nd	Mar. 16-17
Apr. 23 10:26 am-Apr. 25 10:11 am	Taurus	1st	Apr. 2-4
Apr. 27 2:49 pm-Apr. 29 6:25 pm	Cancer	1st	Apr. 6-8
May 3 11:50 pm-May 6 3:00 am	Libra	2nd	Apr. 12-15
May 24 9:42 pm-May 27 12:12 am	Cancer	1st	May 3-6
May 31 5:41 am-Jun. 2 9:56 am	Libra	2nd	May 10-12
Jun. 21 6:58 am-Jun. 23 7:55 am	Cancer	1st	May 30-Jun. 2
Jun. 27 11:11 am-Jun. 27 10:19 pm	Libra	1st	Jun. 6
Jul. 20 2:44 pm-Jul. 20 5:43 pm	Cancer	1st	Jun. 29
Jul. 24 6:08 pm-Jul. 26 9:17 pm	Libra	1st	Jul. 3-5
Aug. 21 3:19 am-Aug. 23 4:50 am	Libra	1st	Jul. 31-Aug. 2
Sep. 1 7:32 pm-Sep. 2 4:43 pm	Pisces	2nd	Aug. 11-12
Sep. 17 2:00 pm-Sep. 19 2:27 pm	Libra	1st	Aug. 27-29
Sep. 29 1:50 am-Oct. 1 2:08 pm	Pisces	2nd	Sep. 8-10
Oct. 16 2:23 pm-Oct. 17 1:03 am	Libra	1st	Sep. 25-26
Oct. 26 8:56 am-Oct. 28 9:15 pm	Pisces	2nd	Oct. 5-7
Oct. 31 7:48 am-Nov. 1 12:41 am	Taurus	2nd	Oct. 10-11
Nov. 22 4:52 pm-Nov. 22 6:21 pm	Pisces	1st	Nov. 1
Nov. 27 4:06 pm-Nov. 30 12:04 am	Taurus	2nd	Nov. 6-9
Dec. 20 1:09 am-Dec. 22 1:45 pm	Pisces	1st	Nov. 29-Dec. 1
Dec. 25 1:12 am-Dec. 27 9:39 am	Taurus	2nd	Dec. 4-6
Dec. 29 2:40 pm-Dec. 30 5:40 am	Cancer	2nd	Dec. 8-9

Companion Planting
Plant Helpers and Hinderers

Plant	Helped By	Hindered By
Asparagus	Tomatoes, Parsley, Basil	
Beans	Carrots, Cucumbers, Cabbage, Beets, Corn	Onions, Gladiola
Bush Beans	Cucumbers, Cabbage, Strawberries	Fennel, Onions
Beets	Onions, Cabbage, Lettuce	Pale Beans
Cabbage	Beets, Potatoes, Onions, Celery	Strawberries, Tomatoes
Carrots	Peas, Lettuce, Chives, Radishes, Leeks, Onions	Dill
Celery	Leeks, Bush Beans	
Chives	Beans	
Corn	Potatoes, Beans, Peas, Melons, Squash, Pumpkins, Cucumbers	
Cucumbers	Beans, Cabbage, Radishes, Sunflowers, Lettuce	Potatoes, Aromatic Herbs
Eggplant	Beans	
Lettuce	Strawberries, Carrots	
Melons	Morning Glories	
Onions, Leeks	Beets, Chamomile, Carrots, Lettuce	Peas, Beans
Garlic	Summer Savory	
Peas	Radishes, Carrots, Corn, Cucumbers, Beans, Turnips	Onions
Potatoes	Beans, Corn, Peas, Cabbage, Hemp, Cucumbers	Sunflowers

Plant	Helped By	Hindered By
Radishes	Peas, Lettuce, Nasturtium, Cucumbers	Hyssop
Spinach	Strawberries	
Squash, Pumpkins	Nasturtium, Corn	Potatoes
Tomatoes	Asparagus, Parsley, Chives, Onions, Carrots, Marigold, Nasturtium	Dill, Cabbage, Fennel
Turnips	Peas, Beans	

Plant Companions and Uses

Plant	Companions and Uses
Anise	Coriander
Basil	Tomatoes; dislikes rue; repels flies and mosquitos
Borage	Tomatoes and squash
Buttercup	Clover; hinders delphiniums, peonies, monkshood, columbines
Chamomile	Helps peppermint, wheat, onions, and cabbage; large amounts destructive
Catnip	Repels flea beetles
Chervil	Radishes
Chives	Carrots; prone to apple scab and powdery mildew
Coriander	Hinders seed formation in fennel
Cosmos	Repels corn earworms
Dill	Cabbage; hinders carrots and tomatoes
Fennel	Disliked by all garden plants
Garlic	Aids vetch and roses; hinders peas and beans
Hemp	Beneficial as a neighbor to most plants
Horseradish	Repels potato bugs

Plant	Companions and Uses
Horsetail	Makes fungicide spray
Hyssop	Attracts cabbage fly away from cabbages; harmful to radishes
Lovage	Improves hardiness and flavor of neighbor plants
Marigold	Pest repellent; use against Mexican bean beetles and nematodes
Mint	Repels ants, flea beetles and cabbage worm butterflies
Morning Glory	Corn; helps melon germination
Nasturtium	Cabbage, cucumbers; deters aphids, squash bugs, and pumpkin beetles
Nettles	Increase oil content in neighbors
Parsley	Tomatoes, asparagus
Purslane	Good ground cover
Rosemary	Repels cabbage moths, bean beetles, and carrot flies
Sage	Repels cabbage moths and carrot flies
Savory	Deters bean beetles
Sunflower	Hinders potatoes; improves soil
Tansy	Deters Japanese beetles, striped cucumber beetles, and squash bugs
Thyme	Repels cabbage worms
Yarrow	Increases essential oils of neighbors

Year 2001 Weather Predictions

Nancy Soller

New England, northern portions of the West Coast, central Alaska, and even Hawaii should experience the coldest weather. Central Alaska will be very cold with above average precipitation. January and the first part of February should see the coldest temperatures because the Jupiter-Saturn conjunction, which brought cold temperatures to much of the year 2000, will still be in effect then.

Much of the East Coast will see above-normal temperatures and precipitation. This forecast extends over much of the area west of the Appalachians and east of the Mississippi to areas on either side of the Mississippi. West of the Mississippi will be drier than normal, although there will be some destructive storms and winds will be prominent.

Spring in New England and northern portions of the East Coast should be cool, dry, and windy. In the south along the East Coast should be cool and stormy with stiff winds. West of the Appalachians and east of the Mississippi temperatures should be below normal, winds strong, and they could see many storms. Areas along the Mississippi and west should be wet and warm, with the West Coast seeing very warm, dry weather. This forecast extends to the Alaskan Panhandle. Central Alaska should have a cold, stormy spring; Hawaii should see seasonable temperatures and excessive precipitation in wet parts of the Islands.

Summer will see excessive precipitation along the entire East Coast with high humidity and the testimony for moisture continuing inland as far west as the Mississippi. Areas west of the Mississippi and east of the Rockies should have seasonable weather, but most of the area from the Rockies to the West Coast will be dry with some excessively hot temperatures. Central Alaska will be very cool and windy and the Alaskan Panhandle will see destructive storms. Nondesert areas in Hawaii should be deluged with precipitation.

Fall will bring mostly dry weather to the northern East Coast with moderate temperatures and precipitation mainly in the form of thunderstorms. Seasonable weather is predicted for most other areas east of the Mississippi.

Most areas from the Mississippi to the Rockies will see excessive precipitation and cool temperatures. Destructive, windy storms are forecast for much of the Rockies. Central Alaska will be chill, dry, and windy, but the Panhandle will see excessive moisture and fog. Hawaii will see some hot, dry, and windy weather.

January 2001

Zone 1: Temperatures will be cold, windy, and stormy north; and foggy and rainy in the south. Watch for precipitation January 1, 2, 6, 9, 14, 17, 25, and 27. Watch for winds January 1, 6, 11, 17, 19, 22, 27, and 28.

Zone 2: Low temperatures are predicted for January and the first week of February growing milder thereafter. The south will experience fog and high precipitation. Precipitation is likely January 1, 2, 3, 6, 14, 17, 25, and 27. Winds are due January 1, 3, 6, 17, 22, 27, and 28.

Zone 3: Areas near the Mississippi will have a relatively mild winter once the Jupiter-Saturn conjunction separates in February. Expect high precipitation with storms and destructive winds west. Watch for precipitation January 3, 5, 14, 16, 17, 24, and 27. Winds are due January 1, 3, 17, 19, 22, 27, and 31.

Zone 4: Windy weather with the potential for destructive storms is the forecast for January. Watch for precipitation January 3, 14, 16, 17, 22, and 24. Winds are due January 1, 3, 17, 19, 22, and 31.

Zone 5: Wind and destructive storms are forecast for this zone this month. Precipitation is most likely January 13, 25, and 26. Watch for winds January 1, 11, 13, 17, 20, 22, 23, 25, and 31.

Zone 6: The Alaskan Panhandle will have windy weather with some destructive storms. Central parts of the state will have extreme cold with much precipitation. Hawaii will see below-normal temperatures with excessive rainfall. Watch for precipitation January 1, 2, 6, 9, 13, 14, 17, 25, 26, and 27. Winds are likely January 1, 6, 11, 17, 22, 23, 25, 27, 28, and 31.

February 2001

Zone 1: A chilly month with much wind and severe storms is predicted north. The extreme south will see much precipitation and fog. Watch for precipitation February 8, 11, 12, 14, and 25. Winds are likely February 3, 8, 9, 12, 22, 25, and 28.

Zone 2: The first week of the month will be very chill, but the rest of the month will be relatively mild in this zone. Watch for precipitation February 8, 11, 12, 14, and 25. Watch for winds February 3, 8, 9, 12, 22, 25, and 28.

Zone 3: Areas near the Mississippi will have a relatively mild month after the first week. To the west there will be much wind, the potential for hail and some destructive storms. Precipitation is likely February 4, 8, 12, 17, and 25. Winds are likely February 3, 8, 9, 12, 17, 18, 25, and 28.

Zone 4: Much wind and some very destructive storms are forecast. Watch for heavy precipitation February 8, 12, and 25. Winds are likely February 3, 7, 9, 15, 17, 18, and 25.

Zone 5: Storms and wind are forecast with precipitation likely February 1, 3, 4, 11, and 23. Watch for winds February 3, 7, 9, 15, 17, 18, and 25.

Zone 6: Central Alaska will be extremely cold with much precipitation. The Panhandle area will be windy. Hawaii will have above average precipitation and below normal emperatures . Watch for precipitation February 1, 3, 4, 8, 11, 12, 14, and 25. Winds are likely February 3, 7, 8, 9, 12, 15, 17, 18, 22, 25, and 28.

March 2001

Zone 1: Northern portions of this zone should have a cold month with winds and storms. In the extreme south watch for rain and fog. Watch for precipitation March 1, 3, 9, 16, 19, 28, and 29. Winds are likely March 1, 3, 9, 10, 19, 21, and 31.

Zone 2: Heavy precipitation and fog are forecast for this zone in March. Precipitation is likely March 1, 3, 9, 16, 19, 28, and 29. Watch for winds March 1, 3, 9, 10, 19, 21, and 31.

Zone 3: Rain and fog are forecast along the Mississippi with winds, some destructive storms, and the possibility of hail further west. Watch for precipitation March 1, 3, 9, 13, 16, 19, and 31. Winds are due March 1, 3, 5, 13, 19, and 31.

Zone 4: Wind and storms are forecast along with the possibility of hail. Precipitation is likely March 1, 3, 9, 13, 16, 19, and 31. Watch for winds March 1, 3, 5, 13, 19, and 31.

Zone 5: Expect heavy storms and stiff winds in March. Watch for precipitation March 2, 16, 24, 28, and 31. Winds are due March 5, 18, and 28.

Zone 6: Central Alaska will be chilly and wet. The Alaskan Panhandle will see storms, and winds. Hawaii's temperatures stay below normal and wet. Watch for precipitation March 1, 2, 3, 16, 19, 24, 28, 29, and 31. Winds are likely March 1, 3, 5, 9, 10, 18, 19, 21, 28, and 31.

April 2001

Zone 1: Cool and windy is the forecast north. Seasonable temperatures and normal precipitation are forecast for the south. Watch for rain April 1, 5, 7, 8, 15, 23, 25, and 28. Winds are due April 4, 5, 8, 10, 11, 13, 15, 18, 23, and 25.

Zone 2: Seasonable temperatures and normal precipitation are predicted for eastern portions of this zone. West, along the Mississippi, it will be wet and warm. Rain is likely April 1, 5, 7, 8, 15, 23, 25, and 28. Watch for winds April 4, 5, 8, 10, 11, 13, 15, 18, 23, and 25.

Zone 3: Most of the plains area will see some heavy rains and be warmer than usual. Watch for rain April 1, 8, 10, 28, and 30. Winds are likely 4, 10, 11, 13, 14, and 18.

Zone 4: Dry with above-normal temperatures. Precipitation likely April 1, 8, 10, 28, and 30. Winds are due April 4, 10, 11, 13, 14, and 18.

Zone 5: Dry weather with temperatures above normal. Precipitation likely April 1, 5, and 10. Winds are likely April 5, 10, and 14.

Zone 6: The Alaskan Panhandle can expect dry, warmer weather, but most of the rest of the state will be very cold and stormy. Hawaii will be warmer, but wet. Precipitation will be most likely April 1, 4, 5, 7, 8, 10, 14, 15, 23, 25, and 28. Watch for winds April 4, 5, 8, 10, 11, 13, 14, 15, 18, 23, and 25.

May 2001

Zone 1: A cool, windy month is forecast north. In the south the weather should be seasonable. Watch for precipitation May 7, 10, 11, 15, 16, 24, 29, and 31. Watch for winds May 3, 6, 7, 10, 14, 19, 23, 27, and 31.

Zone 2: Normal temperatures precipitation are in the forecast with possibility for winds. Areas near the Mississippi may be wet with temperatures above normal. Rain is likely May 7, 10, 11, 15, 16, 24, 29, and 31. Watch for winds May 3, 6, 7, 10, 14, 19, 23, 27, and 31.

Zone 3: Wet and warm is the forecast for the Plains this month. Rainfall is likely May 10, 11, 15, 16, 19, 24, and 30. Winds are due May 3, 10, 16, and 19.

Zone 4: Dry weather with above-normal temperatures. Rains possible on May 10, 11, 15, 16, 19, 24, and 30. Winds are likely May 3, 10, 16, and 19.

Zone 5: This month may be very warm with little precipitation. Rains possible on May 1, 7, 10, 22, 25, and 30. Watch for winds May 1, 6, 10, 15, and 23.

Zone 6: Warm, windy and drier-than-normal is the forecast for the Alaskan Panhandle. Central parts of the state will see cool, stormy weather. Hawaii and the Aleutian Islands will have excessive precipitation. Watch for rains May 1, 7, 10, 11, 15, 16, 22, 24, 25, 29, 30, and 31. Winds are due May 1, 3, 6, 7, 10, 14, 15, 19, 23, 27, and 31.

June 2001

Zone 1: A windy month is predicted north where temperatures will be below normal. Seasonable temperatures are predicted south with normal rainfall. Watch for rain June 2, 6, 13, 14, 16, and 25. Wind is likely June 2, 5, 6, 12, 15, 16, 17, and 19.

Zone 2: Seasonable weather is forecast, but areas near the Mississippi may see excessive precipitation. Rain is likely June 2, 6, 13, 14, 15, 16, and 25. Watch for winds June 2, 5, 6, 12, 15, 16, 17, and 19.

Zone 3: Excessive rainfall is forecast the first two weeks of the month and temperatures will be a little above normal. Watch for rainfall June 2, 4, 5, 6, and 14. Winds are likely June 2, 4, 5, 6, 12 east, 13, 15, 17, and 18.

Zone 4: Seasonable temperatures and precipitation are forecast east; to the west it will be dry and hot. Watch for precipitation June 2, 4, 5, 6, and 14. Winds are likely June 2, 4, 5, 6, 13, 15, 17, and 18.

Zone 5: Hot and dry is the forecast for this zone in June. Rainfall would be most likely June 13, 21, 27, and 30. Winds are due June 5, 6, 16, 19, and 30.

Zone 6: Hot weather with less precipitation than normal is the forecast for the Alaskan Panhandle. Central parts of the state will have cool, stormy weather. Hawaii will have excessive precipitation June 2, 6, 13, 14, 16, 21, 25, 27 and 30. Winds are likely June 2, 5, 6, 12, 15, 16, 17, 19, and 30.

July 2001

Zone 1: Excessive precipitation is forecast for the entire East Coast this month. Temperatures should be seasonable. Heavy rain is likely July 5, 8, 12, 13 south, 20, 27, and 29. Watch for winds July 6, 8, 12, 14, and 29.

Zone 2: Heavy rainfall and seasonable temperatures are forecast. Watch for rain July 5, 8, 12, 13, 20, 27, and 29. Winds are likely July 6, 8, 12, 14, and 29.

Zone 3: Seasonable amounts of precipitation and near-average temperatures are forecast for most of this zone. Areas near the Mississippi, however, will have excessive rainfall. Rain is likely July 8, 13, 15, 21, 26, 29, and 30. Watch for winds July 6, 8, 14, 26, and 29.

Zone 4: Expect above normal temperatures with little rain, but dates most likely to result in rain include July 12, 17, 19–21, and 26. Winds are likely July 17, 19, and 26.

Zone 5: Hot and dry with rain most likely on July 12, 17, 19–21, and 26. Winds likely July 17, 19, and 26. July 17 and 19 may see stiff, destructive winds.

Zone 6: Destructive winds and many storms are forecast for the Alaskan Panhandle. Central parts of the state will be unseasonably cool and windy. Hawaii will be warmer than usual and extremely wet. Watch for precipitation July 5, 8, 12, 13, 17, 19–21, 26, 27, and 29. Winds are likely July 6, 8, 12, 14, 17, 19, 26, and 29.

August 2001

Zone 1: Rainfall, when it comes, will be heavy. Watch for rain August 1, 2, 5, and 22. Winds are likely August 1, 2, 4, 5, 7, 10, 15, 20, 22, and 23.

Zone 2: Rainfall will be heaviest as the month begins. Temperatures should be seasonable. Watch for rain August 1, 2, 5, and 22. Winds are due August 1, 2, 4, 5, 7, 10, 15, 20, and 23.

Zone 3: Areas near the Mississippi will see some very heavy rainfall August 4 and 5, but the rest of the month it will be dry. The rest of the zone will be dry, too. Watch for winds August 5, 7, 10, 18, 23, and 28.

Zone 4: Temperatures will be above normal with northerly winds and much below normal precipitation. Watch for rainfall August 4 and 5. Winds are likely August 5, 7, 10, 18, 23, and 28.

Zone 5: Extreme heat with scant rainfall. Rains due August 2, 4, 12, 21, 22, and 25. Winds are likely August 1, 2, 5, 10, 20, and 21.

Zone 6: Central Alaska will have an extremely chill and windy month, but the Alaskan Panhandle will be hotter and drier than usual. Hawaii will have more rainfall than normal. Precipitation is most likely August 1, 2, 4, 5, 12, 21, 22, and 25. Winds are due August 1, 2, 4, 5, 7, 10, 15, 20, 21, 22, and 23.

September 2001

Zone 1: Excessive precipitation is forecast the first three weeks of the month. The last week should be relatively dry to the north. Watch for rainfall September 1, 2, 5, 6, 8, 11, 14, 17, and possibly the 24 and 28. Winds are likely September 5, 9, 11, 14, 17, and 21.

Zone 2: Expect a wet month rainfall likely September 1, 2, 5, 6, 8, 11, 14, 17, 24, and 28. Winds are likely September 5, 9, 11, 14, 17, and 21.

Zone 3: Seasonable temperatures and below normal precipitation are likely. Rainfall due September 5, 6, 10, and 30. Watch for winds September 4, 5, 6, 17, and 30.

Zone 4: A warm month is forecast with northerly winds. Rainfall likely September 5, 6, 10, and 30. Winds are likely September 4, 5, 6, 17, and 30.

Zone 5: The first three weeks of the month will be extremely hot and dry. The very end of the month should see a big storm. Rain most likely on September 4, 6, 8, 11, 28, and 30. Wind is likely September 4, 6, 8, 11, 21, and 30.

Zone 6: The Alaskan Panhandle will experience a rainy, stormy month. The central area will be unseasonably chilly. The Aleutians and Hawaii will be wet except during the last week of the month. Watch for storms September 1, 2, 5, 6, 8, 10, 11, 14, 17, 28, and 30. Winds are due September 4, 5, 6, 8, 9, 11, 14, 17, 21, and 30.

October 2001

Zone 1: An unusually warm month is forecast. Rainfall will be limited, but some thunderstorms are likely. Precipitation likely October 2 south, October 3, 9, 20, 23, and 29. Winds are due October 3, 13, 15, 23, and 26.

Zone 2: Seasonable weather with areas near the Mississippi experiencing wet. Watch for rains October 2, 3, 9, 20, 23, and 29. Winds are likely October 3, 13, 15, 23, and 26.

Zone 3: Prolonged rainfall on rain dates is predicted in this zone. Temperatures south will be warm. Look for rainfall October 7, 9, 21, 26, and 27. Winds are likely October 6, 9, 13, 14, 19, 21, 26, and 27.

Zone 4: Destructive storms are forecast for this zone. Dates likely to result in rain include October 7, 9, 21, 26, and 27. Winds are due October 6, 9, 13, 14, 19, 21, 26, and 27.

Zone 5: Wind, rain, and many storms, along with low temperatures are forecast. Watch for precipitation October 1, 2, 3, 7, 16, 20, 21, 26, 27, and 30. Winds are likely October 1, 2, 6, 9, 13, 14, 21, 26, and 30.

Zone 6: Excessive precipitation is forecast for the Alaskan Panhandle this month; the interior of the state will be chill, dry and windy. Hawaii will have temperatures above normal and less rainfall than usual. Watch for precipitation October 1, 2, 3, 7, 9, 16, 20, 21, 23, 26, 27, 29, and 30. Winds are forecast October 1, 2, 3, 6, 9, 13, 14, 15, 21, 23, 26, and 30.

November 2001

Zone 1: Northern areas will see above-normal temperatures. Seasonable temperatures are predicted south. Precipitation will be more frequent than last month. Watch for rain November 2, 8, 14, 15, 20, 22, 23, 25, 28, 29, and 30. Winds are likely November 2, 3, 8, 15, 16, 17, 20, 23, 25, 26, and 29.

Zone 2: Eastern portions of this zone will have seasonable weather, but to the west will experience cool and wet. Watch for precipitation November 2, 8, 14, 15, 20, 22, 23, 25, 28, 29, and 30. Watch for winds November 2, 3, 8, 15, 16, 17, 20, 23, 25, 26, and 29.

Zone 3: Low temperatures north, seasonable temperatures south, and much precipitation is forecast. Watch for precipitation November 1, 5, 8, 13-15, 22, 23, 25, and 30. Watch for winds November 1, 5, 12, 15, 16, 17, 20, 25, and 30.

Zone 4: Storms and destructive winds are forecast. Watch for precipitation November 1, 5, 8, 14, 15, 22, 23, 25, and 30. Wind is likely November 1, 5, 12, 15, 16, 17, 20, 25, and 30.

Zone 5: Stormy and windy is the forecast. Temperatures will be chill. Watch for precipitation November 1, 3, 11–16, 17, 20, 23, and 26.

Zone 6: Central Alaska will be chill, dry, and windy this month, but the Alaskan Panhandle will see excessive precipitation. Look for Hawaii to be warmer and drier than usual. Precipitation is likely November 1, 2, 3, 8, 11, 14, 15, 20, 22, 23, 25, 28, and 30. Wind is likely November 1, 2, 3, 5, 8, 11–16, 17, 20, 23, 25, 26, and 29.

December 2001

Zone 1: Northern portions of this zone will be drier than normal and temperatures here will be above normal. Southern portions will have seasonable weather. Precipitation will be most likely December 7, 10, 14, 22, and 30. Winds are likely December 4, 6, 10, 13, 24, and 30.

Zone 2: Seasonable weather is predicted east; to the west it will be wet and very cold. Watch for precipitation December 7, 10, 14, 22, and 30. Watch for winds December 4, 6, 10, 13, 24, and 30.

Zone 3: Precipitation, when it comes, will be prolonged and temperatures will be below normal. Watch for precipitation December 14, 19, and 29. Winds are likely December 4, 14, 19, 21, 23, and 29.

Zone 4: Destructive winds and several heavy snowstorms are forecast. Precipitation likely December 14, 19, and 29. Winds likely December 4, 14, 19, 21, 23, and 29.

Zone 5: Stiff, destructive winds are forecast low temperatures. Watch for some very heavy storms December 3, 7, and 22. Winds likely December 3, 6, 7, 10, 22, 24, and 30.

Zone 6: Very chill, dry and windy is the forecast for the central part of Alaska in December, but the Panhandle will see excessive precipitation and the Aleutians will be warmer and drier than usual. Hawaii will by dry with above normal temperatures. Watch for precipitation December 3, 7, 10, 14, 22, and 30. Watch for stiff winds December 3, 4, 6, 7, 10, 13, 22, 24, and 30.

Earthquake Predictions

Earthquake watching becomes very important as the new millennium dawns because of massive earth changes predicted by various visionaries and psychics in connection with apocalyptic times. These changes include massive earthquake activity, volcanic activity, massive oceanic changes, and the shifting of the magnetic pole. It is predicted that earthquake activity and volcanic activity will not be confined to areas currently at risk, but will include areas presently not considered earthquake zones.

Astrologers have long noted that earthquakes appeared to be related to eclipses, but it was Ann E. Parker of Skokie, Illinois, who devised a method for making accurate predictions. Ann noted that earthquakes were related to both solar and lunar eclipses, that they could occur up to eighteen months before or after a quake, and that Mars was the trigger. Ann used geodetic equivalents to pinpoint high-risk locations—areas where the geodetic midheaven, geodetic ascendant or geodetic vertex corresponded to the sign and degree where the eclipse occurred. Further refining her predictions Ann noted that Pluto, Mars, or Uranus almost always showed up in angular locations in relation to the earthquake site during eclipses within a few months prior to the quake.

The area near the Texas-Louisiana Border is one area predicted as the site of a new rift. The geodetic midheaven, the geodetic ascendant, and the geodetic vertex of points near this border are all in the later degrees of the mutable signs of Sagittarius, Pisces, and Virgo. This suggests that the eclipses of March 14, 2006, at 24 degrees of Virgo and the September 29, 2006, eclipse at 29 degrees of Virgo could result in a massive quake in this area. Since earthquakes connected with eclipses can be triggered up to eighteen months before the eclipse actually occurs, it is possible that the area is in danger as early as 2004.

The Long Beach and Los Angeles areas in California are also hot spots. The geodetic ascendant of this area is 16 degrees of Aquarius suggesting that the February 5, 2000, eclipse at 16 degrees of Aquarius could result in a quake there or in other places in Southern California. An earthquake in this area, however, may be history in 2001. Mars may have triggered it in the year 2000. This testimony is strengthened by the fact that the January 20, 2000, lunar eclipse astrocartography map set for Washington, D.C., shows a Pluto-Mars crossing offshore a short distance north of Los Angeles.

Other eclipse astrocartography maps set for Washington, D.C., and suggesting earthquake activity in California are the solar eclipse astrocartography map of December 25, 2000, and the June 21, 2001, solar eclipse astrocartography map. The December 25, 2000, map shows a Neptune-Saturn crossing at San Francisco. The June 21, 2001, map shows a Uranus-Mars crossing between San Francisco and Los Angeles. Quakes here will likely follow the eclipse.

The July 28, 1999, lunar eclipse at 5 degrees of Aquarius could result in a disastrous quake in Newfoundland, California, Oregon, Paraguay, Pakistan, Brazil, or in volcanic activity at Mount Saint Helens. Danger dates include January 1, 2, 23, and 24; February 10; March 14, 15, 30, and 31; June 10, 20, and 21; July 18 and 19; August 17, 18, 24,and 25; September 29; October 1 and 2; November 3, 4, and 5; and December 5 and 6.

The August 11, 1999, solar eclipse at 18 degrees of Leo could result in a large quake in Alaska, California, Indonesia, the Caroline Islands, Iraq, Turkey, or Brazil. Dates at risk include January 4 and 24; February 21 and 22; March 8; April 9; May 22; July 2 and 3; September 14, 15, and 16; October 19, 20, and 21; November 22, 23, and 24; and December 23, 29, and 30.

The January 21, 2000, lunar eclipse at 0 degrees of Leo could result in a large quake in Alaska, the Philippines, China, Japan, Kenya, Italy, Hungary, Serbia, Croatia, or Bosnia Herzegovina. Dates at risk include January 13 and 14; February 1; March 3, 4, 18, 19, and 20; April 17 and 18; May 31; June 1; July 9–31; August 16; September 21 and 22; October 27 and 28; November 29; and December 29 and 30.

The July 1, 2000, solar eclipse at 10 degrees of Cancer could result in a quake in Indonesia, China, Sumatra, Algeria, Morocco, or the Ryukyu Islands. Danger dates include January 19; February 5; March 8 and 23–25; June 4–5, or June 30–July 3, and July 10; August 6–9, and 15; September 24 and 25; October 30 and 31; and December 2, 3, and 5.

The July 16, 2000, lunar eclipse at 24 degrees of Cancer could result in a destructive quake in New England, New Brunswick, St. Vincent Island, the Virgin Islands, Bolivia, the Dominican Republic, Puerto Rico, Chile, Brazil, and the American Northwest. Dates to watch include January 21; February 19 and 20; March 5 and 6; April 6; May 20 and 21; June 26 and 27; August 6 and 7; September 11 and 12; October 17–20; November 19 and 20; and December 21, 22, 28, and 29.

The July 31, 2000, solar eclipse at 8 degrees of Leo could result in a large quake in Alaska, the Philippines, China, Ethiopia, Kenya, Bulgaria, Greece, Poland, Hungary, Serbia, Croatia, or Bosnia Herzegovina. Critical dates include January 6, and 29–31; February 15; March 20 and 21; February 15; April 7 and 8; May 2 and 3; June 10–13, 14, and 15; July 22 and 23; August 25, 26, 29, and 30; October 2–6; November 8–10; and December 8, 9, and 13–15.

The December 25, 2000, solar eclipse at 4 degrees of Capricorn could result in a large, disastrous quake at the New Madrid Fault, Nicaragua, British Honduras, El Salvador, the Fiji Islands, Iran, Turkey, southeastern Europe, or Paraguay. Dates that such a quake could trigger include January 6, 26, and 27; February 23 and 24; March 10–12; April

12 and 13; May 23–25; July 3 and 4; August 10 and 11; September 16 and 17; October 20–23; November 26; and December 23–25.

The January 9, 2001, lunar eclipse at 19 degrees of Cancer could result in a quake in Indonesia, China or the Philippines. Danger dates include January 12 and 13; February 9, 23, and 24; March 27; April 19 and 20; May 11, 12, and 31; June 1, 17, and 18; July 5; September 1–4; October 10 and 11; November 11–13; December 15 and 21.

The June 21, 2001, solar eclipse at 0 degrees of Cancer could result in a big quake in Sumatra or Northern Ireland. Danger dates include January 18 and 31; February 1; March 2; April 2, 3, 17, and 18; May 2, 17 and 18; June 26 and 27; September 8–10; October 14 and 15; November 19–20; and December 19.

The July 5, 2001, lunar eclipse at 13 degrees of Capricorn could result in a quake in Washington, D.C., Charleston, South Carolina, Miami, Peru, Columbia, Iran, or Russia. Dates when a quake could occur include January 1, 2, 26, and 27; February 12; March 11, 12, and 31; April 1, 29, and 30; May 1; June 11, 12, 20, and 22; July 19 and 20; August 17–19, and 24–26; September 30; October 1–3; November 3–5; December 8 and 10–12.

The December 14, 2001, solar eclipse at 22 degrees of Sagittarius could result in a quake in Kansas, Nebraska, western Oklahoma, Mexico City, Acapulco, Alaska, the New Hebrides Islands, Greece, Hungary, the Czech Republic, or Germany. Danger dates include January 7, 8, 30, and 31; February 14–16; March 19-21; April 7–9; May 3 and 4; June 14 and 15; July 22 and 23; August 24–26, 29, and 30; October 3 and 4; November 8 and 9; and December 13–15.

The December 30, 2001, lunar eclipse at 8 degrees of Cancer could result in a quake in Malaysia, Sumatra, or the Ryukyu Islands. Danger dates include January 13–15, and 31; February 1 and 2; March 3–5; April 19 and 20; May 31–June 14; July 9–August 1; August 16; September 21–23; October 8, 9, 27, and 28; November 29; December 24, and 30–31.

Magic Under Glass

Penny Kelly

Few experiences come close to providing the sense of creating an entire world—climate, soils, plants, insects, animals, foods, and you as the human component—as that of buying, setting up, and growing in a greenhouse. Greenhouses come in all sizes, shapes, and prices. You can buy the free-standing kind, or get one that attaches to your house. Of those that attach to your house, you can choose a lean-to style, or those with one end attached to your house, the length of it stretching out to any number of feet you desire. Prices start as low as $350 and go up to over $10,000, depending on size, style, and how many technological systems you want to install.

We bought a fairly large free-standing greenhouse, 30 feet wide by 100 feet long, for $4,000 about five years ago. It was quonset-style, covered with six-mil plastic that was guaranteed to last at least three years. It's still doing fine without repairs or replacement, after five years. We put the main structure up ourselves in two weekends, orienting it to run in a north-south direction in order to capture full morning, midday, and afternoon Sun. When it was time to put the plastic on, we got a team of eight people together. There was a good breeze that day, which made it a bad day for unfurling over 100 feet of plastic film, and a couple of times one or two people went airborne trying to hold onto it. After several tries we got it over the framework, then snapped the edges into place.

That night we had a rough storm with wind gusts close to seventy miles per hour. We live up on a land formation called the Lawton Ridge and the constant wind here was one of the first things I noticed about the place when we bought it in 1987. My only concern about buying the greenhouse in the first place was for the wind. Would such a flimsy structure stand up to Mother Nature and her elements? As it turned out, greenhouses are not that flimsy. There it was the next morning, shining in the bright Sun. The storm that first night served to ease my mind greatly from then on.

The first year we really didn't know what we wanted to do with the greenhouse, and we didn't want to build in a whole lot of structure that might need changing as we learned more about how to work with it, so we kept things simple and flexible. On one half of the greenhouse floor we made two long raised beds of compost about 15 feet deep and 50 feet long. The beds were about 5 feet wide across the bottom, and 3 feet wide across the top, giving me a total planting area of 300 square feet. We left the middle five feet of the greenhouse as a long center aisle in order to move back and forth freely with flats, wheelbarrows, tools, and sprayers.

On the other half of the greenhouse floor, a section about 15 feet wide by 100 feet long, was covered with black ground cover to keep the weeds down. Rolls of ground cover can be purchased from any good greenhouse equipment and nursery supply center. They will also have things like potting soils, peat moss, plant foods, plastic or wooden plant markers, peat pellets, flower pots, hanging baskets, bedding flats, plug trays, and every conceivable configuration and size of plant cell pack. You will be amazed at the things that are available for greenhouses, and the ideas they will spark in your mind.

Once the ground cover was down, my husband designed and built a wonderful potting bench with a large bin to hold potting soil and soil amendments, shelves for flats, cell packs, and unused pots of various sizes. He also put hooks at both ends of the bench to hold hand cultivators, shovels, rakes, hoes, potato forks, and other garden tools. The potting bench was set up at the south end of the greenhouse on the ground cover. Then we set up a series of benches and shelves in the rest of the space blanketed with ground cover. The benches were to hold the flats of seedlings each spring until they went into the garden or the greenhouse beds, and at first I thought there was far too little growing area in the beds and far too much bench area for the flats.

We had purchased the greenhouse in spring and didn't set it up until midsummer when the main garden was already in for the year. So I decided to seed several flats of cool weather plants and grow them in the greenhouse beds just to see what would happen, and how long I could keep them going when the weather turned cold. The seeds planted included a variety of lettuces and other greens, plus a few vegetables such as kohlrabi, cabbage, peas, turnips, radishes, broccoli, and cauliflower. Due to varying germination, I had somewhere between six and twelve seedlings of each for planting.

The seedlings were transplanted from the flats into the greenhouse beds in early September. I thought that it was much too late to see much success, but planted them anyway because I figured it was just an experiment. I placed them a bit closer than normal, thinking they would be smaller than usual because of the cooler weather, the shrinking number of daylight hours, and the artificial environment of the greenhouse. This was not the case, however. As soon as they were in the ground, their growth took off for two reasons I had never considered.

First, they were growing in a bed of excellent compost. Second, the effect of fifteen inches of freshly piled compost was the equivalent of double-digging the garden beds. The plants were able to work their roots through the compost easily, enabling them to find whatever they needed to grow big and healthy.

Never had we enjoyed such abundant, delicious, and healthy salads. I would go out to the greenhouse every couple of days and pick two or three leaves off each lettuce plant. The leaves were thick, firm, shiny, sweet, or spicy hot (the mustards) and the range of colors created beautiful salads, and two or three would fill a plastic shopping bag. Both family and guests could not get over the creations that appeared in my salad bowl and many insisted on going out to the greenhouse to see the miracle for themselves.

By the time December and colder weather came, the salads were truly treasured, and as the month drew to a close, we began to mourn what we thought was the approaching demise of our lettuce and greens supply. In January, the deep freezes began, and when we woke up one chilly fifteen degree day, we were sure it was over. Out in the greenhouse the lettuces were all down, looking frozen and crispy. My husband went out to the greenhouse that afternoon for something and came back excitedly a few minutes later, insisting that I "come and look." I was amazed to see the lettuces, standing up, straight and tall, looking as healthy and tasty as ever! And for the rest of the winter we witnessed the same phenomena over and over again. The lettuces would freeze by night, thaw by day, and keep producing without interruption.

Since the greenhouse was not heated, I bought a couple fifty foot rolls of white, floating row-cover, and covered both beds to help the plants resist the cold. We ended up supplying lettuces to three other families besides our own that winter, feeding a total of twenty people, plus our occasional guests. The whole experiment turned out to be a powerful lesson in the extraordinary ability of a healthy plant to resist the extremes of weather. Only later did I realize that there was not a single bit of evidence of insect damage either, something that is not always the case in a greenhouse environment.

What happened with the other vegetables in the beds? Everything grew and produced wonderfully except the peas, broccoli, and cauliflower. The peas didn't seem to have enough insects for pollination and so there were only a few peas. The broccoli and cauliflower grew so slowly at first that they were trying to make heads in the darkest, shortest days of winter, and ended up with a poor contribution. In the case of the cauliflower, there was no attempt to head out in over half the plants. In contrast, the kohlrabi was the most tender, most delicious I have ever tasted, the turnips were perfect, and so were the radishes. Once the cabbages were picked, the roots were left in the ground and they continued to produce small side heads from which we continued to pull individual leaves. Eventually, everything went to seed the following summer.

Since then our greenhouse has evolved into an amazingly versatile building. We have four cows, two of which are milked twice a day. The north end of the greenhouse now has a tiny milking parlor in it. Two young steers and one goat have spacious pens next to the milking parlor. Once the spring seedlings are out of the greenhouse and in the ground, the benches are moved. Large round bales of fresh hay take their place from July or August until the cows have eaten it all by the following spring, at which time the benches go up again, and the seeding of flats for the garden begins for the next year.

Using cedar wood, which offers a natural pest resistance, we have built permanent beds in the greenhouse, expanding our growing area to just over 900 square feet. Even with the hay out of the way, we never have enough bench space for spring seedlings, and end up with flats all over the floor and sometimes out the door.

Although we have large, shuttered ventilators and a fan to maintain good air circulation, our greenhouse has roll-up sides, which has proven to be a great asset in avoiding things like fungus and mildew problems, or too much heat and humidity. The thing to be aware of with roll-up sides, however, is that a sudden summer storm can blow right through the greenhouse when the sides are up, carrying any seed packages you've left lying around, whisking empty cell packs and trays into the field, and even blowing trays full of seedlings off their benches, sometimes making it necessary to start the seeds all over again.

Feathered visitors who are adept at identifying and instantly plucking your carefully planted seedlings out of their trays and cell packs are another slight disadvantage to roll-up sides. When the sides are up, the birds come in to enjoy a meal of sprouts. Some of their favorites are the sunflower, morning glory, and corn seedlings. The only thing that seems to work in this situation is the floating row cover to protect the young plants. Other critters sometimes leave evidence of having visited, but so far nothing serious has been lost due to their presence.

Watering is a major task in any greenhouse. After ours had been up for a year, we trenched a water line to both ends, then put in a couple of frost-free water hydrants. We rented the trencher for a day and purchased the hydrants. A 100-foot hose attached to the hydrant allowed us to water all areas of the beds, reach all of the flats on the benches, and even wander outside to water pots and trays sitting outside in the sun.

Spraying, and therefore a good sprayer, is fairly important in a greenhouse, and although we had several three-gallon, hand-pump style sprayers, we eventually went to a fifteen gallon, battery operated sprayer mounted on a small cart with a 100-foot hose. It allowed us to move easily around the greenhouse or the garden when it was time to feed plants or spray one of the herb teas used in organic gardening. The fifteen gallon size also allowed for a minimum of running back for refills, and turned out to be well worth the money, since we are committed to growing our own food.

After several years experience, the greenhouse is still not exactly the way I would like it to be, but we have continued to grow vegetables in beds filled with compost. Our experience with extraordinary plants that

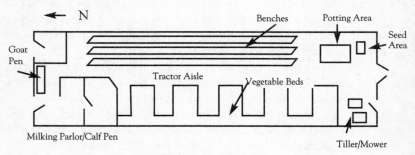

Greenhouse Floor Plan

stand up to all manner of cold weather and harsh conditions is consistent. The high productivity of the plants is also consistent, and it is clear the vegetables have superior nutrition because they refuse to rot. I picked a large basket of cucumbers from the greenhouse in early August this year and put them in the refrigerator to use one by one. Slowly, from August until mid-October, I used all but the last four, which finally began to look more suitable for the chickens than for the dinner table.

If you have forgotten how good food can be, or if you've never known how long it will last, invest in a greenhouse and experience for yourself the miracle of great food almost year round.

The Moon in Your Garden

Roslyn Reid

We've all read articles about planting by the Moon's phase or by the astrological sign the Moon is in at the time of cultivation. While this ancient practice is still followed quite seriously (and successfully) by many of today's gardeners, there are other connections between the Moon and plants in mythology, folklore, and symbolism.

Moon, Plants, and Myths

Sometimes an unexpected lunar connection will show up in the name of a plant. The plant artemisia (commonly known as silvermound because of its round, silvery appearance) is one example. Artemis is the Greek goddess of the Moon and most commonly associated with its waxing phase. Her Roman counterpart is Diana. In *Aradia: The Gospel of the Witches*, Charles Leland describes a society of Italian Witches known as the streghe. To this group, the connection between their deity and the celestial body is so strong that they even call the Moon "Diana" and worship it as a stand-in for the actual goddess.

Other myths may be more esoteric, but they still link the Moon to plant life. In the creation myth of the Makoni tribe of Zimbabwe, the Moon is a man named Mwuetsi. Created by the sky god Maori, Mwuetsi wished to live on Earth, but at that time it was too barren to support life. Seeing this, Maori created a wife for Mwuetsi who bore him grasses, bushes, and trees over the next two years. After this extraordinary accomplishment, Maori showed his gratitude by giving her some competition—he created another wife for Mwuetsi who bore him chickens, sheep, goats, cattle, and children.

This Makoni myth is unusual in several ways—it views the Moon as masculine, it has a woman giving birth to plants, and it considers all life to have arisen from a union of the Moon and the Earth. Many other creation myths use a single creator, or some form of union between the Sun and the Earth.

In the Polynesian lunar calendar, the twelfth day of every month is sacred to Lono, the deity of vegetation. According to their tradition, flowers planted on this night would be round and perfect like the Moon.

Trees of the 13 Moons

One of the most famous and widely-discussed links between plants and the Moon comes from Robert Graves' Celtic Moon calendar, also known as the *Trees of the 13 Moons*. In 1948, Graves, a British poet, published a book called *The White Goddess*, an account of his investigation into the Moon goddesses of ancient religions. Although he postulated the Celtic tree calendar as fact, the consensus today is that he probably invented it, or at least considerably elaborated upon it, for his book.

Graves replaced the familiar twelve month solar calendar configuration with a thirteen month one based on a twenty-eight day Moon cycle. He associating a native tree or plant with each "Moon" (month) and used Gaelic names for most of them. Following is a brief look at his associations, which Graves based on theories of an ancient Celtic written alphabet called the ogham. The Gaelic term for each tree is in parentheses.

December 24 to January 20 is the start of the lunar year, and is represented by the birch (beith). This is a good period for initiations or beginnings. The ghostly white birch tree is also an excellent plant for a Moon garden (discussed later in this article).

January 21 to February 17 is represented by the mountain ash, or rowan (luis). This tree is actually not an ash, but a member of the rose family. One of the most magical of all Celtic trees, the wood of the rowan is prized for protection, especially of cattle herds, which gives it an association with the Moon. (See alder, below, for the cow connection.) This lunar cycle marked the beginning of the growing season.

February 18 to March 17 is represented by the ash (nion). The ash has an unusual connection with the Moon—its wood was favored by sailors as an amulet against drowning; and, as we all know, the sea falls under the influence of the Moon.

March 18 to April 14 is represented by the alder (fearn). The wood from this tree—actually more of a bush—is used to make milk pails (it has a high resistance to the corrosion of moisture). Alder has an unusual lunar connection—the cow who jumped over the moon!

April 15 to May 12 is associated with the willow (saille). The willow has been linked with Artemis, the Moon goddess whom we met earlier through her silvermound. And in his famous *Herbal*, Nicholas Culpeper, the English astrologer and physician of the early seventeenth century says of this tree, "The Moon owns it," apparently because of its folkloric association with Witches.

May 13 to June 9 is represented by the hawthorn or mayapple (uath). In ancient Greece and Rome, this plant was associated with marriage and the honeymoon. However, during medieval times, the honeymoon came to an end when the meaning imparted to this plant was officially reversed. From that time it was considered a favorite plant of Witches, and burned on Walpurgis Night to smoke them out and expel them from villages. But as we shall see later, the mayapple is another good plant for a Moon garden.

June 10 to July 7 is one of the most important in the old Celtic religion because it contains the hinge of the year, or Summer Solstice. Therefore, this period of time is represented by one of their most important trees, the oak (duir). At the Solstice, the Sun reverses direction; and nights (the time of the Moon) begin to get longer. According to legend, mistletoe growing on oaks would be harvested with a golden sickle by the ancient Druids. The use of this tool represented the union of the Sun (gold) and the Moon (the crescent shape of the sickle), another connection between a plant and the Moon.

July 8 to August 4 falls under the auspices of the holly (tinne). The holly blooms in July. Later, its flowers give way to little white waxy berries resembling tiny Full Moons. Also, the first wheat of the year was usually harvested at this time, and the French used this "first fruit" to make the Moon-shaped pastries we call croissants (crescents).

August 5 to September 1 is presided over by the hazel nut (coll). Because this tree is not native to the United States, many Celtic pagan groups in this country substitute the witch hazel in their magical workings. In the original Celtic legend, though, the hazel nut is associated with the tale of the cauldron of Cerridwen—sometimes called the Cailleach, or Moon Crone.

September 2 to September 29 is the vine season (muin). Obviously, this is not a tree, but the type of vine used to represent this period appears to be flexible. Graves seems to indicate a bramble, such as blackberry; but artistically, this cycle is usually represented by a grapevine. Grapevines are the symbol of Dionysus, whose mother was Selene—the Moon.

September 30 to October 27 is represented by the ivy (gort). Again, not a tree. Ivy represents wisdom, which is why colleges like to grow it on the walls of their buildings. Here is another connection with Selene, because in ancient Greece the ivy was one of the plants dedicated to Dionysus. (It seems strange that a vine representing inebriation and a vine representing wisdom were both symbols of the same deity!

Perhaps this is the origin of the ancient Latin saying, *"In vino veritas"*.)

October 28 to November 24 is represented by yet another plant which is not a tree, the reed (ngetal). Reeds could be harvested at that time to fashion a springtime bed for Brighid, a Celtic triple goddess (all triple goddesses are associated with the Moon). In making an inviting reed bed for this goddess, families encouraged her to enter their houses in the spring and bless them with a bountiful crop.

November 25 to December 22 is the lunar cycle of the elder (ruis). This is another "Dark Moon" tree for several reasons—one being its dark blue berries, representing the New Moon. Also, in some cultures, the elder is traditionally associated with the wood used in Witches' brooms for their moonlit flights.

You may notice that there is a leftover day, December 23. Although acknowledging it in a very Celtic fashion as a "time outside of time", Graves is vague on the plant representative for this day. Some Celtic scholars prefer the fir (ailm), possibly because it represents the first vowel in the ogham, while all the trees of the thirteen Moons are represented by consonants. Another possibility is because the fir was harvested on this day for use as a Maypole during Beltaine in the spring. The fir also has its own lunar connection, being one of the plants associated with our old friend Diana.

Other scholars consider the yew (idho) to be a good candidate because of its association with death. Either yew or fir could be appropriate, for the Winter Solstice represents the return of the Sun—and therefore the death of winter, domain of the Moon. The harvesting and erection of the Maypole is a symbol of the connection between the year's division into the realms of Sun and Moon, the time of the dark and the time of the light. Both are necessary to turn the wheel of the year.

Moon Gardens

By now you may be asking, what is this moon garden which we keep mentioning? Consider this: There is no such term as a "Sun garden" because most plants need the Sun to flower, and therefore, would be considered sun gardens. A Moon garden consists of plants which bloom at night.

The idea of the Moon garden most likely originated in Japan; but it was popularized in the West by the Victorians, who wished to enjoy all gardens all the time. Most Victorians liked to build their gardens around a theme: the kitchen garden, the butterfly garden, the color garden (based on several variations of one or two colors). The Moon garden was

a very popular theme at the time. One of the world's most famous moon gardens can still be seen at Sissinghurst Castle in England, former home of Victorian writer Vita Sackville-West.

Flowers and plants best suited for a Moon garden are those which can easily be enjoyed by the light of the Moon, or which release their scents at night. Although most flowers attract bees and other insects for their propagation, some flowers are favored by nocturnal pollinators, such as the sphinx moth. Therefore, the seeds of these night-bloomers are spread in the same manner as their day-blooming brethren and sistern. Night-blooming plants usually use scent rather than color to attract insects. As you might imagine, colors of the vegetation in a Moon garden could be white, silver, lavender, pink, light blue, or any other color which reflects moonlight. This includes foliage as well as flowers—an example previously mentioned is the birch tree, with its white trunk. Striped hostas also show up well and are easy to grow. Even fruit can be used. The Victorians were partial to light-colored melons such as honeydew, which resembles the moon.

Other flowers appropriate for a Moon garden are some night-blooming succulents such as a vinelike plant called cereus (a relative of the Christmas cactus and sacred to the Moon goddesses). Cereus blossoms stay open for only one night, but the plant blooms so quickly that some people actually claim to have watched it open. These fleeting flowers bloom from July to October and can grow up to a foot long. After the blossoms fall, a red fruit will appear. Unfortunately, cereus is a warm climate plant, so if your Moon garden is north of Florida, you must bring it inside for the winter.

Other useful plants include white or pink petunias, trillium, nicotiana (night-blooming tobacco flower), lambs ears, artemisia (silvermound, mentioned earlier), yucca, verbena, datura, cosmos, allysum (whose flowers look like snowballs), pink evening primrose, and even some varieties of white roses. One special category of night-blooming plant is the tropical water lily. Obviously, these require a pond or pool, but all the better to reflect the Moon!

And what Moon garden would be complete without the moonflower? This is a vine, *ipomoea alba*, bearing pink or white six-inch-wide blossoms.

Although it resembles the morning glory, the moonflower is on the opposite schedule, blooming at dusk and closing at dawn all summer long. Its flowers release a lemony aroma which wafts along on the night air. The name alone is enough to justify its place in the Moon garden.

Finally, be aware that if you do decide to try growing a Moon garden, some of the plants which you might want are almost impossible to find in a commercial nursery. You could have some luck by checking around for seeds (see the Bibliography and Resources section at the end of this article). If all else fails, try to locate someone who grows that particular plant and would be willing to barter for it. (This is called pass-along planting, from the book *Passalong Plants* by Steve Bender. The term refers to plants which are obtained from somewhere other than commercial sources.)

For specifics on your Moon garden's planting, location, design, etc., I recommend the excellent article "moon gardens" by Leslie Sturtevant appearing in Llewellyn's *1999 Moon Sign Book.*

Furniture and Accessories

There are other items suitable for inclusion in a Moon garden. Probably one of the most popular, if there is enough room for it, is the Moon bridge. Found in the original Japanese Moon gardens, a Moon bridge is especially appropriate if you have the previously mentioned pond for night-blooming lilies. In certain ancient Asian traditions, the half-moon shape of this bridge signifies good luck and money. But the bridge also makes use of your lily pond in the daytime to reflect itself and turn into a Full Moon, representing the completeness of the well-rounded garden.

Some companies sell Moon benches and tables designed for the garden. These are usually crescent-shaped to resemble a Moon in its first or fourth quarter, or there might be Moon-shaped cutouts in them or decorations on them. And it's all the better if the bench and table are painted white

One of the most unusual accessories for a Moon garden is a moondial. Based on a sundial, the moondial was invented during the Renaissance. Like sundials, some of them bear mottoes in Latin such as *Docet umbra* (the shadow teaches) or *Ut umbra sic vita* (as a shadow so is life).

Moondials aren't really used to tell time, however, because of the problem of conversion—one must know the current phase of the Moon and use a table to convert Sun time into Moon time. This is complicated because the Moon's shadow loses forty-eight minutes for every day after the Full Moon, but gains the same amount of time after the Full Moon. Some moondials have the tables engraved right in them, although it could be tricky to use one of these in the dark. As you can see, figuring out the time from a moondial is probably not worth the trouble, but it makes a charming garden accessory. And one imaginative suggestion is that the entire Moon garden be designed in the form of a moondial by planting flowers in a concentric circle around a tree.

In finishing up our tour of the Moon garden, let's not forget one of the most popular "rustic" accessories—the outhouse. Nonfunctional privies, or some representation of them such as on wind chimes, are used in many places to lend a "country" flavor to the garden. The familiar crescent moon cutout on the door supplies the Moon connection. This design has been traced back to an outhouse constructed in 1820, although why the cutout has assumed the shape of a Moon is not clear. One popular theory holds that customarily there were two outhouses, one for men and another for women—the men's door marked with a sun and the women's with a Moon. There are quite a few holes (so to speak) in this theory, however. How was the Sun-shaped cutout distinguished from a Full Moon cutout? And why would there be two separate out-houses when every home today has a unisex bathroom?

Saluting the Moon

As you can now see, the connection between the Moon and plants is more pervasive than it first seems—it can be found not only in the lunar planting calendar, but in mythology, folklore, and everyday life. In a recent article, Raven Grimassi outlines procedures for using the power of Moon imagery to communicate with plants, giving a whole new meaning to the term "drawing down the Moon." And if you don't have room for a Moon garden, you can scatter synthetic pearls around your regular garden or yard—tiny little imitation Moons, placed on the ground in honor of the real thing.

So in closing, consider this quote from Dan and Pauline Campanelli: "Salute the Moon in her snowy whiteness and breathe in the coolness of her light. The Spirit is most active when the body is most still." Best of all, we don't even have to wait for nighttime to salute the Moon!

Making Herbal Drinks

K. D. Spitzer

Herbal drinks can be served hot, but some of the best are served icy cold and are quite refreshing in the summer months. The best source for fresh herbs to use in your herbal drinks is, of course, the garden. There are some old favorites that need to be included in the garden and then you can experiment with additions around this center core. Most of all, you need the mints: spearmint, peppermint, and all the varieties in between. The fruity mints offer a breadth of flavors that are cooling in the summer months. Orange mint, apple mint, and pineapple mint are personal favorites. And don't forget bee balm (Monarda didyma) Oswego tea of Amerindian tea lore. It's reliably attractive in the garden and its leaves and blossoms are delicious in the glass.

I plant mint in pots because, let's face it, the mint family is about power, takeover, even subversion. Unless you have a forgiving location that won't mind if mints take over, pushing out everything else, plant in pots. Don't believe anything anyone says will contain your mints in the ground. Stainless steel cylinders couldn't hold back the mints, never mind anything lesser. Plant with care, or the next thing you know you will be talking to the mint devas and trying to rip out plants by the handfuls. (Bad idea! In two years all those little pieces you missed will be back in full force and putting out thousands of new plants.) If you are a black-thumb gardener, start with a mint plant. Its survival and thriving will bolster your courage.

While you are contemplating where to plant the water mint—under the outside spigot or over near the water pond—indulge in a cup of the following. Grab a handful of fresh spearmint leaves, add a cinnamon stick, and cover with water just brought to a boil. Let steep for five minutes and sweeten with cane sugar rather than honey. This hot tea is as refreshing on a hot day as when it is served cold. You can use a teaspoonful of dried leaves if its not convenient to raid your mint garden. A traditional alternative is to substitute a licorice stick (the real thing, not the candy) for the cinnamon. Even aniseed or fennel seeds can be substituted, as mint and anise flavors march along quite amicably. Add a slice of lemon or garnish the cold drink with lemon balm.

Moroccan Mint Tea

This world famous tea is very simple to make at home. You'll need Gunpowder green tea and a metal teapot that can go back on the fire. Measure a couple of teaspoons of green tea into the teapot. Cover with just the amount of boiling water that can be absorbed by the tea and let sit for a minute. Then fill the teapot with hot water and put on the burner. Do not allow to boil, but let it steep on the heat for a couple minutes. Remove and add a small handful of spearmint leaves. Return to the heat for one minute, and then add two sugar cubes per serving.

This is traditionally served very hot in small glasses. This should occasion a shopping trip to a Middle Eastern market for the tea glasses. While you're there, search out a source for candied aniseeds—a fun garnish for teas, cakes, or cookies, or just a nibble while you're drinking your tea.

The Mint Julep

Of course, this classic mint drink, which is perfect for slow sipping as you sit on the veranda on a sultry afternoon, is a must. Crush six to eight mint springs in the bottom of a tall glass. Add a tablespoon of simple syrup (recipe on page 342) and continue crushing to extract the flavors. You can use the handle of a wooden spoon. Fill the glass with crushed ice and add a couple ounces of bourbon. Garnish with more mint sprigs.

Lemon, Lime & Lavendar

The lemon flavored plants look great and smell even better. Lemon balm (*Melissa officinales*) is currently enjoying celebrity, but has the best flavor only if used fresh. While lemon balm grown in my garden is slightly harsh, the flavors do vary from garden to garden and soil to soil.

On the other hand, lemon verbena (*Aloysia triphylla*) is an old fashioned plant that, fresh or dried, puts out both great scent and flavor. It takes so well to cutting over the summer months, don't bother waiting until it blooms because the flowers are quite unremarkable in this otherwise wonderful herb. It is, however, very sensitive and for that reason, I usually plant it in a pot, rather than sticking it directly into the ground. When you bring it in for the winter, and you'll want to, this tender perennial will drop its leaves. Don't get hysterical. Every English-speaking herb writer will offer advice on how to avoid this, and I have probably tried more than half of these ideas. If you haven't totally shocked the plant into cardiac arrest by digging it out of the ground, then you have half a chance of wintering over one of the great herbs.

Pick up the leaves that have fallen off and use them to infuse oils or potpourris, or crumble them into nifty little sachets for your drawers. Dried, these leaves will still impart their flavor to teas. Add to a China black. Unlike lemon balm which does not dry well, dried lemon verbena leaves store well, and are flavorful in both hot or cold teas. This plant grows to about forty inches tall. Take cuttings in the spring to reproduce it, and think nothing of pinching back the blossoms when cutting for tea.

You don't need to, but you can bolster its flavor with lemon-scented geranium leaves. Even nutmeg-scented geraniums add a flavor punch. Throw in some lemon-scented basil or even lemon-thyme (a fabulously versatile herb). Of course you'll want to garnish your tea with fresh sprigs of lemon verbena, or for a interesting choice, one of your mints. A tea this old-fashioned and romantic deserves to be served iced in your "good" glass ware. I serve this this lovely Victorian tea in have mismatched antique green depression glassware that are cone-shaped.

Lime and Lavender Iced Tea

Lime and lavender iced tea is refreshingly different. Pour a cup of water brought to a boil over three tablespoons of fresh lavender blossoms or one tablespoon of dried. Let steep until the water cools. In the meantime, zest several long strings of lime peel from four limes. Squeeze the limes, add three cups cold water and enough simple syrup to sweeten to taste. Combine with the cooled lavender tea and serve iced, garnished with the lime zest and stems of lavender blossoms. You can also use frozen limeade. Just follow the directions on the container to prepare.

Licorice-flavored drinks can also be attractively prepared. Anise hyssop is one my favorites. The blossoms can be plucked for garnish, or still on the stem, used as a swizzle stick. The flavor can be enhanced with star anise or aniseed, fennel seed, or green sweet Cecily which is a versatile herb that is often overlooked.

Digestive Aid

Pour water brought to boil over several sprigs of spearmint or peppermint, which you have crushed with a wooden spoon. Add a good pinch of both aniseed and fennel seed. Let steep five minutes. Strain and serve hot with a candied licorice whip or real licorice stick. Serve it cold with crushed ice and thin lemon slices. Use a zester and cut stripes from stem end to blossom end before slicing the lemon to add a little style. While this tea isn't as "enjoyable" for its flavor as some others are, mint and licorice are a stimulating digestive aid.

Tea Times

The English used to favor a drink made from elder flowers as a treat for the hired help brought in for haying time. It's a really thirst quencher, and also quite suitable for a hard-fought game of croquet. Often served as a sparkling beverage, it's a little on the bland side and profits from the addition of lemon slices.

Elderflower Champagne

6 washed elderflower heads
3 cups white sugar
3 lemons
2 tablespoons white wine vinegar
1 gallon of water.

Heat half the water to boiling and dissolve the sugar. Thinly pare the lemons and add the peel (but not the pith) to the sugar. Save the lemons for another beverage. Then combine all the ingredients, stir well and cover. Refrigerate for four to five days. Serve well chilled in tall glasses and garnish with mint sprigs, anise hyssop, or lemon slices.

Elderflowers also make a great wine. If you are not a winemaker, see Llewellyn's *1997 Moon Sign Book* for the complete method of wine-making. Here's the recipe:

Elderflower Wine

1 lemon
1 pint elderflower heads (tightly packed)
1 campden tablet
3 pounds sugar
1 teaspoon pectin enzyme
1 package champagne wine yeast
1 teaspoon yeast nutrient
1 ½ cups orange juice

Try not to gather the elderflowers near a road. If you must, then be sure and wash carefully. Grate the zest from the lemon and add to the flowers in a sterilized two-gallon container. Wrap the lemon well and save. Bring a gallon of water to a boil and pour over the flowers. Add a Campden tablet, cover well and let sit for three days. You don't want to expose this to fruit flies and if you find their little corpses in the batch, dump it! Put the sugar in a stainless steel kettle and pour the flower and water mixture over it. Bring to a boil and then let cool. Strain and pour into a jug with a fermentation lock. Add the pectin enzyme and the juice from the lemon. Mix the yeast and the orange juice which you have warmed to wrist temperature. Let sit until it bubbles, about an hour. Add to the wine and let it get on with its fermentation. You may have to rack it to clear it, but it will probably be ready to bottle in two to four months. Let it develop for six months to a year before drinking.

Pimm's Cup

Pimm's Cup is another English favorite that flaunts the cucumber flavor of borage. The leaves are used here along with the blossoms. This punch bowl favorite is showy as well as delicious. Pimm's No. 1 is a gin-based liquor made in England using dry gin, fruit juices and spices.

To assemble a punch bowl, use about two ounces of Pimm's to twelve ounces of club soda or a citrus flavored seltzer or lemon lime soda. Decorate with slices of orange, lemon, lime, and cucumber. Garnish with lots of the spectacular and blue borage blossoms and leaves. Don't forget the mint leaves. You can substitute champagne for the club soda, if it's a really special occasion; then add apricots or peaches for garnish along with the borage.

Sage Wine

Another herbal drink that is not only delicious, but efficacious to your health is sage wine. This is so simple to prepare. Buy a good sauturne and use it to drown several large pieces of cut sage leaves. Cover and store in a dry, dark, cool cupboard. Taste it for sage flavor ten to fifteen days after storing, letting it sit longer if necessary. When satisfied, then strain and store in an attractive decanter. Use as a digestive by sipping no more than a tablespoon after dinner, naturally from thimble-sized stemware. In the cold months you can warm it in the microwave, along with a stem of fresh sage. Serve an ounce or two in your Middle Eastern mint tea glasses. Add a cube of sugar or a little honey to sweeten.

Simple Syrup

Simple syrups are simple to make. Mix one cup water with one cup sugar; bring to a boil and simmer for five minutes. Let cool and refrigerate. Make a large batch for the summer months because it is so useful. Add to freshly squeezed lemons, along with water or seltzer for a great tasting lemonade. Flavor the syrup with your favorite herb when simmering.

Garnishes

Garnishes can be candied ginger, swizzle sticks, star anise, cinnamon sticks, fresh stalks of herbs, and dried licorice sticks. Make vanilla sugar or anise sugar to sweeten teas. Infuse honey or corn syrup with herbs to give them flavor body, or buy herbal honeys that have been flavored at the source by the bee!

Freeze blossoms in ice cubes. Use herbal teas for the fluid. Any edible flower will do, but borage, clove pinks, pansy, or viola blossoms are quite nice. The red blossoms of pineapple sage are spectacular and I like to toss handfuls of lemon gem marigolds in a glass of lemon-scented teas. Float blossoms from your calamondon orange tree or Star of Bethlehem jasmine to add a special touch to either hot or cold teas. Violet blossoms can be frozen in cubes in late spring and if the trays are emptied into a ziplocked bag can be stored in the freezer to use in the summer months. You need to use this method with "frost free" freezers as, otherwise, they will "dry" out the cubes.

Tea Preparation Methods

I like to steep herbs in the Sun for maximum flavor. Measure fresh or dried herbs into a jar, add cold water to cover and place where it can sit in the sun all day. For added flavor, add some thin slices of lemon or lime. Thin slices of fresh ginger root or lumps and slices of crystallized ginger can also be added to spice it up.

If you are using the hot water method, don't use hot tap water. Water that has been sitting in the hot water heater or pipes leading from it is flat due to a lack of oxygen that brings out the tea flavor. And if you are heating water to pour over your herbs, take the tea kettle off the fire just before it boils. The tea will have a better flavor than if you let the water (and thus the oxygen) bubble away. This is true no matter what tea you are making. Also avoid using water that smells strongly of chlorine.

Use about a teaspoon of dried herbs, or double that for fresh herbs, in every cup of water. Let steep for ten minutes and then strain off. (If using roots or barks, you need to make a decoction by simmering for ten to fifteen minutes before straining.) If making a dried tea blend, then let it sit for a couple weeks after blending and before steeping.

Sonic Bloom

Peter Tompkins

In 1975, in a sports arena in Arizona Jean Dixon prophecied that a small black box would soon be discovered that would revolutionize agriculture allowing the United States to grow food for the whole planet on a third of its land, providing for health sustenance for those starving in the Third World. When the world's population rises to almost three times its present overcrowded 5.5 billion—sometime within the next half century—we'll be feeding 14 billion people. In the Third World, conditions are so appalling that an emaciated child dies every second of every day.

In the span of a half million years we have greedily turned great forests into deserts, caused the extinction of countless plant species, and turned millions of acres of rich soil into unproductive wastelands larded with poisonous chemicals. While farmers struggle in semi-arid regions to grow food on marginal soils, in northern climates others struggle with a short growing season. Our soil is more and more tainted, eroded, and worthless, its trees hacked and uprooted.

The disaster is such that it may require many miracles to reverse the destruction. One solution in particular is intriguing: techology developed by a research scientist from Minnesota, Dan Carlson. His novel system for growing abundant produce, patented as Sonic Bloom, nourishes plants through their leaves to the accompaniment of a special sound.

What motivates Carlson is a horrifying event he witnessed in the early 1960s. In Korea, as an enlisted soldier he was obliged to watch a starving mother lay the legs of her small child beneath the rear wheel of an army truck, creating an authentic cripple and thereby entitling the family to a live-saving food subsidy.

Back home, using his GI Bill of Rights, Carlson spent many hours in the University of Minnesota library, studying plant physiology. Stuck by the idea that certain sound frequencies might help a plant breath better and absorb more nutrients, he experimented with various frequencies until, with the help of an audio engineer, he found one in the 3 to 5,000 Khz range that was consonant with the early morning bird chriping that helps plants open wider their stomata, or mouth-like pores.

On every leaf there are thousands of such small openings. Each stoma—less than 1/1000th of an inch across—allows oxygen and water to pass out of the leaf, or transpire, while other gases, notably carbon dioxide, move in to be transformed by photosynthesis into sugars. During dry conditions, the stomata close to prevent a wilting plant from drying out completely.

Photomicrographs show plant stomata opening wider to Carlson's frequencies, while a Philips 505 scanning electron microscope shows substantially higher stomata density on a leaf treated with Sonic Bloom; additionally, the individual stomata are more developed and better defined.

The Work Begins

As stomata normally imbibe the morning dew, sucking up nutrients in the form of free flowing trace elements, why not, thought Carlson, develop a special organic spray to apply to the leaves along with the sound that induces stomata to open. Even in poor soil, Carlson reasoned, plants could be well nourished with a foliar spray containing the right combination of elements. To develop such a effective nutrient solution took Carlson fifteen years of trial and error experimenting in labs throughout the country with the funding of a caring "angel."

Carlson needed to find not only what elements serve to make a plant flourish, he needed to find the proper balance of nitrogen, potassium, and phosphorus; but not the overdose recommended by the chemical companies which swamp the plant to the exclusion of trace elements vital to its health. Too much of any one element can distort or even kill a plant. Endless testing with radioactive isotopes and Geiger counters to trace the elements' translocation from leaves to stems, from peak to roots was done. Among the first natural substances used was Gibberilic acid, naturally derived from rice roots, needed by every living plant. Eventually Carlson included sixty-four trace elements derived from natural plant products and from sea weed. He also added chelated amino acids and growth hormones, altering the surface tension of the water base to make it more easily absorbed. The end result was Sonic Bloom.

As a test for his brainchild, Carlson induced a common household purple passion vine (*Cynura sp.*)—which normally grows no longer than eighteen inches—to wind its way, room-to-room, throughout his Minnesota home, until it reached a length of 600 feet. This phenomenal growth stimulating researchers from *The Guinness Book of Records* to verify the fact and included the it in their 1976 edition. But that was only the half-way mark: over the next few months the vine grew another 600 feet.

Further tests showed that even without the special sound a plant leaf can absorb 300 percent more Sonic Bloom than any other foliar spray, but when accompanied by Carlson's special frequency the absorption and translocation rate of nutrients rises to an amazing 700 percnet—far more than a plant could possibly absorb through its roots. The result is early maturity, greater yields, improved taste, more nutrition, and longer shelf life. (Sonic Bloomis considered a plant growth enhancer, not a fertilizer.) For normal use Carlson recommends fertilizing the soil, as usual using an organic rather than chemical fertilizer. To check a plants' progress on a larger project Carlson will analyze leaves and mix up a second formula containing any deficit elements.

How It's Done

Ideally, the sound, which is similar to the frequency range of bird calls made by swallows, martins, and warblers, sounding altogether like a flock of barn swallows—is played to plants beginning thirty minutes before spraying, during spraying, and another thirty minutes after. The advantage of this mechanical sound is that it includes frequencies of birds long since disappeared. Carlson's healthy spraying operation is so simple all one needs is a cassette player and nutrient sprayer. The misting should be applied to both sides of the leaves until saturated. For home gardeners, Carlson has developed an inexpensive kit containing a cassette tape, a sprayer, and a bottle of nutrients. It sells for $60. For indoor plants, the chirping sound is imbedded in a tape of classical, easy-to-listen-to music that is played once every morning, preferably between 5:30 and 9 AM, when plants naturally absorb the dew. Maximum results come from such daily sound stimulation that dramatically increases absorption of both nutrients and dew, providing drought protection as well as increased growth. But impressive results can be achieved by using the Carlson system for as little as two hours weekly. As a bonus, the sound appears to attract unusual quantities of birds who add their chorus to the manufactured medley; synchronously, butterflies swarm in greater numbers.

Treatment is basically the same for commercial operations, but the special sound units that do not play music, only the basic high-pitched oscillating frequency. These units can also be activated by a solar cell to turn them on at daylight and off at nightfall. Powered by a 12 volt battery, units can be mounted on poles or trees in the growing area. (Sonic Bloom comes in sizes for five to sixty-acre spreads.) Multiples of these can be used for larger acreage. For still bigger farms, mobile frequency generators are mounted on tractors. The sound does not worry animals, but the larger units should not be too near a house. From a distance the sound blends pleasantly with that of crickets.

Field crops are treated with the nutrient once every ten days or two weeks. One gallon of concentrated nutrient sells for $250: diluted one teaspon to a quart of water, it provides 256 gallons of spray, enough for five treatments on four and one-half acres of crops; the sound units start at $250 for a single high-frequency ceramic speaker suitable for treating up to five acres; a larger model suitable for forty acres costs $550, and for sixty acres $650. The system allows for much larger profits, costing per season about $60 per acre of row crops, and $200 for tree crops. An increase of yield from just 2 to 10 percent is all that is needed to cover the cost of the Sonic Bloom.

Both seeds and cutting from plants benefit greatly from the treatment. Carrot seed soaked overnight in the nutrient solution—one half ounce per gallon of water—with the cassette tape left to play continuously, produced a far greater than normal carrot crop of 400 pounds to each forty-foot row. Soaking ginseng seeds the night before planting resulted in 95 percent germination. Sprouts, alfalfa in particular, soaked in Sonic Bloom and played to for seventy-two hours, developed an edible body with 1,200 percent increase in weight and double the shelf life. Cuttings should be sprayed once a week with 500:1 solution until established, then sprayed once a week with a 250:1 solution. Suckers cut from a tomato plant should be allowed to grow for seven days or until fourteen inches long, then placed in shade a sprayed once a day with one-quarter ounce per gallon solution. In ten to fourteen days, the sucker should be fully rooted and start to grow two inches a day. Fifty-five days later—

instead of the normal production time of nintey days—plants should be seven to nine feet tall, producing 400 to 600 tomatoes, many with a double fruit hand. Five hundred cucumber seeds soaked in a 500:1 solution, serenaded for eight hours, and planted in one greenhouse, matured from seed to harvest in forty days, producing 7,600 pounds of cucumbers, so many they had to be picked daily over a period of thirty-six days lest they grow too long to fit in twenty-inch packing boxes.

More interesting, in terms of the turn-of-the-century debate between Darwinians about inherited characteristics, plants can now be shown to pass on their cultural improvements to their offspring, even when the offspring are left untreated. Any seed or cutting from a Sonic Bloom treated plant is better than its parent. Kidney beans, untreated, usually produce three to four beans per pod. Treated with Sonic Bloom, the increase is up to four to five. Their offspring, untreated, will regularly produce four or five. If treated they will produce five or six. A generational improvement may go on up to eight or nine per pod.

Sonic Bloom is now being marketed and used in forty-eight states and thirty-five foreign countries. *Acres Usa*, the agricultural bulletin, reports that test done with Carlson's tape-and-foliar spray produce impressive results with alfalfa and corn crops. *Landowner*, the bulletin of Professional Farmers of America, reports that laboratory studies of a variety of plants show yields of vegetable and field crops increased by 20 to 100 percent: soy beans by 100 percent, tomatoes by 133 percent. According to *Landowner*, greenhouse plants produce larger root mass, more blooms, and have faster maturity. A Pennsylvania alfalfa grower using Sonic Bloom has won every contest for growth and nutrition in his country, with 29 percent protein, the most tons per acre, and five cuttings instead of three.

Cauliflowers grown with Sonic Bloom are so big that only four will fit in a box designed for twelve. Soybean plants treated in Wisconsin produced up to 300 pods per plant, thirty to thirty-five being the norm. What's more, the beans contained 27 percent protein against a normal 15 percent. Dill plants grow over four feet tall, calla lillies over six feet tall. Bell peppers bear over fifty peppers per plant instead of the norm of four or five per plant. In River Falls, Wisconsin, corn grows sisxteen feet high, and young evergreen trees grow three to four feet annually. In Florida, orange production has increased by 66 percent, with a whopping vitamin C content 121 percent above normal, and fruit in all stages of growth on each tree, making for a perpetual harvest.

Bill Bostwick, a grower of high potency American ginseng in the Midwest, obtains 5 thousand pounds an acre, whereas the state average is a mere 13 thousand pounds per acre. Bostwick grows plants to five year maturity while most others are obliged to harvest at

three to four years. Despite the propensity for molds and fungi to form on ginseng, his plants have minimum disease, his roots are the largest and of best quality. Test a St. John's University in Jamaica, New York, Bostwick's ginsenocide level—the active ingredient in ginseng—was four to five points above the average. With Sonic Bloom, his seeds are much larger, enabling him to sell his seeds for $50 a pound whereas non users get only $8 to 10.

Cranberry growers using Sonic Bloom for the first time have achieved novel results. Nathaniel Shurtleff, Jr. of Fox Island Corporation in South Carver, Massachusetts, a cranberry grower for sixty years, says he has never seen anything like the increase in quantity and quality: 209 barrels per acre instead of the average 125 barrels, an increase of 66 percent, with a sugar content of 8.92—much higher than normal. All of which rewarded him with $80 a barrel, or $6,000 an acre.

Wilson Mills of Circle K Apple Orchard, using Carlson's foliar nutrient for the past eight years, gets larger, healthier trees with increasing yields, higher fruit quality, less insect problems, increased sugar levels, earlier maturity, reduced fertilizer, and an improved shelf life (five months instead of thirty days). Whereas the state average is 290 bushels per acre, he exceeded 400 bushels. Lab reports showed his fruit had a 400 percent increase in copper, 1,700 percent in zine, 300 percent in chromium, and 126 percent in potassium. Increase zinc give pliability to boughs allowing trees to hold more fruit. Lack of these four elements in man's diet leads to male impotence.

At Melody Farms, in Arkansas, where the average crop of tomatoes from a 4 thousand square foot greenhouse was in the range of 9 to 10 thousand pounds, Charles Dodge, its owner, now gets 19 thousand pounds. Once picked, his tomatoes have a shelflife of up to twice as long, many three times normal. Their taste is considered superb, and Dodge reports no problem with tomato disease.

Blueberry bushes grow towards the source of sound and are ready for picking ten days or even two week earlier than usual, and they are exceptionally sweet. Grown with no chemical commerical fertilizer, herbicide, or pesticide, they can be sprayed with blackstrap molasses and hydrogen peroxide to deter the few pests which do occur.

The Lily Hill Company in Lawton, Michigan, has grown fourteen acres of concord grapes which, having withstood several freezes down in the midtwenties, reached an excellent sugar level twelve days earlier than any other grape crop in the area. Vines that usually produce eighty to ninety buds per vine producded between 150–170.

Used on ancient open pollinated seeds collected from Central and South America, Sonic Bloom produced impressive results with a 100 percent increase in peppers and melons. In San Juan Pueblo, a Native American communty not far from Sante Fe, the corn produced 17.5 percent more ears with 16 percent more height. Amaranth weighed two pounds per plant, and quinoa grew nine to eleven feet tall with over two-pound heads. Open pollinated seeds reproduce forever and are considerably more nutritious.

Carlson claims his system substanially increases not only yields but quality, all at a fraction of the cost of chemical fertilizers. He says the common method of crop production, with its overreliance on chemicals, is producing plants that are stressed out. Remove the stress and the plants become more adaptable and pest and disease resistant. Carlson's plants exposed to recorded sound units and foliar spray not only grow bigger and faster but are better able to adapt to adverse soil and water conditions with increased ability to adjust to unstable climate; this makes them excellent for drought-stricken areas. Tests in arid environments show a 50–60 percent reduction in watering needs since larger and deeper roots tap additional reserves of ground water. Fruits, grains, and vegetables, all with heavier sugar content, are not only disease-resistant but the sugar levels adversely affect the digestive tracts of insects, keeping them at bay. Balance growth of fruits and vegetables leads to early maturity—often within fifty days—followed by an extended shelf life, plus a dramatic improvement in taste.

Rose bushes yield up to seventy flowers per bush compared to a normal eight to ten. Chrysanthemums achieve double production while reducing their maturity time from ten to six weeks. The added shelf life for flowers greatly increases their sale value. The faster turnaround time in greenhouses provides for an extra crop per year.

Carlson has had many offers to sell, but he remains in control because of his prime concern for the world's hunger problem. Sonic Boom is now a potent force in Australian agriculture. Using the foliar spray, John Fergusson of Orange, New South Wales, obtained 160 percent increase in plums, 130 percent in nectarines, 100 percent in apples; all were larger, had increased sugar content and a longer shelf life. In Medowie, New South Wales, Nick Falko obtained such gourmet prices for his gourmet-sized peaches and nectarines that on the profits he quit his job as a prison guard to help his wife beat cancer.

In the Philippines, Carlson has helped farmers renew land destroyed by toxic ash spewed from Mount Pinatubo's eruption. In Israel, 450 endangered North African varieties of shrubs, fruit, and nut trees are being successfully treated with Carlson's formula to prevent them from becoming extinct.

Working with the Chinese government in the province of Sinhiang in Inner Mongolia, Carlson demonstrated how to grow plants in one of the worst areas of the world. Dr. Hou Tian Zhe from Xinjiar Academy of Forestry reports a 30–90 percent increase in food crops such as melons and potatoes. In Thailand the product is being marketed by Dr. Don Nielson, and in Malaysia by Tham See Lin of Senagor with the result that the Malaysian hospices for the unwanted elderly now enjoy highly nutritious food from their own produce.

After addressing a bioresearch committee in Japan, consisting of 8 thousand organic farmers, Carlson received a special award from the Minister of Finance.

But the most sensational development has occurred in Mexico where Raul Mendez of Quimcasa in Huixquilucan grows and markets produce all over Central and South America. Raul has developed a fungicide that causes to grow extremely well, obtaining increases of as

much as 200 percent. Combining his fungicide with Sonic Bloom, he now claims to get increases of up to 500 percent: 300 bushels of corn per acre, and 137 bushels of soybeans per acre, whereas in the U.S. on some 50 million acres of soybeans the average harvest is only between forty and forty-five bushels pers acre. Raul's soybeans respond to the spraying by lifting their leaf tips erect.

With this joint venture, Carlson hopes to bring the northern and southern parts of this hemisphere closer together in peace and growth, both materially and spiritually, using Sonic Bloom to replace the culture of noxious drugs.

Preserving Endangered Trees

One of Carlson's more positive ventures with his foliar nutrient is the protection of trees, especially endangered species, which can now be salvaged and perpetuated by use of Sonic Bloom, leading to the prospect of preserving such national treasures as the Black Forest in Flanders and the centennial redwoods in California.

Noting that a row of pine trees closer to the source of his chirping boxes were much more developed than others planted at the same time but out of range of the sound, Carlson decided to devote a major effort to the improvement of the many species of nut trees he raises on his Wisconsin farm—endangered American chestnuts, horse chestnuts, butternuts, beechnuts, heartnuts, hickories, hazels, and filberts—growing them to maturity much faster with his nutrient spray, producing walnuts twice the normal size, and endangered butternuts with thirteen nuts per cluster. A great source of food, if spread around the country, healthy nut trees, larger, and faster growing, could go a long way to feeding the hungry, and they are an ongoing self-perpetuating investment: butternut trees live 125 years, black walnut 175 years, and the American Chestnut—which can grow 250 feet tall and eighteen feet through—can live up to 600 years.

As hardwoods treated with Sonic Bloom grow at the same rate as soft woods, the average yearly girth increase is of one-and-one-quarter inches. Minnesotan chiropractor Bryan Zins, using Sonic Bloom for ten years on his three thousand black walnut tree farm, obtained a yearly increase in size up to 400 percent. A black walnut seedling bought for $15 is worth more when matured to a tree of fourteen inches in diameter, all of $1,500. Eighteen inches across, it can be worth as much as $20,000. Simple multiplication shows that instead of having to wait fifty years for his profit, Dr. Zins' thirty-two acres of black walnut trees should be worth $60 million in fifteen years. Hard to beat as a retirement investment! Plant trees as your children are born and your can send them to Harvard when they are eighteen. And if you plan to return to this planet in some future life, cleaning up and replanting its forests may be one of the most salutary endeavors you can perform.

Poets, musicians, occultists, and now even scientists, realize that the many frequencies to which we are being exposed can dramatically effect our spiritual and physical well-being. Rudolf Steiner, perhaps the most impressive clairvoyant philosopher of the century, whose brilliantly shamanic biodynamic system of agriculture produces increasingly healthy soil, describes the intimate effect that birdsong and even the sound of birdwings has on the development of plants, all part of the magical interconnection between the planet's physical and spiritual beings. And if, as Steiner maintains, inferior food tends to trap human beings in their bodies, delaying their necessary development of clairvoyance, Sonic Bloom may be as spiritually liberating as it is physically invigorating.

What propelled me to write this article was an apple tree, probably not more than thirty years old, viewed from the kitchen window of my eighteenth-century farm in West Virginia. Every fall since I bought the place some twenty years ago I have looked at that tree wondering what the devil could be done about its ugly misshapen inedible fruit the size of golf balls. Last year I sprayed the darn thing three times with Sonic Bloom to the accompaniment of Carlson's chirping soundbox, then sat back. That's all: no fertilizer, no rock dust, no special care. By September, I had a tree totally covered with orange-sized apples, beautifully colored, delicious to eat. Such palpable proof led me to review what has been happening to Sonic Bloom since I reported on its apparent marvels in

Secrets of the Soil almost ten years ago. Now, as a result of what I have learned, I plan to travel to Mexico with Carlson to see with my own eyes if his Sonic Bloom combined with the Raul Mendez' organic fungicide, really can, as claimed, produce a 500 percent improvement in yields, a potential abundance that is staggering, opening the limitless abilities of nature to support all existing life on the planet, healing the wounds inflicted on it by greed and folly in the past.

If true, Carlson may be on his way to solving malnutrition on this planet, a way that can provide healthy abundant produce for every man, woman, and child in God's own Garden of Eden where, so far, we have done little but sin.

Could Jean Dixon, with her clairvoyant vision, have forseen Carlson's small black sonic box?

Magical Garden

Skye Alexander

Since ancient times, the garden has been a symbol of sanctuary in cultures around the world, a haven of peace, harmony, and abundance. The Bible even depicts Paradise as a garden. We go to the garden to escape from the chaos and rigors of modern life, to commune with nature and reconnect with our inner selves. Without oasis such as New York's Central Park and Boston's Emerald Necklace, our steel-and-concrete urban centers would be harsh environments indeed.

Gardening is good for the body, a pleasant way to get exercise and fresh air, but more importantly, it's good for the soul. Cultivating a garden is an act of creativity. As we watch the seeds blossom and bear fruit, we become participants in the timeless magic of fostering life. Gardening is also a lesson in karma, where we reap what we sow. It's an example of give-and-take: we nourish the plants and they in turn nourish us.

A lush and lovely garden endears you to your neighbors, as well as to the birds, insects, faeries, and elementals who, like us, are seeking sanctuary in a world where natural refuges are dwindling.

You needn't live in the country or even have a yard to enjoy a garden of your own. By using containers, hanging planters, climbing vines, and solar fountains, you can transform a rooftop, porch, or fire escape into an idyllic, private retreat.

Feng shui, the ancient Chinese art of placement, recognizes five elements: earth, water, wood, fire, and metal. If you wish to take advantage of the mystical benefits feng shui offers in order to attract health, happiness, and prosperity, you'll want to include symbols of these five elements. You might also choose to lay out your garden according to feng shui principles, using either the compass directions or the bagua as your "blueprint."

Creating Balance and Wholeness in the Garden

One reason why gardens have such a restorative effect on us—and perhaps why they play a central role in spiritual art and literature—is that they bring together the elemental archetypes earth, air, fire, and water, which are astrology's building blocks. When all four elements are present in our environment, we experience a subconscious sense of balance and wholeness. As you design your garden, make sure to include representations of these four elements.

Fire • The Sun is a natural symbol of fiery energy. You can enhance the fire element by hanging faceted crystals to reflect and refract the Sun's light. Burning incense in your garden, perhaps on an altar or shrine, combines the elements fire and air. If you plan to use your garden sanctuary at night, you might consider adding lanterns, strings of electric lights, or votive candles to embody the fire element.

Earth • The earth element is symbolized by the soil in which your plants are nestled. You may also wish to include other representations such as terra cotta planters, special stones, ceramic sculptures, or marble statuary.

Air • Gentle breezes wafting through your garden provide the air element. You can enhance this by adding wind chimes, mobiles, or whirligigs.

Water • If you aren't lucky enough to have a natural stream, pond, or waterfall in your garden, you can incorporate the water element by installing a birdbath or an electric, solar, or battery-powered fountain. Another option is to simply fill a shallow dish with water, then float a flower in it.

Wood • The stems and trunks of plants bring the wood element into your garden. You might also want to include decorative pieces of driftwood or wooden outdoor furniture in your sanctuary.

Metal • Metallic urns or planters, a decorative wrought-iron railing or gate, or metal outdoor furniture are good ways to incorporate this element into your garden plan. A copper weathervane, sundial, wind chime, or lantern will also do the trick.

Magical Plants

Long before the advent of chemistry and modern medicine, herbalists used botanicals to cure illness and save lives, which may be one reason plants were initially linked with magic. Countless generations of wise men and women throughout the world have tapped the secrets of the plant kingdom, using roots, herbs, flowers, bark, and leaves in potions and amulets to promote healing, provide protection, attract love, induce insight or visions, and increase prosperity.

However, magical practitioners will tell you that a plant's physical properties are only part of the story. When working in the magical

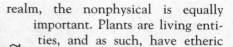

realm, the nonphysical is equally important. Plants are living entities, and as such, have etheric bodies as well as physical ones. They also possess a type of intelligence and an ability to communicate with us and with each other, as polygraph expert Cleve Backster's experiments proved (see *The Secret Life of Plants* by Peter Tompkins and Christopher Byrd).

When planning your garden, pay attention to the mystical powers inherent in plants, and choose those that support your own purposes. Even if you never use them in magical work, their presence in your environment can have an impact on your life. Because plants are complex organisms, most of them have a variety of applications and faculties. The following lists include some common herbs, flowers, shrubs, and trees you may wish to include in your garden, along with their magical uses.

For best results, consult some good books on the subject (such as Paul Beyerl's *Master Book of Herbalism*), as the time of the day and lunar phases may influence a plants' development. It's also a good idea to familiarize yourself with the physical properties of the species you include in your garden some popular and beautiful plants, such as foxglove and wolfbane, are poisonous.

Protection • snapdragon, peony, verbena, valerian, anise, sage, thyme, fennel, garlic, dill, chives, ash, pussy willow, and pine.

Love • primrose, roses, pink or red clover, marjoram, jasmine, periwinkle, lemon balm, basil, marigold, daisy, orchid, anise, and geranium.

Prosperity or success • alfalfa, all mints, lavender, cedar, money plant, vervain, and parsley.

Insight, inspiration, and wisdom • lavender, peppermint, marigold, yarrow, anemone, apple, cornflower, elm, heather, narcissus, violets, watercress, and wisteria.

Astrological Correspondences

Astrologers believe that all things on earth have affinities with certain celestial bodies. Early healers, herbalists, and magical practitioners were familiar with zodiacal and planetary connections to the plant world, and utilized them to facilitate their work. According to Hippocrates, a physician must consider a patient's birthchart before attempting treatment, and Culpeper wrote "first consider what planet causes the ailment," and "you may oppose ailments by herbs of the planet opposite to the planet that causes them."

Some flowers and plants bloom during the month when the Sun is in their corresponding zodiacal sign. Jonquils and daffodils, for example, generally blossom during the spring months Aries and Taurus. In other instances, the plants have certain properties that are similar to the astrological signs with which they are associated. Hemp is known for its hardiness—a quality astrologers connect with Capricorn. Water lilies and lotus flowers grow in water, so they are related to the water signs Cancer and Pisces.

In your garden, you may wish to include plants that harmonize with your own astrological energies. Also consider cultivating those species that contain qualities you'd like to encourage in yourself or to strengthen weak factors in your birthchart. For example, if you're an "idea" person who has a preponderance of air signs in your chart and you want to be able to apply those ideas in practical ways, put in plants that are associated with the earth signs Taurus, Virgo, or Capricorn.

Aries • holly, aloe, dogwood, jonquil, daffodil, hyacinth, honeysuckle, snapdragon, cactus, gentian, sweet pea, chrysanthemum, onion, basil, and garlic.

Taurus • columbine, daisy, larkspur, lily, daffodil, orchid, clover, lilac, sage, thyme, birch, and ivy.

Gemini • azalea, honeysuckle, lily of the valley, cedar, vervain, yarrow, heather, parsley, lavender, ferns, valerian, and endive.

Cancer • iris, jasmine, water lily, white rose, lettuce, willow, watercress.

Leo: red rose, larkspur, poppy, marigold, peony, dahlia, sunflower, chamomile, ash, and rosemary.

Virgo • aster, heather, lavender, myrtle, pink geranium, fern, fennel, azalea, dill, and mulberry.

Libra • cosmos, apple blossom, daisy, gardenia, pink rose, violet, hibiscus, thyme, wild strawberry, and peppermint.

Scorpio • chrysanthemum, orchid, violet, dogwood, eucalyptus, foxglove, periwinkle.

Sagittarius • paperwhite narcissus, Christmas cactus, dandelion, magnolia, red clover, oak, sage, maple, pinks, chestnut.

Capricorn • holly, carnation, mistletoe, pansy, hemp, comfrey, wintergreen, moss, thistle.

Aquarius • carnation, arbutus, wild rose, and lady slipper.

Pisces • violet, heather, passion flower, wisteria, narcissus, and lotus.

The creation of a garden is a deeply personal and ongoing process. As you grow and evolve over time, so will your garden. If you've never planted a garden before, start small. Choose a few favorite plants to begin with, then add more gradually. If you already have a garden, don't hesitate to make changes until your sanctuary suits your needs and preferences. Include objects that have special meaning for you: an inspirational saying on a plaque, a spiritual icon, artwork, or labyrinth. Do whatever pleases you there: meditate, play music, write, draw, dream, relax, reflect, pray, celebrate, perform rituals, work magic, make love. Above all, cultivate your relationship with your garden and the living entities who are a part of it, for the garden is a metaphor for life.

Controlling Your Garden's Climate

Harry MacCormack

Most serious gardeners listen to weather forecasters and hope that their analysis of atmospheric conditions contains some element of accuracy. We need the information to plan planting dates, transplant opportunities, and to nurture and stimulate plants that will feed us. A climate is generally understood as the prevailing or average condition over a period of time in a locality. If you intend to stimulate health-giving, timely, abundant plant production, knowledge of the climate in which you are gardening is of primary importance.

Readers of this *Moon Sign Book* are also probably aware that climate reflects cosmic conditions. Lunar periodicity is very important to calculations involved in decision-making regarding all aspects of growth. For instance, depending upon where you live, an average frost date in late spring or fall will often vary a week or even more depending upon the tendencies of a particular season, and often the peculiar intensities around the Moon's phase. Climate knowledge is necessary if you intend to garden successfully. Ultimately, you cannot rely on reports and charts totally. They are indicators of how conditions have tended to be over the years. You must be as "in tune" with subtle wave energies as your plants are. You must be able to smell the air and know it will rain. You must know that wind of a certain direction has a potentially damaging quality setting up young plants for insect infestation. Of primary importance in growing vegetables, fruits, nuts, grains, herbs, and flowers is the Sun. Without Sun there would be no biological life—at least not the kind of life we know on this planet. Much of what we need to manage in garden climate has to do with solar presence.

Influencing how Sun and earth relate in our garden is various seasonal weather patterns. Earth's atmosphere goes through somewhat predictable cycles. For instance, here in the Pacific Northwest, I need to have mature vegetables ready for market by April 15 when our farmer's markets begin. I need to have tomatoes ready by late May or early June if I want to be competitive with other farmers, and our weather has a direct

impact on my success. Our rains, modulated by ocean temperatures, plummet the soil until at least April. There are patterns of weather: one to two days rain usually separated by periodic sun occurs about twice a week during this crucial growing period. Without weather knowledge and climate management, crops like tomatoes, peppers, basil, cucumbers, squashes—our major market crops—would be impossible to grow. However, if you have this knowledge, you'll have crops that few other growers have. With climate management, we have warm weather crops growing through all kinds of weather. It does cost time and money, but surprisingly little of either once you get a system going.

Soil Temperature

What you are actually managing is soil temperatures. Good organic growing practices always begin with nutrient cycling through good, organically enriched soils. What is important to realize is that living soils rely upon incredible populations of microorganisms to cycle the nutrients we add. And, these creatures—invisible to the naked eye—need optimum soil temperatures to stay in balance and break down rocks, composts, animal by products, etc., into compounds which plants will utilize in order to mature for harvest.

So what you need to create with your management is *microzone* climates, or microzones. Different plants have different microzone needs. Lettuces, for instance, for the April market, can be grown in beds managed with plants. Those same beds would be too hot in midseason for any leafy crop such as spinach, lettuce, collards, etc.

Most land grant universities have someone on staff whose specialty is watching "degree hours of heat and light" for a given region. For instance, while I write this article the weather lab behind me is watching with elation and fear the degree hours needed for maximum sugar set in the wine grape harvest, which is about two to three weeks late this season. It happens that fall weather is remaining hot at the moment, necessary for sugar set in all fruits. But we are now at a time where an early frost could damage melons, squash (winter), peppers—all of which like the grapes are fending for themselves without some control elements.

During a plants early growth periods we need to maintain durable levels of moisture to sustain growth. However, the soil should be neither too wet (a condition which drops soil temperatures and therefore microbial activity) nor too dry (drought also severely limits microbial activity.) The reason so many fruits and vegetables are late this season is that we had prolonged cloudy skies late into mid-July, followed by periodic cloudy skies all summer, and then intense Sun-heat for a few days in September. Through all of this I am in a situation where I've got customers who expect tomatoes, peppers, basil, squashes, melons, etc. "ahead of the curve", or before they are in overabundance. To accomplish that task is a little bit like playing garden god. But, year after year in this increasingly unpredictable climate we pull it off with the following management techniques.

How To Manage Garden Climates

We grow our own seedlings. Much of the seed we grow we have carefully saved over the years from plants we've selected because they grow well in our maritime climate. The first lesson in managing climate in your garden has to do with timing. If I were to plant a tomato seed in the field on December 28 or even January 15, nothing would happen because germination requires soil that is generally around 70 degrees Fahrenheit. That temperature must be maintained for days. This is easily accomplished inside by filling germination trays, usually plastic, with a good quality organic potting soil, then providing bottom heat on the tray during the germination and young seedling phase of growth when the root development is taking place—generally about a month. I have several germination tables set up with heat cables to set the trays on. Before I started using heat cables, I used heat pads. You can even use a heating pad such as are available for medical purposes. The soil needs to be kept moist. I usually water with a can or a squeezable plastic bottle that has had tiny holes drilled in the top for this task. And in the early stages, while the weather is cold, I often use warm water, so as not to cool the soil by adding moisture.

I start tomatoes, peppers, and onions so early because they require a long period of growth before they will produce a crop. In mid-January and into February we start lettuces, spinaches, collards, various squash varieties, and other plants with shorter period growing requirements for early markets. Home gardeners can do the same if you really want to eat from your garden. You need to set up some kind of condition where the soil can be warm for germination. An easy one is to use an old table with a thermostat-controlled electric heater placed underneath, and draped with old blankets to hold the heat in. We have a setup like this, with a plastic cover over hoops on the upper table. We germinate in the lower space, then move the plants upstairs to the table top where they can get the residual bottom heat plus sunlight.

Once the plants are up, you need to control soil temperature and light. In midwinter there isn't enough daylight to get plants growing fast enough to have them ready for transplant when spring arrives. So for tomatoes, onions, peppers, and other plants that are set out very early (January–February) once they have germinated they receive extra light hours. I have "grow lights" set up to give six, then four, then two extra light hours per day as the Sun is moving toward Equinox. For plants set out from germination, but still in germination trays after late February, there are enough light hours from sunlight.

Germination trays are crammed with plants. When they hit their second leaf stage they must be transplanted into pots, unless they were germinated in individual containers or in plugs. This task is done while it is usually still quite cold and cloudy. For fast growth the pots are then set over heat cables. Tomatoes and peppers require more warmth to get a good start. Cool weather crops like lettuce, broccoli, etc. can be transplanted and will generally take off if they are inside a clear plastic hoop house or greenhouse. You don't want them to get too hot before transplant.

From my point of view, if you are a serious gardener and you want to eat from or sell from your garden, various forms of "hoop houses" are necessary. Hoop houses can be built easily from various materials. I will briefly discuss two variations. The first uses hoops made from #12 wire (usually used for fencing). We bought rolls of wire years ago. We've cut it in four-foot lengths for our beds. You can custom cut to any size, and may want to vary the size for taller crops like beans, peppers, or tomatoes. We use these wires to support spun polyester floating row cover. We have also used these wires to support clear plastic, netting, or shade cloth. We generally place these hoops over a raised bed on three to five foot centers after a crop has been transplanted. Spun polyester fiber or floating row cover material can be purchased from nurseries and seed companies, or from agricultural greenhouse companies. It comes in various thickness, usually a very light form used mostly for insect and warm weather protection, a medium which will give some frost protection, and a heavy which is used in cold weather. Light penetrated this white material as does water. Its great advantage is wind protection. Placed over broccoli or kohlrabi transplants in March, beside a control which is not covered, it is amazing how fast the transplants take off. We often set transplants in beds worked the previous fall, that in early Spring are essentially mud. But by market time in late April–May we've got a crop producing. Lettuce, spinach, all kinds of "cool weather" crops thrive in this kind of managed cover condition.

We usually set out early-midseason tomatoes in hoop houses covered only with floating row cover. We do this in mid to late March. They will reach full production in July. We also use floating row covers mid summer on cool weather crops to protect them from too much sun. And as one attempt to keep deer from having a feast in the night. We use the same setup, actually the same covers, later in May when setting out melons, cucumbers and tomatoes for late harvest.

Why got to all the trouble of transplanting rather than direct seeding all of these crops? Again, it's climate management. It is simply too wet and cold to get any growth. Often direct seeding in April, May, or even June results in rotted seed for us. This year, for instance, our most productive winter squashes were transplanted and therefore had many light/heat hours of advantage, and were able to produce on time. Direct seeded squashes produced almost nothing because of inclimate conditions.

A second line of construction for hoop houses is larger and usually covered with six mil clear plastic. There are many ways to build a larger hoop house. Most are done with either twenty-foot lengths of rebar or plastic pipe. I have used both. I have built structures as long as sixty-five feet. I would, however, suggest the efficiency of a hoop house in the thirty to forty-foot range. Usually twenty foot hoops cover a ten-feet wide piece of ground, allowing you to make either a two or three-bed system inside. We generally use these hoop houses for transplants of warm weather crops, tomatoes, peppers, basil, and squashes, although early in the season we use them to sneak through early peas or beans, cucumbers, even carrots. We create trellises for many of the crops we grow in hoop houses to help with rapid growth, to help with slug damage, and to cram more plants into a small space on highly fertile beds. Location of a plastic hoop house in full Sun means that you can easily generate daytime temperatures over 90 degrees Fahrenheit even when it is cloudy and relatively cold outside. Frost protection is excellent, as high daytime temperatures warm the soil sink which can radiate warmth and modulate cold nighttime temperatures. There have been situations in late March, after we've transplanted tomatoes, etc. into these structures where temperatures have dipped outside into the low to mid-twenties and we've had to put floating row cover over plants inside the plastic hoop house to save them.

Plans for the construction of hoop houses are available from many publishing houses. Simply speaking, you need to get the twenty-foot rebar or plastic pipe into a hoop. Rebar hoops are fairly easy to bed. I make a jig in the driveway by pounding short stakes into the ground ten feet apart, measuring up seven feet at the center, placing a double stake there, then placing two sets of stakes on each side to form the arch. Then place the rebar around the stakes to get the first arch bend into the soft steel. To finish the bed, I use a telephone pole or other post. With help from another person, gently jerk some bends that are more severe.

Small hoop houses need center post support. Steel fencing posts work well. A length of rebar between posts, wired to the posts acts as the center support. Rebar or plastic pipe should be set every three feet and wired to the center bar after being pushed into the ground. A side support bar is wired to the sides at about four feet up, or in the case of plastic pipe can be screwed on with bugle screws and a screw gun. An angle support from ground up to the outside arch should be placed at each of four corners. Doors are easily constructed of 1 x 4 wired to the base of the outside arch and angles up to the apex of the arch where they are also wired. Then a 1 x 4 is screwed horizontally across the two angle boards at chest level. A roll-up door cover, 2 x 4 base and 1 x 4 upper is screwed on the horizontal member. To leave open, which you will want to do much of the time simply roll up the plastic sheeting door and use strings to tie it to the horizontal cross member. In high wind we weight the 2 x 4 base of the door with dirt.

To cover, spread 6-mil plastic over the structure and use lath and screws to attach plastic to the angular end piece of each 1 x 4. We load dirt on the base plastic along the ground. We also screw 1 x 4s outside and inside the structure to lock the plastic to the rebar, because of high wind. Plastic pipe can be screwed in a similar manner with the plastic hoop house structures to hold the plastic down in wind.

Hoop houses can be used year round. In cold weather they are warm enough to grow lettuces and other cool weather corps. So, we keep them heavily composted. Compost is used like a mulch. And we keep their soils well fertilized with fish base fertilizers and rocks dusts.

Controlling water in such artificial growing conditions is essential. I highly recommend a drip irrigation system, usually two lines per bed. It is easy to over water and create plant disease. It is also easy to underwater and create artificial drought. In our area, we have to be aware that ground water from outside rain actually keeps beds very moist in the spring.

Who Benefits From Climate Management?

Germination for extended season crops requires intensive climate management. Seedlings grown for transplant allow a grower to grow almost all year round as long as you provide the proper climate for them to thrive. Growing your own seedlings is an advantage for several reasons. Primarily, they allow you to time your growing season, regardless to some extent of normal weather patterns. For organic growers, we use transplants to get by at least on weeding, the major negative factor in organic growing. And growing your own seedlings is the only way to know what you have in terms of open pollinated stock. If you plant by the Moon and use other astrological timing factors, the only way you know the life cycle of the plant is by germinating you own seedlings.

In the field, transplants grow faster and stronger with less insect damage with floating row cover. Under plastic hoop houses, we can have what our customers expect, tomatoes ripe in late May or early June, and throughout June and July until the field tomatoes, which were aided by floating row covers, ripen. The row covers are removed as blossoming occurs.

A final aspect of climate management to consider is the shade factor. We use hoops to build shade houses for lettuce and other cool loving crops in the heat of summer. We also use a companion planting strategy for some crops. For instance, artichokes like it cooler. They grow best in foggy, coastal regions. So, I've got them planted where the shadow of a large tree protects them from morning Sun, and sunflowers give them a bit of shade in the afternoon. We've used corn as a shade crop for bell peppers which also, for whatever reason, maybe moisture, do better with a little afternoon shade. Some herbs do much better in a partial shade partial Sun situation, basil being one, ginseng and goldenseal being others.

A reminder, much of what we do with mulching, watering, and even tillage practices is directly related to managing climate in our gardens. Strawberries get their name from growing better in mulch, which keeps the soil cooler, retaining moisture, which they need in constant supply. One could say that gardening in climate management before it is tillage, fertilization, and finally harvest.

Bibliography:
1. MacCormack, 2000, 2000 MOON SIGN BOOK, Llewellyn, St. Paul, MN.

for the best new book on subtle wave energies:
Tiller, William A., SCIENCE AND HUMAN TRANSFORMA-TION, Subtle Energies, Intentionality, and Consciousness, PAVIOR, ISBN 0-0642637-42

MacCormack, THE TRANSITION DOCUMENT, Toward an Environmentally Sound Agriculture, Oregon Tilth, Salem, OR.

LLEWELLYN'S

Personal
Lunar
Forecasts

Understanding Your Personal Moon Sign

Gloria Star

The ever-changing reflection of our Moon in the night sky has always been a source of fascination. As Earth's constant companion, the Moon has a power all her own. Physically, her cycles have the power to control the continual ebb and flow of Earth's tides. Yet there is something more which has led to our unique and eternal fascination with the Moon. Since the time of the Sumerians, written records have linked the Moon's cycles with changes in nature and alterations in behavior. Recorded musings about the Moon and her influences are scattered over time and throughout the art and literature of human history. But do you realize that you have your very own personal Moon? It is one of the many features of your astrological chart, and it is a significant indicator of your emotional nature and the way you express your needs.

Your horoscope is based upon precise calculations, and an astrologer will chart the positions of the Moon, Sun, and planets based upon the exact date, time, and place of your birth. This detailed picture of your horoscope symbolizes the complex levels of energy which are part of your whole being. You probably know about your Sun sign, which describes the ways you express your ego and channel your drive to be recognized— something easy to see and even easier to show to others. Your Moon tells a more intimate story, describing your subconscious nature. You feel your Moon.

To find the degree and placement of your personal Moon sign, you will need to obtain a copy of your astrological chart based upon your personal birth data. To obtain your chart, you can visit a competent astrologer or order your chart calculations directly from Llewellyn Chart Services by using the "Astrological Services Order Form" in the back of this book. You may also use the handy tables and simple calculation method described on page 62 of this book. These guidelines provide a close approximation of your Moon's sign, but to determine the precise placement of your Moon, you'll need a copy of your astrological chart.

While you may think that you're unfamiliar with the astrological concepts associated with your Moon, you are better acquainted with this energy than you may realize. Whenever you tune into your basic feelings about anything, you're connecting through the energy of your Moon. Your habits and attitudes reflect the qualities of your Moon.

Each planet, the Sun, and the Moon are in specific signs in your astrological chart. An analysis of your Moon provides insights into your inner strengths, but it also shows where you feel most susceptible. This energy shapes your thought patterns and is the repository of your emotions, stimulating your underlying emotional nature. The attributes of your Moon sign represent the filter through which you absorb your impressions about your life experiences. As you learn more about yourself and your needs, you may find that by concentrating on the nature of your needs, as illustrated by your Moon sign, you can establish an environment which provides true comfort, security, and safety. Once you're in the flow of the energy of your Moon, you carry your sense of home into every life situation.

You're using your lunar energy whenever you express nurturing and support toward others and yourself. Whether you're male or female, your Moon indicates the way you "mother" others. Psychologically, your Moon portrays your archetypal feminine and represents your relationship with your mother, with women, and with the feminine part of your own psyche. Your Sun, on the other hand, represents the archetypal male quality and illustrates your connection to men, your father, and the masculine elements of your inner self.

When you probe more deeply into the mystery of your Moon you uncover the cradle of your soul. At this level, your Moon contains all that you have been, and therefore influences all that you can become. Shining forth from deep within your eyes, the light of your Moon reflects the inner, soulful aspects of yourself. Your Moon represents your most dominate emotional tendencies and needs; it is the part of you that has flown to the pinnacle of ecstasy, and remembers the true emptiness of despair. Your capacity for contentment increases when you strive to fulfill the needs defined by your Moon's sign.

This part of the *Moon Sign Book* is designed to help you understand the basic planetary cycles throughout the year 2001 that influences you at an emotional level. Transits to your Moon stimulate change, and you may discover that some of the cycles help you reshape your life, while others stimulate a desire to delve into the mystery of yourself. Astrology can show you the cycles, but you are the one who determines he outcome through your responses. By opening to your own needs and responding to the planetary energies in a way which allows you to fulfill these needs, you can experience a renewed sense of self-confirmation and a deepened feeling of personal security.

Aries Moon

Since childhood you've preferred to take the lead, and your pioneering drive stems from your need to feel free while thoroughly enjoying life's challenges head-on! Your eager Aries Moon can be a mighty force, keeping your warrior spirit alive and invigorating your ability to embrace leadership. You're the one who opens the doors for the underdog, and you can tap into courage ignited by the flame of desire and forge ahead, undaunted by obstacles.

You're at your best when you feel free to exercise your spontaneity, and you love the adventures of life. Consequently, situations which are too predictable can become boring, and you'll lose patience with others who fail to value personal autonomy and mutual independence. Intimate relationships work best for you when you have room to try new things, and if your needs are not being met you prefer to deal with problems directly and immediately. Even in your career you perform at your best when your passion is fully engaged and you're free to develop your distinctive talents.

You choose to take the initiative, and when others are paralyzed by apathy or lack conviction, you start the wheels of progress turning. Your laserlike focus in a crisis can be ready at a moment's notice, and situations ranging from sports or military action to politics, counseling, or medicine can be especially gratifying to you. In your heart of hearts, you have the exuberance of a child, and may opt to maintain your daring (and occasionally impertinent) drive to have what you want, when you want it! Flirting with disaster can keep your spirit alive, but others may feel alienated and insecure if you carry things too far or leave the impression that you're only around when you can have fun. Developing the finesse required to balance your passion for love and life with responsible action may take time and maturity. By the same token, locating the place that feels most like home can seem to be a process of trial and error, but once you're in a place that gives you freedom of expression and plenty of room to exercise your individuality, you'll put your mark on it!

Famous Individuals with Aries Moon

Marlon Brando, Peggy Fleming, Luciano Pavarotti

The Year 2001 at a Glance for Aries Moon

During the early part of this year you may still feel that fulfilling your needs is just beyond your reach, but after April the carrot comes off the stick, and you're feeling more self-assured and emotionally stabilized. You're still making changes, and while some things are happening around you and beyond your control, your ability to express and assert your particular needs may be getting easier. Your intuitive abilities continue to improve, and by listening to the whisper of your inner voice you feel that you're definitely gaining in clarity. The primary downfall of the cycles influencing your Moon can stem from a tendency to become too self-absorbed, or to think only about immediate possibilities, failing to take into account long-range effects.

Jupiter's influence during the first half of 2001 continues the theme which began last July: increasing your optimism and confidence by learning more, and by making connections to others who understand your needs and desires. After July 12, when Jupiter moves into Cancer, you may be tempted to overdo it. Your tendency to forget about limits can lead to trouble before you know it, and although this can be a good period for making improvements at home, your needs for space can be costly. Look inside: You probably want more emotional space, and need the physical environment to complete the illusion that you have plenty of breathing room!

Saturn's cycle moves into the sign of Gemini, and after April you'll feel your enthusiasm returning. If your Moon is from 0 to 15 degrees Aries, you'll even feel the positive support of Saturn stimulating your desire to prioritize. You have plenty of time and energy to do the things that enhance your emotional and personal security. The extremely slow-moving transits of Uranus, Neptune, and Pluto have a specific influence, too. If your Moon is from 5 to 9 degrees Aries, you're experiencing the stimulus of Neptune's cycle, bringing an enhancement of your creativity and deepening your desire to explore your spirituality. Listen to your intuition and trust your visions, since the clarity you're experiencing now can have a direct impact on your future! You're feeling positive, healing cycles if your Moon is from 11 to 15 degrees Aries, since Pluto is transiting in trine to your Moon. This can be the perfect year to renovate or move, and you are in the perfect cycle to alter your habits and attitudes so that you can experience healing at the deepest level. If your Moon is 18 to 25 degrees Aries, you're feeling the impact of Uranus traveling in sextile aspect to your Moon. This cycle stimulates a need to break free, and anything or anyone standing in your way is likely to be history by the end of the year! If your Moon is 25 to 29 degrees Aries, you'll be completing your period of trial and error under Saturn's influence by the end of April. Then, for the remainder of the year, you're breathing easier and looking for fresh adventures to excite your interest.

All Aries Moons can experience profound insights into relationships this year, and you may finally feel ready to give yourself and those you love the freedom you've always craved. It starts with a sense of self-acceptance, and extends to your ability to accept and embrace the diversity of life.

Affirmation for the Year
My heart overflows with joy and abundant love!

January
Your impatience with others who need to justify the practicality of solutions or actions can lead you to wonder if you'll ever feel fully satisfied! Fortunately, the lines of communication open up after the Moon's eclipse on the 9th, and talking over possibilities with a close friend inspires your faith that things will work out, even if some of your plans have fallen apart. Your romantic passions stir during the New Moon on the 24th, although you can fall victim to mixed signals if you're not careful. Instead of acting on assumptions, you'll be much better off if you clarify what someone else really wants before you take action, since regrouping can leave you feeling both frustrated and disappointed. It's a good thing you thrive on challenge!

February
Love opens your heart, and whether you're funneling your energy into a romantic passion, your creative artistry, your family, or even redecorating your living space, others cannot help but notice that you're inspired! Problems arising near the Full Moon on the 8th can result from simple misunderstandings, although you'll resent attempts to manipulate you. After all, you're more comfortable with the direct approach. It's easy to go overboard from the 15th to 24th, when you may be spending money for the wrong reasons. Even though it's a bother, think twice before you agree to overextend your finances—or if you're tempted to take up the slack for someone else who's in a bind.

March

The excitement of this month keeps your heart singing, and your creative drive continues to burn brightly. Even though you may ultimately feel the need to question your emotional attachments, your confidence about forging full-steam ahead into a relationship can set the stage for an unforgettable and passionate encounter or a complete change of course in your love life. You can also feel inspired by to change your life, although there may not be sufficient time to follow through with all the ideas filling your fertile mind. The initiation of Spring on the 20th adds fuel to the fires, and your ability to focus on your priorities seems easier, too. You're relishing your independent spirit, which is a good thing—since others may not be able to keep up with your pace!

April

Opportunity knocks, and you're on the road to adventure—or at least you'd like to be. Eliminating obstacles, including your own resistance, is easier when you tune in to your inner voice. Instead of just thinking about what you want, you're distinguishing wants from needs, and can find it much easier to give voice to those needs from the 6th to 20th. Striking a balance between your personal priorities and the requests of others is important during the Full Moon on the 8th, since you may be accused of selfishness if you fail to acknowledge your obligations to those who are counting on your support. A new chapter begins after the 20th.

May

Reaching out to others to form a network of understanding and support allows you to accomplish things you could not do as effectively on your own. While you may prefer to forge singular pathways, drawing upon your connections can strengthen your sense of emotional stability, and you'll find that your confidence inspires others to trust their own value. You can then do what you do best: ignite hope and meet challenges head-on as you speak your mind about issues that matter most to you. Just because others may not agree, you're not likely to back down. Right now, following what you know to be the higher road, without compromising your principles, can send the message loud and clear that you're not playing around!

June

You may welcome the chance to take a second look at some of the things you've missed over the last couple of months. With Mercury and Mars both in retrograde, you're challenged to be more attentive to your promises, especially promises to yourself. Yes, there are second chances, and this month you can make amends where necessary. Returning calls or getting back in touch with someone can lead to amazing revelations and give you a firmer foothold on the best ways to make your dreams come true. You may even run into unresolved feelings that have been blocking your ability to attain satisfaction. Turn inside during the solar eclipse on the 21st to uncover the reasons for your fears.

July

Maintaining your objectivity can be difficult, since everyone else seems to have priorities that involve you! Before you cave in to pressure, make an attempt to clarify what's going on, since you may have fallen victim to unspoken expectations. This is the time to turn around behaviors which can lead to those ridiculous assumptions, and to establish a more meaningful way to communicate with others about your needs and abilities. Even though you may feel a little awkward around someone who's attempting to take care of you, letting them know what genuinely feels good and what makes you uncomfortable can lead to improvements in the relationship. If not, you're likely to pull away in order to regain a sense of control over your life. August

Breathing easier, you're feeling more alive, and during the Full Moon on the 4th you may decide that it's time to take a different course of action. Power plays are evident, so at least you'll be able to tell where others are standing, although the outcome of changes can be highly uncertain. It's clear that you need to align yourself with situations that give you ample room to exercise your independence while still fulfilling the obligations near and dear to your heart. At home, you may feel the urge to make changes or you may even be thinking about a move. It's the need for space that's driving you, and expensive options can be enticing. First impressions may be right, but do yourself a favor and check out hidden costs before you decide.

September

Realizing that you're not interested in divulging all your secrets, you may feel that you're not being honest with someone you love. However, before you spill the details of your past or share your secret fantasies, consider your motivations. You may be looking for more attention or even be seeking out permission to do something you are not allowing yourself to accomplish. Or, you could just be hoping to share your guilt—but that way everyone could end up feeling hurt. Talking over your concerns with a counselor or close friend helps clarify the situation, and you may discover options you've failed to consider. If you're looking for a way out of a tough circumstance, finding the path of least resistance may be easier if someone else is there to offer an objective point of view.

October

You may respond as though you have a chip on your shoulder, since during the Full Moon in Aries on the 2nd your feelings of emotional vulnerability are elevated and you can overreact before you know it. An unconscious motivation to fill in the gaps of your life that are the result of frustrations with relationship or career can stimulate your tendency to get into situations which are difficult to control, like overspending, or making promises which are impossible to fulfill. You're more aware of the long list of things you want which seem to be out of your reach, and instead of taking careful steps toward fulfilling your desires, your impatience can propel you into ill-conceived action. Staying physically active can help, and you may also benefit from meditation.

November

Instead of just thinking about it, you're eager to put your ideas and hopes into action. Complicated relationship issues emerge and can lead to confusing communication from the 1st to 13th. Although there may be changes around you, your ability to respond in ways that support your deepest needs comes to the rescue. In fact, your courage and desire to keep moving forward has its own reward. Before the end of the month you're seeing results and fulfilling some of your immediate goals. Staying out of the way of manipulative individuals requires a bit of finesse, but fortunately you know how to move quickly, and can remain outside the battle zone by refusing to become involved if it's not your fight!

December

Your playful attitude harmonizes beautifully with this festive season. Reaching out to heal old hurts allows you to move quickly toward more rewarding connections with friends and family, and your sense of family may become much more expansive near the time of the Sun's eclipse on the 14th. Your knack for coming directly to the point works to your advantage, and can be the catalyst which escalates an intimate relationship. At the end of the month you'll appreciate time in your own comfort zone, or might even decide that getting away from the daily grind is just what you need to close out a very productive year. Invite the vision for the year ahead to your dreams during the lunar eclipse on the 20th.

Taurus Moon

Stable and enduring, your Taurus Moon helps you shape a powerful connection with the practicalities of life. There's an earthiness about your needs, and you'll feel happiest when you're standing on solid ground and enjoying the sweetness of the fruits of life. You seek out reliable people and situations, and can be a fortress of strength for those who are part of the circle of your life. Even if some parts of your personality are not conservative, when it comes to important choices you're most comfortable with high-integrity options that promote healthy growth.

The force which sustains you is love, and by opening your heart to the power of love, everything comes alive! Yet rushing into commitment is definitely not your style. Taking time to determine the depths of your feelings is important, since once you've promised yourself to an idea, a person, or a situation, you're likely to remain committed. For this reason, you'll find that adapting to change to be a difficult assignment, especially if changes arise outside your control. Anything that seems to compromise your feelings of security can give rise to fear, which can quickly overtake your confidence. It is during such times that it's crucial to determine whether you're holding your ground through life's storms, or you're stubbornly resisting necessary change. After all, you could probably win the prize for stubborn resistance!

Your heart sings when your life is a reflection of quintessential beauty—whether you're developing your artistic sensibilities, creating a lovely home, or nourishing those who share your existence. However, when it's time to let go, bidding goodbye to something or someone can feel like you're losing part of yourself. Those who are an integral part of your life understand how deeply you care, although they will appreciate being given the latitude to make their own mistakes or to follow a path you might not have chosen for them. Fortunately, your patience reminds you that personal development and evolutionary change require trust, time, and most of all love.

Famous Individuals with Taurus Moon

Carol Burnett, Ronald Reagan, Mike Wallace

The Year at a Glance for Taurus Moon

During the last two years you've been taking a careful look at your needs, and you may have felt that you've been striving to create a more solid security platform. The influence of Saturn transiting in Taurus has also helped you become more realistic about the manner in which you experience and fulfill your needs, and you may have made serious commitments which you hoped to make permanent part of your life. Saturn leaves Taurus in April, and moves into Gemini. With this passage, you may feel a bit lighter. However, you're also discovering that some of the foundations you thought were carefully secured are undergoing change, and some of those changes are happening due to situations you cannot control. If, during the last two years, you've been resistant to change, the influences of this year will illuminate the areas where your deeper needs may have been left behind!

Fortunately, Jupiter's influence in July helps open the way toward filling in some of those gaps, especially if you're willing to put forth the effort and take advantage of arising opportunities.

The most influential cycles are specific to the zodiac degree of your Moon. If your Moon is from 0 to 4 degrees Taurus, this will be an excellent year to assess your personal environment, and a great time to develop more trust in your intuitive abilities, since Uranus is transiting in quintile aspect to your Moon. However, if your Moon is from 5 to 10 degrees Taurus, you may feel extrasensitive emotionally under the influence of Neptune, which is transiting in square aspect to your Moon. You're more susceptible to falling victim to illusions or deception, but, if you make an effort to remain emotionally grounded, you can use this time to become more in touch with your spirituality.

If your Moon is from 11 to 16 degrees Taurus, you're experiencing a year of major adjustments, since Pluto and Saturn are each influencing your Moon. Pluto's transit in quincunx to your Moon can leave you feeling that the fulfillment of your needs is just beyond your grasp, while Saturn's transit in semisextile to your Moon helps take steps you need to heal some of the wounds you may have suffered last year. The link between your physical and emotional well-being is highly apparent under these influences, and finding the best way to integrate healing change into your life may require that you ask someone you trust for help.

If your Moon is from 17 to 25 degrees Taurus, you may feel that your life is not exactly under your control. Your needs are changing, and, symbolized by Uranus transiting in square aspect to your Moon, you may feel that you're riding an emotional roller coaster. If your Moon is from 25 to 29 degrees Taurus, it's important that you establish reasonable emotional priorities, since the foundations you create now will have to sustain a series of changes next year!

All individuals with Taurus Moon are experiencing a period of awakening, and you may feel that, on some level, you're seeing certain things about yourself that were previously hidden or repressed. With your needs exposed to the light of understanding, you can now find effective ways to fulfill them.

Affirmation for the Year

I trust the guidance of my inner self, whispering through
the voice of my intuition.

January

Your feelings of passion intensify. Whether you're directing your energy toward a lover or a creative project, you're not likely to be satisfied unless you feel that you've thrown yourself fully into it. Clarity about a love relationship emerges near the time of the Moon's eclipse on the 9th, but changing circumstances can test your commitment from the 22nd to 31st, leading you to wonder if you're making unrealistic choices or assumptions. It could be that your loved one is encountering changes, too, and you'll both have to determine how to incorporate them into your relationship. Yet, you're also facing the need to move beyond your old patterns, and it's more likely that the true test arises from the fact that compromising on deeper issues will make you feel like you're going backwards.

February

Your preferences and needs seem to be at odds with those who share your life, particularly near the Full Moon on the 8th. This can result from breakaway changes in the life of a child or new opportunities for your partner. The changes challenge your desire to keep a firm grasp on the way things have been. The more you resist your needs to change or stand against the desires of others challenging the old structures, the more frustrating the pressure becomes. Ask yourself what you have invested in keeping things the same, since making reasonable alterations could give you the break you've needed, allowing you to try something different for yourself! Fear is your enemy, but by identifying your fears, you can shrink them to a manageable size.

March

Although you may be fascinated with the prospect of using unusual ideas or making alterations to accommodate unexpected changes, you can still feel on edge emotionally. The little things may be most annoying, if others are making assumptions which obligate you and your time. You can be just as uncooperative as they are unreasonable. Talk about your concerns early in the month, since jwaiting and hoping things will get better could result in nights of restless sleep. You'll appreciate the support and objectivity offered by a counselor or good friend, especially if you're feeling uncomfortable about the best way to address a pressing issue. At home, concentrate on getting rid of clutter, since you're also clearing away old attitudes. One action aids the other.

April

You've never been fond of tossing the old because it's old. In fact, your fascination with the tried and true has always been part of your value system. But you're learning that holding on for the sake of holding on can be frustrating. You may wonder about the values which drive others, but you're not likely to force the issue. Fortunately, the fluctuations calm down near the middle of the month, and after the 20th your patience is rewarded. Establish fresh priorities during the Taurus New Moon on the 23rd, when your practical insights can form the framework of positive and lasting commitments. Make a successful move or significant changes in your personal environment from the 23rd to the 30th.

May

While others may make promises, you listen carefully to their words and look for proof that they mean what they say. "Walking the talk" is not easy, and the inconsistencies are apparent from the 1st through the Full Moon on the 7th, allowing you to determine whether or not you're willing to be part of another's plans. Of course, allowing room for the unexpected is necessary, since disruptions are almost a sure thing. But a clear commitment to the integrity of a relationship or a professional promise can accommodate many of life's surprises. It's time to invite fresh ideas after the 23rd, even if you are unsure of some of them. Just tell yourself that you're "considering" them, since making long-term changes will seem more natural after you've gotten used to the idea.

June

It's a good thing you can remain calm in a crisis, since you may be surrounded by them! For those you love, there's little you would refuse if your help or resources are necessary, and, in some instances, you may also discover that you have some valuable assets which are even more valuable because you have safeguarded them. Although you may be tempted to drop your emotional boundaries, be cautious, and if you sense any deception from the 6th to 16th, check it out. Your intuitive feeling about a person or situation can keep you and your vulnerabilities safe. The solar eclipse on the 21st seems to bring a kind of relief to the insanity you've witnessed, and by the end of the month you're ready to let down your guard, especially in matters of love.

July

Since your heart is open to the total experience of loving, take advantage of the energy building from the 1st through the lunar eclipse on the 5th. This is a time to show your feelings, making special moments and memories with the one you love. If you're still feeling a bit vulnerable, you might prefer a more casual atmosphere. After the 13th your feelings of self-assurance can give you the courage you need to tackle important projects, or to deal with personal issues with greater confidence. Explore your plans for the future during the New Moon on the 20th, when you're ready to make alterations that will give you the opportunity to step onto a different platform, professionally and personally.

August

It's a good thing you're feeling generous, since there are plenty of demands on your time and energy. The most draining experiences can come from trying to keep everyone happy. Since your top priority is more likely to fall under the canopy of "reasonable options," you can keep damage control within moderate levels. Underneath it all, you may feel frustrated with the pace of change, especially if you seem to be falling behind. It's more likely that you'll have to accommodate the practical choices, even though you're becoming more and more fascinated by those options with all the bells and whistles!

September

Setting priorities for your most pressing emotional needs requires you first to separate your needs from the demands of others. While you cannot ignore the necessities, you're on the way toward connecting with others who share your interests or whose fortunes are aligned with yours. For that reason, situations at work may be improving, but daily relationships at home ease, too. The music of love can be dissonant through the 21st, but healthy assertive actions on your part after the 9th can help keep the song playing. Taking time to share special moments can turn the tide during the New Moon on the 17th, but you may not feel particularly satisfied with romance until next month.

October

Despite pressures in other arenas, you're finding great satisfaction in the relationships that fill your soul. The flow of giving and receiving love is strengthened, and expressing your passion seems more natural. The only problem can be having time to indulge in lifes pleasures, since your hunger may outweigh the realm of possibility. But these are the things which spur your creativity and encourage you to take steps to let others know how you feel. Your connection to your common sense values fortifies your convictions, and even in the face of conflicts you are likely to show calm, steady, and reassuring support, inspiring others to trust their ideals. You're feeling pretty sensitive by month's end, as the Moon heads toward its fullness in Taurus late at night on the 31st.

November

Since the month begins with the Taurus Full Moon, you may feel a bit exposed. How you handle your vulnerability depends a great deal upon whether or not you're making realistic choices. Emotional energies run high, and your fantasies can outweigh reality from the 1st to 13th. You may see only what you wish to see. Simply slowing to enjoy the beauty of the moment without turning everything in your life upside down can be difficult. The secret is knowing when to take control and when to step away and allow things to move at their own pace. If you're feeling confused, withdraw into private moments to connect with your inner self. Unexpected elements begin to calm down after the 15th.

December

There are definitely a few topsy turvy moments early in the month. The potential for others to take unanticipated actions near the solar eclipse on the 14th makes you feel pretty unsettled. This is one of the times when you might prefer to allow someone else to take the lead, while you play the supportive role. After the 16th, you'll have a clearer idea of the best ways to exert your influence, and your close relationships prosper as a result of your understanding and compassion. You're eager to celebrate the joys of love in a manner that will sustain your relationships for years to come. Your artistic sensibilities are awakened, too, and it's time to allow your playful side to emerge, as you share your bounty with those who mean the most to you.

Gemini Moon

Driven to learn about the perpetual variety of life, your Gemini Moon is nurtured when you exercise your curiosity and feed your mind. You feel most alive when you're heading out for a journey, starting a class, reading a good book or engaging, in stimulating conversation. These things nourish your soul. You are constantly on the watch for fresh horizons, new ideas, or different ways to approach life. Keeping an open mind is important for you, and forging mental connections with others—including people of all ages and backgrounds—will help you stay young at any age.

To develop a close relationship, you first need to feel that your love of freedom is respected. You'll be drawn to those who share your enthusiasm and curiosity. Situations that inhibit your independence can prompt you to withdraw your affections, and you'll definitely feel a dampening of your interest and passion. Facing a crisis, you can find humor which lifts the spirits of others and helps you maintain an objective viewpoint. However, heavily charged emotional situations can be uncomfortable for you. In your heart of hearts you need to be revered for your intelligence and wisdom, but it can take years before you feel fully appreciated by the world.

You're capable of carrying a sense of home with you as you travel through the kaleidoscopic experiences of life, since your feeling of connection to people and situations is strengthened through your shared interests and ideologies. Sometimes, though, you can distract yourself, or feel emotionally scattered because you're juggling too many things at once. To feel safe, certain, and settled, you must first embrace the personal freedom that stems from an outpouring of the unfettered expressions of your mind, as it links harmoniously to higher principles and the wisdom of the ages.

Famous Individuals with Gemini Moon

Shirley Temple Black, Leonard Nimoy, Nolan Ryan

The Year at a Glance for Gemini Moon

It's your turn to establish a more reliable foundation based upon your highest needs, and you're more likely to make choices which reflect a true understanding of your inner drives. In some ways, the most innovative options will be the ones which provide the greatest satisfaction, although you're also learning the value of integrating what you've gleaned from your past with what you're creating for your future.

The year commences with Jupiter in Gemini, a cycle which began last July and will last through July 12, 2001. Your desire to have it all can be the primary drive during this time, but you can go too far if you're not careful. In some instances, this influence leads to a lazy attitude, since you may feel reasonably content. However, putting your energy into positive growth will set you on a path of tremendous change and true prosperity. By April, Saturn enters its two-year cycle in Gemini, slowing your pace and stimulating your drive to be more responsible for your emotions and needs.

The zodiac degree of your Moon will determine the impact of planetary influences. If your Moon is from 0 to 15 degrees Gemini, this is the year Saturn will conjunct your Moon. Since this cycle only happens every twenty-eight years, you'll definitely feel the impact, and the first influence can be a sense of heaviness and a more serious attitude. You're not one to become excessively intense, but you may be inclined toward more negative thinking than in the past. It's time to make serious commitments to yourself and to others, and those commitments are likely to last. This cycle will be especially influential in your consideration of settling down or creating roots. If your Moon is from 5 to 10 degrees Gemini, you're also feeling the influence of Neptune transiting in trine aspect to your Moon, adding a powerful boost to your intuitive insights and creativity. The greatest challenges arise for those with the Moon from 12 to 16 degrees Gemini. You're feeling powerful transformational changes while Pluto transits in opposition to your Moon. Old emotional supports are dropping away, and you're experiencing a series of endings as you bid goodbye to the things and people you've outgrown.

If your Moon is from 17 to 25 degrees Gemini, you're feeling alive and free while Uranus transits in trine aspect to the Moon. This is an invigorating cycle, and you may decide to move, travel, or take off in an entirely new life direction. Choices will reap their karmic rewards next year, and, since you're more interested in maintaining your freedom than losing it, breaking free of negative attitudes and inhibiting circumstances can lead to powerful and positive change. If your Moon is from 26 to 29 degrees Gemini, the first four months of this year hold the greatest challenge, since you're taking steps which will place you on the best platform for growth during 2002.

All Gemini Moons are likely to feel a stronger connection to their drives and needs, and you're learning the truth of the cosmic law, "What you think, you become." It's your time to explore the true nature of mindfulness.

Affirmation for the Year

I wholeheartedly welcome responsibility for my thoughts, actions, and desires.

January

Emotionally intense situations can cloud your objectivity, particularly if others are overreacting or abandoning what you see as reason or logic. It's like a virulent epidemic, everyone has the same symptoms! Your drive to make sense out of situations takes charge on the heels of the lunar eclipse on the 9th, and for the remainder of the month you may be the one who seems to possess the capacity for solutions. Fresh ideas enliven your energy during the New Moon on the 24th, when your dreams and intuition can prompt you to follow the most rewarding paths. Romance may be on your mind, too, especially if you've found someone whose ideas and intelligence really turn you on!

February

Mercury retrograde cycles, like the one happening from the 4th to 25th, can be troubling, since communication breakdowns are a common occurrence under this influence. By keeping your priorities straight, you can at least maintain strong connections with the people who matter most, and, during the Full Moon on the 8th, may have a chance to delve into the core of recurring relationship problems and arrive at potential resolutions. Watch for a tendency to jump in before you're sufficiently acquainted with the ins and outs from the 21st to 28th. If you get in over your head it can take a lot of doing to catch your breath! The biggest trap rests in the possibility that you're distracting yourself from finishing an obligation which no longer holds your interest.

March

Are you feeling like you're in a rush? A number of things can trigger the sense that you're running out of time, and more than likely it's an illusion created by the scattering of your energy. Instead of putting more on your plate, you might make more meaningful strides by funneling extra time and energy into your most pressing responsibilities. Oh, you can have fun, and can even find a way to squeeze in play time with those who bring the most joy. From the 1st to 16th it's also easier to talk about your needs, even if you're just in a chat room or e-mailing a friend. Initiating a different focus in a relationship or pursuing a new interest fares best after the 25th. Maintain an inviting, nonthreatening attitude, since you can set others on the defensive if you're too bright, too soon!

April

Everything's clipping along quite nicely, and if you're eager to make headway on a project at home or within the context of a close relationship, set aside some extra time the weekend of the Full Moon on the 8th. This period can be especially significant for creative or artistic endeavors, and your involvement in a favorite activity can open doors to greater satisfaction or enthusiastic response from others. You may feel like somebody's putting on the brakes after the 20th, since Saturn moves into Gemini, and you're also seeing evidence of polarization from special interest groups. If you're called on to make a choice, decisiveness is important. Fence-sitting now can be misinterpreted as weakness.

May

Competitive situations can actually spark your interest, particularly if there's a mental challenge. Your ability to focus is strongest from the 1st to 14th, although you may have brilliant ideas throughout the month. Leave plenty of room for spontaneity: If your schedule is too structured you may feel extremely frustrated. You need a chance to respond to the moment, particularly from the 23rd to 31st, when your innovative concepts and occasionally radical ideas can fill your soul with hope and your mind with clear vision. Be careful with your words, though, since speaking before you've had a chance to consider the impact can lead to that terrible condition which requires foot extraction.

June

You may feel that you're walking through a minefield during much of this month. Once you figure out that there are dangers in the emotional territory you're traversing, you can be more attentive to the hot zones. Be particularly alert to any circumstances which place you within a competitive arena, since you can feel especially vulnerable during the Full Moon on the 6th. In fact, you could even feel ambushed if you've been ignoring pleas from others for more attention! Mercury is retrograde in Gemini, giving you a chance to think back about situations from the past which relate to current emotional issues. You could even run into an old "friend," stirring emotions you've long since forgotten. Most likely, your response will be something like a quick hello, and then getting the heck outta there!

July

You're feeling rather self-indulgent, which is fine if you can afford it. The only problem from the 1st through the Moon's eclipse on the 5th is knowing your limits, and, paying attention to them! Venus transits over your Moon this month, softening your heart and stimulating your desire to express your feelings. Since you can be the master of communication, you're likely to arrive at a pretty fabulous way to show how much you care. There is a tendency from the 14th to 20th to abandon one situation in favor of greener pastures, although your obligations may prevent you from making all the changes you desire. Review your options after the 22nd, and try to include the needs of others in your plans.

August

A playful attitude and an open mind can open the way for lots of joy in your life. Making a move or changes in your personal environment can be especially exciting from the 1st to 12th, but after the 17th you're probably better off staying put and concentrating on the demands of your daily schedule. Power plays within the bureaucracy at work or even in the family can be troubling, although you may be able to stay out of the line of fire by paying attention to the subtle signals. Okay, so some of the signals may not be so subtle, and those are the ones you really need to watch! If you are directly involved, you'll probably be one of the people calling the shots. That means taking responsibility for your actions and thoughts is more important than ever.

September

Complex circumstances can be troubling during the Full Moon on the 2nd, but you can sort through the situation and decide the first things to address. Family problems can be convoluted, and if you're not sure where to start, stepping outside the action for a while allows you to gain perspective. Emotional tensions cool as lines of communication are established. After the 8th, you're feeling more confident that things are working out for the best, and your attentions can turn to someone or something stirring your enthusiasm. Passionate and on fire with ideas, you're eager to share your thoughts and dreams if you're met with some-one whose intelligence and wit compliment your own. Stay alert!

October

This time, the Mercury retrograde cycle from the 1st to 22nd can work to your advantage. While some gadgets may break down and structures may change several times, your flexibility and open-minded attitudes allow you to make the most of situations. Even the detours can be an adventure if you keep a positive outlook during the Full Moon on the 2nd. And around the New Moon on the 16th you can experience true serendipity. Argumentativeness can be a problem after the 23rd, although you may wonder in the end what's upsetting everyone. Good humor comes to the rescue, and you may even find material for your next exciting project in the ridiculous workings of life on planet Earth.

November

From the 1st to 7th you're eagerly working on relationships or projects close to your heart, and it's a marvelous time to reach out and invite oth-ers to share your joy. Keeping an alert mind from the 7th to 15th helps you avoid potential traps—like those offers which seem too good to be true. Your vulnerabilities can be easier to spot by those who would take unfair advantage of your honest desire to help, and if you're working from a hidden agenda yourself, then things can get really complicated. Keeping busy with mentally challenging projects can help you stay out of trouble, and even the naysayers who've been critical of your "far-out" ideas may finally get on the bandwagon by the 23rd. It's a good thing you don't harbor a grudge!

December

If you're involved in a mutually supportive relationship, you might enjoy accompanying your partner as he or she leads the way during a fun-filled month. Your agenda reads more like, "I'd really like to have some time off." A small adventure or a captivating idea can stir your creativity, and if you have the time and energy to follow the untrodden path, you may discover possibilities others have overlooked. Be aware of your deeper motivations, since you could unwittingly send mixed signals this month, creating quite a stir if someone thinks you're making promises when all you were doing was waving hello! These things can get out of hand near the time of the Moon's eclipse on the 30th, so it's a good idea to clarify your New Year's Eve plans to make sure you and your date are on the same page.

Cancer Moon

Through your Cancer Moon you embrace the natural rhythms of life and feel a profound connection to the tides of human emotion. You've always had an awareness of your inner being, and you may have clear intuitive sensibilities which allow you to feel the eternal power of the soul. Your ability to allow the essence of tenderness, nurturance, and comfort to flow through you draws others closer, and you may be the first person others seek when they need a haven or support. Not one to stand on the sidelines, you prefer to become intimately involved, and when you make a connection to others, you know how to make them feel like part of your family. Although home and family may be your central life focus, your insightful, protective guidance and care shine through whether you' re raising children, encouraging students or directing a company.

Your physical home maintains a high priority, and it forms the anchor in your own life. You may not feel that you' re truly thriving until you have a nest filled with the things and people you adore. Even in love relationships your need to establish a secure home and strong family will be necessary if you are to feel a true bond with your partner, whether or not your have children of your own. Anyone under your care can rest assured that you take your commitment to heart, and you may also feel that, to some extent, you' re a caretaker of the traditions of the past. You understand the value of the things which tie people together, and may have a passion for history, antiques, genealogy, or collecting. It's letting go that can be painful, particularly when it' s time for your innocents to face the world. Letting go of the past can seem harsh, and sometimes changes which require you to step into the unknown can leave you feeling unsteady. Yet the connection you' ve created will always remain, if you have faith in the purity of your love.

Trusting what you know, that all of life has an ebb and flow, you can become vibrantly confident and feel more positive about the alterations which happen over the course of a lifetime. As you merge with this flow, your eyes will shine with contentment as you absorb the peace arising from your awareness of the timeless truth of life.

Famous Individuals with Cancer Moon

Walter Cronkite, Sydney Omarr, Mary Tyler Moore

The Year at a Glance for Cancer Moon

The stability you've been creating during the past two years will serve you well during 2001, since this year you're ready to expand your options and open your heart to new possibilities. Of course, the world continues its dynamic changes, but while some things can seem unsettling, you may also feel a quality of excitement which kindles your creativity and strengthens your insight.

The cycles during the early part of this year stimulate your need to establish clear priorities as you adapt to new possibilities. You may even find a level of consistency which can be quite helpful as you look toward the future. It is when Jupiter enters Cancer in July that your confidence gains momentum, and then, through the remainder of the year, you may feel that you're on the receiving end of the good things for a change!

Specific cycles which will have more notable influences are those which have a direct connection to the degree of your Moon. If your Moon is from 0 to 4 degrees Cancer, you may feel more emotionally centered and peaceful this year while Neptune transits in biquintile aspect to your Moon. Focusing energy on enhancing the comfort and beauty of your personal surroundings, and enjoying the special bonds you have with those who share your home, can be especially rewarding. If your Moon is from 5 to 10 degrees Cancer, you are experiencing a more uncomfortable cycle while Neptune transits in quincunx aspect to your Moon, and Uranus transits in sesquiquadrate to your Moon. These influences prompt you to turn inside and explore the subconscious responses you have to the world around you. You can become more sensitive and intuitive now, but you may fight it. By becoming more connected to your inner self, you can gradually alter many unconscious fears and reactions standing in the way of your happiness.

If your Moon is from 10 to 16 degrees Cancer, you're feeling the stimulus of Pluto transiting in quincunx to your Moon while Saturn travels in semisextile to your Moon. These two cycles together signify a period of deep emotional change, and can be accompanied by a move, change in family structure, or a period of profound psychological insights into your needs. If your Moon is from 17 to 25 degrees Cancer, you may feel especially unsettled and insecure, and have to deal with a series of unpredictable changes while Uranus transits in quincunx to your Moon. Be careful of a tendency to jump into situations before you have all the facts. If your Moon is from 26 to 29 degrees Cancer, you're creating a more stable emotional platform and may be getting settled into a home that feels just right, while Saturn completes its transit in sextile to your Moon from January through April. From July onward, you're feeling the pressure of increasing responsibility, but you are capable of handling it with style!

All Cancer Moons need to become aware of the differences between needs and wants, since the awakenings during the lunar eclipses in January, July, and December emphasize the importance of embracing your deepest and highest needs.

Affirmation for the Year
My words and action support the growth of my soul.

January
Your enhanced intuitive sensibilities seem to be working overtime in the realm of romance, although your desire and ability to express yourself in all areas of your life is also empowered. Reflect on your top personal priorities during the lunar eclipse in Cancer on the 9th, and then look around to determine where you should make changes to fully manifest your needs. you're not likely to be distracted from your primary drives, although out of the corner of your eye you may realize that people seem to be embroiled in what appear to be superficial issues. Since you're targeting the substance, you may wonder what all the fuss is about, but stay alert to avoid being blindsided by unanticipated changes from others after the 22nd.

February
Despite a difference of opinion or in the style of expression with a friend or loved one, you may be holding fast to your ideas. Leave room for the possibility that these differences could lead somewhere, and do yourself a favor by keeping an open mind without compromising on what's truly important to you. After the 18th, the emotional climate changes, and you reap rewards for your care and hard work. However, there may be others tangled in disputes who are calling out for you to take sides. Before you move one way or another, ask yourself about potential long-term implications, since your decisions ultimately influence your reputation. While you may not reach a peaceful resolution immediately, you might serve yourself and your needs better by bowing out before the shooting starts!

March
Making room for the variations between your own and another's priorities can save you a lot of grief, since there' s ample evidence that some people are clueless about the impact of their actions and decisions.

While you like to protect your loved ones, you may have to let them find out for themselves that some of the things they want are not good for them. Fortunately, your past experiences offer a bit of comfort near the Full Moon on the 9th, and after the 18th you may even have a chance to talk about your concerns with those who are out stirring up trouble for themselves. Meanwhile, forget about finding that chicken soup for the soul on your grocery shelves. Dinner and conversation with your friend does the trick quite nicely, thank you very much!

April

If you can feel yourself pulling up your shields, it could be because you've tried too hard to assure that everybody else is okay, and now you're realizing you've left yourself open! While you can still get your point across from the 1st to 6th, you may feel like the resident alien for a while. After the 19th you'll see evidence that even the most rebellious fledglings are winging by the nest for comfort, but this time, you're likely to be more cautious. Wisdom is, after all, gleaned from experience! Try the practical approach during the New Moon on the 23rd, when something as simple as the bottom line cost can make a real impact, especially if you're not covering the difference! (Even though, inside yourself, you're crumbling at the thought.)

May

Although you may not fully appreciate the motivations which are distracting some of the people around you, you're feeling much more tolerant now that you're turning your attention to the things that will help you bring your life more in tune with the times. You may experience a spiritual and emotional rebirth during the Full Moon on the 7th, when paying attention to your motivations helps you accept that you must, first, answer to your true needs. Surrounding yourself with forward-thinking individuals, reading literature which challenges your mind and spirit, and taking a fresh approach to daily tasks makes a huge difference. It's like transplanting when the flower has outgrown its container—you need room for your roots to spread, and to encourage you to fully blossom!

June

By observing the effects that the people and situations of your life have on your emotions you may reach enlightening conclusions. You've always been sensitive to circumstances where highly charged emotions are at play, but now you can take one step back and get out of the line of fire, placing yourself in the position of observer. If it's not your battle, stay out of it! You're likely to find that you're gravitating more toward those who are interested in viable solutions, and putting your energy and efforts into two-way relationships can be a breath of fresh air. With the solar eclipse (and Moon) in Cancer on the 21st, you are feeling much more at home with your decisions, even though you can still hear the battle in the distance.

July

Early in the month, through the time of the lunar eclipse on the 5th, you're seeing evidence of the things which are dissolving away and may wonder if your security is in jeopardy. This could be a test of your faith, since the rewards suggested by Jupiter moving into Cancer on the 12th can be plentiful, indeed. Letting go of what you no longer need is important if you are to fill your soul and life with the treasures that lift you up and allow you to enjoy a true sense of personal fulfillment. Taking the time to listen to the urging of your soul, you may discover that you already have a lot to celebrate, and from there, you're on your way to an experience of true abundance. By the time the Cancer New Moon rolls around on the 20th, you're ready to put plans in motion that will help you make your dreams come true.

August

Some people do spring-cleaning, but you may feel like getting rid of clutter and cobwebs around the house and in your heart now! You need the best way to show off the gifts you're attracting into your life, and putting them on a dusty shelf is not exactly doing them justice. Most of all, you feel like inviting others to share in your good fortune. Relationships can flourish under these aspects, since you're dropping some of your shields in favor of riding in style down the freeway of love. Showering someone with affection does your heart good, too, whether it's a child, coworker, or the love of your life. Just as important, if you're developing a real trust with someone, let him or her know what you want and need. They'll love you for it!

September

The fruits of your labor taste sweet during the Full Moon on the 2nd; but there's more to come. Although Mars moves into Capricorn opposing your Moon sign, there's no need to panic. You may feel pretty impatient, though—especially if you seem to be doing all the giving. Remember that part about asking for your needs? Now you may have to ask again, but more directly. The trick is to avoid becoming too demanding, since that can backfire. If you're still chasing after a romance, the game heats up, and your passions can run red-hot. Making room for the joy without getting caught in the small stuff allows you to create something memorable. If you're moving or starting something new, the time from the 17th to 29th promises better success.

October

One of the features of Mercury retrograde (from the 1st to the 22nd) is the potential to repeat something. If you need to stress the point about an important issue, you can make excellent headway from the 1st to 14th. Watch your tendency to overdo it, paying special attention if others seem to be stepping back or avoiding you! Test the waters during the Full Moon on the 2nd, since you can gauge your feelings and another's reactions very easily. You can be pulled into a tense dispute after the 21st, and it could be the result of an unresolved situation or a misunderstanding. Before you determine the outcome, make an effort to find out the details. The matter could be less difficult than you thought, but you'll never know if you don't check it out!

November

There's plenty to stir your imagination, and your fervor for a special someone can be purely wonderful during the Full Moon on the 1st. But be careful about the way you're interpreting subtle signals from the 4th to 12th, since you could be reading something into them that' s not there! Although you prefer a little intrigue when it comes to love, you just hate it when you're confused, and expectation can be a trap. If you can't get a clear picture, then take a deep breath and try the direct approach. The same's true of your own communication: if you want to be coy, just be sure you have a pretty good idea how the other person is likely to interpret your signals, since everything can turn on a dime from the 13th to 15th. You'll feel more at ease from the 18th to 29th.

December

Holiday traditions always spark your enthusiasm, although you may be distracted by a few changes in plans from the 1st to 9th. Fortunately, you'll be back on track after the 10th, and doing things which allow you to give of yourself and harness your nurturing creativity gives you a burst of energy. If your feelings are hurt near the Sun's eclipse on the 14th, it's more likely to be because of somebody' s lack of consideration or forgetfulness, so before you take it personally, decide if it's really worth your effort. After the 16th your mind is on more important things, and turning your attention to your hope for the future seems highly appropriate during the lunar eclipse in Cancer on the 30th. Remember: You can't get what you want if you don't know what it is! Let your dreams thrive!

Leo Moon

There's a powerful light shining from within your soul which radiates from your heart. This is the essence of your Leo Moon—the part of you that yields an ability to bring drama, passion, and fiery intensity into the world. You don't do anything halfway. In fact, when more is at stake, you're likely to do your very best, since the thought of letting down those who count on you is unacceptable. Others rely on you for inspiration, and your enthusiasm and faith in them can lift their spirits when they need it most. You need to feel the admiration and respect from those you hold in high regard, since this is what feeds your soul and gives you the courage to step into the spotlight when your moment arrives.

You invest a lot of yourself in your home and your personal relationships, and those who share the circle of your life are nourished by your warm hugs and generosity. Your home may be a showplace—the perfect setting to nourish the talents of your family and friends. Promises are serious business for you, and anyone who violates a promise or shows disloyalty can hurt you deeply. While you can be generous, you can be equally selfish, and, if you're feeling insecure, you can be too self-absorbed to realize that you're alienating those you most want to impress. Falling into a rut of stubborn willfulness can also undermine your security, since others are less likely to show generosity to you if you seem immovable. Through developing a more flexible and open-minded attitude you'll become better able to cope with life's inevitable ups and downs, and can be much more confident in using your will to make healthy decisions. Feeling that you are in control of your life is very important; even when changes arise from the outside, you do have choices about how you respond. However, your first reaction to unwelcome change is likely to be dramatic resistance, hence your reputation for the sensational!

Immersing yourself in creative endeavors invigorates your soul. While your artistry is your way of giving love to the world, it also helps to assure that your bond with a higher power is strengthened. As the ultimate performer in the drama of life, you are truly never far from the hearts of those who adore you, even when you cannot hear the applause.

Famous Individuals with Leo Moon

Jane Fonda, Paul McCartney, Gloria Steinem

The Year Ahead for Leo Moon

Although you may have felt a little frustrated by Saturn's inhibiting influence during the last two years, you've probably established a new set of priorities and have been closing away your involvement with the people and situations you' ve outgrown. This year, you're breaking free more easily, and it' s time to make empowering and confidence-building changes in your daily routine and habits.

Jupiter's influence is one of abundance and expansion, and from January through July you're feeling a strong stimulus to reach out and explore fresh options and situations. These give you room to grow during Jupiter's supportive cycle. Then, from July through December, become aware of your motivations, since there are ample opportunities to get ahead, but some can be more costly than you first realize.

The strongest influence of the longer lasting cycles is determined by the time these planets make an exact aspect to your Moon, and that' s dependent upon the degree of your Moon. If your Moon is from 0 to 4 degrees Leo, you're experiencing a positive period of emotional stability and confidence in your ability to make changes which will enhance your life during the first half of 2001; after that, the longer-lasting planetary cycles are not strongly influencing your Moon. However, if your Moon is from 5 to 10 degrees Leo, you're feeling the energy of Neptune transiting in opposition to your Moon. This is a spiritualizing influence, and it motivates you to let go, surrendering your need to be in control of everything. However, you can also become unrealistic about your needs, and may make choices which place you at the mercy of others who would take unfair advantage of you. From April through August of this year, you'll gain the benefit of Saturn transiting in sextile to your Moon, and during this time you can make moves and changes with the confidence that you're building realistic foundations for your dreams.

If your Moon is from 11 to 16 degrees Leo, you're feeling empowered while Pluto transits in trine aspect to your Moon and Saturn travels in sextile aspect to your Moon. This is your year to make major alterations in your daily routine, place of residence, work, and personal relationships with the confidence that you're opening horizons which allow you to feel self-assured and trusting of your own and others' promises. You may feel ready to break away from the past if your Moon is from 17 to 25 degrees Leo, since Uranus is transiting in opposition to your Moon. This once-in-a-lifetime cycle is invigorating and inspires you to release old inhibitions in favor of a need to allow your true feelings and creativity to emerge. Other people may be surprised if you seem to be changing too quickly, though! If your Moon is from 26 to 29 degrees Leo, you need to cool your jets for the first four months of 2001 while Saturn completes its cycle in square aspect to your Sun. Taking steps to complete your obligations during this time will lead to a strong and secure foundation for making future changes.

Affirmation for the Year

My goals reflect my true connection to the
wisdom of my Higher Self.

January

If you're feeling that everyone else is making things too complicated near the time of the Moon's eclipse on the 9th, you could be right. But you could also be skirting the issue when it comes to questions about the real give and take in a relationship. Before you shut out the noise, try to assure that you're hearing the important messages, and make an attempt to reach out and connect when it really counts. Making time for play or getting away from the tensions of daily life can invigorate your love life, and you may even feel like a playful flirtation during the New Moon on the 24th. In pursuit of a person or a dream, you could be in for a delightful ride, but be sure to secure your seat belt, since there are definite ups and downs!

February

Tangled and emotionally intense situations can lead to accusations or hostility during the Full Moon on the 8th, although you're probably familiar with the players and the game by now. What you have to ask yourself is whether you still want to play, since you may be very clearly aware of the circumstances that nourish your needs and those that are simply frustrating. Although rash action is not exactly your style, you may feel that it's time to at least bring your concerns into the open. Fortunately, your good intentions will shine through, and even if you are not quite sure which is the best direction to pursue, it's a good time to let go of destructive attitudes and begin the healing process. Keep your expectations in line with reality.

March

While you're eliminating a few old habits standing in the way of your contentment, you're also challenged to find new ways to satisfy some of your needs. Confronted by unforeseen circumstances or unusual people, you may wonder if you've awakened in a parallel dimension, but when the fog clears you're seeing all sorts of fresh possibilities. With the advent of spring you're also ready to initiate a relationship or pursue different directions professionally. However, it's a good idea to first complete unfinished business, since your path becomes more clearly defined next month, and opportunities to make changes without dragging old baggage along are waiting in the wings. Concentrate on making simple changes in your daily routine during the New Moon on the 25th, allowing more time for pleasure.

April

Your creative and inspirational leanings are on fire, and you're making headway toward satisfying some long-held dreams. In personal relationships, it's much easier to make your intentions and feelings known from the 1st to 20th, and you may be feeling particularly amorous during the Full Moon on the 8th. You may be questioning your ties in a love relationship, or even your own feelings, but if you're feeling a return of affection, it's more likely that your old anxieties are just getting in the way. Although Saturn is leaving its tense influence toward your Moon on the 20th, you may still be feeling emotionally exhausted after dealing with resolutions of long-standing problems. However, you can feel the weight lifting, and hope illuminates your path.

May

It's more than just springtime: You're filled with a sense of renewal—emotionally and spiritually—and can find plenty of ways to refresh even the most mundane elements of your life. While you may need to turn your attentions toward someone else during the Full Moon on the 7th, you are not likely to lose anything in the process. In fact, by enlarging your inner circle of friends and family, you may find your heart filling with joy. By staying in contact with those whose ideas and energy can be instrumental in helping your fulfill your fondest hopes, you have plenty of chances to exchange favors which can be helpful to all concerned. At home, this is the time to move, renovate, or improve your personal environment, with special success after the 23rd.

June

Eager to make the most of the momentum you're feeling, you may be tempted to get too many things going at once. This is actually a time to pull back and enjoy the ride itself, and if you're trying too hard to maintain a sense of control or giving in to old fears and shutting out joy, you'll know you're missing something. Although you love entertaining, it can be wondrous to be entertained, and now you have a chance to revel in the experience of cheering the talents of others. Meanwhile, showering attention and affection upon those you love has its own rewards. When the dust settles and you turn to see what's ahead, the most notable change is the stronger understanding you feel with those who share your passions. Looking back is the last thing on your mind!

July

The fur may be flying in the dance of love, particularly if somebody's feeling overlooked or jealous from the 1st through the lunar eclipse on the 5th. Of course, pouting is also an option, although either way, feelings can be unnecessarily hurt if anybody's playing a teasing game with no intention of serious follow-through. You're in the mood to have fun after the 6th, so if you're feeling a bit vulnerable earlier, consider taking time for reflection before you arrive on the scene in full regalia. You might find it worthwhile to concentrate on familiar situations until the 23rd, since it's difficult to get in the groove, due to a series of disappointments from those who are unsure of themselves. Of course, that would NOT be you!

August

You've been wondering when it will be safe to get rid of that junk in the closet or your attic, and this is the time to remove clutter. You need more room to breathe. The same's true of relationships: You're eager to find a way for your fantasies to take flight with the one you love. You're likely to single out family members and friends who appreciate your special blend of humor and drama during the Full Moon on the 4th, since sticking around to hear people complain will not be your idea of a good time. Certainly you take your commitments seriously, but by the time the Leo New Moon rolls around on the 19th you're also thinking about whether or not they truly fit your needs. If not, you're likely to break away and try something out of the ordinary, even if only for a little while.

September

Venus kisses your Moon, and your most loving expressions of care and passion are in the forefront through the 20th. Fortunately, it's easy to repair a rift with another now, although situations during the Full Moon on the 2nd are better left alone until a damage assessment is available. Situations at home are ripe for improvements throughout most of the month, but keep your eye on the budget since you're likely to be drawn to fanciful and expensive options that could exceed your credit limit. You may also be drawn to some fascinating people, and through your connection can step into a highly innovative endeavor or be positively influenced by their insights. On the other side of it, your special talents are sparkling!

October

During Mercury's retrograde from the 1st to 22nd you have a chance to delve into a project or situation and retrieve the most viable elements. There are plenty of distractions to throw you off track, but your intuitive sensibilities can be a helpful compass. It's important to take the time to express your sentiments and show your support to those you love now, since outside demands begin to pull you away next month. There are some lovely moments to cultivate during the Full Moon on the 2nd, and periods of easy tenderness during and after the New Moon on the 16th. Be on the alert for your own increasing emotional sensitivity after the 25th, and a tendency to jump to the wrong conclusions if your feelings are hurt by someone dear to you.

November

Emotional turmoil during the Full Moon on the 1st can leave you feeling vulnerable, although your objectivity quickly returns if you talk about your concerns with someone you trust. Your nerves may be easily frayed, and if you're anxious about a situation, worry can be your constant companion. Periods of vague communication from the 7th to 16th are accompanied by mixed signals, leaving you to doubt your own judgment of a person or situation. Taking the time to sort through the details can lead to a more reasonable conclusion, since the circumstances change again after the New Moon on the 15th. Your comfort zone at home may be anything but, and that's what has you feeling on edge. Aim for a long weekend away at the end of the month.

December

The insanity almost calms after the 8th, although there are still plenty of irritating people and situations to distract you from your enjoyment of seasonal festivities if you allow it. Turning your attention to your personal preferences is easier now, particularly if you have a chance to share time with your favorite people from the 2nd to 27th. If you're in a party mood, organize a gathering near the solar eclipse on the 14th, when there are likely to be some pretty fascinating fireworks! Your warm generosity will be welcomed this month, especially by those shy types cowering in the corner, when a small gesture can go a long way toward turning a downcast face into a smile. By the time of the lunar eclipse on the 30th, you're ready to withdraw from the action, at least for a little while. Even your sunny disposition needs the comfort of the night!

Virgo Moon

Your Virgo Moon provides an amazing awareness of detail, giving you a highly perceptive view of life and strengthening your powers of discrimination. The pure and perfect capture your attention, although you may find that most of life's experiences fall short of the ideal. Your preferences are well defined, and your mental filters give you the ability to distinguish infinitesimal variations when you're evaluating anything or anyone. Your practical, conservative attitudes are more readily discernible, so others may not realize the extent of your emotional sensitivity.

As the master of analytical thinking, you may find that you're constantly taking things apart in your mind, considering how something might be improved, or wondering what makes somebody tick. You like it when things fit into sensible categories, and while that works rather nicely when you're completing your tax return, it can play havoc with your emotions, since they're not always sensible or easy to categorize. You can be a first-class worrier, too, but there are few prizes for this attribute. To counterbalance the resulting scattered feelings of emotionally charged situations, natural surroundings or a pristine environment can calm frazzled nerves and help improve your perspective. Exercises like tai chi, yoga, dance, or other such activities help immensely, too, especially if you're caught up in fretting over the inconsequential.

You need a partner who appreciates your perceptive abilities and will understand your grumbling when things don't work out as planned. Since you're seeking excellence, you can be overly critical of yourself and others. If critiques get out of control, you can alienate the affections of those you adore. Believing in yourself can be a challenge, and when you're most insecure you can deny your true needs. For that reason, finding the inner peace you crave and embracing the transcendent qualities of love with another can be difficult, unless you focus your attention on eliminating a few points on the long list of requirements masquerading as expectations. Remind yourself that although you may think you need perfection, in truth you may simply desire unqualified acceptance. It starts by looking in the mirror and allowing the light from your soul to reflect through your eyes. Therein shines perfection!

Famous Individuals with Virgo Moon
Art Bell, Steven Hawking, Michelle Pfeiffer

The Year at a Glance for Virgo Moon

The foundations you've been working to establish during the past two years are tested during 2001 to determine whether you've included room to accommodate the ever-changing influences of the world around you. Other people in your life may be changing their roles, too, and the manner in which you respond to those changes will determine whether or not you're feeling good about yourself and your choices. Fortunately, most of these changes can lead to greater contentment and increased levels of creative productivity, and your ability to make space for them is likely to increase, too.

Jupiter's influence of rapid expansion continues to test your awareness of personal limitations, although you may be more confident about the manner in which you answer opportunities during the second half of the year, when the implications may be easier to discern. Saturn moves into Gemini in late April, helping you become more aware of the costs of your choices, and the responsibilities entailed in fulfilling your true needs. These cycles suggest endings and new beginnings happening together, which is always more welcome than just endings alone!

When the slower-moving planets make a long-lasting connection to your Moon you feel the most intense changes and developing awareness. This is determined by the degree of your Moon. If your Moon is from 0 to 4 degrees Virgo, you'll feel the greatest emotional tension from January through May, while Saturn is transiting in square aspect to your Moon. This is the time to shoulder responsibility for your emotional needs and to eliminate habits which stand in the way of growth. If your Moon is from 5 to 9 degrees Virgo, Neptune's transit in quincunx to the Moon will last all year, marking a time of deepening emotional sensitivity, keeping your boundaries can be almost impossible. It's important that you spend time each day connecting to your inner and higher self as a means of maintaining your emotional perspective, so that you do not feel too confused by the influences surrounding you.

If your Moon is 10 to 16 degrees Virgo, you're feeling the powerful impact of Saturn and Pluto both transiting in square aspect to your Moon. This can be a difficult year emotionally, since many of the structures in your life which have symbolized security are falling away or changing—some without your consent! Knowing when to let go and when to fortify requires that you develop a powerful connection to your inner being, although you may welcome the challenge of fine-tuning this connection. If your Moon is from 18 to 25 degrees Virgo, you can feel unsettled emotionally throughout most of the year as Uranus transits in quincunx to your Moon. If your Moon is from 25 to 29 degrees Virgo, you're solidifying your emotional and security base while Saturn transits in trine aspect to your Moon from January through early May.

All individuals with Virgo Moon can feel emotionally vulnerable during 2001, but that same openness helps you grow closer to your spiritual Source. Loving yourself is extremely important now. Just remember that you do deserve the love you need!

Affirmation for the Year

I can move gracefully through change and welcome a more refined expression of my true and highest needs.

January

Your high hopes are supported by situations that provide a strong platform from which to launch them. Emotionally, you're feeling more courageous, and your insightful perspectives help to assure that at least a few of your fantasies survive. During the lunar eclipse on the 9th you're likely to be in a position that allows you to reach out with support without compromising your own stability. Exploring love can be positively invigorating, although you may have to make room for the differences in the way you and your sweetheart show affection. Adding artistic details and making improvements to your personal environment increases your connection to your nest from the 8th to 20th. Since the daily grind can be taxing, you'll appreciate that comfort even more.

February

Unanticipated changes from others can shatter your emotional serenity, and if you're on edge everyone is likely to hear about it. If you're feeling testy during the Full Moon on the 8th, you'll do yourself a favor by first exploring what you're feeling before you try to fix it. You may just need some time to yourself to sort through your priorities or focus on an important project. Running headlong into the limitations of reality generates the most tension by month's end. Although you may be able to see the potential in someone, he or she may not rise to the occasion, and you can feel personally responsible. Stepping back allows you to see the boundary lines more clearly. Maybe it's not your fault after all!

March

You're not really being singled out, but during the Virgo Full Moon on the 9th you may feel that the weight of the world rests on your shoulders.

To eliminate some of that accumulated tension, first give your body a break. Gradually increasing your physical activity level not only feels great, but is the perfect way to vent bottled up anxieties or unresolved anger. It's repressed anger that can get you into trouble. Even justifiable indignation may leave you feeling vulnerable and exhausted unless you can find a healthy way to express it. Maybe this would be a good time to start self-defense classes, or to pound out your frustrations on a remodeling or building project. In the meantime, watch yourself to see what really provokes you, since there may be more at work than you realize.

April

Although it's a good idea to end situations which that closure, rushing into the process can leave you feeling undone. Trying to make sense out of another person's actions or reactions can be puzzling and emotionally draining, and you'll do yourself a favor by walking away from circumstances where you don't belong, instead of trying to chisel a little niche for yourself. By letting go of the things you do not need, you're actually opening the way toward creating more satisfaction. There are ample opportunities to focus your energy and attention on the people and things needing and appreciating your attention, and by the New Moon on the 23rd you're making recognizable progress with your efforts.

May

You could blame Mars and Saturn for your anxieties, but the most productive attitude would be to understand that you're running headlong into your own self-criticism. Certainly you, of all people, know that everything has room for improvement. Explore options that give you room to breathe. You're seeing the results of the promises you've made, and the weight of your commitments can leave you feeling emotionally drained unless you get everything into perspective. A retreat during the Full Moon cycle on the 6th–7th can bring renewal and help you let go of some of your old emotional baggage. Watch out for distractions after the 22nd, since you could be tempted to pick up more than you just dropped!

June

If you're feeling emotionally fragmented, it could be that you're juggling too many obligations at once. Now, the rationalization, "It just couldn't be helped," might actually be true, but you can still wonder when you'll get some relief. Chipping away at your commitments one at a time does work, and while you may be at your wits' end during the Full Moon on the 6th, you can also see the light at the end of the (long) tunnel. Simple things like settling into your favorite chair with a good book for an hour or so, sharing afternoon tea with a friend, or arranging fresh cut flowers to brighten your desk at work can have an amazing effect on your psyche. After the solar eclipse on the 21st, you're aiming at personally fulfilling choices, and that's been the point of all this anxiety in the first place.

July

Power struggles continue around you, but you're less likely to get involved. You're looking for the good things life offers, and during the lunar eclipse on the 5th you're finding ample evidence that your needs can be fulfilled. Sorting through a change of heart or ending your connection to circumstances that fail to provide emotional support can be unsettling, but you're ready to move ahead. Watch your emotional filters, though, midmonth you may fall into the rut of feeling that you're being overly criticized, and react with too much whining or grumbling. The New Moon cycle on the 20th marks an excellent time to make alterations at home or start new routines, since you're thinking beyond mere obligation as you seek contentment.

August

You're clearing out clutter from your soul and you'll see the evidence when it's garbage day at home. Anything that's gathering dust is likely to be in your way, and if your relationship feels stale, you may be losing patience with the same old routines and responses. It's easy to go overboard and toss things you might later want, but with your powers of discrimination you can tell pretty quickly if anything passes inspection. Driving your list of wants and needs are categories such as the need to immerse yourself in creatively stimulating experiences. Another thing that's changing is your realization that you can ask for and receive help when you need it, and, after the 23rd, you may even discover that someone is volunteering assistance. Now, that's a gift!

September

Your emotional house-cleaning escalates through the Full Moon on the 2nd, and after a short rest period you're ready to focus your energy and attentions on highly productive endeavors. In some ways, you're leaving behind your old security blanket, and as a result you can feel stripped of a comfortable part of yourself. Your new paths and awareness of your needs, however, helps you remain focused on the most positive part of change and growth. Your obligations continue to require ample attention, yet you now have more effective ways of dealing with them. If you're thinking about moving, starting a new job, or making significant strides in a new endeavor, target the Virgo New Moon on the 17th to inaugurate these changes.

October

You can maintain your focus even while things are changing around you, unless something you really want comes across your path. Even that won't be a problem unless you fail to return to your task. Reviewing your situation after the Full Moon on the 2nd, you may realize that you have a different perspective on yourself and your commitments. Part of the problems arising now stem from Mercury's retrograde from the 1st to 22nd, since during this cycle you interrupt yourself to make repairs, take up the slack for others who seem to fall behind, or deal with a series of unanticipated problems. For this reason it's a good idea to keep a list of important meetings, calls, or projects so you don't end up losing track of them.

November

The early part of the month is filled with confusing circumstances. If you're emotionally upset, you can also be physically drained as a result. Pamper yourself on the 1st, when a massage or dinner out could help ease your tensions. Your talents for organizing and making sure that everything is done perfectly are likely to be in high demand this month, and while you can enjoy the attention and may even prosper as a result, you may not be entirely happy with the results if those working with you fail to fulfill their end of the bargain. That's why, all too often, you prefer to just do it yourself. All in all, though, you're enjoying the creative challenges, and may even have time for some romantic frolics.

December

Since you prefer to do things with at least some preparation, you might be put off by others who have gotten into something unprepared or without thinking. Fortunately, you're very talented when it comes to thinking on your feet. Your nerves may be a jangled mess, but you do your level best to pull things off. That would be fine if you felt appreciated, but you may run into a situation where you save the day and seem to be forgotten. Breaking with an old pattern, you're likely to speak up about your feelings and needs now, even if it means alienating someone. It's not what you say, but how you say it. And, with all that out of the way, by the time the lunar eclipse comes around on the 30th you're ready to envision a more gratifying and satisfying year ahead.

Libra Moon

Your Libra Moon longs for peace, and you thrive when your life is a reflection of harmony and beauty. Through an unmistakable style and grace you express the essence of your artistic soul, and you're drawn to charming places and breathtaking creative excellence expressed by others. In your ideal world, you would live a serene life with the perfect partner by your side, since your subconscious need to feel a connection is extremely powerful. However, the spaces of your heart can also be filled by time shared with family and friends whose values are similar to your own.

You appreciate a home filled with beauty, reflecting your elegant tastes and sense of style. Your deepest yearning is to feel acceptance, a challenge from your inner self is to embrace your strengths and liabilities in equal measure. Driven by a hunger for perfection, you'll go out of your way to refine yourself and your personal expression, and you appreciate others who make an effort to smooth their own rough edges. While searching for your soulmate, you may explore several companions, since finding the right ingredients for a healthy relationship can be the ultimate learning experience. However, even in love you realize that the ultimate goal is to make room for human imperfections and the ever-changing balance of needs that make up the tapestry of life experience. You're certain that all the fairy tales need to be rewritten!

In career choices, personal matters, and at home you strive for balance, and the resulting decision-making can be frustrating to you and to those waiting for you to choose. When you determine what you really want, you're likely to take a passionate stand for your needs, and, when logic dictates that it's time to re-evaluate, you can keep an open mind. Your vulnerabilities arise when you're confronted by hostility or anger, leaving you feeling shattered or uncertain. It is through developing a strong connection to your inner self that you stabilize your emotions and know that you can fight your own battles. The bond you create with your inner partner helps you mirror a self-assurance which will ultimately attract your yearned-for mate.

Famous Individuals with Libra Moon
Maya Angelou, Billy Joel, Sulamith Wulfing

The Year at a Glance for Libra Moon

You're flying high this year, feeling more emotionally satisfied and finding healthier ways to fulfill your most powerful needs. While you may still have to allow for adjustments in other issues, symbolized by planetary cycles in your chart, your most fundamental needs and sense of security are strengthened during the cycles involving your Libra Moon. This can be an excellent year to establish a strong home base, make or renew commitments, or take on family responsibilities.

The opportunities and good fortune represented by the transits of Jupiter also come with a challenge this year. During the first six months of 2001, Jupiter transits in Gemini (a cycle which began last summer), and you're in safe territory when it comes to welcoming abundance into your life. Handling your resources can also be less stressful. In July, Jupiter moves into Cancer, and for the remainder of the year this influence adds a restless quality to your emotions. As long as you honor reasonable limitations and continue to fulfill your responsibilities, you're not likely to go overboard, but failing to pay attention to limits can tempt you to overextend yourself emotionally.

By April, Saturn's cycle moves into Gemini, marking a two-year period of increasing emotional stability. The year Saturn and the slow-moving outer planets are most influential to your Moon is determined by the exact degree of your Moon. If your Moon is 0 to 4 degrees Libra, you're experiencing an awakening of your hidden talents while Pluto transits in quintile aspect to your Moon and Uranus transits in sesquiquadrate to your Moon. These two cycles have a subtle influence, and by spending more time in reflection, meditation, or creative endeavors you are likely to develop this level of enhanced consciousness more quickly. If your Moon is from 5 to 9 degrees Libra, you're feeling the wonderful influence of Neptune transiting in trine aspect; you're finding more reasons to trust your intuitive insights and can let go of old hurts that are standing in the way of your happiness. This is a year of forgiveness and spiritual insight.

If your Moon is from 10 to 16 degrees Libra, you're feeling empowered while Pluto transits in sextile aspect to your Moon. This is your time to renovate on every level, eliminating attitudes and habits that block your sense of security, and welcoming healing energy into your life. You're feeling the strongest impact of Saturn's support, stimulating your ability to make choices which sustain your highest needs. If your Moon is from 17 to 25 degrees Libra, this is your year to break free and exercise your independence while Uranus transits in trine to your Moon. You may still maintain some of your relationships, but the way you handle them will change! Finally, if your Moon is 26 to 29 degrees Libra, you're experiencing the challenge of Pluto transiting in semisquare, marking a year of eliminating old fears by facing and understanding their origins. It's like clearing cobwebs from your psyche.

All individuals with Libra Moon can take advantage of this year as a time to exercise greater freedom of choice in the manner in which you gain a true feeling of satisfaction with yourself and your life.

Affirmation for the Year
I know my needs and deserve to fulfill them.

January
Impassioned arguments can lead you astray and away from your comfortable space of logic, particularly if someone's throwing up a smoke screen to conceal his or her true motives. Your objectivity improves after the Moon's eclipse on the 9th, although you're still vulnerable to your own delusions. To determine whether or not you're on the right track, consult with a trusted friend or advisor, since trying to sort through everything alone can lead you down the wrong path. Exercise your creativity during and after the New Moon on the 24th, when taking time to develop an idea or produce something meaningful helps you transcend the ordinary bounds of earthly existence. The spiritual realm becomes your ultimate stronghold.

February
To stay in safe territory at work or within personal relationships, watch out for the danger zones you already know while listening carefully to your intuitive guidance for emotional land mines. Lines of communication can break down during Mercury's retrograde from the 4th to 25th, although your ability to sort through the debris of misunderstanding can help you stay on track with your obligations. A new intellectual challenge presents itself after the 15th, although old prejudices can raise their heads in anger near the New Moon on the 23rd, especially if you step into territory someone else considers to be his or hers. Your ability to finesse your way through the rough spots may leave you unscathed, although you can attract the dust of resentment from those who would be jealous anyway.

March
Although you may be questioning your involvement in some situations, changing them may not be as easy as you imagine. Deciding exactly how

far you're willing to go to satisfy someone else leads you to consider your own motivations, and sends you into an exploration of your values and self-worth. The odd thing may be that you're realizing how many of your values rest in your need to be accepted, and the person or situation you're trying to please may not be important to you after all. Venus retrogrades from 3/8 to 4/19, and during this time you're finally facing what you want and need. Think of this month as closet cleaning, since you have your eye on something you'd really like to put there, but have to make room for it first!

April

The Libra Full Moon on the 8th marks a significant time of release, when you're ready to embrace your soul and express your feelings with power and passion. A dialogue with your partner exposes issues at their core level, allowing you to decide if you're willing and able to make changes to improve or alter your relationship. Instead of protesting the fairness (or lack thereof) of a situation, think about its value to your life and security. You can almost feel the shifting of the planets at the 20th, when all you have to do is take a clear look around you to see things from a different perspective. What you thought you were missing may have been there all along!

May

Progress arrives in the form of a message that confirms your recent choices, opening the way for you to exercise your considerable creativity. Bringing together people of variable talents and divergent ideologies after the 7th can lead to amazing discovery and progress, although it might work better if you oversee sensitive communication. During and after the New Moon on the 23rd you're feeling more emotionally stabilized, even if you are still recovering from a series of changes or the impact of new experiences. A change of scenery can do your heart good, and may even help restore your self-confidence, since you're needing fresh input and will blossom in the heat of newly born ideas stemming from interaction with others.

June

Fasten your seat belt, since the pace of changes arrives with a wild intensity! Initiating a different routine from the 1st through the Full Moon on the 6th can help you increase your productivity, and may also expose the weak links in your personal life. However, since Mercury is retrograding from the 4th to 27th, you may end up dealing with issues you thought were resolved, only to discover that there's another layer beneath those already exposed. These discoveries can lead you to rethink your attitudes about a situation, particularly if you've made choices that have left you feeling discontented. Fortunately, your optimism remains strong all month, reinforcing your faith in your ability to accurately assess your needs.

July

Until the lunar eclipse on the 5th, you may feel an uneasy truce with someone close to you, and if you can maintain open lines of communication even difficult problems head toward solutions after the 6th. In circumstances that support your visions for the future, you're feeling nourished and alive, although the temptation to move into situations before you know all the facts can get you into trouble after the 13th. The problem lies in taking risks for which you are unprepared, and even if you can convince someone else to go along with you, that may not offer sufficient protection! Maintaining a strong base while making changes is possible, but only if you're thinking long-term. Regroup after the 22nd, when you can see more clearly.

August

The changes happening around you can be disruptive, but your response to them will determine whether or not you feel safe. A leap of faith taken just before or during the Full Moon on the 4th helps to confirm your options, and you can also evaluate the reactions of others to determine who's standing on principles similar to your own. Improvements on the home front can accommodate your needs, and you may also be driven by the desire to include innovations that instill the feeling that you have finally moved completely into the twenty-first century! Connections to friends and loved ones are improving, and you're likely to be in the right place at the right time to form a union which fills a long-standing hope or dream.

September

Including beautiful touches is one of your trademarks—whether it's at home, in your creative efforts, or in your manner of dress—and now, the results can be out of this world! You're eager to step into the forefront, and can strike just the right balance between risk and caution from the 8th to 15th, when you might even feel like making a bold statement on the romantic front. Although you're trying to communicate your intentions with clarity, you may be receiving signals that lead to frustration after the 23rd, since your own or another's expectations may stem from unrealistic assumptions. Try to reach an understanding before the 30th, since confusion escalates next month. The same's true of agreements or projects related to your home or property.

October

The Mercury retrograde from the 1st to 22nd can seem especially bothersome, since Mercury is in Libra, and making important decisions can be excruciating. Instead of forcing yourself into a choice that seems inappropriate, decide not to decide. That is, after all, a decision. Besides that, you're feeling some pressure to accommodate people or situations which seem to push your limitations, and you're in no mood to take unnecessary risks, especially where your heart is concerned. Your confidence during the Libra New Moon on the 16th can be high, but you're also experiencing some outside agitation and may have unkind thoughts or be angered by another's lack of consideration. Take a stand for yourself support your own needs now; or it may take a long time to forgive yourself.

November

Your peacemaking abilities come in handy, and negotiating details of an agreement can be advantageous for you from the 1st to 7th. Loving expressions underscore your deeper feelings for someone, and making time to share beautiful moments can have a definite impact on the outcome of your relationship. An assertive support from Mars helps you continue forward toward important personal goals this month, although your desires may take an unexpected turn after the 23rd, when someone new enters the picture. Getting projects done around the house can be a top priority, but expect a few distractions mid month.

December

Excitement builds, and the momentum to fulfill your desires can be exceptionally strong from the 1st to 8th. Although taking a few emotional risks can be safe now, you'll only feel good about it if you have some idea of the outcome. Certainly life does not offer guarantees, but one thing is certain: Foolish choices have a higher percentage of dreadful results. For that reason, even if you're feeling playful, caution is definitely on full alert in the back seat. During the Sun's eclipse on the 14th you can experience a personal breakthrough leading to more adventurous options. From the 22nd through the lunar eclipse on the 30th you can be feeling extra sensitive, particularly if you've been disappointed. Fortunately, it's a good time to withdraw and reflect, and then to let go.

Scorpio Moon

I t's the hunger from your Scorpio Moon that prompts you to look beneath the surface, since the mysteries of life are forever fascinating to you. Your penetrating gaze offers only a hint of your trademark intensity. To others, you can seem like a mystery, and it's unlikely that you'll fully reveal yourself or your feelings to anyone unless they're proven worthy of your trust. You definitely lean toward emotional extremes, since you rarely have lukewarm feelings about anything.

The domain of your subconscious mind is filled with a deep awareness of the true nature of rebirth and healing. You'll feel most sheltered in a home off the beaten path, or a place which encourages your needs for introspection and creativity. You respond best to pure motivations and honesty in others, since you can almost always "feel" when there's a hidden agenda at work. Those who are satisfied with emotionally sterile experiences will find you confounding, although they may still be drawn to your natural charisma. In relationships, you seek others who share your fascination with the ever-changing process of life, and who are willing to share their own feelings with you. While you are not likely to appreciate it when someone exposes your secret self without your permission, you do relish the experience of intimacy. Nonetheless, there are some secrets that you are not likely to share with anyone—and you may even have a few hidden from yourself. The vault in your psyche containing self-doubt, shame, guilt, and unresolved anger is covered with layer after layer to protect your vulnerability, but it is through releasing repressed emotion that you invite true healing into your life. Learning to forgive yourself when negative feelings or experiences arise can be the first step toward living the life you deserve. Then, and only then, can you rise to the heights of ecstasy you imagine, and share the experience of bonding with your soulmate.

You have a capacity for healing which few posses. As a result, the course of your life has probably had many twists and turns. You can become a true healer through harnessing the power resting in the core of your being, allowing you to uncover and maintain insights about the pure essence of life itself.

Famous Individuals with Scorpio Moon

Warren Beatty, Bernadette Peters, Elizabeth Taylor

The Year at a Glance for Scorpio Moon

The restraint you've felt during the past two years while Saturn has opposed your Moon is finally moving away during 2001. Fortunately, it's likely that you've learned the lessons of your emotional priorities, and have found new meaning in the term "emotional boundaries." Now you feel prepared to greet the world from a fresh perspective.

Jupiter's transits to your Moon mark times of outreach, and while you may feel a bit uncertain about boldly opening to new situations from January through June, you're ready to entertain the prospect of allowing yourself to be nourished more fully. In July, when Jupiter moves into Cancer, you're feeling more self-assured and confident about the choices and directions which are unfolding, suggesting more fulfilling ways of experiencing your career and relationships. Soul food seems to be abundant, and everywhere, and that's not just black-eyed peas!

Depending upon the degree of your Scorpio Moon, you'll experience the influence of certain slow-moving transits throughout longer periods this year. If your Moon is from 0 to 2 degrees Scorpio, you're feeling the challenge to drop some of your emotional barriers while Pluto transits in semisquare to your Moon. You may feel these challenges more strongly during April and May, when Saturn is also quincunx your Moon, and you're dealing with endings. If your Moon is from 3 to 9 degrees, you're letting go and facing your need to forgive old hurts while Neptune transits in square aspect this year. This influence prompts you to turn to your inner self and forge a true connection with your spiritual needs, but you can also be susceptible to deception from others if you're denying your true feelings and needs.

If your Moon is from 10 to 16 degrees Scorpio, you're changing old habits and clearing out the things you no longer need while Pluto transits in semisextile; you're also feeling the impact of Saturn's transit in quincunx to your Moon from July through December, when you can feel compelled to finish old obligations so you can move forward. If your Moon is from 17 to 25 degrees Scorpio, you're feeling a wild, restless impulse stimulated by Uranus transiting in square to your Moon. This cycle marks a time of internal revolutionary change, when you may find it impossible to contain your real needs. If you move, you may move more than once under this influence! Finally, if your Moon is from 25 to 29 degrees Scorpio, you'll feel the restraints of Saturn's transit in opposition to your Moon from January through May. While some of your obligations can feel emotionally heavy and draining, you're also recognizing the things and people you truly value, and may gladly embrace the opportunity to forge solid commitments in harmony with your higher needs.

For all individuals with Scorpio Moon, this can be a year of breakthrough, when making changes that improve the quality of your life takes a high priority. Knowing what you need is definitely becoming easier.

Affirmation for the Year

My heart dances with joy as I open my life to fresh possibilities!

January

Your emotional sensibilities are highly charged while Mars transits over your Moon, although your drives may be wide-ranging. Venusian energy is also a bright spot, and with these connections your romantic urges can be exceptional. During the lunar eclipse on the 9th, an existing relationship can grow stronger, and you may also find that it's easier to forgive unintentional hurts. Choosing the right time and place to express yourself can be problematic later, since an unusual impetuosity enters the picture from the 17th to 31st. You can even fall victim to mixed signals from someone whose intentions do not match your own near the New Moon on the 24th, or you may simply misread somebody. Jumping to conclusions could cause damage, so remind yourself to aim for patient understanding.

February

Unreliable or irresponsible attitudes from others can leave you with the sense that you're out in the cold, especially if you're counting on someone who fails to follow through. Your reactions during the Full Moon on the 8th stimulate your desire to close your heart, and you may simply need to withdraw for a while to gain a different perspective on the situation. If you are seeing someone clearly for the first time, then you'll have to determine how that changes your involvement. Perhaps you simply need to set new rules or define your relationship in a different way. Moving with care after the New Moon on the 23rd helps to assure that you don't jump into anything with unrealistic expectations.

March

To some degree you're focusing on your personal needs without involving others unless they're trustworthy. While this could be an attempt on your part to maintain the status quo, you may still need guidance or support, and reaching out to someone you know is nurturing can feel really great near the Full Moon on the 9th. Consider sharing lunch or dinner, and take the time to just catch up on news or explore future hopes together. Otherwise, those outside your inner circle are likely to remain there, since you have bigger fish to fry! Your tolerance for anyone showing hypocrisy is also measured now. Oh, you don't have to actually do anything confrontational. That "look" of yours will convey all that needs to be said.

April

Exploring your past can be illuminating, and from the 1st to 6th you may uncover answers to mysteries you've long pondered. The stimulus to discover why you've attracted certain relationships can also be powerful, and by exploring the motivations you may finally reach an understanding of your desires. Whether you want to change them or not is another story, although you may discover that you're on a different playing field after the 20th, when you're seeing fresh possibilities and may even feel rather enchanted by the prospects of trying something extraordinary. Experimenting with unusual recipes or stopping in the new restaurant in town will do for starters after the New Moon on the 23rd. Remember to keep your eyes open to see who's there!

May

Changes can leave you feeling pretty unsettled, but getting in touch with your inner self during the Scorpio Full Moon on the 7th can help you pull everything into its proper perspective. You may be extra sensitive, although this can be channeled quite effectively into your needs for a spiritually enriching experience. Healing touch can make a huge difference, too, and whether you're focusing on getting closer to your intimate partner or giving in to your need for a long-overdue visit to your massage therapist, you'll gain tremendous benefit from physical tension release. Think of this as a month of fine-tuning, since first attempts can fail, but may expose the best path for success the second time around.

June

Overtures from others garner your attention, although you may question the sincerity of apparently last-minute plans. Romantic notions can be rather enticing from the 7th to 16th, although you'll be happier if you maintain your emotional boundaries, since illusion and fantasy may be overpowering. Mercury's retrograde from the 4th to 27th can be a good time to retrace your steps or resolve issues standing in the way of your close relationships. During the solar eclipse on the 21st you may feel a strong surge of self-assurance, and reaching out to someone in need of your support can turn around an otherwise awkward situation. You're still not likely to drop your shields for a while, but you may be more comfortable with a friend or lover than you've felt in a long time.

July

After a getting off to bumpy start, the energy this month begins to smooth out for the lunar eclipse on the 5th, although you may still be at odds over unfinished business with anybody who's left you in the lurch! Mercury and Jupiter bring harmonious influences your way starting the 13th, when you're more likely to feel that your concerns are being heard. On top of that, you're attracting more trustworthy supporters, and can even see the strengths and weaknesses of your adversaries more clearly! Some people are drawing battle lines and playing power games, but you can see through them and are more likely to watch from the stands. However, if you are drawn into conflicts, advise your opponents that they may want to set their shields on high power!

August

Right in the middle of the third quarter, it appears that the rules are changing: Saturn and Pluto are in opposition and the old platforms are challenged by problems which are finally rising to the surface. You can appreciate the needs for change, but during the Full Moon on the 4th may feel that there's little hope for an immediate solution. Diverting your attention to a creative project can help, but if you working on renovations (including your home), pay careful attention to the things being thrown in the garbage. Some of that trash might be treasure! Consider digging through the attic and making a careful assessment before you eliminate anything—and that includes a few bothersome relationships, too!

September

It's a mixed bag: You're feeling reasonably productive, but differences of opinion divert your attention from the things you really want or need. Spending time in reflection or contemplation during the Full Moon on the 2nd yields exceptional rewards, since by removing yourself from a difficult situation for a period of time you can determine the most creative response, particularly if others seem to be rushing headlong toward disaster. After the 9th you may feel more confidently assertive, but be aware that you can get in over your head if you're trying to fix things that are not your responsibility to repair! Your own passions run hot after the 23rd, when what was a flirtation can become a rather delectable main course.

October

From the 1st to 14th you may be experiencing an intense rush of emotion, and, with a hopeful heart, may finally be willing to expose your innermost feelings. The wonder of it all can be the pure joy of knowing your own desires and needs, and giving love to another can be a reward in itself. Patient understanding may be required if your expectations are not immediately realized, although the power of your vision can inspire others to follow your lead. This is a time to open your heart and allow love to guide you, recognizing that the path may lead to unanticipated changes in your life. After the 24th, small steps will have significant meaning, but be watchful for your tendency to be distracted by illusion. Intuition works like fog lights for the heart: Turn it on!

November

The month begins with a Scorpio Full Moon, and you may feel that you're right on the brink of significant changes. Patience is your friend from the 1st to 6th, when stepping away from the action to observe the situation more clearly can prove to be quite illuminating. Your ability to spot false fronts from others allows you to avoid being drawn into a circumstance that could leave you feeling vulnerable. If you feel like pulling up your shields, it might be helpful, but only if you're not inhibiting the growth of a trusting relationship. Separating the things that are happening in the outside world from your personal life can be a big challenge. You're in the perfect place to start again or initiate changes during the Scorpio New Moon on the 15th, and continue with refinements through the remainder of the month.

December

The hustle and bustle of the season can get on your nerves from the 2nd to 8th. After the 9th you may feel more festive, and certainly will enjoy spending time with those who bring joy into your life. The stimulating energies of Mars and Jupiter can prompt your desire to take the initiative in a relationship, especially if you have evidence that the other person involved is serious about getting closer. Your hopes may dim a little during the solar eclipse on the 14th if outside problems distract from your own plans, although things seem to be back on track by the end of the weekend. By the time the lunar eclipse on the 30th arrives, you'll welcome an opportunity to relax with family or your sweetheart, enjoying the bonds of love you share with one another.

Sagittarius Moon

Your soul relishes adventure, and it's your Sagittarius Moon that drives you to explore the unlimited possibilities of life. Whether you're traveling, in a classroom, reading a book, or engaged in philosophical debates at the dinner table, you love the quest for wisdom, and perform best when you feel unfettered. Those who foster your idealism warm your heart, but you'll resist anybody's attempts to contain your boundless spirit. You were the child who needed a harness, but you always found a way out of it!

Your drive for independence is no accident, since your greatest hunger is to feel the spark of inspiration guiding you to explore the path of truth and wisdom. Your ability to uplift others is accompanied by a true candor, with your ideas frequently right on the mark. For this reason, cultivating your speaking and writing abilities can be especially gratifying, and keeping a personal journal can be an unparalleled way to open dialogue with your soul. You'll even welcome others whose philosophical values differ from your own, as long as they do not try to force you to adopt ideals which contradict your sense of truth. In relationships, you can be exhausted by situations which require your continual presence or attention. Certainly you can be loyal and loving, and may give of yourself without a second thought, but you'll be most committed in situations which nurture your higher values and spirituality. Those who are emotionally insecure may feel that you're lacking in commitment, since your tendency to yield to your wanderlust and desires to follow your own path can leave the wrong impression.

For you, home may not be a particular place, but a feeling you carry with you throughout life's journey. Your restlessness can stem from a yearning to cover mile after mile or explore as many cultures as possible, and adapting to different surroundings can be exciting to you. When you look back on your life, you may find that you have "homes" scattered around the planet! Once you determine that it's time to feather your nest, you'll appreciate an inspirational environment that's close to nature. In your heart, mind and soul you will be forever journeying, questioning, and wondering, ever following your quest for the grail of truth.

Famous Individuals with Sagittarius Moon

Neil Armstrong, Sylvia Brown, Ivana Trump

The Year at a Glance for Sagittarius Moon

This will be a year of extremes for you, and the ride can be a pure delight! You enter 2001 with a feeling of confidence and are exceptionally successful at attracting situations which can be fulfilling on many levels. The planetary cycles also fuel your courage and drive, and even if obstacles arise in your path, you can be ready to deal with them.

Jupiter's transit in opposition to your Moon during the first half of the year can stimulate your desire to have what you want—now! Setting limits can be difficult, especially if you're faced with opportunities that seem too good to pass up. Certainly you can make choices which lead to strong satisfaction, but you can also make promises which are difficult to fulfill. By May, Saturn will enter an opposition to your Moon sign indicating that there are changes around you which can prompt you to make large-scale alterations in your life. You'll appreciate finding relationships and circumstances that give you a sense that you're safe and secure.

Depending upon the degree placement of your Moon, the longer planetary cycles can have a strong impact on your emotional stability. If your Moon is from 0 to 4 degrees Sagittarius, you need to be especially watchful for the best options arising from January through May, since Jupiter will first oppose your Sun, followed by Saturn's opposition during the spring. It's a good time to make significant moves which fit with your long-range plans. If your Moon is from 5 to 9 degrees Sagittarius, you're feeling a strengthening of your spirituality while Neptune transits in sextile aspect, helping you reach deeper into inner realms while opening your heart to others. From May through August, Saturn's influence tests your ability to make realistic choices.

If your Moon is from 10 to 16 degrees Sagittarius, you're feeling the impact of Pluto's conjunction and Saturn's opposition, testing your ability to determine what you truly need and want from your life. You may feel that you need to move or renovate your home, but can run into obstacles which test your personal responsibility and self-discipline, especially after July, when Saturn sits in opposition to your Moon for the remainder of the year. If your Moon is from 17 to 26 degrees Sagittarius, you're feeling the uplifting energy of Uranus transiting in sextile aspect, aiding your desire to express your real needs and to exercise your uniqueness in ways that emphasize your special talents. Moving can be fun, and may open the way for opportunities you haven't previously considered. If your Moon is from 27 to 29 degrees Sagittarius, you're making a series of adjustments from January through April which will add stability while Saturn completes its transit in quincunx to your Moon.

All individuals with Sagittarius Moon will face the questions of what you truly believe, and will be testing the clarity of your ideals. It's time to take a stand for truth, even if it is in conflict with current trends!

Affirmation for the Year
In all things, Truth is my guiding light.

January
Your focus can shift, or you may have a change of heart, which can be disconcerting if someone presses you to stay in a situation you're ready to abandon. It's unlikely you will be able to remain if circumstances beyond your control dictate change, but if it's up to you, explore the nature of your discontent, since you're probably ready to alter an old psychological pattern. Sometimes, though, when you're breaking a habit, you need a change of scenery to underscore your commitment! Small steps taken during the New Moon on the 24th can be a good test, exposing the weak links in your plans. Your obligations can also limit your ability to break away, and by paying attention to your priorities you can make great strides toward satisfying them so you can ultimately move on.

February
After a few spurts and sputters, you're feeling more alive. Inspiration arrives in the form of a new interest or challenge to learn something extraordinary during the Full Moon on the 8th, although you may not be able to focus your full attention until after the 15th. Even then distractions abound. If your heart's not really in what you're doing, your attention is likely to be diverted just to keep boredom at bay. Be careful, since you could accidentally hurt somebody's feelings if you fail to show up for an appointment or do not give him or her the full attention he/she feels is warranted. Fabricating excuses makes a bad situation worse, even if your heart is in the right place. So, to avoid that hot water, think before you make promises this month!

March
If others seem to be overreacting around you during the Full Moon on the 9th, it could be a signal that your attitudes or actions are somehow creating irritation. Mars will be transiting near your Moon for the next four months, and it's easy to say or do things that have a stronger impact than you first realize. Your passions are growing stronger, and while your intentions may be honorable, if you're pushing, you could end up alienating the very person you want to impress. By reading the signals, you can gauge the

timing and get right in the groove from the 1st to 8th and again after the 20th. This is an excellent time to move, renovate or make changes at home, and you'll feel strong momentum if you start a significant project during the New Moon on the 25th.

April

With high hopes and support from the right people, you're making progress from the 1st through the Full Moon on the 8th, when it's time to fulfill important needs. Your fervency inspires others who may lack inspiration of their own, and bringing together others of like mind can be gratifying for you, too. Continuing with ongoing projects works to your advantage through the 20th, but after that you may feel a need to re-evaluate your situation. Almost like a change in the weather, the planetary cycles stimulate different needs after the 20th, when taking a serious look at your habits and needs can expose the areas in your life which need extra attention. A love relationship may be the key to unlocking your resistance or fear of change.

May

Taking stock of your life situation helps you determine a fresh set of priorities, although juggling current commitments from the 1st to 20th can take all your energy and attention, postponing expected changes. Your offer of support to others can be endearing, however, and is likely to be greatly appreciated as long as you can follow through with your promises. Striking a balance in your close relationships takes top priority during the New Moon on the 23rd, when your emotional bonds grow stronger if you share dreams and ideals. Just connecting with someone because you feel obligated won't cut it, in fact, you could end up feeling resentful if that's the case. However, if you do have a responsibility, failing to uphold your end of the bargain can leave you in a world of regret.

June

You may feel that the universe is not cooperating and your quest for immediate gratification can work against you, since you may get what you think you want, only to discover a more satisfying option later. However, you're in the perfect position to explore your feelings and real needs during the Sagittarius Full Moon on the 6th, when adventurous situations can lead to pure joy. There's a catch, though: Anything that's out of harmony with your true needs can leave you feeling exposed and vulnerable, particularly if you're jumping in before testing the water. It's a good thing you know how to make the most of situations, since you do get a second chance after the 14th; this time, you'll be ready.

July

Taking more deliberate steps and slowing your pace just a little can actually get you where you're going more quickly. From the 1st to 13th you're also more inclined to reach out and make amends for any situations that have gotten out of hand in recent months, especially if the relationships involved are worthwhile. It's also conceivable that by returning to the scene you'll see things differently, feeling more confident about the choices you make. Your penchant for pointing out the obvious can be irritating to those arguing for the logical option (in your mind, they may be babbling), and you're ready to get down to the core of a situation to determine whether or not you'll still be involved. Your impulse may be to disappear into the sunset after the 23rd, and this time, you may not return.

August

Your dreams are calling to you, and with Mars completing its cycle in Sagittarius you may feel that if you fail to act now that it will be too late. To determine whether or not you're overreacting, think about your goals and consider withdrawing for a few days to reflect on your deeper needs. During the Full Moon on the 4th your clarity improves, and explaining or describing what you want can be much easier. Funneling your increasing passion toward an existing situation or relationship which needs extra energy can be quite gratifying, especially if changes beyond your control give you more latitude to exercise your creativity. Wait until the New Moon on the 19th to move or start a new project, since you're much more inspired then.

September

Adding special touches to your home and personal environment warms your heart, although you're likely to feel extra sensitive if others take a critical attitude during the Full Moon on the 2nd. Before you respond, decide if you're happy with the situation. That will make it easier to avoid saying those words you cannot retract! Intimate relationships improve through better communication from the 1st to 20th, and special times with loved ones can lead to a deeper commitment. You may be inclined toward grand romantic gestures after the 18th, but try to ascertain if your intended is open to your words or actions to avoid creating an awkward situation. It may just be a question of choosing the appropriate time and place.

October

You understand why people make assumptions, yet problems resulting from the wrong expectations can be really uncomfortable. Although it may not be your intention, you could be sending mixed signals, and taking time to observe reactions before you continue can save you (and someone else) a lot of heartache. However, if you're waffling because you simply do not know what you want or how you feel, then taking time out can serve the best interests of all concerned. Mercury's retrograde from the 1st to 22nd can work to your advantage, since you're likely to discover that you're not the only one wondering or confused! For that reason, taking slower, more deliberate steps with anything that affects your security will leave you feeling happier in the long run.

November

From the 1st to 7th you're likely to feel inspired and full of hope, particularly if you're getting affirmative responses from someone about a proposal or idea. It's a great time to put finishing touches on a renovation or project, and can also be the perfect time to enjoy travel—alone or with your sweetheart. Complex and emotionally-charged situations seem to be building around you from the 8th to 20th, and you'll do yourself a favor by staying out of the line of fire, particularly if the circumstances do not directly involve you. Changes after the 25th give you an opening, when you can interject your opinions or provide objective guidance without garnering a negative response.

December

You're feeling much more comfortable from the 1st to 25th, and your confidence and charm (yes, charm!) can attract positive attention. Feelings of generosity and creative inspiration abound, and you sense that you're on the brink of major changes. The Sagittarius solar eclipse on the 14th marks a powerful time, when you're at a crossroads and can confidently initiate changes or take new directions which lead to more gratifying relationships and circumstances. Breaking free of destructive habits can be much easier too, and if you're considering transplanting yourself to a different environment, moving forward with confidence seems to bring you to the perfect situation—just in time to celebrate! It's time to adopt a lifestyle which truly nourishes your needs on every level: Emotional, physical, and spiritual fulfillment can be yours to claim.

Capricorn Moon

You've never been surprised to discover that life is filled with challenges. In fact, when things are going too smoothly you may feel that something's wrong! It's your Capricorn Moon that hungers to feel the self-respect which comes when you're standing tall in the light of your accomplishments. Forging a steady, sure path, you feel recharged when you're climbing toward your goals. Yet even as you stand at the summit of achievement, your desire to fortify your security prompts you to reach toward new peaks. In some ways, it's the process of living a productive life that feeds your soul.

Your dedication to family and home can be behind your motivation for hard work, and because you take your responsibilities seriously, you'll also respect others who have the dignity to honor their own. A conservative home environment in a natural setting feels best, and you may need space to showcase family heirlooms. Work itself can become an addiction, and because you naturally tend to shoulder responsibility, you may be drawn to relationships that invite others to rely on you to carry the heaviest load. To avoid the resentment which can arise, it's necessary to keep your eyes open for times when you can relinquish burdens to others. Personal and professional relationships will prosper if you keep these limits in their proper perspective.

Your sense of humor can break the ice during tense times, and more than once your dry wit has come to the rescue when reality presses too hard against sensitive issues. Besides that, you're not all work, since when the job's done (or under control), you do love to let your hair down and play. It's just that you feel guilty when you know you're wasting time and effort. You'll feel a flow of contentment when you open your time and your heart to those who love you, since allowing the flow of tenderness and love can only happen when you drop your walls. It's your need to feel that you're in control of your emotions all the time that can block the love and support you so deeply crave. Protecting yourself is one thing, but shutting out the joy of life diminishes the returns on your hard work, and that simply would not be very practical, now would it?

Famous Individuals with Capricorn Moon

F. Lee Bailey, Cher, Anaïs Nin

The Year at a Glance for Capricorn Moon

You'll appreciate a chance to expand your horizons this year, since you've probably been working at a steady pace, and the change of scenery will do you good! The year 2001 marks a period of adjustment, when alterations in your routine that afford you a sense that you're getting more out of life can be emotionally invigorating. It's not a time to try to keep things the same: if you do you may find yourself wondering how the rest of the world lives while you're hitting the 9 to 5. Instead, you're trimming down your burdens. That makes it much easier to dance to the music.

Saturn, the planet ruling your Capricorn Moon, is moving out of the earth sign Taurus and into Gemini, and as a result you may be craning your neck to see what's around the corner. Unfortunately, you won't know 'til you get there, but you can be better prepared by using the influence of Saturn's cycle to accept the responsibilities that are yours and relinquishing those you no longer need to carry. Jupiter, the energy of expansion and abundance, presents the first challenge to alter your habits and make room for greater joy, and by doing just that you may find other eyes looking deeply into your own with appreciation and love after Jupiter enters Cancer in July.

Depending upon the degree placement of your Moon, other cycles will have a yearlong impact. If your Moon is from 0 to 3 degrees Capricorn, make creative changes at home while Saturn transits in biquintile to your Moon from January through April. Then, during July and August, when Jupiter opposes your Moon, you'll feel ready to expand your living space or your family. If your Moon is from 3 to 10 degrees Capricorn, you're experiencing a need to eliminate habits that undermine your health and emotional security as Uranus transits in semisquare aspect to your Moon this year. You're also feeling the influence of Neptune traveling in semisextile, stimulating your need to reach inside and embrace your spirituality, making time in your routine to connect with your inner self.

If your Moon is from 10 to 16 degrees Capricorn, you're feeling the impact of two cycles: Pluto is transiting in semisextile and Saturn transits in quincunx aspect to your Moon. The Pluto cycle is the first you'll feel from January through June, when you may actually experience a kind of emotional purging as you eliminate unhealthy attitudes and habits. Then, from June onward, Saturn adds its influence, and you'll need to watch a tendency to fall into depression if life is not changing when and how you want it to. If your Moon is from 17 to 25 degrees Capricorn, you're breaking out of your shell while Uranus transits in semisextile to aspect all year. Finally, if your Moon is from 26 to 29 degrees Capricorn, you're feeling the support of Saturn during the months of January through May, when emotional stability provides a strong platform for decision-making and personal commitments.

All individuals with Capricorn Moon will feel a need to take a personal inventory during January, July, and December, when the lunar eclipses stimulate your need to turn inward and explore your deepest feelings.

Affirmation for the Year
I hold an attitude of acceptance and forgiveness in my heart.

January
You're ready to take the leap and reach out with loving arms from the 1st through the lunar eclipse on the 9th, when letting someone know how you feel can lend strength to each of you. Making changes or improvements at home works best through the 19th, but you may be worried about the budget after the 15th and decide to regroup and think over your options before you continue. You're looking for substance, and from the 24th to 31st you may run into situations which look good on paper, but when you try to make them reality—they just don't stand up to the test. You can be especially concerned if someone you care for seems to be following a wayward path, but the question is whether you can do anything about it. Keep the doors to communication open, just in case!

February
It's a good thing you appreciate practical considerations, since those are the options which continue to slow progress for those in such a big hurry until the 15th. After that, watch out! Those pressing for answers before you're ready to give them can get on your nerves, and you are not likely to jump into anything if you sense that it's too risky or could undermine your stability. By taking an approach to changes or innovations that is more comfortable, you'll experience an outcome that's more acceptable, too. This is one of those periods when your patience is definitely tested, and even you may be willing to take limited emotional risks after the 23rd if there are some assurances that you can trust another's involvement and commitment.

March
You're not the only person reconsidering your emotional entanglements, since Venus is in retrograde, stimulating the need to reflect on true feel-

ings and values. You are likely to have a problem if, during the Full Moon on the 9th, you feel others are rushing to judgment before considering the impact of their actions or decisions. You're seeking substantial support, and may find that you're aligning with the underdog if that's where true self-respect resides. Be on the alert if your tendency is to hold a negative attitude toward progressive change, though, since you'll do yourself a disservice if you cannot incorporate innovation into your current situation. Simply resisting can actually block your ability to maintain your security, when all is said and done.

April

Giving others leeway and opportunity to forge new paths works fine, as long as they're not digging in your backyard. You may feel that your needs and concerns are simply being ignored, and while you can interject some timeworn wisdom, those who are most impetuous may simply not hear you. After the 19th there are changes which help to underscore the value of your conservative, down-to-earth concerns, although you may still have to move over a few inches for the liberal innovators. Putting your plans or projects in motion during the New Moon on the 23rd works nicely, since you'll feel more self-assured about the quality of the foundation you're creating. This works for business and family matters alike.

May

Just when you thought you had everything under control, unanticipated changes or unexpected guests can throw the best laid plans into disarray from the 1st to 5th. Calling in your allies and those who understand your needs and way of doing things helps bring the situation under control, and by the Full Moon on the 7th you may feel that you're back on track. But don't count on it, since others in crisis may need your reassuring shoulder before month's end! There can be fortunate changes involving children or young people in your life, and making time to enjoy their talents and company can give you plenty of reasons to smile. After all, your inner child is always looking for a chance to laugh!

June

You've always known that rushing into anything before you're ready does not work, and that theory will be tested this month. If you're lucky, you'll have a chance to live it vicariously by watching others jump from the frying pan into the fire. One thing seems certain: You're finding amazing ways to stretch your resources, and your conservative attitudes work to your benefit when it comes to family matters and relationship issues. The solar eclipse on the 21st can bring relationship questions to a critical point, and afterward, when the noise settles to a dull roar, you may want to say, "I told you so," but your better judgment is likely to whisper a message of restraint. Sometimes it is the acceptance of changes beyond one's control which calls certain levels of creativity in action.

July

The Capricorn lunar eclipse on the 5th can stimulate feelings of raw vulnerability, particularly if you've been feeling that your needs have not been given the attention they deserve. This is a good time to explore your priorities and to reflect upon whether or not you've been attentive to your own needs. With Jupiter's ingress into Cancer there's an additional stimulus resting on the ground of unspoken assumptions from and toward others. To avoid the ravines of disappointment, target the New Moon on the 20th as a time dedicated to striking a balance between your personal and professional realms. Funnel more time toward the relationships that nourish your soul and the activities that allow you to provide reassuring support and tenderness toward those you adore.

August

The embrace of nature can fuel a renewed sense of stability, especially if you're seeing the manmade structures around you falling apart! You always gain fresh momentum when you take the time to connect with the earth in some way, and whether it's a camping trip, hiking a mountain path, building sand castles, digging a new garden, or climbing trees, you'll feel more alive by making these contacts. Of course, holding someone you love close to your heart can be the best thing of all, and receiving affection and appreciation from others can soften the rough edges of your life. Venus and Jupiter work together to open this flow, and, after the 15th, you may even find talking about your feelings is easier, even if you do keep the conversation brief!

September

Old barriers break down during the Full Moon on the 2nd, when you may discover that the resistance you've felt from someone else has been due to their misreading your intentions, or could there be an old grudge in the way? Even though it may mean breaking your promise to never let 'em see your weakness, sharing your anxieties with someone you trust can actually open the way to deeper levels of intimacy. After Mars enters Capricorn on the 8th, you'll feel an increase in your ability to assert yourself. Taking the lead in matters which require you to engage the courage of your convictions inspires a fresh energy during the New Moon on the 17th, and you can set a precedent which others confidently follow.

October

A few awkward moments can arise on the days around the Full Moon on the 2nd, especially if someone your actions show a lack of social grace. You're probably not concerned with such trivialities, since you're looking at the long-range picture and taking actions which uphold values you deem to be important. Once you've explained yourself, everything falls easily into place and hurts can be quickly forgiven (just be sure you don't walk away with negative feelings!). Working on projects at home which are functional and enhance the beauty and value of your property proves to be successful, and if you've fallen behind, then this is the time to cross a few tasks off your "to do" list. Target time for romance after the 27th.

November

If you're having mixed feelings about all the distractions keeping you from your priorities near the beginning of the month, keeping everything in perspective helps you avoid saying or doing things that get you into trouble. After the 7th you're feeling more self-assured, and can begin to cultivate areas in a relationship which have been faltering. You're rarely comfortable putting resources into risky situations, even if someone is pushing you to get into something you question. While holding your ground can be tough, you may at least give a proposition its due attention before you say "no." From the 15th to 22nd you may have sufficiently tested a situation and can confidently agree to participate.

December

Circumstances you think have little consequence can be disturbing to others around you, and if you adopt an attitude which appears to be uncaring, then others may feel hurt. Although the signals can be subtle, you are capable of reading them, and by taking an active approach you can quickly diffuse these misunderstandings. After the 15th, communicating your deepest affections and showing your support to others strengthens ties to those sharing your life. Taking time away from work and enjoying the rewards helps you appreciate yourself and others more. The challenge of the lunar eclipse on the 30th is to find a way to integrate into your life the experiences that feed your soul, and to make a commitment to maintain and support those needs beyond the celebrations of the season.

Aquarius Moon

Your deep yearning to honor the true spirit of good will toward all reflects the needs of your Aquarius Moon, through which you also feel the urge to express your individuality. You thrive when you're part of the leading edge of evolutionary change, and your fascination with uniqueness inspires joy in your heart. While you treasure your friendships, you can be a loner, since your need for self-realization may take you along the untrodden, singular path. Throughout your life, your visionary soul has sought to lead the charge which can liberate humanity from ignorance and prejudice. These desires and needs beckon to that which is extraordinary within yourself and in the world.

Your intuition can be laser-sharp, and when you're in a quandary, surrendering to your intuitive voice helps illuminate the best path. The manna of your life is logic, and when you're upset, finding the logic behind the situation helps you cope. Unfortunately, feelings and emotions frequently do not make sense, yet your need to understand allows you to rise above selfish desires—at least some of the time! In most cases, you may have to allow your feelings to be what they are, and adopting an air of unconditional acceptance is part of what makes you such a valued friend. The ideals are easier to visualize than create, and understanding the entrapment of being merely human helps you accept that you're working toward the unconditional. Only those at ease with your independent way of operating will be able to handle getting close to you, since you need your time to reach toward the abstract and value those who allow ample room for your eccentricities.

You like doing things your way, and can appear aloof or uncompromising. But you can reach out toward others and embrace the importance of allowing the same independence you value for yourself. It is when your urge for freedom is strong that you can seem cold to someone who needs to know she or he is special, and even though you may not mean to break hearts, you sometimes do. Welcoming the experiences and expressions which shatter the boundaries of the ordinary sustains your connection to your soul, and ultimately these are the things which lead you into unity with the ultimate intelligence of the Source.

Famous Individuals with Aquarius Moon

Henry Ford, Tipper Gore, Debbie Reynolds

The Year Ahead for Aquarius Moon

Finally, it feels as though it's your turn! Although there are still a few tests on the proving ground of life experience, the cycles for 2001 support your ability to fulfill and express your true needs without the inhibitions you've felt in the past. Since you tend to push the envelope, you've gotten flack for sometimes being radical, although you've cooled your jets a little during the past two years. Now, the sky's the limit, but you understand the value of creating a secure launch pad and landing site!

The first quarter of the year marks a time to complete ongoing projects or finish obligations, since Saturn continues its trek in Taurus through April. However, after that time the planetary cycles support your needs to break free and experience life on your own terms, as long as those terms are in harmony with your highest needs. Jupiter's transit in Gemini adds feelings of optimism through July, and after that, while Jupiter travels in Cancer for the remainder of the year, you'll need to be aware of a tendency toward self-indulgence.

The degree of your Moon defines when the long-lasting cycles will have their greatest impact. If your Moon is from 0 to 3 degrees Aquarius, you're ready to establish a strong foundation which will serve as your touchstone during the months from January through May. It is in these months that Jupiter and Saturn transit in trine to your Moon, helping you keep your priorities on the things you need the most. If your Moon is from 4 to 9 degrees Aquarius, your intuitive insights are becoming almost uncanny, since Neptune is traveling in conjunction to your Moon. Additionally, from May through July your visionary abilities can serve to help you move to the right place at the perfect time.

If your Moon is from 10 to 16 degrees Aquarius, you're carving an exceptional space for personal fulfillment and security while Pluto transits in sextile and Saturn transits in trine to your Moon. This is your year to determine what you need in terms of home and family, and the foundations you create now can serve you for many years to come. If your Moon is from 17 to 25 degrees Aquarius, you're experiencing the marvelous influence of Uranus transiting in conjunction, an aspect which is not likely to happen again (unless you're very young). You may feel that you've been waiting for this time to arrive, and you're likely to make significant moves and changes which allow you to feel fully alive and to openly and freely express yourself and your needs. If your Moon is from 25 to 29 degrees Aquarius, you're eliminating self-defeating attitudes while Pluto transits in semisquare and Saturn completes its square aspect cycle. The changes you make now will make it possible to embrace and express your deepest needs next year. Think of this as the time to pay old debts and bid goodbye to things you no longer need.

All individuals with Aquarius Moon can feel especially blessed during 2001, since the generational influences of Uranus and Neptune traveling in your moon's sign are indicative of a period when individuality and tolerance are among humanity's important learning tasks, and you are the one who can illuminate the path for the journey.

Affirmation for the Year
I accept my uniqueness and encourage others to embrace their own!

January
Divisive situations separate logic from passion, and while objectivity is difficult to recover, it is the practical thinker who wins the day during the lunar eclipse on the 9th. Those adhering to tradition can seem in the way, but once you give their ideas room to grow, you may find that you're leaning toward the idea of incorporating change within the framework of existing structures. Your visionary sensibilities awaken during the Aquarius New Moon on the 24th, when your suggestions and insights help shine the light on possibilities others would never see. Although there may be resistance, you can help build the bridge between yesterday's values and today's challenges. After the 28th, rash action by those with little patience can be damaging.

February
The cycles near the Full Moon on the 8th stimulate a feeling that you're spread too thin, especially if you're carrying family responsibilities and work demands. You may want to throw in the towel and take a long vacation, but may have to settle for ten minute coffee breaks until midmonth, when the pressure become less intense. Mercury's retrograde in Aquarius offers an opportunity for you to bring an old project out of the closet to determine if it's worth completing, or if you should abandon it once and for all. You may feel the same way about some relationships—especially those which tend to demand more than they return. Search your heart for your motivations; if guilt alone is why you're there, reconsider.

March
Power struggles may surround you, but you're the one people seek out for an objective solution to their dilemmas. Although you may not need to keep your shields up, it's a good idea to maintain a healthy distance if

you're being pushed to choose sides. You know that if it's not your battle, there's no reason to join. Fortunately, your personal relationships offer great satisfaction, and while temporary setbacks can be disappointing, you're willing to give the ones you love room for human error. Venus enters a retrograde cycle, marking a time of questioning personal values and feelings of love, but in the process you may also discover an old love that's been sleeping in the corner of your heart. Whether these feelings create a yearning for a person or stimulate your desire to dust off your creativity, their awakening happens for a reason.

April

Allowing ample time to explore the urging of your desires can set your heart ablaze, and during the Full Moon on the 8th, with a little help from the right ambiance, you're ready to drop your shields and let the feeling move you. An existing relationship can rise to a new plateau, but new love can be rather delectable, too. Your artistic expression begs for extra attention, and dancing with your muse from the 6th to 30th can be pure delight. A transition period begins on the 20th, when Saturn changes signs, and for the next several days you may be scrambling to re-establish your balance. On the home front, a move from the 6th to 19th can be especially positive, but changes made after the 22nd can lead to confusion. This can be a good period to regroup, review, and set up plans you'll initiate next month.

May

You have the qualities which can attract precisely what you need. In relationships, intimate understanding can arise as you abandon old inhibitions that stand in the way of the kind of connection that sets your heart soaring. Misunderstandings can arise near the Full Moon on the 7th, due to a series of events beyond your control, but fortunately open communication and objective viewpoints allow you to transcend the temptation to close the door too soon. Initiate changes during and after the New Moon on the 23rd, when a move or renovation can be the perfect way to create the home you've always wanted. Changes in family structure that incorporate greater tolerance can come about through your insightful encouragement.

June

A series of fast-paced changes may leave others breathless, but just puts color in your cheeks! Reconsidering your involvement in a relationship or career endeavor with an eye on future developments allows you to see a different perspective. By reopening discussions you may also be able to establish a much better understanding during the Full Moon on the 6th. Renovations can be especially exciting, since you may actually expose something of merit in the process, in addition to incorporating the innovations you desire. If you're moving, expect things to be confusing, but enjoyable. Expenditures can be out of bounds unless you keep an eye on them, since everything has a tendency to go to extremes this month.

July

From the 1st to 12th your time may be spent dealing with a series of meetings, calls, or projects, putting on finishing touches. Launch important innovations before the lunar eclipse on the 5th, or after the 23rd. Loving relationships are more rewarding now, probably because you're taking more time to accomplish a true meeting of the minds. Your fascination with a special someone can be particularly enjoyable after the 6th, although you may see only what you want to see for a while. Some clarity emerges as circumstances change late in the month, and even then, if you've formed a connection, the charms of love can be purely wonderful. You may sense that you're on the brink of change—but it's not just you. Restructuring is happening everywhere.

August

The Aquarius Full Moon on the 4th can be a time of wonder and blessing, and, since you've been releasing some of your fears about commitment, you may also discover that forging a positive bond with another adds such enrichment that it becomes a real win-win situation! You may need to offer comfort to those who are fearful about the changes happening in their lives, especially if your visionary sensibilities offer a clue about where things are going. Working in partnership with others or in tandem with a like-minded community can be especially gratifying now, since you can focus on innovation while others use their practical aptitudes to forge new foundations. Think of yourself as the architect of change in your family, too!

September

Early in the month you may feel ready to make the final push on a significant plan, and by presenting your ideas to others you can relinquish some of the control and watch while things take shape. It's time to use your influence to make connections for those whose talents you appreciate. You may also feel that you need to pamper yourself by stepping out of the limelight and enjoying the performance. It's almost as though there's a changing of the guard, and whether these shifts represent the natural course of events in family affairs or the way things are going at work, you need to feel a sense of completion and closure, so that you can move forward with a new lease on life.

October

During the Full Moon on the 2nd you'll feel a surge of confidence as you witness new imperatives appear while old pathways dim. Although it's tempting to try to move in both directions at once, your focus is on the future, and the best you may be able to do is to take all that you've learned into a fresh situation, blending tradition with innovation. It's tempting to initiate changes during the New Moon on the 16th, and while this can be a good time to continue with ongoing negotiations or to keep working on issues in a relationship, you'll be happier starting something on your own terms after the 26th. Watch out for your own illusions, since there's a test of your ability to distinguish between the visions that work and the dreams which are only an escape from your obligations!

November

From the Full Moon on the 1st through the 6th you may struggle within yourself to determine the best choices. Your needs may not actually be new, but what you are experiencing is a different awareness of the best ways to fulfill them. For that reason, alterations in your relationships can arise. Although you can reach a workable agreement early in the month, your promises are tested from the 11th to 15th. Is it the universe asking if you're really serious, or are you simply uncertain about the situation? Either way, illusion plays a big role in the test! Breaking away from old habits is never easy, even when you want to change, but once you're beyond the test, you're ready to initiate the journey toward exciting horizons after the 23rd.

December

Celebrate! The solar eclipse on the 14th marks a time when you're eager to follow your unique path, armed with information and truth, on your side. From the 1st to 14th every minute can be filled with planning, revising, and collecting—all necessary to make major modifications. Sharing your dreams with someone who understands and supports your urges can corroborate your own ideas, and while it's great to know that you're not actually alone on the planet, you're likely to feel sufficiently confident to proceed on your own if necessary. Your friends are there beside you, though, cheering your success and may benefit from your good fortune. Dedicating some quiet time during the lunar eclipse on the 30th helps you bring everything into perspective, and prepares you to invite the vision for yet another new year ahead.

Pisces Moon

T hrough your Pisces Moon you experience a profound need for inner peace, and your desire can lead you to establish priorities in your life that center around spiritual and artistic experiences. You may be especially sensitive and emotionally expressive, and while some may wonder if intuition really works, you know that it does. Your sensitivity to the intangible elements of life allows you to surrender to the realm of pure imagination, and as a result your feelings for art, music, and drama are finely tuned. Most of all, you exude an otherworldly quality giving you the capacity to bring magic into any situation.

Sometimes you may feel that you are perched on the narrow boundary between fantasy and reality, and your special talents shine when you integrate these realms. You prefer to think of life as it should be, filled with serenity, peace, and forgiveness, and when you're confronted with harsh situations you often feel that you simply must reach out to help. You prefer to offer tolerance in the face of bigotry and embrace misery with compassionate care. The challenge is to become aware of your own emotional boundaries, since, especially in your personal life, you are prone toward sacrificing your own needs in favor of more pressing demands you feel from others. To preserve your compassionate sensibilities without being take in by unscrupulous characters, you need to create an emotional filter which will give you the ability to discern situations with greater clarity. Otherwise, you can become a victim.

Since your deepest urging is to transcend the bounds of the earthly plane, you can fall prey to addictive behaviors, and may also be drawn into traps set by deceitful people who would steal your power. By determining healthy choices which encourage you to release the heaviness of everyday life, you can more readily maintain your emotional integrity. Balancing tools like meditation, yoga, dance, chanting, or playing and listening to music can be welcome. You also need a home which allows you to drop your cares and encourages you to exercise your creativity—a place where you can nourish your dreams. Ultimately, it is the nurturance of your faith which can illuminate your path and may, in turn, inspire the world to become more loving for all.

Famous Individuals with Pisces Moon

Audrey Hepburn, Paul Newman, Robin Williams

The Year Ahead for Pisces Moon

Having spent the past two years strengthening your foundations and establishing a home base, you may feel that you're ready to dig deeper into your needs and feelings during 2001. While some changes continue to happen without your invitation (or permission, for that matter!), some planetary cycles serve to stimulate a reaffirmation of your confidence and optimism. This is the year to remind yourself that you are safe in the midst of change and to put to use your exceptional adaptability and tolerance.

The first four months of 2001 provide a mixture of cycles which test your ability to stay within your personal limitations, and you'll make the best use of Jupiter's and Saturn's transits by determining what you can afford emotionally. By the summer, Jupiter enters Cancer, forming a supportive connection to your Moon, helping you maintain a positive outlook and strengthening your faith in yourself and those who share your life. During late spring, Saturn leaves Taurus and enters Gemini, and for the following two years you may feel that you're missing something when it comes to comfort and fulfillment. This cycle tests your ability to clarify the best ways to nurture yourself and others.

By determining the exact zodiac degree of your Moon, you can zero in on the long-lasting cycles represented by the slower-moving planets during 2001. If your Moon is from 0 to 4 degrees Pisces, you're not experiencing the impact of the slow transits to your Moon except during April and May, when Saturn will square your Moon. During this time you may feel some level of emotional deprivation, particularly if you're leaving a situation behind, but, fortunately, during July you'll have every reason to celebrate when Jupiter trines your Moon! If your Moon is from 5 to 9 degrees Pisces, you're feeling more emotionally sensitized while Neptune transits in semisextile to your Moon. This can be an excellent time to develop your creativity or to reach out to others in charitable efforts.

If your Moon is from 10 to 16 degrees Pisces, you're feeling the impact of Pluto transiting in square aspect, and then after July you'll experience Saturn's square to your Moon. Expect that you will be dealing with a series of challenges related to your need to eliminate old attitudes, bad habits, or destructive situations. In some ways, these cycles mark a period of rebirth, but that means you leave the comfort of the womb and emerge into a different awareness of yourself and your needs. If your Moon is from 17 to 25 degrees Pisces, you're feeling a strong sense of emotional freedom and release while Uranus transits in semisextile aspect and Neptune transits in semisquare. It's time for you to feel the wind beneath your wings as you expand your awareness! If your Moon is from 26 to 29 degrees Pisces, you're completing a rebuilding and stabilizing phase from January through April, while Saturn finishes its cycle in sextile aspect. Now, it's easy to say, "I know what I need," and to find ways to fill those needs.

Affirmation for the Year

I am stepping onto a brighter horizon with hope and self-assurance.

January

Venus and Mars lend their passionate drives to your emotional expression, making this a highly romantic and inspirational month. During the Moon's eclipse on the 9th your inclinations lean toward private time with the one you dearly love, but your children and family can also provide their own unique comfort and joy. From the 10th to 18th you're uncovering the truth about situations which may have been filled with deception, and, at the very least, you're clarifying for yourself exactly how you feel about someone. Acting on your convictions can be easier if you truly sense that you're making things better, but where matters of the heart are concerned it can be difficult to let go when you see unrealized potentials. But you can't make them happen all by yourself!

February

Your compassion goes a long way toward bridging gaps, although you need to be careful about putting yourself in the middle of volatile situations. You can see the egos operating big-time, with others jockeying for positions of recognition during the Full Moon on the 8th, but you may not be able to keep someone from getting hurt. Fortunately, you can be there with emotional first aid. At home, you're ready to make a few changes, and during the Pisces New Moon on the 23rd you may decide to get rid of some of the stuff cluttering your space, while you break away from habits and attitudes that stand in the way of your contentment. You're entering a cycle that challenges you to develop your assertiveness, but it may be the iron hand in the velvet glove kind of power!

March

If somebody's pushing you around, you're not likely to appreciate it. The question is, what can you do about it? Exploring your life for situations that show your tendency to step aside when you feel insecure, and examining your relationships to determine whether or not your needs are given priority may lead you to wonder how you're going to get out of a few messy circumstances. Think of it this way: It's time to identify where you are, how you feel, and what you want. You don't have to change everything overnight, but now is the time to begin. Start during the Full Moon on the 9th by talking over your concerns with your partner. Then, from the 18th to 31st, make a concerted effort to communicate more openly with others. Little by little, the light grows stronger!

April

Clarifying the intentions of others from the 1st to 6th helps you determine whether or not you want to become further involved, since you're seeing evidence of empty promises and cavalier attitudes. Using the time from the Full Moon on the 8th until the 20th to get rid of things which no longer have value can have a remarkable effect on your self-confidence. Clearing out closets, shrinking inventory, or going through treasures from the past has a way of helping you refine your priorities. Then, during the New Moon on the 23rd, you may feel more sure about building toward a more stable future. You're also integrating other responsibilities into your life, changing the dance as the music shifts to a different tempo.

May

It's difficult to avoid being pulled into changes happening beyond your control, but fortunately your flexibility allows you to shift along with the tide. Your affections for your lover may deepen during the Full Moon on the 7th, although that does not assure that everything is going smoothly. The greatest difficulty you're facing is how to deal with the endless stream of distractions that present themselves, since it's hard to know whether you're supposed to do anything about them. While sitting back to wait for the storms to subside or seeking out an escape seems like a good idea, it may not be possible. Integrating healthy escapes into your routine may be necessary after the 22nd if you want to maintain your peace of mind. The trick is to maintain your balance during a stormy time. Call it a test of your "sea legs."

June

The roar of excitement around you can get on your nerves, and if others are doing things which seem insensitive, you'll do yourself a disservice by withdrawing and doing nothing except feeling sorry for yourself. After all, if you're pouting too much things are likely to get worse before they get better, since emotionally you may be responding to your worries and imagination just as strongly as you respond to the "real" world. During the Full Moon on the 6th your tolerance is tested, but that doesn't mean you have to roll over and play dead! Gradually the external pressures begin to subside, and you may feel that you can peer out from your shell. By the time of the solar eclipse on the 21st you're beginning to feel more self-assured, although donning battle gear is not on your agenda. Take a long walk in the morning sun, and plan for an optimistic summer

July

Pace yourself from the 1st to 12th, since the temptation to jump in feet first before testing the water can lead to unpleasant surprises. Watching from the stands while others take sides works best during the Moon's eclipse on the 5th, although you can enjoy a powerful period of romantic intrigue! After Jupiter enters Cancer on the 12th you'll be facing more palatable and satisfying options, but you're still getting rid of bad habits and healing old wounds. Turning your attention to your nest makes a big difference, and throughout the month you can make alterations, which give you the feeling that you're finally home—in every sense of the word. If a move is on your agenda, target the New Moon on the 20th to transport your stuff to new digs.

August

Your artistry and imagination need somewhere to go, and whether you're zeroing in a relationship, a dramatic performance, work of art, or an exciting renovation in home decor, it's time to let your inner voice sing while you dance along. From the corner of your eye you'll see a few motions from others definitely lacking in grace, but you're not letting that stop you! Love may also be in bloom during the Full Moon on the 4th, despite objections from the naysayers who fail to recognize the power of devotion to the song of the heart. As your optimism grows, you're lending hope to those needing inspiration, and sharing your good fortune makes things better. Working in harmony with others on projects that benefit community or family can be especially satisfying.

September

Lending your applause to the success of others gives you great joy, and during the Pisces Full Moon on the 2nd you're at a significant milestone emotionally. Your ability to objectively explore your life and your relationships can be very powerful, and, like looking into a mirror, you may see the imperfections just as clearly as you see the reflections of beauty. Whether or not you feel happy is determined by your response to the whole picture: Simply focusing on the flaws can leave you feeling raw and exposed, but looking only at the things you like can be a sign of denial. It's important to know how you feel and what you want, while also listening to the concerns and demands of others, but now it's easier to say "no" when it's appropriate!

October

From the 1st to 14th you're making strides on the home front, although rebuilding or decorating efforts can be especially gratifying all month. Despite Mercury's retrograde you're seeing progress in matters that are personally important. The troubles can manifest in circumstances which seem to be more "outside world," although there are disruptions due to lacking or poor communication. Soliciting help from others on important causes allows you to feel that your efforts are making a difference, since you may be the visionary of the group, but others need to bring their talents into the fold to keep progress on track. After the 23rd you're feeling more at ease, and you may finally have a chance to enjoy your love life.

November

The emotional storm clouds emerging with the Full Moon on the 1st are likely to be due to misread signals, so to avoid being accused of saying one thing and doing another, explore your own motivations and desires. If you're not happy or upset and hiding it, it's going to show, particularly to another who's sensitive to your innermost feelings. However, if you're seeking a time to explore and express your affections in a more intimate way, it's a good time to deepen ties. After the 8th the emotional climate improves, and until the end of the month you're focusing your energy toward creative outreach. Your generosity during the New Moon on the 15th brings loved ones closer, but it can also enhance your reputation on the career front!

December

What you want for someone and what they want for themselves can be in conflict, and since this is a gift-oriented time of year, do yourself a favor by asking for a list if you're uncertain. Despite your intuitive senses, after the 2nd you may be influenced by insecurity and go overboard. With Mars in Pisces after the 9th your needs for passionate play intensify, and sharing love can become delightfully erotic. However, the right time and place may not manifest immediately, so you may have to content yourself with flirtatious games. Of course that builds tension, and by the time the lunar eclipse arrives on the 30th, the excitement can be quite enticing. A vacation or time away from normal routine can be just what you need to awaken romance, or, if you prefer, to dance with your artistic muse. Either way, you're feeling alive and full of hope.

About the Authors

Gloria Star has been an internationally renowned astrologer, author, and teacher for over two decades. She has been a contributing author of the *Moon Sign Book* since 1995. Her most recent work, *Astrology: Woman to Woman*, was released by Llewellyn in April 1999. She is also the author of *Optimum Child: Developing Your Child's Fullest Potential through Astrology* (Llewellyn Publications, 1987), now translated into four languages. She edited and coauthored the book *Astrology for Women: Roles and Relationships* (Llewellyn, 1997) and contributed to two anthologies, *Houses:*
Power Places in the Horoscope (Llewellyn, 1990), and *How to Manage the Astrology of Crisis* (Llewellyn, 1993). Her astrological computer software, *Woman to Woman*, was released by Matrix Software in 1997. Listed in *Who's Who of American Women*, and *Who's Who in the East*, Gloria is active in the astrological community and has been honored as a nominee for the prestigious Regulus Award. She has served on the faculty of the United Astrology Congress (UAC) since its inception in 1986, and lectures regularly throughout the United States and abroad. A member of the Advisory Board for the National Council for Geocosmic Research (NCGR), she also served on the Steering Committee for the Association for Astrological Networking (AFAN), was editor of the AFAN Newsletter from 1992–1997, and now serves on the advisory board. She currently resides in the shoreline township of Clinton, Connecticut.

Skye Alexander is the author of *Planets in Signs* (Whitford Press, 1988) and the astrological mystery *Hidden Agenda* (Mojo Publishing, 1997). She may be reached through Mojo Publishing, P.O. Box 7121, Gloucester, MA 01930, or mojo@shore.net. Her website is www.shore.net/~mojo.

Stephanie Jean Clement, Ph D. (Minnesota) is an accomplished astrologer with 25 years of professional experience. She is on the board of the American Federation of Astrology and has degrees in English Literature, Humanistic Psychology and Transpersonal Psychology. She has had numerous articles published in astrological magazines, and has written several books: *Planets and Planet-Centered Astrology, Counseling Techniques in Astrology* and *Decanates and Dwads.* Her most recent book, *Charting Your Career,* gathers together the threads of her experience in astrology, psychology and esoteric studies. Currently, Stephanie is preparing a book and computer program for journaling your dreams and daily experiences, as well as a book about the Midheaven in the astrological chart. She also writes a monthly astrology column for a financial institution and serves on the faculty of Kepler College.

Estelle Daniels has been a professional astrologer since 1972 and is the author of *Astrologickal Magick* (S. Weiser, 1995), and coauthor of *Pocket Guide to Wicca* (Crossing Press, 1998). Estelle has an astrological practice in Minnesota, and lectures around the U. S. Her work appears irregularly in *The Mountain Astrologer,* and she has been contributing to Llewellyn's annuals since 1997. She is an Initiate and High Priestess of Eclectic Wicca and teaches the Craft to students of varying interests and levels.

Alice DeVille is an internationally known astrologer and writer who has been practicing for twenty-five years. Alice conducts workshops and lectures on a variety of astrological, spiritual, and business topics, including a popular workshop called "Finding Your Soulmate." Her focus is on helping clients discover the psychological and spiritual attunement that supports their life purpose. You can reach Alice at: DeVilleAA@aol.com.

Kim Rogers-Gallagher is an astrologer and author of *Astrology for the Light Side of the Brain* (ACS Publications). She also writes columns for the magazines *Welcome to Planet Earth, Dell Horoscope,* and *Aspects.*

Heyde Class-Garney is an astrologer, spiritual counselor, and certified tarot grandmaster. She has a B.S. in metaphysical ministry and is currently the vice president of the American Tarot Association (ATA). She has written her own column for the ATA newsletter titled "Astro-Tarot" since 1995. Heyde has studied many new-age topics, including herbs and aromatheraphy. One of her specialities is baking, which she has done for thirty years.

Verna Gates teaches folklore classes at the University of Alabama at Birmingham, and has been featured on *NBC Nightside* as a folklorist. She was a writer for CNN and has been a freelance writer for fourteen years. Her specialties are wildflowers, moonlore, and storytelling.

Madeline Gerwick-Brodeur is a certified astrologer, who specializes in business astrology. She received her BA degree with honors in economics and is listed in many of the Who's Who books. She is the coauthor of *The Complete Idiot's Guide to Astrology*. Please visit her web site at www.astrocycles.com.

Kenneth Johnson was born in southern California, where he obtained his degree in the study of comparative religions at California State University, Fullerton. He has been a practitioner of astrology since 1974 and is the author of six books published by Llewellyn, including *Mythic Astrology: Archetypal Powers in the Horoscope* (1993) and *Jaguar Wisdom: An Introduction to the Mayan Calendar* (1997). He has lived in London, Amsterdam, San Diego, Santa Fe, and currently resides in California.

Penny Kelly has earned a degree in naturopathic medicine and is working toward a Ph.D. in nutrition. She and her husband Jim own a fifty-seven-acre farm with two vineyards, which they are in the process of restoring using organic farming methods. Penny is the author of the book *The Elves of Lily Hill Farm* (Llewellyn, 1997).

Gretchen Lawlor combines twenty-five years as an astrologer with more than ten years as a naturopath in her astromedical consultations and teachings. Regularly traveling around the U. S., U. K., and New Zealand to visit hospitals and alternative medical practitioners, Gretchen teaches natural approaches to common health problems. Her work has been published in almanacs for the past twenty years. She can be reached for consultations at P.O. Box 753, Langley, WA 98260, e-mail:light@whidbey.com.

Harry MacCormack is an adjunct assistant professor of theater arts (play writing, screen writing, and technical theater), and owner/operator of Sunbow Farm, which is celebrating a quarter century of organic farming.

Caroline Moss holds workshops in Cheshire, England to teach about growing and using herbs, and designs herbgardens to commission. She shares her home with a husband, two children, and their menagerie of hens, ponies, and rare-breed sheep.

Dorothy Oja has been an astrologer for twenty-eight years in a practice called Mindworks. Her specialties include electional work, composites, and Davison relationship analysis. An active writer for numerous magazines, her articles are available on request. Dorothy now acts as cochair of AFAN's legal information committee, dedicated to protecting the constitutional rights of astrologers when faced with anti-astrology ordinances.

Leeda Alleyn Pacotti embarked on metaphysical self-studies in astrology and numerology at age fourteen after a childhood of startling mystical experiences. After careers in antitrust law, international treaties, the humanities, and government management in legislation and budgeting, she now plies a gentle practice as a naturopathic physician, master herbalist, and certified nutritional counselor.

Louise Riotte was a lifetime gardener from Oklahoma and the author of several gardening books from Storey Publications, including: *Sleeping With a Sunflower* (1987), *Carrots Love Tomatoes* (1998), *Roses Love Garlic* (1998), *Planetary Planting* (1998), and *Catfish Ponds and Lilypads* (1997).

Bruce Scofield currently maintains a private practice as a full-time astrologer in Amherst, Massachusetts. He works with clients by telephone and mail. He has a masters degree in history, is the author of twelve books, and has researched the mysterious astrology of the Aztecs and Maya. His website, www.onereed.com, contains articles and information about his services.

Kaye Shinker teaches financial astrology at the Online College of Astrology (www.astrocollege.com). She serves on the National Council of Geocosmic Research (NCGR) board of examiners and is active in the Chicago and New Orleans chapters. A former teacher, she and her husband own racehorses and travel around the U. S. in an RV.

Maria Kay Simms is the author of *The Witch's Circle*, and also of a new book, *A Time for Magick*, to be published by Llewellyn in 2001. She has also authored several astrology books and computer texts from ACS Publications; the most recent books: *Future Signs* and *Your Magical Child*. Maria is the President of National Council for Geocosmic Research, Inc., a professional organization, and is certified as a professional consulting astrologer by NCGR and also by American Federation of Astrologers.

Nancy Soller has been writing weather and earthquake predictions for the *Moon Sign Book* since 1981. She is currently studying the effects of the Uranian planets and the four largest asteroids on the weather. She has lectured at the Central New York State Astrology Conference.

K. D. Spitzer is an accomplished astrologer and tarot reader. She teaches, consults, and writes about the planets and the Moon, contributing articles to various magazines. She gardens, cooks, and cuts her hair by the Moon, which hangs in the clear sky over seacoast New Hampshire.